The Mosquito Bowl

ALSO BY BUZZ BISSINGER

Friday Night Lights

A Prayer for the City

3 Nights in August

Shooting Stars (with Lebron James)

Father's Day

The Mosquito Bowl

A Game of Life and Death in World War II

Buzz Bissinger

HARPER LARGE PRINT

An Imprint of HarperCollinsPublishers

Insert art credits: Page 1, top, courtesy of the Estate of John J. McLaughry; page 1, middle, courtesy of the Estate of John J. McLaughry; page 1, bottom left, courtesy of the Estate of John J. McLaughry; page 1, bottom right, courtesy of Judy Corfield; page 2, top, courtesy of Judy Corfield; page 2, middle, courtesy of the family of Odette Hendrickson Davis; page 2, bottom, courtesy of the family of Odette Hendrickson Davis; page 3, top left and right, courtesy of the family of Odette Hendrickson Davis; page 3, middle, courtesy of Judy Corfield; page 3, bottom, courtesy of Roger and Mary Parmenter; page 4, top, United States Marine Corps; page 4, middle, courtesy of John Steele; page 4, bottom, courtesy of John Steele; page 5, top, courtesy of the Bauman Family Legacy; page 5, middle, courtesy of the Bauman Family Legacy; page 5, bottom left, courtesy of the Estate of John J. McLaughry; page 5, bottom right, courtesy of the Bauman Family Legacy; page 6, top, United States Marine Corps; page 7, top, Bettmann/ Getty Images; page 7, bottom, Bettmann/Getty Images; page 8, top, Paul Popper/Popperfoto/Getty Images; page 8, middle, the Asahi Shinbun/Getty Images; page 8, bottom, Bettmann/Getty Images.

HarperCollins books may be purchased for educational, business, or sales promotional use. For information, please e-mail the Special Markets Department at SPsales@harpercollins.com.

FIRST HARPER LARGE PRINT EDITION

ISBN: 978-0-06-324225-8

Library of Congress Cataloging-in-Publication Data is available upon request.

22 23 24 25 26 LSC 10 9 8 7 6 5 4 3 2 1

To Neal McCallum—
Veteran of the 6th Marine Division and Okinawa.
Sailor. Scholar. Student of history. First responder to
my endless questions. Best of all my great friend.

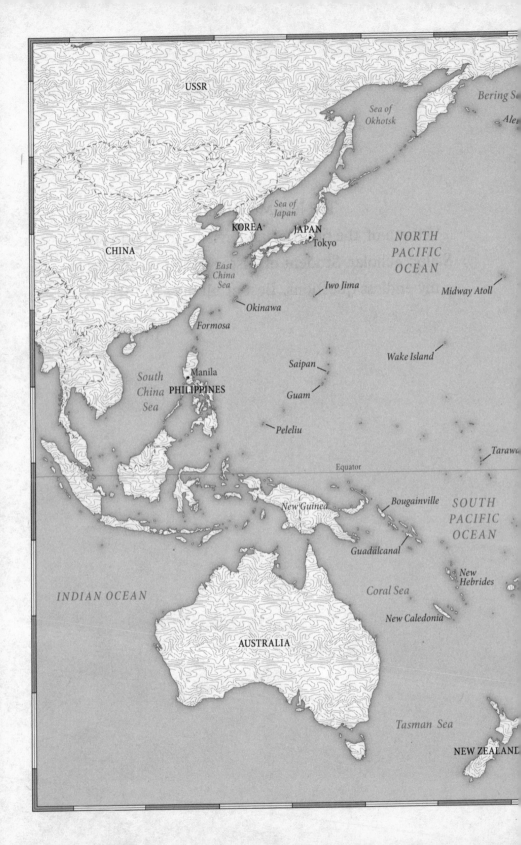

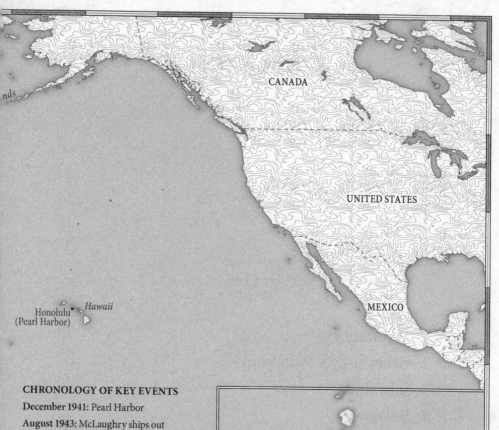

CANADA

UNITED STATES

MEXICO

Honolulu
(Pearl Harbor) • *Hawaii*

nds

CHRONOLOGY OF KEY EVENTS

December 1941: Pearl Harbor

August 1943: McLaughry ships out

November 1943: Tarawa

January 1944: Schreiner and Bauman
    ship out

May 1944: Murphy ships out

June 1944: Saipan

August 1944: Guam

September 1944: Butkovich ships out

December 24th of 1944: Mosquito
    Bowl on Guadalcanal

April 1st of 1945: Okinawa begins

June 22nd of 1945: Okinawa ends

August 15th of 1945: Japan announces
    it will surrender

East China Sea

IE SHIMA

*Motobu
Peninsula*

▲ *Mt. Yaetake*

OKINAWA

*North Pacific
Ocean*

*Hagushi
Bay*

*Horseshoe
Ridge* ▲▲ *Sugar Loaf Hill*
Naha ▲ *Half Moon Hill*

PACIFIC THEATER
AND OKINAWA

0   500   1000   1500
Scale of Miles at Equator

0   4   8   16
Scale of Miles

Contents

Part Two

Part Three

Author's Note

This is not an all-encompassing account of the Battle of Okinawa in the spring of 1945. Because of the nature of the book, the focus is on the 4th and 29th Regiments of the 6th Marine Division. As a result, the bravery of the 22nd Regiment of the 6th Division, the 1st Marine Division, and the 7th, 27th, 77th, and 96th Infantry Divisions of the army are only briefly noted. To the men who served in those units and their families, please do not take this as a slight.

Only the last names of marines are used when mention is brief. Marines in general referred to each other by last name, nickname, or simply "mac." First names in many instances were not even known.

Preface

My father was a marine at Okinawa.

He was drafted in 1944 during his freshman year at Dartmouth College. He told me he had actually been taken by the navy but had enlisted in the United States Marine Corps because he did not want to die on board a ship. Knowing even as a kid a smidgen of the history of the marines in the Pacific, that struck me as the strangest logic I had ever heard. But he was suited to the corps. He was tough, an excellent football player at guard in high school despite being only five foot nine and 165 pounds, once separating his shoulder and having his coach pop it right back on the sidelines.

He never talked about Okinawa except for little odds and ends: being in a foxhole at the end of the campaign with a little guy from Brooklyn who prayed a lot, dying for a bottle of booze, coming down with something, and getting shot with a needle bigger than his body. My sister, Annie, and I sometimes marched around the apartment with my dad, the cadence sounding like *hup-a-left hup-a-left hup-a-left left right left*. He made it fun, as other marines who had been at Okinawa did to avoid the irreversible scars that lay underneath. I did ask him once if he had used his rifle there. He said he had. I asked him if he'd hit anything. He said he'd had no idea and hadn't been about to find out.

That was all he said, going outside to smoke a cigarette when the subject of Okinawa came up. It was his private space; to ask further would have been to violate it. I know he had seen things he could not bear, so at odds with his humanity and pacifism. He hated guns. But he did what he did because there was no other choice. Duty back then was not up for discussion. I will not embellish. He was not wounded. I can't say for sure how much action he saw. But I know he was there, and that's enough for me and should be for the rest of us. He was a hero because he was in the war. He was not a war hero.

When I embarked on *The Mosquito Bowl* in 2017 with the eighty-two-day Battle of Okinawa in World War II integral to the book, it was not because of my father. It was not some search-and-discovery story. I had no idea what regiment or battalion and company he had been in and had never searched for information.

As I was doing a book proposal, I looked up the military records of the men I might be writing about. Because many of them had died at Okinawa, I wasn't sure I could do the kind of reporting that was necessary. My other nonfiction books had been based on being there, so-called immersion journalism. This was the opposite. I wanted the men to come alive as flesh and bone before their deaths. I went back and forth on whether I could really get to their core and do them the justice they deserved. As I conducted my inner debate, the irony of researching the careers of others but not my father's seemed crazy. I wanted to respect his privacy, but I realized I had to know.

I hate the use of the word *destiny* as a force that leads you to something. The only destiny I can guarantee is that I will eat the last cookie in the jar late at night and then lie to my wife, Lisa, about it.

A significant part of *The Mosquito Bowl* deals with the 4th Regiment of the 6th Marine Division, which fought at Okinawa. Because online records can be spotty, I assumed I would never find his name. But Ancestry. com makes it effortless, and records are remarkably accurate. It took me minutes.

There was my father, Harry G. Bissinger, on a muster roll attached to the 1st Battalion of the 4th Regiment of the 6th Marine Division as a private. It was a rifle company.

In other words, he was in the very same regiment and battalion that are so central to *The Mosquito Bowl*. Because many of those I wrote about were great college football players and my dad was a great sports fan, I have no doubt that he knew of them and maybe met some of them.

It was that discovery that made me realize I had to do it; it *was* destiny, after all. I would be writing exclusively about other marines, but I knew that I would be writing about my dad.

He left us far too soon, dying at the age of seventy-five roughly six weeks after 9/11, invaded by leukemia that devoured him four months after diagnosis. I so terribly wish he was here for so many reasons, a man of incredible charisma, charm, and humor who wasn't above taking a drink or two or three because that's the way his generation rolled. He was one of those rare people you always wanted to be around. For all his ebullience with others, he was so very hard on himself. He rarely took pride in anything he did despite all of his accomplishments, one of which was being a marine.

I so terribly want to tell him how proud I am of his duty on those killing fields. The book is my way of doing it.

Prologue

As October bled into November and then December in the iron lung of heat and humidity, the greatest enemy of the 6th Marine Division on the island of Guadalcanal in the fall of 1944 was boredom. Boredom led to anxiety; anxiety led to sights and sounds and smells you could not shed of shit and blood and once-human carcasses turning black with bloat or green with flies or white with a million squirming maggots, which led to fear, and fear never relented no matter how much you had already witnessed and how numb you already felt. The military was encumbered by a thousand rules, but for the veteran marine there was one that stood out, the rule of three: if you had already survived two campaigns in the war, you would not survive a third. Your luck, which any soldier would tell you was the only difference between life and death, would run out.

The marines of the 6th Division were from every state and region: the Brooklyn boys who spoke their own patois and should have been in prison but could hot-wire any army vehicle and therefore were heroes; the southerners, who liked to kill; the stoic midwesterners; the self-collected westerners; the Ivy League easterners, who could fight like hell with a little more smarts. They came together in the great pot of World War II and learned that their differences were far less than their commonalities. They trusted one another. They learned respect for one another. Most of the time they liked one another—except when they didn't and fought it out. It was the only sustained period in American history when socioeconomic difference was no difference (as long as you were white).

Most of the roughly twenty thousand marines of the newly formed division were veterans of at least one battle. The longer they were in combat, the more they knew when to hold 'em or fold 'em or go all in. They used judgment, as much as they could in war. The ones who were impulsively brave were too often the ones who did not come home. But the untested ones were different, just out of basic and field training, some naturally terrified but others eager and excited. Once they had arrived at Guadalcanal in the southwestern Pacific for training, there was a certain amount of swagger, as though they had been in the war since the attack on Pearl Harbor. The military liked the young ones, seventeen, eighteen, or nineteen, too confident against death to know any better and therefore willing to do anything. They had the excess that comes with youth, all of it just a grand adventure, a way off the dimly lit lamppost corner where the shadows never varied. They wanted to be in the marines because of the great tales of the South Pacific they had read as kids, only to end up here on this jungle-rotted shithole of Guadalcanal, where the million-crab march to the ocean took place with regularity, infesting tents, boots, and fart sacks.

The untested did not yet know that the 320 mm spigot mortar, as big as a trash can and sometimes called a "screaming Meemie," had lousy aim for all its thunder and rarely hit anything. They did not know what it was like when a mortar shell hit and men were blown apart and shredded by shrapnel and graves registration could not figure out which leg belonged to whom as the dead bodies were recovered for burial. They did not know what it was like to hear a wounded man screaming in agony and telling him to shut the fuck up because otherwise he would give away the location to the enemy. They did not know about the Japanese snipers who concealed themselves in the tops of palm trees and could stay there for long stretches at a time, subsisting on a small bag of rice and a canteen of water. They had never smelled burning flesh with its strange sweetness like scorched marshmallow. Or the melting flesh left in the sun for several days that slicked the ground with a skim of greasy entrails that caused soldiers to slip and covered their uniform with the slime and stink of the dead. Or the open flesh of infection layered with the yellow jelly of pus. They had not seen the two-ton trucks loaded with the feet of marine corpses sticking out of the back.

They did not know anything. But they would learn.

The 6th Division lived in tent cities on Guadalcanal generally separated by regiment, battalion, and company, in rows of tents, eight or nine to a tent with folding cots on a flooring made of wood and corner posts to support the mosquito net. The camp was basically a small city with clothing stores, recreation fields, a post office, a radio station, a barbershop. The scuttlebutt was that a battle was coming in the spring of 1945, a big one, as the Americans moved closer and closer to the Japanese home islands. When the marines were finally told where they were going, the word was that the casualty rate might be as high as 80 percent during the beach landing alone.

Marines crave rumors. They depend on them as they

wait, feeding their eternal persecution. Each rumor passed on only ratchets up the embellishments; it's the war version of the telephone game. But given the size of the marine and army infantry forces initially landing, somewhere around sixty thousand, an 80 percent casualty rate sounded preposterous. Maybe the men could take comfort in that.

But it was a false comfort.

The campaign they would ultimately enter into, the Battle of Okinawa, would turn out to be one of the bloodiest battles of the twentieth century and one of the least known, fought in the shadow of the western theater and for a country that was already exhausted by the war. A rough average of three thousand people, including US and Japanese forces and Okinawans, died every day for the length of the eighty-two-day campaign that began on April 1st of 1945—maybe somewhat fewer, maybe more, including an unknown number of Japanese soldiers and civilians sealed up in caves by explosives and suffocated to death.

As each day on Guadalcanal in December of 1944 passed with the rumors of when the marines would ship out, more and more of them adopted that faraway gaze known as "the thousand-yard stare" or "going Asiatic" or "going rock happy" or whatever else you wanted to call it, the eyes blank and deadened like shark's eyes, seeing but not seeing, the mouths talking but not talking. Some went deep into their heads and never came out. One soldier scrubbed his balls raw every night. There were suicides. The wait. The interminable wait.

Marines didn't like to wait; it was better to know you were going to die than play it over and over in your head. *Let's just fucking get it on.* Semper Fi. Semper Die. The army liked to hang back, as far as every marine was concerned, hiding behind artillery and mortar when the only way to conquer was to advance, a foot into a yard into a mile. Men were meant to be sacrificed, if that was what it took, not saved. Be a sightseer in the Pacific, join the army. Fight a war in the Pacific, join the marines.

Much of it wasn't true. Much of what the marines thought about everything wasn't true. But it fired up the chip on the shoulder necessary to make them fight and kill and be killed. They believed themselves to be alone, and when you are alone, you reach into yourself and fight like hell to get out. The navy. *The navy?* They ate like kings on board ship, fresh fruit and vegetables. The merchant marine. *The merchant marine?* It had published a 358-page cookbook with recipes, including for raisin bread and braised spare-

ribs. Worst of all: the army. It got the best of everything; soldiers left shit lying all over the place like
kids at the beach, which was why the marines stole
from them whenever they could. It wasn't simply to
even the score; it drove the doggies absolutely nuts,
whining to some marine colonel who looked at them
with the patented marine look of *Fuck off.*

Fights erupted in those waning months of 1944, ac-
cusations of cheating in ten-cent pinochle with one
partner telegraphing his bid to the other with a hand
signal, a cough, or a scratch on the neck, the only reason the fights did not become free-for-alls being the
admission that everyone was cheating. Too much
money was lost at craps behind the sleeping tents off
of the Henderson Field airstrip at the canal, where
the southern crackers were outhustled by the northern Blacks (who in combat were only assigned to haul
heavy supplies and man ammunition dumps so they
would not touch whites), the marines the most segregated and racist of all the services. Some marines
became animals before combat, like the kid from Alabama drunk on beer, down on all fours, howling at
the moon, and challenging every other marine in his
platoon to a fight. There were no takers except for his
gunnery sergeant, who gave him a chance and told

him to straighten his shit up, then, despite giving away thirty pounds in weight and ten years in age, took him behind a tent, hoisted him onto his feet, and broke his jaw with one punch. That was another unwritten rule the untested would learn one way or another: never fuck with a gunny behind a tent.

Relief from the drudgery came at chow time. It was the great equalizer and social hour once a medic popped the antimalarial, a hideous-tasting pill called Atabrine, into your mouth with a grizzled sergeant there to make sure you swallowed it. There was a wooden mess hall with a canvas roof for each company. The enlisted men and officers usually ate in the same facility. The officers also had their own club, where there was beer and whiskey.

It was over a few beers that former collegiate football players in the 29th Regiment of the 6th Marine Division stood toe-to-toe with former collegiate football players of the 4th Regiment and made the emphatic claim that the 29th would kick the 4th's ass if there was ever a football game between the two, which of course was preposterous in a place like Guadalcanal with a war going on.

They were not run-of-the-mill former collegiate football players.

The 29th included an All-American running back

from Purdue who had set a scoring record in the Big Ten; an All-Missouri Valley Conference end who had caught nine touchdowns in a single season; starters from Cornell, Notre Dame, Illinois, and Duquesne; and five former captains, including from Notre Dame, Illinois, and Purdue.

The arrogance of the 29th infuriated the 4th, which had ample bragging rights of its own: a two-time All-American wide receiver from Wisconsin and another at center from the University of California, an Ivy Leaguer who had started with the New York Giants for a year, starters from Wisconsin, Michigan State, Fordham, Montana, and Ohio Northern.

If you merged the players from the 29th and the 4th into one team, it would not only have posed a challenge to any National Football League franchise, with proper training it most likely would have beaten most of them, as the aggregate included sixteen players who had already been drafted by pro football or would receive offers.

The men of the 29th and the 4th continued to banter as they waited and waited. It was just talk.

Until the talk became as wonderful as it was improbable.

There would be an organized football game on Guadalcanal on Christmas Eve of 1944 between the 29th and 4th Regiments of the 6th Division, as close as you could get to the real thing.

There was a name that would forever become associated with it: the Mosquito Bowl.

Sixty-five marines of the 29th and 4th Regiments suited up. The field was carved out of the 29th Regiment parade grounds, dirt and pebbles and shards of coral. Cut-off dungarees and shorts served as football pants. The 4th wore green T-shirts with numbers stenciled on the front and the 29th white T-shirts with numbers similarly stenciled. They all donned marine field shoes since the quartermaster had not anticipated a need for football cleats in the Pacific war. A minimum of fifteen hundred marines ringed the field. Much had been bet on the outcome, making the game even more special.

It was broadcast on the Guadalcanal-based Mosquito Network to various parts of the Pacific. The score was flashed to destroyers at sea. Radio silence was supposed to be observed because of the ever-present possibility of Japanese attack, but snatches of commentary were listened to by sailors on one ship. The captain wasn't simply livid when he heard it; he assumed that the war must be over if the marines were playing a football game on Guadalcanal.

The game quickly devolved into semitackle, and some said it was tackle. It was a street fight, a sanctioned marine street fight without the military police trying to club the bejesus out of you and throw you into the brig on a diet of piss and punk. A footnote to the Pacific war—until it was forgotten like most everything is forgotten.

For roughly two hours the Mosquito Bowl wasn't simply a reminder of what life had once been like for the players but freedom and abandon, with the spectators captured in the same moment, screaming their heads off, whether drunk or sober. The beauty of sports, the ultimate power of it to carry you away, had never been stronger. Many of those who played in the Mosquito Bowl had been molded into officers during stateside training, told over and over to tear up every shred of their former lives. They were no longer college boys but men in their early and mid-twenties there to lead eighteen- and nineteen-year-olds of lesser rank into battle and never let any decision be influenced by how many would die or be irreparably wounded physically and mentally. The overall number of casualties in the Battle of Okinawa among the marines, army, and navy, roughly fifty thousand, not including as many as twenty thousand taken off the line for combat fatigue, would be beyond imagination. The number reportedly became a crucial reason that President Harry Truman ordered the dropping of the atom bombs on Hiroshima and Nagasaki in August of 1945. He was not going to lose another American boy, and his conclusion was that the only way to put an end to the war in which the Japanese had caused the deaths of roughly 30 million civilians and military, and continued to act with stubbornness and arrogance as if they had some bargaining power when they had none, would be with shocking obliteration.

World War II was a total war in which the ends justified any means, the creativity with which a man or woman could die: Bullet. Mortar. Rocket. Bomb. Artillery shell. Naval shell. Shrapnel. Choked. Set on fire. Crushed. Drowned. Amputated. Vivisected alive. Contaminated by typhus from carefully cultivated fleas. Blown up by their own hand. Morphine injection. Land mine. Poisoning. Starvation. Suffocation. Malaria. Snake bite. While taking a piss. While taking a shit. Left to rot. Jumping off a cliff. Beheaded.

That was what a marine of the 6th Division thought about. That was what he knew could happen. That was what would happen too many times. But at the Mosquito Bowl they were college kids again. They were not going to die or see others they loved die. They were going to do what they had done for so much of their lives.

They were going to play football.

The world should have changed course on that field of coral and dust. The rickety ships and transports that had taken them thousands of miles across the sea to this place nobody had ever heard of should have taken them back home, the whole thing turning out to have been some government snafu and FUBAR. The Japanese, knowing they could not win the war the very second the first bomb was dropped on Pearl Harbor but deluding themselves into thinking the Americans had no stomach for the fight and would negotiate a settlement, should have surrendered as early as May of 1942 after the decimation of much of their carrier fleet at Midway. Some top commanders acknowledged after the war that the loss of four carriers there had made victory impossible, without acknowledging the tens of millions who died over the next three years, the vast majority from neighboring countries as well as their own, hopelessness perverted into hope.

Those who played, those who watched, should all have had the chance to see how their lives would have turned out. They should have all experienced success and failure, love and heartbreak, joy and sorrow, babies becoming sons and daughters with their own legacies: growing gray; growing old; dying with as much dignity as one can ever die with; the chance to say goodbye to those they loved and those who loved them. But the world did not change.

By the late spring of 1945 at Okinawa, more than a dozen of the sixty-five who had played in the Mosquito Bowl had been killed and roughly twenty others wounded, a total casualty rate of 54 percent. It was by far the largest collection of athletes ever to die in a single battle. In the entirety of the war in both the eastern and western theaters, twenty-one NFL players died in combat. There were two killed from Major League Baseball.

It wasn't the best game played or the greatest or some other marketing hyperbole, but it was the most tragic in terms of its later repercussions. Just pause and think about it: a football game in which almost a quarter of the players were dead six months later.

Those who died weren't the most skilled ever to play, despite their remarkable skill. They didn't run the fastest or throw the longest or tackle the hardest. But if you measure sports by the values that have since become so blurred by money and fame—pure brotherhood without a guaranteed contract, sacrifice of self, the ability to rise above pain, the refusal to quit, values so important that the US Navy believed football to be the single best training for combat and saved the college game during World War II—then those who died were the best who ever played.

They are all but forgotten now, as all men in war are ultimately forgotten. They are eternal, as all men in war are eternal. Who they were, where they were from in an America both blessed and brutal, the gung ho innocence that turned into the darkest horror as they traveled through the maze of being a marine, is not some period piece or contrived cautionary tale but the most timeless story of all: of humanity in the face of all that has become inhuman, the inhumanity of all that once was human, the remarkable sacrifice that men are still willing to make even when the world has gone mad, united by that thing you cannot ever control in war, however brave or careful or fearful or raging with revenge: *who dies*, because so many died after that game; *who lives*, because many did live despite combat and serious injury.

The Mosquito Bowl.

Part One

1
McLaughry

The procession of the 358 graduating seniors of Brown University started at the Van Wickle Gates and wound its way along Waterman Street in Providence in Rhode Island, through the campus to the great white steeple of the First Baptist Meeting House. It was the end of something, the beginning of something, the sliver of time in between the two that was commencement on June 17th of 1940.

There had been a dinner dance the Saturday before, not quite as spectacular as the junior promenade in the Hotel Biltmore ballroom with Louis Armstrong and Jolly Coburn and His Orchestra playing until 3:00 a.m., but perhaps more let loose given that nothing could happen to you anymore. Some of the graduates were undoubtedly the worse for wear than others. One beer too many, or maybe three or four or five depending on the level of relief and mood and celebration and skating by in French or maybe it was English lit, freedom from four years of being told what to do by crotchety men in bow ties who spoke in stilted and stentorian tones like failed try-outs for Shakespeare. Not to mention those ridiculous brown caps with white buttons known as "dinks" they had been expected to wear as freshmen in all of Providence except on Sundays and not walking on the campus grass and having to make a deferential greeting to all upperclassmen, the regulations enforced by the Brown Gestapo of the Cammarian Club. It didn't matter how hungover you were at graduation anyway; nobody in history had ever looked bad in a cap and gown as long as the tassel wasn't on the wrong side.

Commencement processions were hierarchical, who led the line carefully chosen. It was an exceptional honor, something in your life you would never forget.

No one in the class could compare to John Jackson McLaughry, selected by his peers to be the marshal of the 1940 commencement. He was class president. He was a member of Alpha Delta Phi, the supreme of the supremes when it came to fraternities. He was also the football captain in a program that was highly competitive nationally at a time when the East was still the beast of football, fielding six of the top twenty teams in the country in 1940.* Everybody knew who John McLaughry was, not just at Brown. Playing the utterly unglamorous position of blocking back, he had become known nationwide for crushing his opponents without mercy on offense and defense. He had thrown the hammer in track, having unofficially set the national schoolboy scholastic record at Phillips Academy in Andover in Massachusetts; had broken the Brown record in the hammer as a freshman; had won the Penn Relays; had finished second in the Amateur Athletic Union championship; and had been in the running for a spot on the 1940 US Olympic team until the games were canceled because of the cauldron of Europe. He had also been Brown's reigning heavyweight boxing champion for two years. But he wasn't some one-dimensional jock.

He was an artist of budding potential, an uncanny gift that had begun as a child when he had been bedridden with an illness that had forced him to learn to walk again; he had drawn soldiers and historic figures

---

* The teams, according to the Associated Press poll, were Boston College (5th), Fordham University (12th), Georgetown University (13th), University of Pennsylvania (14th), Cornell University (15th), and Lafayette College (19th).

and landscapes, imitating Winslow Homer and N. C. Wyeth. When he was twelve, he had won a scholarship for Saturday classes to the prestigious Rhode Island School of Design. As he had gotten older, he had become a student of military history and what made a man heroic in the face of great obstacle. What were the qualities someone must possess? He had no idea how important that search would become.

At the traditional "Under the Elms" exercises held on the Friday before commencement, McLaughry gave the welcoming address. The speech was short and unadorned, a little bit dour. The lighter side of his personality came through in the drawings and caricatures he created, a side of whimsy and cleverness and affection that were not in his personal demeanor, although there were moments of great animation. He had had his fun in college, and his grades were a reflection of that: two A's (both in art), two B's, twenty-six C's, and six D's. He was the proverbial big man on campus, strolling down Brown's Middle Campus with eyes upon him, six feet tall and close to 200 pounds, big for a back in the 1930s. He knew how to clean up and looked Gatsbyan in white coat and tie at the spring Alpha Delta Phi dance. But in pictures you rarely see him smiling; instead there is an aura of seriousness defined by the blunt force of his chin and a surprisingly well-proportioned nose despite his having broken it five times while playing football. He had done so in the 1937 game against Dartmouth College on the opening kickoff, and then a second collision during the same game had actually reset it.

McLaughry and his classmates had entered Brown in 1936 in the grip of the Great Depression. Four years later, the economy was recovering somewhat, with the banks in better condition and the beginnings of job creation by the country's naval rearmament program. It was also the beginning of a new decade, and beginnings implied possibility despite the seemingly unstoppable advance of the Nazis. In September of 1939, they had invaded Poland, which had prompted declarations of war against Germany by England and France. Americans had watched with wary eyes. British prime minister Winston Churchill emphasized to US President Franklin D. Roosevelt that the United States must become involved for the preservation of democracy. Roosevelt knew that Churchill was right, but the American public was determined not to engage in the war beyond the sending of military supplies to the Allies. No one had forgotten the legacy of the

Great War: some 20 million dead, including more than 116,500 Americans, in a cause that had only precipitated the fracturing of Europe.

Americans had felt duped, manipulated, guilted, and goaded by the British, fighting *their* war thousands of miles away across the Atlantic. They were determined never to be put into the same situation again. On June 14th of 1940, three days before McLaughry graduated, 79 percent of Americans told a Gallup Poll that they wanted to stay out of the war. On college campuses, sentiment against entering the war in Europe was even greater: a month before graduation, the *Brown Daily Herald* reported that only 2 percent of undergraduates nationally surveyed believed that the United States should immediately join the Allies. The story, in the lower left-hand corner of the front page, was dwarfed by the one in the top left-hand column recapping the formal dances of eleven campus fraternities. Both Delta Kappa Epsilon and Pi Lambda reported record attendance, 225 persons swaying and swinging to the Lee Cross Orchestra at the former and 200 jamming the latter. Not to be outdone, Billy Burke played at the redbrick mansion of Delta Upsilon and Ed Drew and his swingsters at Phi Kappa Psi up on Waterman Hill.

The bands played on.

McLaughry had choices after college, remarkable ones: graduate school in art, an executive training program in business, maybe even a career in pro football. His last season at Brown in 1939 was not his best, as he was beset by injuries. The talk that he could be an All-American got whispered out. But the New York Giants drafted him in the third round, making him the twenty-fifth pick of the draft. He wasn't sure he would pursue the opportunity. The pro game was not held in particularly high esteem; many of those who played were considered one step up from felons or maybe they were felons, roughhouse thugs whose diet consisted of beer and more beer and who could maybe get the alphabet right on the second try. There wasn't much money. College coaches, even greater islands of sports than they are now, were decidedly against the pro game, seeing careers that led to nowhere once they were over. Many of the nation's best players in 1939 had no interest in playing pro whatsoever. McLaughry was different, perhaps because he knew that even if a career in the pros did not pan out, he would still have plenty of options.

Of all the marines who would play in the Mosquito Bowl on Guadalcanal before shipping out for Okinawa, no one had lived a more rarefied life. The McLaughry family in America went back to the Revolutionary War, when Richard McLoughry, who had emigrated to New York from Ireland, had served as a private soldier in the New York militia. John McLaughry had grown up in the neighborhood surrounding Brown, his block filled with private school teachers, administrators, lawyers, and businessmen. He had gone to the finest high school in Providence, Moses Brown School, where he had been football captain, followed by a postgraduate year at the even more prestigious Andover.

He was being groomed for success, plenty of pressure without Tuss.

With Tuss . . .

2
Everybody's Watching

In a picture taken in the 1930s, DeOrmond "Tuss" McLaughry is wearing baggy football pants and an athletic shirt with the initials BUAC for Brown University Athletic Council. Spinsterish black socks are pulled up to the knees; his feet are encased in ankle-high football shoes. He looks like the original inspiration for Bill Belichick.

He stands between his two sons, John and Robert. They are in football uniforms, John a young teenager and Robert four years his junior. In another picture taken the same day, Tuss watches as John, already big and brawny, practices his tackling technique against the appreciably shorter Robert, laughing either because he's having a ball or because he is trying to be cheerful in the face of being pulverized into dust. In another John is hiking the ball to Robert in the style of the game then, in which the backs were roughly a yard behind the center. The field is otherwise empty. Tuss hangs back, seemingly reluctant to coach his sons, his instinct to let them have fun and find their own way. He knew something about pressure because of his chosen profession, how it could corrode, the best thing to do to find ways of minimizing it. He knew that his boys felt pressure enough. To become intimately involved in their practice would only heighten that pressure. Fathers had a way of doing that when it came to sports, living vicariously through their kids, pushing them to heights they themselves could never attain, the common delusion that a child who excelled in sports enhanced their own immortality.

Tuss wasn't simply the father of two fine athletes;* it would have been so much simpler if he had been. He was a college football coach—a very famous college football coach at the time, a dean among his egocentric peers for his innovativeness and graciousness and levelheadedness. He had become a living legend at the age of thirty-two in 1926, leading in his first season a Brown team

---

* The younger Robert was actually a better natural athlete than his older brother and one of the best high school running backs in the country. He suffered a hairline fracture in his back in a skiing accident and never played at Dartmouth.

that not only went undefeated but became known as the "Iron Men" in which the eleven starters played two consecutive games without substitution and almost a third until Tuss replaced them with ten minutes left.

John McLaughry attended all but one of the ten games of the Iron Men team. They were magical for a nine-year-old, in particular the Harvard game, when the stadium in Cambridge was so crammed that spectators spilled out into the aisles like tossed peanut shells. His father was a superstar, and the son felt the burden of that the moment he began to play football competitively.

"If a son of a coach does not excel in athletics or doesn't care for them he is looked down upon and is considered not to be a 'chip off the old block.' Secondly, if he does make good in a moderate way he is said to be living on the reputation of his father," he wrote in a personal autobiography as part of a school assignment. The pressure had started in high school, at Moses Brown School. He was big for his age, 155 pounds, and as a freshman made the starting varsity in the backfield. Moses Brown played Rhode Island State's* freshman team in the first game of the season. He was nervous enough, but then the nervousness multiplied when his picture was in the

---

* Now the University of Rhode Island.

paper the morning of the game, holding a football with an accompanying story about how he was following in his father's footsteps. He played with the yips and fell out of the starting lineup.

The attention at Moses Brown died down, particularly as he got better. But it ratcheted up again, actually getting worse, when he took the postgraduate year at Andover in 1935–1936. Andover football was a big deal then, routinely written up in the New York and Boston papers, its rivalry with Phillips Exeter Academy the high school equivalent of Yale versus Harvard. The school was a bastion of wealth, prestige, and conservatism, 79 percent Republican, according to a straw poll. Ninety percent of the students disapproved of the New Deal. An astounding 304 alumni were in *Who's Who in America*, slightly less than 1 percent of the total.

Close to ninety out of roughly 175 seniors went to Yale in 1936, the year McLaughry graduated, a glaring example of the white privilege that had a lock on the country. During that time period, one out of every ten students at Yale was an Andover graduate.

Postgraduates, or "ringers," as the student body called them, were usually excellent high school athletes, particularly in football. McLaughry was highly touted in the newspapers with the unofficial asterisk next to his name. "Every account of any of the games in the New York or Boston papers, when mentioning me, never failed to state that I was the son of the Brown football coach," he wrote at one point. "The feeling that it was imperative to do well was constantly with me at Andover, and during the Exeter game I had the feeling that a lot of people were watching me to see how many mistakes the son of the Brown football coach made. I made a lot of mistakes [a punt of his was blocked when a player on his own team ran into him] and lost the game for Andover because of them. I think I was not at my best because of the nervous strain I was under in trying to do as well as many expected me to do. It is a hard thing for a person to understand who has never been in the same position as I was and still am."

Andover was the greatest challenge of his life up to that point, no longer in the Providence cocoon. Academics were a struggle; he did more work in one year at Andover than he had done in four years at Moses Brown. His teachers did not hold back on criticism, one he had in the fall term of 1935 noting, "He knows a great deal, but his paper is messy and not conspicuously literate. He would have done better, I suggest, to have thought more and written less." He skated by with a 63-point average in the class but an admirable A/B for effort. His Latin was a mess. His French wasn't so hot, either.

During the winter term his grades improved appreciably, 80 points or better in three courses, English history and two art classes. He was a runner-up for the prestigious Yale Prize for an English history essay he wrote, a shock to his professor and for that matter to McLaughry himself. He won the award for best athlete, not just for football but also for track with a 206-foot throw of the eleven-pound hammer during practice that would have broken the national scholastic record by an astounding eight feet, eleven inches.

As a student on scholarship, he waited on students in the commons and cleared tables, by his own typically precise calculation carrying off 140 milk bottles and 168 glasses every meal. He learned the Andover ropes, noting that the best place for a minivacation was the new infirmary, where the night nurse gave you a glass of milk with a scoop of ice cream in it as well as access to radios, magazines, and playing cards. Although he never tried it himself, he knew some students went to the infirmary and while there surreptitiously leaned against a radiator in the hope of getting a temperature and a few more days in Heaven.

Socially he fit right in, becoming a member of one of Andover's prestigious societies after successfully going through initiation. All members had to be addressed as "sir" or "master." In one rite of passage, he and the other pledges were forced to eat sandwiches with everything imaginable and unimaginable in them. Three cups were passed around into which everyone had to spit. Then they were blindfolded and forced to drink from what seemed like one of the cups; it didn't hold the spit, just a raw egg. He was used as a human tennis ball with "players" at each side of a long bench armed with broomsticks and mop handles hitting McLaughry back and forth across a "net." Another "good game," as McLaughry called it, was pushing a penny up and down a rug several times with your nose. Wrinkles in the rug were effective obstacles. The first night he rubbed almost all the skin off his schnozz, and a scab developed; the second night the scab fell off, and blood dripped the whole way. Every time a pledge smiled during the initiation period, he had to drop and wipe the smile off on the floor, accompanied by the smack of a paddle. McLaughry's mother was quite upset, but he reassured her that "it wasn't half as bad as it sounded." As further reassurance, he told her that the initiation was a lot easier than in prior years, when some pledges had been beaten so badly that they'd had to go to the infirmary.

It would have been easier had McLaughry gone to Yale; Tuss's looming presence would have been at least somewhat alleviated. But he chose Brown. It was a foregone conclusion. He felt obvious loyalty to his father, whatever the added pressure. But the decision unleashed a new slew of stories, not simply of the son with a football coach for a father but of the son playing for a father who was now his coach. As John got better and better during his career, becoming an honorable All-American in 1938 and routinely heralded as one of the best blocking backs in the country as well as a vicious linebacker, coverage about the two McLaughrys multiplied in dozens of papers. They were news from Los Angeles to Boston with St. Louis, Cincinnati, Minneapolis, and Indianapolis in between.

There was another level of subtext to it all: the son as savior of the father.

II

The Iron Men of the 1920s had given way to a string of lousy teams in the 1930s. Even living legends had a shelf life. A chorus of voices rose to say that it was time for Tuss to go, and in 1935 it was reported that he was going to resign after nine seasons. He needed a star of follow-my-example leadership. He needed a balls-out blocking back. He needed his son. "Other coaches have had their sons playing football for them," wrote Harry Grayson, the sports editor of NEA Service. "Other sons have done fairly well, but historians cannot recall another who was quite as valuable as John Jackson McLaughry is to his dad and Brown."

In 1935, Brown went 1–8 and was shut out in seven games. In 1936, the varsity went 3–7, outscored by Harvard, Dartmouth, and Penn by a total of 110–6. The only bright spot was the undefeated freshman team with John as captain. The 1937 season wasn't much better, with John now on the varsity, Brown losing to Harvard, Dartmouth, and Yale by an aggregate score of 91–6, the highlight being the introduction of "Butch Bruno" the bear as the new Brown mascot to consensus approval. The alumni wanted Tuss out more than ever. The school stood by him. The team, anchored by John, had winning records in both 1938 and 1939, defeating not only the usual suspects but also Harvard and Columbia.

The father had turned it around. It would not have happened without the son.

They had one final ride together after John graduated.

Tuss had been selected as the coach of the Eastern College All-Stars in its annual game against a pro team, in this instance the New York Giants. So had his son as one of the studs of the East. Tuss had seventeen days to put a squad together. A crowd of forty thousand at the Polo Grounds watched in shock on September 4th of 1940 as the All-Stars won 16–7. Tuss reestablished his reputation as a coaching genius. The *New York World-Telegram* called him the coach of the year, and the Giants' head coach, Steve Owen, complimented him on "a superb job." The *New York Times* called him "magnificent."

Praise was also lavished on John, who was cocaptain of the team and called the plays. The *New York Herald Tribune* said he "really had the Giants running around in circles." The *World-Telegram* said he ran the team "with poise, confidence and enough daring." The *New York Times* wrote, "Perhaps the key to the whole success of the All-Stars was John McLaughry's direction of the team. The big youngster did his father proud."

John signed a contract with the Giants for $2,000. As usual exceeding expectations, he started several games, beating out a first stringer. When it came time to renegotiate his contract with the Giants the following season, 1941, he did not like what he was being offered. So he quit and entered the executive training program at Bethlehem Steel's Fore River Shipyard in Quincy, Massachusetts. On the day that every American alive would remember where he or she was, December 7, 1941, McLaughry was in New York. He had gone to the Giants game against the Brooklyn Dodgers to see his old teammates, before a crowd of 55,051 at the Polo Grounds. The Japanese attacked right before the start of the game, and the boys in the press box knew but not the fans, somehow coping without smartphone alerts.

McLaughry was in a cab down Eighth Avenue in Manhattan. He was half listening to the radio when the news came that Pearl Harbor had been attacked by the Japanese.

Six days later he took the physical examination for pilot training for the US Army Air Corps. He was one of five who passed out of about forty who were there with him in Boston that day, but there was a hitch: he was still at his playing weight of two hundred pounds, good for football but nine pounds overweight for his height by air corps standards. He was given two weeks to lose the weight and promptly dropped eleven pounds, his tipping of the scales covered by the newspapers, given his celebrity.

Almost immediately afterward he married Jane Pitts on January 10th of 1942 in the chapel of St. Martin's Church in Providence. She had grown up in the city, the daughter of a prominent doctor, and was the sister of a friend of McLaughry's from Brown.

She had graduated from Bennington College with a degree in art the same year McLaughry had graduated from Brown, then had moved to New York when he played for the Giants. In a caption accompanying a lighthearted illustration of her shortly after their marriage, he wrote in the form of a scroll:

> An artist by trade and a
> Liberal in thought, whose love
> For ale is more than a lot
> —With Love from Hubby

In a corner on the same page was a smaller illustration of his wife leaning against an easel, emblematic of her skill in art, graphic design, and drafting—which made sense as Bennington, all female at the time, had produced a remarkable number of accomplished artists.

McLaughry reported for duty at Maxwell Field in Alabama to begin his training at the end of January in 1942. He was in the army now.

It was the worst decision of his life.

3
Schreiner

On the same day in December of 1941 that John McLaughry enlisted in the army air corps, a twenty-year-old football player from the University of Wisconsin named David Schreiner sat down at a table in perhaps the finest house in all of Lancaster, Wisconsin, the one his prosperous father had built in the midwestern Prairie School style, and in studied script gave himself a typically thorough beating.

> Lives are lived to learn. One should profit by his mistakes and live in the future a life picketed by the errors of the past. It sometimes takes many mistakes not just one to indelibly print on one's mind the meaning and true worth of the errors he has made.

I believe that I must begin to rebuild my character. This is a slow process at its best, and can only be done by having dogged persistence and determination. One thing must be concentrated on at a time; character and personality being built like a wall, foundation first which is the most important, and then the virtues which come as a result of a strong foundation.

The coming year, I am convinced is going to be my year, because I am going to accomplish the things which will stand me in good stead in later life. Although to an outsider it would appear as if I have made a great success of myself, I know that I have let more important things slip behind during my past achievements.

I set out to make myself a better man. I must, to begin with, forget a false sense of pride which is inherent in me. This means forgetting about trying to make impressions on people, or being afraid that people will think me self-centered or conceited. I am as good as other people—I must believe this. My main downfall, is, perhaps, lack of will power. I must dominate myself—I must be "the master of my fate" and "the captain of my soul."

He then wrote down sixteen different items he wanted to improve upon in the coming year:

More thoughtful of God

No smoking or drinking

Never be silly

Respectful of my parents

Never talk about anyone

No promiscuity of any kind with a girl

Regular habits of exercise

Slower eating, more regular, and better balance

More sleep

Ambition—drive, drive

Relax when necessary—be relaxed all the time

Sit up straight

Be more cheerful

Be more helpful

Do not be at all self-conscious

Date only nice girls

Wow . . .

Schreiner cleared tables at breakfast and dinner in the Ann Emery Hall women's commons at Wisconsin to make some extra money, even though his family, through the mercantile store they owned in Lancaster as well as savvy investments, apparently had plenty of it. The women ogled Schreiner, who was an inch over six feet with facial features like smoothed stone in which all cracks and fissures had been filled in; traditionally handsome without the slightest intrigue of imperfection, a soft smile of shyness. He rejected the advances, of course, his only observation being that the coeds ate ravenously and his presence had not caused them indigestion.

He was a member of the Phi Delta Theta fraternity, where he also lived, and he was a varsity football player for the Wisconsin Badgers, first starting as a sophomore. He played both ways at end—wingman, as it was called in those days—often going sixty minutes. Though he did acknowledge having some success, the itemization of faults in his New Year's resolution indicated that he felt it had been of no merit; unsatisfied, never satiated Schreiner.

The puzzling thing about Schreiner's self-assessment was his play on the football field in 1941 as a junior, when he was named first-team All-American by the Associated Press. Most young men his age would have puffed out their chests at least a little bit, a fine cigar moment. The Wisconsin football team in its muddled history in the Big Ten had little to brag about, the idea of any player being named to any All-American team a rare comet. Schreiner could have swaggered about, and no one would have protested. Instead, when a reporter for the *Capital Times* in Madison informed him that he had been named to the All-American list by United Press, his reaction did not have evidence of joy. "What for, I haven't done anything."

He had a complicated self-image that was infused with the ideal that the essence of humankind was rooted in humility. It had to do with the roots of his family and where he was from, a small place in the heartland of the heartland, a place to come to from Europe or places in the East and find work as long as you were willing to work, the conversational swell of "gosh" and "golly" and "gee whiz," the sounds of war still surreal and far away despite the bombing of Pearl Harbor twenty days before Schreiner had made his vow of contrition. He would serve, as 12 million others would in some capacity. But only a minority would serve on the front line of combat as he would ultimately do. Even fewer would be marines, roughly 475,000 at war's end in 1945.

II

The Schreiner family embodied the nineteenth-century immigrant experience that had put the United States onto the path of unprecedented economic

might: strong hands and backs, the bounty of the fur-
rowed fields of the Midwest, acceptance by those already here once Americans' instinctive hatred of new
immigrants wore off in the cyclical pecking order, the
acceptance of the Germans and the Nordics because
they were white and capable of melding in without
bringing alien traditions and religions. Immigrants
became coveted in the mid-1800s, competed over
to the degree that Wisconsin, like many states, had
an office in New York trying to entice them to move
there. Twenty thousand pamphlets were printed in
German.

In 1853, eighteen-year-old John Schreiner,
then named Johannes, living in Dexbach, Hessen-
Darmstadt, Germany, and fatherless since the age of
nine, joined the wave of immigrants from Germany in-
undating Wisconsin. He arrived in Lancaster in Grant
County in 1853, one of 893 living there. He was eager
for success, or at least steady work without the threat
of turmoil, revolution, and oppression, and America
represented shiny hope. Lancaster was virginal then,
newly incorporated, in a setting of hills and forestland
that reminded those from the homeland of their own
country. Grant County had a gift, the same American
gift that stretched from the flatlands of the Midwest
to the prairies of the Dakotas to the Palouse of Idaho

and Washington: the gold of the soil unlike any in the world, yielding in Grant County white and yellow hybrid corn, clover, barley seed, fruit, and milk from the roaming cows who had found their Xanadu.

In 1855, John Schreiner married Sophia Nathan, perhaps the wisest move of his life. Her grandfather Jacob had come to the United States in 1849, leaving behind his Jewish religion "in the Atlantic Ocean" because of a fear that persecution in Europe would follow him to Wisconsin. Jacob Nathan started out as a butcher, then began a mercantile business in Lancaster, ultimately inviting his grandson-in-law John to become a partner in 1868. Their company, Nathan, Schreiner & Co., bought items from forced sales in the East, aware of the midwestern inferiority complex when it came to fashion, and offered them to customers at 30 percent off: ladies' hose at eight cents a pair, spring shawls for a dollar, Japanese silk and linen fans, parasols in all grades, and groceries. It did an average annual business of $75,000 in the 1860s. But its big money was made as a dealer of Wisconsin-raised cattle, hogs, and sheep, shipping them to the stockyards in Milwaukee and Chicago.

John Schreiner gained sole ownership of the mercantile side of the business in 1882, changing the name to John Schreiner & Sons. One of those who worked there was Dave Schreiner's father, H. E., or Bert, as he was called. The success of the business led the Schreiners to become not just the first family of Grant County but highly respected in the corridors of power of the state capital in Madison. They were prosperous, but they were also imbued with a civic responsibility to make Lancaster a place of community. In 1926, when his son David was five, his father became the mayor of Lancaster by a landslide margin of 241 votes, 551 to 310. He served on the Lancaster District school board as treasurer and was also a board member of the Lancaster Country Club.

Bert and his wife, Anne, were woven into the fabric of a town whose residents, like most in America, desired safe predictability, an ebb and flow without surprise, punctuated by trips to Milwaukee and maybe even the Windy City on the Chicago & North Western Railway. Good schools were promoted. So were churches: Baptist, Catholic, Congregational, Episcopal, Methodist.

It was a life of pleasant obscurity with Lancaster doing what it did best, sowing the soil, milking the cows, slaughtering the hogs, letting it loose every now and then with fine food and drink. Until Dave Schreiner came along.

As his career flourished nationwide, he became a symbol of hope and pride, certainly the biggest thing in the county since Omar Koopman, the "corn husker king." He wasn't perfect. In an incredible admission when he was thirteen, he left a scribbled note for his mother telling her he was playing hooky from school to go fishing with Leroy Temple, Cecil Fosberg, and a couple of other buddies for the opening of trout season. He packed a lunch and promised to be back before suppertime.

"Do not send anyone after us."

In the summer he and his best friend, Mark Hadley Hoskins, looked like Tom Sawyer and Huckleberry Finn as they played outdoors, Schreiner in striped pants hiked far above the waist like a stretched rubber band and Hoskins in overalls. In the fall they did what most boys across small-town America did: when they weren't in school they spent their time outdoors playing sports. They were inseparable until the war. They went to Lancaster High School together, then to the University of Wisconsin in Madison, where they were both starters, their legend such that they became known as the Touchdown Twins. They lived together and were in the same fraternity together. Hoskins became a pilot for the Army Air Forces. Schreiner became a marine. He was in Guadalcanal when he learned that Hoskins had been shot down in Hungary and had bailed out; there was no word on whether

Hoskins was still alive. Schreiner called it the worst day of his life.

He played fullback at Lancaster High, where, according to him, he was one of the "worst fullbacks" ever to play the game. That wasn't true, of course, since none of Schreiner's self-assessments were true. But Mark Hoskins was the bigger attraction at Lancaster High and was considered both a better athlete and a better student; Schreiner's grades were mediocre, B's and C's. He wrote earnest but unimaginative essays on the evils of fascism and highway safety. When they entered Wisconsin in 1939, Hoskins was the one who got attention. There were no write-ups about Schreiner, just another kid from small-town Wisconsin trying to make the leap to a Big Ten program, grousing to his parents that nobody knew his name and the other players were soft. He made the starting freshman team, but the transition to college was difficult.

He criticized himself for being a slow thinker. He found some relief in pledging to a fraternity, particularly enjoying a prank on a frat member involving hiding alarm clocks in his room that went off every half hour. His course of study was premed, a big reach given his academic record in high school; it was mostly the desire of his mother. He needed a minimum of a 2.0 grade point average to be accepted to medical

school, and as a freshman he hovered in the range of a
1.5. During the spring he contemplated quitting football because the grind of practice and interference with
studies no longer seemed worth it.

He fretted to his parents about his grades in physics,
French, and economics. At least his social life started
filling out, sort of. He met a girl he thought was swell
and was going to take her home for his parents to meet.
But she turned out not to be so swell, and he never did.
He dated a woman named Barbara, whom he liked for
a while until he once again became "fed up." When he
went home for Christmas in December of 1940, he told
his mother he wanted to be as inconspicuous as possible: "You know how bashful I am."

III

Schreiner came to the attention of college football as
a sophomore. He could not have chosen a better place
than when Wisconsin played Columbia University in
New York City in 1940. The game was a 7–6 loss, but
Schreiner caught a forty-yard touchdown pass from
Hoskins, which was when the "Touchdown Twins"
label originated. He also intercepted a pass. He received
admirable notice from the sedentary grumps of New
York covering sports. The game was incidental to the

magic of the weekend itself, an era of college football that no longer exists. Wisconsin coach Harry Stuhldreher had put Columbia onto the schedule not for gate receipts but to show his boys the great wide world. Many of them, including Schreiner, had never seen the ocean, so the train from Madison stopped in Asbury Park on the New Jersey shore for the players to see the Atlantic, and they stayed at the swanky Berkeley Hotel there. There was a special dinner at the Waldorf-Astoria in New York City the Saturday night after the game when the team stood and sang "On, Wisconsin!" to rousing applause; then it was on to the Winter Garden on Broadway to see the Olsen and Johnson farce *Hellzapoppin*. They hit the nightlife after that, the details of which went with them to their graves. They stayed at the Waldorf, followed on Sunday by a four-hour tour of the city, including Radio City Music Hall, and lunch at the famed Jack Dempsey's on Forty-ninth and Broadway, where the boxing king himself often held court and the cheesecake was said to be the best in the city. As a local newspaper later put it, "Hadley Hoskins and Dave Schreiner both had the time of their lives."

All without earbuds, video games, or streaming. Imagine . . .

In 1941, as a junior, Schreiner was on the cusp of becoming one of the greatest ends in a decade, proving the unstoppable weaponry of the forward pass along with his hitting. In letters to his parents, he wrote about how nice it would be to be home with "you folks" the weekend before the huge Ohio State game and said he would make sure that his sister, Betty, and brother-in-law, Hal, would have tickets in plenty of time. The Ohio State coaches were dazzled by Schreiner that day in November of 1941 even though Wisconsin lost, 44–36.

He never said a word about his performance.

After the Mosquito Bowl had been played, McLaughry wrote to his father that Schreiner and an All-American center from the University of California named Bob Herwig were by far the two best players out there. But he was wrong, at least by the measure of future potential and destructive power and speed. There was someone else, a name so beautifully born for football that there had been no choice but to play it.

Butkovich.

4
Butkovich

There were seven Brothers Butkovich.

They all had nicknames, and it was easy at first to get the nicknames mixed up, which one went with whom and why. Emil, the oldest, was called "Scrap," and not even his nephew Larry Krulac was sure where that had come from. Frank, the second oldest, was called "Jargo," and that, too, was something of a mystery. Edward, the third oldest, was "Boul," and since there was a Bill in the family, it just seemed common sense that Boul would be Bill but Bill wasn't Boul. John, the fourth oldest, was "Diz," named after the Major League Baseball pitcher Dizzy Dean, which actually made sense since he was considered kind of goofy. Louis, the fifth oldest, was called "Koja." Tony, the sixth oldest, was called "Blondie" because of his hair color. Bill got the name "Sonny," as in "Hey, Sonny," because he was the youngest, although he was also mouthy and talky and that made "Sonny" seem too benign. Or maybe he was mouthy and talky because he was called Sonny and always had to fight upstream in the sibling order.

Spanning in age from Emil, born in 1907, to Bill, born in 1924, the Brothers Butkovich were great athletes, among the best group of siblings ever in Illinois. Jargo (Frank) was a giant and knew his way around a football field. Boul (Edward), who later owned a bar in a beer-and-a-shot-now-it's-Friday-night-let's-fight town legendary for its saloons, was a catcher with the biggest hands and fingers anyone had ever seen and had played semipro up in Wisconsin. Dizzy (John) was a good baseball player until his leg got shattered while he was working in the coal mines like his dad. Koja (Louis) was an all-state running back at Canton High, a behemoth in the late 1930s at six foot three and 198 pounds, and played football at the University of Oregon. Sonny (Bill) was the starting quarterback of the University of Illinois football team for two seasons and started at second base in baseball.

They were the sons of Croatian immigrants from a coal mining town in Illinois called St. David where there was never enough of anything except the love of the parents that encircled all their children. There were eleven in the family, crammed together in a tiny hothouse of athleticism and competition and perpetual motion that could have ignited were it not for the presence of their father, Blaž, who spoke softly—actually he did not speak much at all—but kept strict order with a single look.

The other Brothers Butkovich might not like to hear it, but the second youngest, Tony, was the best athlete. In football he led Lewistown High School to an undefeated season in 1938 and appeared destined for Big Ten greatness. In basketball he was a starter on the Lewistown High team that became "the legend of Fulton County," second only to when Abraham Lincoln had spoken about the sanctity of the Declaration of Independence in 1858. Some felt his best sport was baseball and that he had true pro potential, just as he had true pro potential in football. He was hitting .455 with the Canton Fans in the Illinois State League the summer after high school graduation, the game against Delavan memorable for the Brothers Butkovich, with Tony and John going a combined seven for nine with three home runs in an 18–0 blowout.

After he joined the marines, he liked to send pictures home from Guadalcanal of a parrot perching on his shoulder. He was innately bighearted, a kid in many ways. He wept in the locker room. He hated to take off his uniform after an upset win; he wanted to make the moment last forever. He played with blood and dirt on his face. He liked to tease and taunt.

A year younger than Schreiner, he had been far more touted coming out of high school and one of the best all-around athletes in the history of Illinois up to that time. But he did not have a similar success in college. He was in his ascendance to what many hoped would be a great season of his own in the Big Ten in 1942 as a junior, or at least come closer to the hoopla that had surrounded him. His sophomore year at the University of Illinois had been mediocre at best.

Maybe all Butkovich needed was another year of physical and emotional maturity to have the kind of season in 1942 that so many had expected. Maybe he needed to remind himself where his father, Blaž, had been at the same age: underground, the living spat out begrudgingly at the end of the day only to be pulled back in the next, the cycle of the mines where workers' bodies gave out in their forties unless the phlegm and blood of black lung or an accident got to them first. Or maybe what he really needed was a pep talk and thrashing from the Brothers Butkovich that he had better get his act together and not squander the speed and strength he had been given.

Baseball was the game of choice in St. David. Everyone played; it was an inclusive game in which even the slightest of athletes could always be tucked away in right field without ever being heard from again. Mothers who had come to the United States from Croatia or southern Italy cooked up a feast fit for kings and queens and sat on a hill on Sunday afternoons in the shade of the summer sun to watch their boys born in America playing in an American ritual. Sometimes the games were held on the field near the Burlington and Northwestern Railway tracks bisecting the town, and that was always a bonus because it was flat and unencumbered. Other times they were played in "Sheepshit Stadium," a pasture from which the residents were temporarily relocated but left behind their calling cards. Calcified dung patties were used for bases, making slides uniquely exciting when the bases were not quite calcified. When the weather was good, they played past twilight until they could not see the ball anymore and then played some more. Bats were precious, nailed back together when they broke and stinging like hell when you made contact.

The legacy of the Brothers Butkovich was remarkable coming out of a town of less than one thousand in midstate Illinois built by coal, sustained by coal, surrounded by coal, living by coal, dying by coal. The three young-est brothers all used their skill in sports to attend major universities. Few working-class families in America could claim that, much less the family of a coal miner born across the Atlantic. It was an American story, the kind of story Americans bragged about, leaving out the parts about hatred and racism and degradation that Blaž Butković and so many of the roughly 15.7 million other immigrants like him had faced when they had decided to leave their homeland and build the United States into the most powerful country the Earth had ever witnessed.

II

The municipality of Mrkopalj in Primorje-Gorski Kotar, Croatia, about thirty miles inland from the Adriatic port then known as Fiume and now called Ri-jeka, held the myths of fables, giants and faeries and unicorns hidden within its rolling forests, watched over by the mountains of Viševica and Bitoraj. It was in the tiny village of Sunger, a satellite of Mrkopalj, that Blaž Butković was born in 1874, the son of Anton and Ana Butković.

Dependent on timber and sheep herding and sub-sistence farming, the area, though beautiful, was im-poverished; their faltering fortunes caused Butković and roughly 170,000 other Croatians to emigrate to the United States between 1900 and the beginning of the First World War in 1914. They were part of the wave of millions, almost all of them from southern and eastern Europe who came to the United States during that period in the greatest wave of voluntary emigration in the history of the world. Blaž took with him no particular professional skill. He was a hardworking laborer; that much he knew about himself. He traveled alone, as many men did. He knew he would most likely go to either the coal mines or the steel mills, as the vast majority of Croatians did. He had contacts from Mrkopalj in the United States if he could only get to them—unless a railroad conductor, knowing he spoke no English upon his arrival, shunted him to a different destination in return for a tidy payoff from an employer desperate for labor.

There was potential reward in going to America; as the lowliest worker, it was possible to make more than seven times in a year what he had in his native land. There was an enormous demand in a country bursting with new industry, its share of worldwide manufacturing output growing from .8 percent in 1800 to 23.6 percent in 1900 and the number of industrial workers from 6 million in 1870 to 25 million in 1910. But the need varied depending on supply and demand and recessions and minidepressions. There was cyclical un-employment, too, and immigrants were the first to be fired.

It wasn't only the lack of regular employment that ultimately drove some Croatians back home. It was also the physical relocation to urban places of concrete where land was there only to be developed, no stars at night in the twenty-four-hour-a-day belch and haze of factory smoke, the monotonous maddening sound of machine on the warehouse floor, the withering looks by subway passengers as they cupped their hands over their mouths and whispered the word *vermin* to their companions. Living in America often caused the ache of loneliness, a life turned inside out and upside down, sealed and shuttered. The word *assimilation* was tossed about, but it was a code word for admitting the right, "pure" stock, as defined by nativists and restriction-ists and eugenicists. Which was why as many as 40 percent of those from Croatia made as much money as they could by working twelve to sixteen hours a day and then returned home, prompting one Slavic writer to observe, "My people do not live in America; they live underneath America. America goes on over their heads."

As emigrants returned home to Croatia to tell their stories of an America no one wanted to believe, Blaž

Butković undoubtedly listened. Just as he also must have heard the stories of those coming back in a made-in-America blue serge suit and a rainbow-colored tie, bragging of the riches they had made regardless of whether the stories were true or not. According to them, the streets of America would always be paved with roses.

The immigrants themselves were gold for the transatlantic steamship lines. Thousands of so-called runners working on commission for ticket agents traveled from city to village in southern and eastern Europe peddling Pied Piper tales of the sublime life in America with plentiful jobs and cushy living for young men and women. In some instances they used priests and their reputation for honesty to talk villagers into emigrating, the holy fathers taking the holy water of a kickback. They talked families into selling everything they had before they left, even though they knew that certain members had physical or mental afflictions that would surely bar them from entry.

The runners did not mention that after their arrival, some women, under the pretense of a better life in the United States, would be recruited into forced prostitution by men describing their work as a "livestock roundup," enticing them by promising easy-money laundry work or becoming a housemaid, searching for them in employment agencies and the waiting rooms of large department stores, where new arrivals liked to sit and dream of all the riches of America, thumbing through catalogs glittering with goods like gold.

They did not mention where the new arrivals, female and male, would live after they arrived in New York and settled there, as the largest percentage did: maybe in a tenement on West Houston Street with dirt on the walls so thick it could retard a fire from a stove spark. Or in a *drustvo*, a communal boardinghouse catering to Croatians and Slavs. Or in one of a row of "lodging houses" on the Lower East Side, sleeping in a filthy bed covered by a filthy blanket rented by the day or night depending on one's work shift. Entire families were forced to live in a single bed that took up an entire room. Some mothers rolled over in the night and suffocated their babies—maybe accidentally or maybe on purpose, no one knew. The runners talked instead of going to see vaudeville shows at the Orpheum Theater and shopping in R. H. Macy's department store, which took up a block of New York, an *entire block*!

Butković was thirty years old when he left Mrkopalj in March of 1904 for the French port of Le Havre. Upon his arrival it was standard to be greeted by a welcoming committee of con artists, hucksters, and flimflammers. Fly-by-night doctors in European port cities offered remedies for the contagious eye disease trachoma, the number one bar to entry by US immigration officials: drops that would blind a person if overused. A fake dentist made the rounds, telling travelers that it would be impossible to get affordable dental care overseas and pulling the three remaining teeth of one unsuspecting woman. Merchants at the edge of the dock sold worthless seasickness charms. Organized crime ran a profitable racket in which you could buy anything if you could afford it: fake passports, fake naturalization certificates, fake doctor's stamps claiming a clean bill of health since steamship lines required medical examinations before boarding.

Blaž Butković arrived in the United States on April 14th of 1904. The ship docked at a pier on the West Side of Manhattan; then he and the other new arrivals were transferred by barge to Ellis Island, once the site of an ammunition depot, now the entry point into the United States. It was a madman's palace, thousands of arbitrary and at-whim decisions made during the peak years of the 1900s, when as many as five thousand people went through in a single day. It was dreaded by immigrants, who feared that they would

be barred from entry for reasons they did not understand and were never fully explained. The rate of rejection was actually minuscule, less than 2 percent:
immigrants as laborers were too essential to the country's growth. But those forced to return went back to
countries where they no longer had homes or possessions because selling them had been the only way to
raise enough money to come to America.

Butković and the thousands of others were herded
into cattlelike pens of wire mesh and waited for hours.
They eventually lined up in single file, and a doctor
from the US Public Health Service quietly sized them
up from top to bottom in all of two minutes each for
such issues as flat feet, gait, goiter on the neck, scars,
acne, spinal deformity. Those deemed "suspicious" for
whatever reason received a chalk mark on their clothing that to a terrified immigrant was the same as being
branded: *B* for "back," *C* for "conjunctivitis," *CT* for
"trachoma," *G* for "goiter," *K* for "hernia," *S* for "se-
nility," *X* for "suspected mental defect," circled *X* for
"definite signs of mental disease." A second doctor
flipped up an eyelid with a thumb and finger to make
sure that there were no signs of the highly contagious
trachoma or instead used a metallic instrument plunked
into a pail of disinfectant after each exam.

Butković received no chalk marks based on his available records. He was considered neither an imbecile nor an idiot.

Blaž Butković avoided the ghettoized pockets of despair in the cities, where roughly two-thirds of immigrants settled. The community of Mrkopalj, like thousands of other villages throughout Europe, had developed a word-of-mouth network about where to emigrate, places that members of the community had already gone to and could vouch for in terms of decent jobs and a hospitable environment. Those from Mrkopalj and the surrounding region gravitated to mining towns: the Radosevićs to Gallup, New Mexico; the Starcevićs, Kazlarićs, and Majnarićs to Roslyn, Washington; the Stankovićs to Calumet, Michigan; the Zaboraćs, Sepićs, and Butkovićs to the small city of Canton in Fulton County.

Welcome to America.

5
Land of the Free

The United States was a country of immigrants who hated each new wave of immigrants. Southern Italians were filthy dagos. Croats and those from other eastern European countries were dumb hunkies. Jews were kikes and believed to have a heightened capacity for insanity. Almost 16 million people emigrated to the United States between 1903 and 1924 in what detractors described as the continent's "garbage bin" of southern and eastern Europe, supposedly poisoning and polluting the country's Anglo-Saxon and Teutonic bloodlines.

Beginning in the late nineteenth century and for the next twenty-five years, there came a hostility from self-referenced "pure Americans" that would evolve into detestation and not only culminate in the banning of virtually all immigration from Europe in 1924 except for a tiny quota but become an impetus for the Japanese declaration of war. Those who were most publicly outspoken in their loathing were not individuals on the fringe; they were politicians, judges, powerful business leaders, eminent authors, acclaimed professors, university presidents, and federal immigration officials. They found expression not in basement printing press pamphlets but in books published by such eminent mainstream publishers as Charles Scribner's Sons and Dodd, Mead and magazines such as the highly popular *Saturday Evening Post*, the single greatest source of anti-immigration rhetoric.

In describing "the poor Italian and Slav" working in the coal mines in 1892, the social scientist Henry Rood described them as "the scum of Europe . . . content to swarm in shanties like hogs, to contract scurvy by a steady diet of the cheapest salt pork, to suffer sore eyes and bodies rather than to buy a towel and wash-tub, to endure typhoid fever rather than undergo the expense of the most primitive sanitary apparatus." A cross section of how they were referred to in other popular published writing: as "morons," "imbeciles," "bacteria," "scarcely superior to an ox," "vermin infested," "thieves and murderers," "queer alien mongrelized people."

II

Blaž Butkovich, his last name now changed from Butković as it had been for virtually every last name ending in "ić," arrived in Fulton County somewhere around 1904. Illinois had become the second largest coal-producing state in the country next to Pennsylvania. Fulton County was an agricultural community, one of those places where there were three times as many swine (153,253) as people (roughly 50,000)—along with 47,293 cattle, 25,993 horses, 764 mules, 12 asses and burros, 13,163 sheep, and 2,657 bee colonies—in 1910. The number of bushels of corn harvested that same year: 5,820,479; the number of gallons of milk: 3,304,130; the number of eggs by the dozen: 1,238,719. Farming was the bedrock, but the economy changed as coal mining exploded in Fulton County in the first decades of the twentieth century.

In 1904, a few months before leaving Croatia, Blaž Butković had married Ana Grubisić, who emigrated from Mrkopalj in 1906. They settled in St. David in the eastern part of Fulton County. Their first child, Emil, was born in 1907, followed by Frank in 1909. In

January of 1910, after living in the United States for the required five years, he and his family became naturalized citizens, their desire to be not simply of America but American.

The lifeblood of the region was the mines: Panic, Pee Wee, Hoodoo, Big Creek, Saline, Truax-Truer, and Little Sister, the bigger ones owned by out-of-town corporations and the tiny ones by locals hoping to pick up a little work when the corporate boys closed down the shafts because the price of coal was too low. St. David barely ever had more than a thousand residents, always a distant cousin to what passed for major metropolises in the county, Lewistown, the county seat, about ten miles south, with a population of nearly three thousand and the even bigger Canton, about five miles north, with twelve thousand.

The Butkovich family lived on Fulton Street, in a home they bought with a mortgage in 1906 for six hundred dollars. They later purchased it outright, common among immigrant families no matter what the financial sacrifice because of their intrinsic belief in home ownership and the laying down of stable roots. The house was small for a family that would grow to eleven: seven boys, two girls, and the parents. But it was bigger than the so-called batch houses where many miners lived:

one room with a window on the front and another on the side. The Butkoviches had a living room, a dining room, and a kitchen in front and two bedrooms in back. The seven brothers sprawled in the front rooms until several of them were old enough to go out on their own. The two sisters slept in one bedroom and the parents in the other. Eventually a porch was added.

Ana Butkovich, the family matriarch, and other like-minded residents of the neighborhood had bountiful vegetable gardens next to their homes, the magical green thumb transplanted from the old country. She planted fulsome rows of tomatoes, beans, and sweet corn. A hog was kept in the backyard until the annual slaughter, which became a community event, every inch of the animal preserved and the whole thing able to sustain the family for weeks, if not months. They ate well since Ana was something of a legendary cook, stuffed peppers, steak and polenta, cabbage rolls. Her pièce de résistance was povitica, a Croatian pastry made from thin layers of dough, covered with brown sugar, walnuts, and spices, and then baked. The dough stretched all the way across the dining room table as she made an enormous one every year and then raffled it off to raise money for St. Michael's, the Catholic church in town conveniently located next to Ma Caster's saloon, nothing better than a Sunday sermon and a shot, or maybe it was a shot and a Sunday sermon, or maybe just a shot and screw the sermon.

The block they lived on in St. David was defined by its diversity, a distinctly American diversity. It was a melting pot, which, as many historians of immigration point out, was rarely the case, particularly in the bigger urban areas. The Tomyanoviches, the Housers, the Stepiches, the Yadros, and two families of Butkoviches were from Croatia, the Villelmos and Peronas from Italy, the Larkins and Aunears from England, the Kennedys from Ireland, the Chimas from Poland. The languages spoken included English, Croatian, German, Polish, and Italian.

All of the men on the block but one worked in the coal mines. They lived their lives by the whistle: three long blasts at the end of the day signaling "work tomorrow," one long blast meaning "no work tomorrow," the dreaded sustained blast signaling that there had been an accident. They worked in blackness except for the light from kerosene or carbide lamps, excavating thousands of feet below the surface like ants burrowing tunnels, the "roofs" above them nothing but thin timbers that could collapse or catch fire, the "rooms" in which they excavated the coal having such low ceilings it was often impossible to stand up, the "cages" that took them up and down a metaphor for a miner's life, men in a cage just hoping to hear the three whistles at the end of the shift.

Coal dust stuck to the skin and clothing and got into the miners' lungs, which became black and hardened as if painted with shellac. There were troughs of water at the mine to wash off what they could with Castile soap, but they never got rid of all the grime. They often worked standing in water, and when the temperature dropped during the Illinois winter, they went home frozen. They suffered in subhuman conditions to provide warmth to others. But there was never enough money, never enough of anything. So in the winter in St. David, a miner or one of his sons would climb to the top of a railcar carrying lump coal. As the train approached a cluster of homes, he would throw the coal overboard for the families living there to burn for heat. When the air turned frigid, families gathered around the radio near the stove to listen to *The Lone Ranger*, *The Shadow*, and *National Barn Dance* out of WLS-AM in Chicago, featuring the singer Gene Autry and, best of all, Smiley Burnette on the accordion.

Work was good for Blaž Butkovich in 1910, after he become naturalized. He was unemployed for only twelve weeks that year, which, by the standards of

mining and considering the fickleness of the market-
place, was remarkable. Steady employment fed the
ever-growing Butkovich family, Emil followed by
Frank followed by Victoria in 1911 followed by Edward
in 1913 followed by John in 1915 followed by Mary in
1916 followed by Louis in 1919 followed by Tony in
1921 followed by Bill in 1924. But having steady work
only increased the risk of never coming back when the
miners trudged out in the morning in beaten-down,
black-spotted indigo overalls from Stifel's, the men
whose faces had lost individual expression many years
before and all looked the same, eyes that were milky
clouds, always wondering what might kill them.

Employers, and even some miners, were not known
to shed a tear when immigrants were killed, believing
that they took stupid risks to make money and that it
was their own fault they could not read English and
did not understand warning signs. Between the years
of 1883 and 1904 in the state of Illinois, 1,705 employees lost their lives in the mines, an average of 77 a year.
Wives and children stood in a circle around the lip of a
mine waiting for what many of them already knew, the
bodies of their husbands and fathers being slowly lifted
out by rope and pulley, not knowing whom the body
belonged to until the stretcher reached the surface and
hung there in the haloed light.

On November 13th of 1909, the year Blaž Butkov-ich's second child was born, a fire started in the St. Paul Coal Company mine in Cherry, Illinois, when a kerosene torch ignited bales of hay in a pit car, which in turn spread to the timbers above. It took eight days to bring the fire under control enough for the twenty-one survivors to be rescued and two months for all the bodies to be recovered. It was the third deadliest accident in US history at the time. The nationalities of those killed formed the immigrant anthem of America: 64 from Italy, 62 from Austria-Hungary, 17 from Lithuania, 11 from France, 9 from Sweden, 8 from Poland, 8 from England, 6 from Belgium, 3 from Russia, 2 from Ireland, 2 from Greece, 2 from Wales; 212 in all. One hundred seventy wives became widows. Four hundred forty-five children, 39 of them under the age of one, became fatherless.

III

St. David was scrappy and pugnacious, with the vinegar of proud cantankerousness. The railroad went through hauling bins of coal. The whistle blew every day at 4:00 a.m., which became a favored time to get pregnant since you had been woken up anyway and might as well get to work.

Main Street ran parallel to the tracks. It wasn't paved until the 1930s, so until then it was either dirt or mud or dust. There wasn't much there: Bima the grocery store, J. Honey Drug for medicine and ice cream, one-stop shopping for hardware and furniture at E. M. Reynolds. But if you wanted a drink, you had found the right place. There were ten saloons up and down Main Street at one time, or maybe it was six, or maybe, who knows, beer and the newspaper and sass from a woman barkeep who kept an eye out for underage drinkers with her special greeting: "You little son a bitch, you're not old enough." There was poker and other backroom gambling, and inevitably there was someone who lost his week's wages and had to borrow from the saloon owner to make it through until the next payday. There were fights among the miners that started over nothing and ended over even less.

Blaž Butkovich was big and imposing, his smile lost long ago in the Devil's work. He told his boys never to brag, to let their actions speak for themselves, although the collective athletic brilliance of the Brothers Butkovich made that difficult. He worked long and he worked hard as a coal miner. He believed in St. Michael's and the Croatian Fraternal League. He sat ramrod straight in church with his ample mustache. He sang in the church choir. Ana Butkovich was simply a sweetheart. Bit by bit his life and that of his family became more stable. They had found a place in America, a good place, even as the future of the immigrant in America only became more precarious. Eugenics had broken through to the masses, the idea that reckless breeding, the pollution of American blood by the southern Italians, the Slavs, the Polish Jews, and the Blacks, was killing America.

It wasn't simply that Americans hated "the new immigration"; the country was at complete odds with the way it viewed and sold itself as humane, kind, all-embracing. It had the profound beauty of its democratic principles, but they were terribly lost in the early 1900s in ethnic subjugation. Immigrants were considered pollutants, even though they had built the subway tunnels in New York, stripped the fat off the cows in the stockyards in Chicago, mined the mines in Pennsylvania, West Virginia, and Illinois, forged the steel in Pittsburgh. In 1917, a literacy test was imposed by Congress by which an immigrant had to show her or his ability to read thirty to forty words in the language of her or his choice. It did not do nearly enough to restrict immigration in the eyes of politicians. In the aftermath of World War I, because of which Americans now viewed Europe as a bastion of radicals, Communists, and warmongers, an act was passed in 1921 placing a severe quota on European immigration with particular bias against southern and eastern Europeans. The Immigration Act of 1924 made the quota even more restrictive, essentially closing US borders to Europeans for forty-one years until the passage of a new immigration act by President Lyndon B. Johnson as part of Great Society legislation.*

The end of the immigration era meant that the story of success that Blaž Butkovich and others symbolized would not occur again for the next four decades. Under the immigration restrictions of 1924, Blaž Butkovich would not have even been allowed into the country had he tried. There would never have been three first-generation children going off to major universities to play football.

The Brothers Butkovich still living at home in the 1930s threw themselves into sports as a way of maintaining some rhythm in their lives. Tony played basketball at St. David Elementary, newly built, with *steam heating*. There was, of course, Sunday-afternoon

---

* Under the Bracero program, established in 1942 because of a shortage of farm labor, Mexicans were legally allowed to come to the United States as contract workers without rights of citizenship. Some five million took advantage of the program over the next two decades. At the same time, some four million Mexicans living in the United States were deported.

baseball. He went to Lewistown High, a feeder school, where he was arguably the best football player ever in the history of the program, maybe the entire county. Competition came from his brother Lou, who had gone to high school in Canton (St. David kids were given a choice) and become the first-team all-state running back.

It was in basketball that Tony received the most attention. He helped lead Lewistown High to March Madness for the first time ever, in this case the original March Madness, a term coined just a year prior. The great sporting event of the Illinois High School Boys Basketball Championship began with 893 teams, cut down to the final 16, who played at Huff Gymnasium at the University of Illinois. The three-day event attracted 46,256 spectators.

Lewistown drew Hebron in the first round, locals paying a dime each to cram into the high school gym and listen to the game as it was relayed over telephone and amplified by a loudspeaker. Lewistown High had all of 355 students, but that was massive compared to Hebron's enrollment of 101. Everybody loved Hebron, cloyingly called *Little* Hebron by the sportswriters. They were also good—championship-caliber good— with a record of 31–1 that included beating defending state champion Rockford. Lewistown came in with a terrific record of its own, 26–4, but it didn't have a single starter six feet tall, compared to Hebron's four. Butkovich, about five foot ten, started at guard. He had great speed, given his brawn, but sometimes he was overly aggressive and prone to fouling out. He did engineer a rule change when he purposely threw a foul shot against the backboard to get the rebound: it became a requirement afterward that the ball had to touch the rim.

With four minutes left, Hebron held a very healthy 30–23 lead. Butkovich had led Lewistown in scoring with ten points, all of them in the first half. He had disappeared after that. The team itself had scored only nine points in the second half. Hebron's players should have played ball control. Instead they continued to shoot. Butkovich suddenly showed flash, hitting a shot on a fast break to narrow the score to 30–25. He scored again on another fast break to bring Lewistown within three points of Hebron, 30–27. With about ninety seconds left, Jimmy Jackson sank one from the circle to make the score 30–29. Don Ford, a Lewistown substitute, intercepted a pass and made a layup as he was going underneath the basket.

The final score: Lewistown 31, Hebron 30.

Lewistown went back to normal the next day in the quarterfinals, losing to Moline, 49–32. That was irrelevant. The game against Hebron became legend, and so did Tony Butkovich. Without his having scored on those two fast breaks, Lewistown would not have won. He had led all scorers with 14 points. He had made Lewistown, even if momentarily, the toast of high school basketball in Illinois. Little towns never forget something like that, an epic victory in Lewistown's first trip to March Madness and the only one it ever made.

The legacy of Tony Butkovich only seemed poised to grow further. He was set to go to Bradley University in Peoria and play baseball. But suddenly there was a change of heart: he decided to go to Illinois and play football.

As a member of the freshman team in 1940, he ran over several starters in the annual freshman-varsity scrimmage, which drew the attention of the coaches. He played only haltingly on the varsity in 1941, not unusual since sophomores rarely started. But 1942 would be different, just as it would be for Dave Schreiner—unless they both ran out of time.

A war was on, and there was only so long they could make it wait, no matter how entirely fucked it was at the beginning.

6

The Army Way

On January 24, 1942, married for exactly two weeks, John McLaughry left for training in the army air corps. He boarded a train from New York for Maxwell Field in Montgomery, Alabama. The trip took nearly twenty-eight hours, the leg from Greensboro to Atlanta on the filthiest train he had ever been on, ragged, bug-infested, stopping at every speck on the map in between. The air corps required specialized training, and the selection to become a combat pilot would be rigorous. Training took seven and a half months and under different circumstances should have taken more. But there was no time to waste; the Japanese were dominating the air with their superbly made Mitsubishi Zeros and years of training. American boys had to get up there. It was elementary, except that it was the "army way" and virtually nothing in the army way at the beginning of 1942 was elementary.

There were eight thousand cadets in the army air corps program at Maxwell, though McLaughry thought the capacity was five thousand, and more were coming in every day. There was no housing at the field itself, so McLaughry and other cadets from Squadron E were put up in an old cotton mill, then moved to a different airfield and lived in relatively spacious tents with floorboards. At least the amenities were better. The food, served at tables by Blacks, who were considered incapable of doing little more by the all-white military establishment than being waitstaff, service staff, and supply staff, was excellent. The cadets had frequent chances to go to the PX, and there were movies every night. He missed the one film he wanted to see, the Alfred Hitchcock psychological thriller *Suspicion* with Joan Fontaine and Cary Grant. There was no pilot training in sight, even in the classroom. What was strange was the utter lack of urgency, the war across two vast oceans still an abstraction. Men like McLaughry wanted to fight. Instead, they found themselves buried in the bureaucracy: *Go here, go there, no, back here, who are you again? A war? Where?*

In 1940, the US Army ranked nineteenth in size in the world, just ahead of Portugal's. With great cajoling,

President Roosevelt overcame the isolationists and America Firsters and pushed Congress to approve the first peacetime draft in US history on September 14th of 1940. The goal was to build up its strength to near 1 million. But the draft, like everything else, was politicized and offered appeasement to the lobby of American mothers among other groups. There was grave concern that they would be unable to bear the loss of their teenage and young adult sons, which was why the category of eighteen- to twenty-year-olds initially remained exempt despite their superiority in combat.

A limitation of one year* was placed on service to placate isolationists, which happened to also make raising an effective army untenable; by the time soldiers were trained and acclimated, they were out. The length was ultimately extended to eighteen months in August of 1941, passing by a single vote in the House of Representatives, 203–202. That made little difference in creating a prepared military. As many as 40 percent regretted being in the army, according to a survey in *Life* magazine. They considered military life boring, monotonous, arbitrary, and pointless. The idea of mobilizing to guard against attacks on home soil, given the distance from Germany and Japan, seemed absurd.

---

* Ten years in the reserves was also required, subject to call-up in case of war.

The argument that the United States would ultimately need to supply troops to Great Britain to aid in its fight against the Nazis only infuriated them; most Americans had not forgiven Great Britain for the snookering of them into World War I.

Japan never entered the equation until Pearl Harbor, when a 550-pound aerial bomb hit the seaplane ramp on Ford Island on December 7, 1941, and a radio signal went out at 7:57 a.m. local time: "AIR RAID ON PEARL HARBOR X THIS IS NO DRILL." The reaction over the next twenty-four hours was shock and racist screeds against the "yellow bastards." As the preeminent historian of Japan, John W. Dower, put it in an essay in depicting the prevalent attitude: "The Japanese were subhuman. They were little men, inferior to white Westerners in every physical, moral and intellectual way. They were, as a collectivity, primitive, childish and mad." The Japanese, in turn, considered Westerners weak and cowardly, setting up a conflict that in terms of brutality and hatred was worse than the United States' war against the Germans.*

Thirteen days after Pearl Harbor, draft eligibility

---

* The death rate for Western prisoners taken by the Japanese was 27.1 percent, seven times higher than the rate of Western prisoners taken by the Germans and Italians. It is believed that the death rate for Chinese prisoners taken by the Japanese was close to 100 percent.

was changed to make twenty-year-olds eligible to fight. But eighteen- and nineteen-year-olds, incredibly, continued to be exempt from actual fighting, the only requirement to register with the local draft board. The army still felt it would have no problem reaching its goal in 1942 given the potential pool of men of more than 40 million. But the army's standards for induction were far too high, given the atrocious physical and mental state of many American men: lazy, out of shape, not terribly bright.

Based on a survey by the Selective Service, 50 percent of those physically examined were not qualified for any type of military service. The rate of syphilis among recruits was a little over 5 percent.

At least McLaughry's Squadron E had a lot of laughs together, although that may not have been the point.

They went into town on open posts and got crazy fucked-up bonkers out-of-your-mind shitfaced in a way that made the frat parties at Brown look like penitence sessions. They gambled and beat the hell out of one another for fun. They gained a reputation for being perhaps the worst outfit in the current crop of cadets, embracing a former artillery sergeant who first showed up under armed guard for hitting a fellow sergeant with a metal chair and fracturing his skull. It was with pride that McLaughry told his parents that his squadron was considered "the gamblingest, hard drinkingest and most hard to handle outfit that has been around in a long time."

Fun and laughter were not part of the Japanese playbook.

Movies were forbidden at the Imperial Military Academy. Letters, the lifeblood of American servicemen, were discouraged. Soldiers were required to go on *setchu kogun*, or "snow marches," to acclimate to the cold, five days in the bitter winter in which they bivouacked out in the open. During the summer, to acclimate to the heat, marches as long as forty miles were carried out in peak temperature, with no head protection except a service cap.

On the very first day of training, the officer in charge went down the line of recruits, punching each one in the face. Afterward, any man who outranked another had the right to give him a face slap, a kick, or a beating into unconsciousness. A perceived infraction by one member of a barracks resulted in a beating for all. A first-year Japanese soldier was slapped across both cheeks several dozen times just to be made an example of for other soldiers, then forced to jump over each bed in the barracks, making the sound of a bush warbler, and finally to mimic a prostitute beckoning to a potential customer. A favorite cause of beating was for an officer to mention the name of the emperor and see if a soldier came to attention. It was the same with accidentally stepping on a newspaper left on the floor with the emperor's picture on it. The implements used in beatings included shoes with thirty-six tacks in their soles, wooden rifles, clubs, bats, whips, cleaning rods, tent poles, broomsticks, bamboo swords. Face slapping was a particular favorite anytime and anywhere: soldiers' teeth were knocked out and their ribs broken. The only retaliation was for a soldier to scratch flakes of dandruff into the miso soup and rice served at mealtime to officers who had administered beatings. Some soldiers preferred to commit suicide.

The treatment was inhumane. It also had its intended result: to make the soldiers of the Imperial Japanese Army inhumane, transfer the sadism used against them to the enemy and non-Japanese civilians. The command wanted the rank and file to simultaneously hate its officers and fear them, instilling what the historian Jay Fagel described in his study of Japanese army brutality as a "bloodthirsty desire to slaughter their enemy."

Soldiers were forced to memorize the Senjinkun military code of January 1941, which stated, "Never live to experience shame as a prisoner. By dying, you will avoid leaving behind the crime of a stain on your honor." They were frequently ordered to go on banzai attacks, made legendary by Western propaganda and silly war films but, in reality, mass suicide missions: wounded and exhausted soldiers running into machine-gun fire to fulfill the Imperial Rescript of 1882 with the famous phrase "Duty is heavier than a mountain; death is lighter than a feather." The Japanese believed themselves to be the world's superior race, and the military leadership was convinced that the spiritual will of its soldiers would make up for the glaring lack of modern weaponry to the point where it was considered irrelevant. They had been taught to believe in death as much as life, or even more so, that the beauty, poetry, and traditions of a culture must be subsumed by nationalists, extremists, and militarists, in devotion to an emperor considered to be a living deity. As the United States foundered in 1942, the Japanese were prepared, devoted, and formidable. Fighting to the death was their only option. Anything else was disgrace.

It wasn't until July 8th of 1942, six months after he had arrived, that he actually flew an airplane. He went up with an instructor for thirty-five minutes, taking the controls to do some turns, banks, climbs, and level flight. McLaughry had routinely worked through obstacles. But the moment he climbed into that plane, he crumbled. For the first time in his life he was confronted by the shock that whatever he did, he might not make the cut.

The number of maneuvers he did multiplied: 90-, 180-, and 360-degree turns, banks, climbs, glides, power-on and power-off stalls, tailspins, "S" turns, and takeoffs. He had yet to solo; his instructor was concerned that he would crash if allowed up there by himself. His pride was at stake, and he assumed that it would be the same for others in his class in overcoming the embarrassment of washout. He discovered instead that very few of the trainees in his class cared anymore whether they made it or not. Because of all the delay and moving around and what he termed as "military school child's play," they had lost their enthusiasm. The more poorly he flew, the more he told himself it did not matter anymore. Although he tried to minimize the feeling, he also had to grapple with the success of his younger brother, Bob, who was a natural-born flyer poised to get his wings with the navy.

As the weeks passed, things only got worse, to the point where the flight commander said he was a danger to himself and had frankly scared the shit out of his instructor on a few occasions. On so-called Black Friday, July 31st of 1942, he joined the ranks of what was known as "Le Squadron des Éliminés."

McLaughry had the option of trying to become either a navigator or a bombardier, for which the requirements were not as stringent. The earliest he could be commissioned as an officer would now be May of 1943, *seventeen months* after war had been declared. In a difficult and heartfelt letter to his father, he wrote that he had decided to get discharged, which was his right after being eliminated from piloting: "My patriotism is at a low ebb after all this stuff, and they apparently don't care much here about time, money or efficiency. . . . I have tried very hard not to get the attitude so many of us have—they just don't give a damn—but I fear I have lost the battle, for ever since I've washed out, it's become more and more apparent to me that I really don't care much one way or another what I do."

For someone who wanted to serve and fight, his attitude was not surprising. It reflected a country chaotically playing catch-up after having ignored sign after sign that war was coming, gone blind because of misguided diplomacy, the dismissal of Japanese culture as inferior and irrelevant because it wasn't the culture of the United States, the fatal ramifications of legislating racism and white supremacy.

II

His name was unknown, but his motive for suicide in a Tokyo garden was not. In a letter he left for the US ambassador to Japan, Cyrus E. Woods, he had written, "I pray God for the removal of the injurious anti-Japanese clause from the immigration bill, which has subjected the Japanese to great insult and humiliation." The letter was signed by A NAMELESS SUBJECT OF THE JAPANESE EMPIRE. It galvanized his country into a swell of grief and anger.

Several other suicides occurred in June of 1924 over the sweeping immigration act passed by Congress. At an anti-US rally in Tokyo with a capacity crowd of thirty-five thousand, amid cries of "Banzai!," a resolution was adopted stating that the United States had committed "an unforgivable slight upon the Japanese people" and was "encouraging the calamity of racial hatred." The *Japan Times and Mail*, in an editorial titled "The Senate's Declaration of War," wrote that the bill had "given a shock to the whole Japanese race such as has never before been felt and which will undoubtedly be remembered for a long time to come." Signs went up all over Tokyo urging citizens to "hate everything American." Doctors and hospitals were urged not to treat American travelers. Women were told not to use American-made cosmetics. Members of the Japanese intelligentsia who had been openly pro-American turned their backs on the country and vowed never to set foot in it again.

The day the Immigration Act of 1924 was signed into law by President Calvin Coolidge became known in Japan as "Humiliation Day." It all but shut off immigration from Europe into the United States. But there was something else, a single phrase seemingly sneaked in to avoid controversy and diminish its inevitable repercussions. It excluded from entry "any alien who by virtue of race or nationality is ineligible for citizenship." That seemed vague, except that it only applied to Asian countries.

Japanese were blocked from any further immigration into the United States, with a few isolated exceptions. They were considered too hardworking, too industrious, too clannish, too intent on moving from economic dependence to independence, daring to think that they were on an equal footing with white Americans.

The presence of immigrants from the Far East had always been detested in the United States, even when workers had desperately been needed to build the railroad tracks, plumb the mines, and do every other form of miserable and backbreaking work. The Chinese had already been permanently excluded in 1902, although, as one nativist author nostalgically admitted, he missed their work ethic of "perfect human ox." Japanese immigrants began to fill the void, initially applauded for picking sugar beets and crops because of their supposedly short legs and ability to squat. But California farmers quickly became resentful of their buying up of land and achieving enormous success in crop growing. The accusation was spurious: the Japanese often bought up land that white farmers considered impossible to develop and then used innovative agricultural techniques that could easily be copied by everyone. They were improving farming, not harming it.

In 1906, the San Francisco Board of Education had passed a resolution excluding Japanese (and other Asian) students from its public schools even though there were fewer than twenty of them. President Theodore Roosevelt found the exclusion appalling, but something had to be done. In a so-called gentleman's agreement with Roosevelt in 1908, the Japanese government promised to restrict immigration by barring laborers from obtaining passports and limiting their issuance to travelers, students, merchants, diplomats, and families of people already in the country. Some people said the Japanese government was vigilant; others said the opposite. But an indication of its good faith was its agreement to no longer give passports to so-called picture brides, who had previously been allowed to go to the United States even though their husbands to be had never seen them.

In a treaty signed in 1911, Japanese were no longer permitted to become US citizens unless they had been born here. Over the next fifteen years, their presence in America only became further loathed. Congressman Albert Johnson from Washington State, a small-town newspaper publisher who was anti-Semitic, a darling of the Ku Klux Klan, and the president of the Eugenics Research Association, in other words impeccable credentials at the time, led the anti-immigration crusade. The greatest proponent of the bill outside Congress was a former publisher of the *Sacramento Bee*, V. S. McClatchy, who in testimony on March 11, 1924, before the Senate Committee on Immigration and Naturalization, which was chaired by Johnson, said of the Japanese, "Of all the races ineligible to citizenship under our law, the Japanese are the least assimilable and the most dangerous to this country. . . . They do not come to this country with any desire or any intent to lose their racial or national identity. They come here specifically and professedly for the purpose of colonizing and establishing here permanently the proud Yamato race."

In 1924 there were 125,000 Japanese in a country of 106 million, or .001 percent of the population, 100,000 of them in California and the Pacific Northwest. But the eugenicists, the Yellow Peril preachers, and the nativists had taken over immigration policy. Supporters of the bill said the Japanese should not take it personally—*we really like you, we just don't want you.*

The Japanese, understandably, did take it personally. Nothing was more unforgivable to the Japanese soul than dishonor. Saving face was a crucial pillar regardless of the cost. Insult and humiliation could not be forgotten or forgiven.

The 1924 Immigration Act marked the beginning of a fatal turn by Japan against the United States. The country increasingly perceived democracies as cesspools for the spoiled: materially hedonistic, single homes that could have housed an entire village, mounds of food dumped down greedy throats to feed and fatten the already fat, the endless need for distraction and diversion without any moral or intellectual rudder, no conception of sacrifice for the greater good, no grace or literary memory.

The act was among the most damaging pieces of legislation ever passed by Congress, insulting US allies in Europe and fueling a conflict with the Japanese that turned into war. The passage of the bill opened the gap between the two countries. Japan had always engaged in a schizophrenic relationship with the United States and vice versa. In 1854, US Navy Admiral Matthew C. Perry sailed into Edo Bay, forcing Japan by threat of force to open up after nearly two centuries of isolation. Japan went on a westernization frenzy, the fastest economic and cultural conversion in world history, far beyond just modern industrialization: Western-style haircuts, gold watches and diamond rings, mustaches and beards, arguments for adopting the Western alphabet, a love of French food.

It seemed to some observers that Japan had become ashamed of its own culture in its freneticism to copy and impress the West. By the 1900s, increasing numbers of Japanese began to believe that their country's obsession with the West had become self-defeating, destroying the country's heritage and traditions without getting it the respect it deserved, treated as a child by the United States and Great Britain.

Japan was in pursuit of establishing its own empire in East Asia, the so-called Greater East Asia Co-Prosperity Sphere, ostensibly to unite the mutual interests of the region and protect against US and British encroachment. It became clear that Japan wanted to subsume other countries to rape their natural resources and turn their citizens into serfs. They used as justification the efforts of the United States in amassing its own colonial empire. How could a country that had taken Guam and the Philippines tell another country not to seek its own territorial possessions? The United States had never supplied a satisfying answer. Neither had the British Empire.

In 1933, Japan abruptly withdrew from the League of Nations after the League issued a report criticizing the country for taking Manchuria from China and creating a puppet state. In 1934, it walked away from the Washington Naval Treaty, which had been in force for twelve years, angry that it was not being treated on an equal footing with the United States and Great Britain and was expected instead to build warships at a smaller ratio than the two other countries. In 1936, the military took over the government. In 1937, they went to war against China. Later that year, the Japanese went on a spree of murder and rape in Nanking.

After August of 1941, when the United States said it would no longer trade with Japan and imposed an embargo on supplying it with aviation oil for its refusal to withdraw from northern China and Indochina, war was only a matter of time. Right up to the attack on Pearl Harbor, Japan and the United States continued to negotiate, but Japan's diplomacy at that point was a cover to prevent the United States from becoming suspicious of its intention to attack. For the Japanese, the itch to go to war was too great, the need to save face regardless of the consequences—a concept of honor alien to the West and therefore considered crazy. They considered it a divine stroke when a final telegram from Roosevelt to Emperor Hirohito in December of 1941 to prevent war arrived too late, thus avoiding, as Prime Minister Hideki Tojo put it, "more of a to-do."

The end of 1941 and the early months of 1942 made the Japanese drunk with victory. With the United States shockingly unprepared, it went on a blitzkrieg of its own: coastal China, the Philippines, Hong Kong, Singapore, Burma, and parts of Malaysia all fell, establishing an empire stretching seven thousand miles at its perimeter and controlling the Pacific.

The best moment of McLaughry's eight months in the air corps came when he appeared before the faculty board just prior to discharge. The board told him he had passed the psychological exam for both bombardiering and navigation. They thought he would be happy, so it gave him a special delight to refuse both options.

On December 2nd of 1942, he once again found himself on a rickety train, this time to Marine Corps Base Quantico in northern Virginia as an officer candidate. His train arrived late, which immediately put him into the shithouse with the drill instructor who was picking him up. After arrival McLaughry asked the sergeant in charge where the "latrine" was.

Latrine?

LATRINE!!!!!!!!!!

Only the army used the word *latrine*. The correct term was *head*.

McLaughry had been in the *army*.

Now he was really in the shithouse.

Welcome to the corps.

7
The Letter

Going into the 1942 season at Wisconsin, Schreiner felt better physically and mentally than he had during the three previous years. The first game, a 7–0 victory over Camp Grant, was a tune-up to shake out the summer rust. It was dull and boring like the opponent, a group of army trainees. But the next, against Notre Dame, was the biggest of Dave Schreiner's career, an opportunity for Wisconsin to show its aspirations and for him to prove that he was without a doubt the best end in the country and deserving of appearing on every All-American list.

But he was about to write a letter that could irrevocably change his life, addressed to local draft board No. 1 in Lancaster, trying to determine his place in the war like millions of others who had registered.

Schreiner, although twenty-one, had received a deferral until the spring of 1943 on the basis that he was preparing for a medical career, which was deemed essential to the war effort. But he was struggling in premed and continued to do so despite concerted attempts to improve. "Premed courses don't fit me too well," he wrote his parents. He told them he was considering a switch of major to economics, even though he knew he would jeopardize his deferral under Selective Service rules and be a lottery call away from active duty.

His parents were concerned. They were fearful of his going off to war until he had to, as all parents are fearful of their sons going off to war. They wondered if it was really necessary to let the draft board know of his change in status, which would keep his deferment intact at least until he graduated in the spring of 1943. Or he could simply continue as a premedical student and avoid the issue altogether.

Schreiner was swimming in the system of the Selective Service, which was both a marvel and a political mire of lobbying and favoritism. The United States' armed forces grew from 334,500 in 1939 to more than 12 million by the end of the war in 1945. It was a testament to the system that processed that many and to the armed forces that trained them in such a short period of time. But it seemed as though every group and constituency wanted to fight in World War II initially, as long as they didn't actually have to fight: the Greatest Generation had its limits.

Finding enough men to serve was not easy. More than 5 million at one time or another received deferments after the draft went into effect in 1940. Roughly the same amount were classified as 4-F, unfit for military service. In other words, to get to the 10 million the draft contributed to the war effort, the Selective Service System had to draft 19 million. As Iowa State University history professor Amy J. Rutenberg pointed out in her book *Rough Draft: Cold War Military Manpower Policy and the Origins of Vietnam-Era Draft Resistance*, "Many, many individual men were more than happy to take advantage of the legal deferments offered them by the Selective Service during the early years of the war, and they resisted the loss of those deferments as the war progressed."

The Selective Service System was bewildering and confusing; rules were issued and then rescinded, depending upon politics. Employees in dozens of occupations and businesses sought deferments from service on the basis that they were essential to the war effort. Some deferments were borderline. Some seemed ridiculous. Deferments were temporary, for a maximum of six months, but they could be renewed. Local draft boards had enormous autonomy. They interpreted Selective Service rules as they saw fit.

The motion picture industry at one point convinced Selective Service that actors, directors, writers, and technicians were essential because of movies' positive impact on the morale of both the public and the armed forces. Large numbers of federal workers were deferred, some of them clerks claiming to be essential on the basis of fancy job titles. Farmworkers were deferred depending on what crops they grew. Even typewriter repairmen could at one point get a deferment if they were married.

As Schreiner weighed his dilemma over the draft, he still had the protection of being a premedical student. No profession was more effective in receiving deferrals for its members than the medical profession. Deferrals were granted not just for physicians but also for students in medical school and even in undergrad premed programs.*

Schreiner listened to his parents' concerns about his changing major. He carefully listened to them about everything. Whenever a big decision was to be made,

---

* In 1943, Roosevelt removed the deferral for premedical students but gave them until June of 1944 to enroll in med school. In other words, he did and he did not.

he went to them for advice and counsel. But in this instance, he had made up his mind. "I don't think it is fair to keep from the draft board the fact that I am no longer a pre-medic, that being the reason I was deferred," he wrote. He hoped that he could join an army officer training program. If that did not work out and he was immediately inducted, "I'll do a good job as a private."

He contacted the draft board to advise it of his switch in major. He already had a good idea of what he was going to do anyway, even if it vastly increased the odds of his going into combat. As he waited for a response, he did what he did best: he got ready to play a football game against the most famous team in the land.

8
Murphy

There were few honors in college football as prestigious as being named captain of Notre Dame, and in 1942 it fell to a local boy from South Bend named George Murphy whose father was a clerk for a large employer in town. Notre Dame was set to play Wisconsin in September and the newspapers made a meal out of Murphy and Schreiner, both playing end and now facing each other, doggedness and determination versus doggedness, determination, bigger size, and a rare gift for catching, blocking, and tackling. Neither of them could have imagined that two and a quarter years later, with their college football careers long behind them, they would play against each other again in the Mosquito Bowl on a Pacific island in the middle of nowhere.

The 1942 season was perhaps the strangest in Notre

Dame's history, not because of its won-lost record or its failed expectations but because of the behavior of its second-year coach, Frank Leahy: so dapper each Saturday afternoon of fall in double-breasted suit and tie and fedora hat, yet spartan and hairshirtish in his lifestyle, clinically pessimistic about his teams, fretting about lousy cupcake opponents to the point that other coaches found him a phony, his manner of speaking a kind of archaic old English in which the words of a sentence wrapped over and under and through and around one another like a poorly designed intersection.

He had the strange habit of being offered a cigarette and saying he would take one later but never taking one later, and he had a work ethic beyond all reason that almost killed him on the field. He affectionately called his boys "lads" and insisted on addressing them by their formal first names; Heisman Trophy winner John Lujack John instead of Johnny, tackle Zygmont Czarobski never just Ziggy. His players liked him, even though they privately made fun of his verbal style and thought his practices were too brutal. They knew he was odd, so far into himself and his coaching that even at a funeral he could not stop speaking about the next opponent, so nervous at halftime of close games that he was on the verge of collapse and had to be helped back onto the field, admittedly neglectful of his wife, who developed a drinking problem, and son, who would have issues with drugs. He rarely went home during the season, living in room 7 of the local firehouse to be as near to the school as possible, a simple bed and desk and soft-backed rocker. He spent little time there anyway, up by 5:00 a.m. and rarely back before midnight, watching grainy black-and-white films of opponents over and over for tiny revelations of tendencies that might have been missed.

He was enormously successful as a coach but also a tragedy as a man, afflicted by anxiety and painful illnesses, failing in business after he left Notre Dame and investigated by the Securities and Exchange Commission for an allegedly fraudulent stock transaction, shunned by the College Football Hall of Fame for sixteen years because of his unpopularity despite his record of 107–13–9 and four national championships in his thirteen seasons as a head coach. He grew hobbled and stiff and was killed by leukemia in 1973 at the age of sixty-four, although it was hard not to think that the agony and pressure of football at Notre Dame had hastened his death even though he lived for twenty years afterward, the fear of losing corroding him inside.

He arrived at Notre Dame in 1941 from Boston College, where he had led the team to an undefeated season and a win in the Sugar Bowl. In his first year, the team went unbeaten. He wasn't high on his future captain

Murphy, who was then in his junior year. He thought he was undersized for an end at six feet zero and 175 pounds and saw that he got pounded on kickoffs. But Murphy worked his way into the starting lineup and mostly stayed there.

In Leahy's second season, 1942, he junked the beloved box formation made famous by the untouchable coaching legend Knute Rockne and installed the T formation. It was time for Notre Dame to modernize, no longer treat the pass as civil disobedience. But sportswriters and alumni were horrified; they felt it was an unforgivable insult to Rockne. During the 1942 season, Leahy was hospitalized for three weeks at the Mayo Clinic in Minnesota for what was diagnosed as spinal arthritis, likely aggravated by overwork and nervous tension. Without Leahy much of the burden of team motivation fell upon Murphy as captain, his local roots only adding to the pressure. He also was the inheritor of Notre Dame tradition, his brother John having been on the team in the late 1930s.

Just as the 1942 season was different, so was the era in which Murphy started at Notre Dame, a school trying to balance its Catholic heritage with academic enlightenment. The school had made significant improvement, particularly in the graduate schools. Several foreign lecturers were brought in to teach to expand the breadth of the faculty and more lay professors were being hired. But liberal arts lagged, English literature considered a dangerous minefield in which Hemingway, as writer Robert E. Burns noted in his fine history of the school, was banned as being "pornographic."

The school conducted a remarkable study, known as "the religious survey," of roughly 10,000 students and alumni. During the years of the survey, roughly between the years of 1920 and 1936, it was found that 4,998,329 Communion wafers had been distributed. But over the last ten years the daily average had been about 1,400, which school officials found disappointing. The students were encouraged to go to confession to help them "live habitually in the state of sanctifying grace," but many acknowledged that they avoided it, due mainly to shame (38 percent) followed by the gravity of their sins (15 percent) and cowardice (14 percent). A hefty number said that they prayed for scholastic success, followed by strength against impurity. Among those polled in the 1935–36 survey, 262 (46 percent) said they used prayer to fight off temptation.*

Five took cold showers.

---

* Seventy respondents said they resorted to "ejaculatory prayer," meaning the spontaneous exclamation of a short prayer, although the wording could not have been worse and was defenseless against misinterpretation.

By 1942 the war in Europe and the United States' entry into it had forced Notre Dame into the real world beyond its manicured quadrangles. Faculty could no longer abide by the steadfast policy of not being allowed to talk about politics outside the school. Since most of the faculty had year-to-year contracts (the football coach was an exception), it was effortlessly easy for the school to get rid of a professor perceived to have broken the rules. But in the context of war those were issues of literal life and death. To stay silent was to reject the bedrock principles of free speech around which American society pivoted, what made the country profound and special as fascism overran Europe. Except at Notre Dame: for the first time ever the school received sustained publicity for something other than football—all of it negative—when a professor was fired after giving speeches condemning anti-Semitism at home and abroad and urging greater wartime cooperation with the Soviet Union.

Notre Dame could not shut out the war during Murphy's senior year. Students, faculty, and alumni were serving in the military; at least twenty-four of them would die that fall. The school was also flooded by navy trainees learning to become officers, turning Notre Dame into more of a drill ground than a campus.

In the midst of the upheaval the school continued to abide by its Catholic traditions. The daily *Religious Bulletin*, a staple of Notre Dame life since the 1920s, admonished students for the "scandal" of coming late to Sunday Mass, declaring it "a sin" to arrive so much as a minute after the priest had started the prayers at the foot of the altar. There was a satirical letter written in the mocking name of Lucifer: don't listen to the priests and their sermons on the dangers of women and wine. There was an insistence on premarital chastity: "God has shared with every man and woman His power of creating life. In the use of that power God has attached a pleasure. The pleasure is for legitimate use in marriage." There was the reminder that the only permissible divorce in the Catholic Church was divorce from Satan with "a good confession."

It was considered essential to go to Saturday-morning Mass to pray for the health of the football team. After the Michigan game in 1942, the *Bulletin* wrote with fury about the lack of support for the team, intimating that poor attendance at Holy Communion and Mass beforehand was linked to three players having been injured early in the contest. "You have failed to pray for the team, and the full measure of God's blessing on the squad has been withheld. . . . Because you have been lame in prayer, notable inconveniences have overtaken your pals on the team."

The routine for every game was basically the same: the team met at the chapel in Dillon Hall to pray for protection from injury and victory in honor of Our Lady. A blessed medal was then given to each player to wear on his uniform or suspend from his neck during the game, just as it was given to Notre Dame men going off to war. Murphy, as captain, led the team in the Litany of the Blessed Virgin. The players then went to the Communion rail where each one was blessed with a relic of the True Cross, injured parts of the body also touched. Before the away game against Wisconsin, the team traveled to Chicago Friday night, went to Old St. Mary's Church for Mass and Holy Communion early Saturday morning, then proceeded to Madison by train.

The game on September 26th of 1942 between Notre Dame and Wisconsin ended in a 7–7 tie, essentially a victory for Wisconsin since no one had given it a chance beforehand. The face-off of Murphy versus Schreiner was less dramatic than advertised. Murphy caught two passes for twenty-four yards. Schreiner didn't catch anything, although he played well on defense.

The following Saturday, Wisconsin went against Marquette University. Schreiner showed his All-American credentials by catching three touchdown passes in one period in an easy 35–7 win. Murphy's captaincy did not get any easier in Notre Dame's second game, when it lost to Georgia Tech, 13–6. Leahy, with his history of illness,* had been terribly sick with the flu the week of the game but, typical of his asceticism, had still slept at the firehouse every night for only a few hours and held those early-morning meetings. Several days after the game, he was ordered by school officials to go to the Mayo Clinic in Rochester in Minnesota for tests. He was diagnosed with spinal arthritis and bedridden for the next three weeks. He insisted on having a telephone installed in his room at the clinic so he could stay in touch with acting head coach Ed McKeever.

The team beat Stanford 27–0. It then faced the Iowa Pre-Flight Seahawks. It was an odd name for a team, but it was made up of players from the navy's V-5

---

* He would collapse in the locker room at halftime of the 1954 game against Georgia Tech. It was first thought to be a heart attack, and a priest was called to give him last rites. It turned out to be pancreatitis. He retired from coaching forever after that season, the nervous tension during games too much for him. Notre Dame administrators insisted that he had not been fired, but they had grown weary of his imperiousness by then and felt football needed to be de-emphasized at the school.

Naval Aviation Cadet program, loaded with great players and undefeated. Notre Dame won 28–0, a stunning win for a team in its infancy with the T formation. Leahy, still bedridden, wrote Murphy a seven-page note the day after the game. It revealed the multiple sides of the coach: thoughtfulness, anguish, stilted formalism, the desire to connect but not knowing how, hyperbole, the relentless push to win at all costs. "In my opinion George, your men yesterday afternoon turned in the greatest football performance ever witnessed in South Bend. In fact it was N.D.'s finest victory in 100 years," he wrote melodramatically. But you could feel the rising nervous tension within him as he anxiously worried about the next game against Illinois and told Murphy, with more than enough pressure on the captain already, not to allow a letdown. "After such a glorious victory as you enjoyed yesterday there usually is a tendency to relax somewhat. Let's not make that mistake. If you and the other seniors start working Tuesday harder than ever before, everyone else will do likewise. We must strive each day for improvement otherwise decay sets in. . . . Keep working hard George and ask all others not to let up for one minute."

He thanked Murphy for the autographed football he had sent him. "Your thoughtfulness is deeply appreciated by the sender of this letter," he wrote, and he asked

Murphy to thank the team for how well they had carried on without him. "Someday I'll repay all of you." He ended the letter with what for Leahy was a highly personal note: "Please remember me to your Dad."

He returned to the team in time for the game against Navy, a 9–0 win. Then Army, 13–0, in front of a crowd of seventy-six thousand at Yankee Stadium in New York, for the team's fifth straight victory. The season went sideways after that, Notre Dame finishing 7–2–2. Murphy had his moments—touchdown catches against Stanford and Army. He was a good and valiant end in a strange and disappointing season for Notre Dame, the opposite of Wisconsin and the soaring Schreiner.

II

Eight thousand spectators flooded the lower campus in Madison for the Friday-night pep rally before the Ohio State game. Both teams were undefeated, Ohio State number one in the country and Wisconsin number six; the game would be broadcast over two hundred stations coast to coast by the National Broadcasting Corporation, and a record crowd of forty-five thousand was expected at Camp Randall Stadium. Schreiner spoke at the rally in his familiar style, leading by example and not by eloquence: "This is the greatest opportunity the Wisconsin boys have ever had in football. We're going to meet the top team in the country. The boys are really primed for this game."

Wisconsin played the best football in its history, beating Ohio State 17–7. Schreiner's play on offense and defense was encapsulated by *Chicago Sun* sportswriter James S. Kearns: "Mr. Schreiner played 60 minutes against Ohio State . . . caught four forward passes for 52 yards, scored the clinching touchdown and bounced his blocking targets around with a vengeance all day."

The undefeated season fell apart the following weekend when the team was upset by the University of Iowa in Iowa City. A dog roamed the field for much of the game, driving Wisconsin head coach Harry Stuhldreher mad as he wondered if the creature had been let loose on purpose. Wisconsin won its last game of the season against Minnesota, 20–6, to finish the season 8–1–1. Schreiner caught a thirty-two-yard touchdown pass and had another called back after officials ruled that he had been inches out of bounds. The team finished ranked third nationally, arguably its best season ever. Schreiner finished third in the nation in receiving yards, with 350. The honors poured in; he had made good on his private promise to improve. He was named first-team All-American by every major outlet, the only one he failed to make being the annual All-American "Jawbreaker" team.* He finished tenth in the voting for the Heisman Trophy, remarkable for an end.

The season ended on November 21st of 1942. Fourteen days later, he made official application to the Marine Corps Reserves as an officer candidate. He capped off his college career in the East-West Shrine Bowl, played in San Francisco. Cocaptain of the East team, he caught a touchdown pass in a 13–12 win. The Detroit Lions selected Schreiner as the first pick of the second round of the NFL draft, although it was moot.

His quasi-rival George Murphy graduated from Notre Dame in December of 1942, majoring in physical education and ranked 283rd out of a class of 346. On the second day of the New Year, he married his high school sweetheart from Central High School in South Bend, Mary Katherine Miles.

---

* For the twelfth year, Dr. Lucien Stark from the University of Nebraska picked his 1942 All-American "Jawbreaker" team: Czarobski of Notre Dame, Cycenas of Purdue, Domnanovich of Alabama, Fekete of Ohio State, Jarmoluk of Temple, Kuczynski of Penn, Joe of Penn State, Radulescu of Michigan State, Ryckeley of Georgia Tech, Susoeff of Washington State, and Vuksanovich of Fordham. Yank magazine, for one, was puzzled how the name "Joe" had gotten in there.

Several months later, on March 9th of 1943, he entered the marines as an officer candidate.

Schreiner graduated from Wisconsin on April 29th of 1943. Entering the war, leaving the warmth of Madison and Lancaster, where he was the brightest star, would be momentous. But the defining moment of his life had already happened.

9
Odette

Odette Hendrickson had grown up on the near west side of Madison, a life of dance recitals and performances by pupils of the Woman's Club School of the Dance to the accompaniment of the Little Symphony of the Wisconsin School of Music. She was confirmed along with twenty-three others at Luther Memorial Church. She went to Madison West High School, where she and some fellow students made a presentation to the local Lions Club, and was part of the mix that attended the semiformal "March Mistake" dance at the Hotel Loraine.

Her father was Joel Hendrickson and her mother, Lula. Joel Hendrickson was a certified public accountant, had been the chief financial officer of the manufacturing giant, Allis-Chalmers, and ultimately the head of the income tax division of the Wisconsin Department of Revenue. The family lived in the fine neighborhood of Nakoma, its homes ranging in style from Prairie School to Craftsman to Greek and Tudor Revival, the streets curvilinear and the lawns without a defiant blade of grass, surrounded by shade trees and shrubs. Their home was a Tudor Revival brick with an attached garage, the roof deeply pitched and a chimney that spanned the entire height of the house.

The living was extremely comfortable, until Odette's parents divorced when she was in high school in the 1930s. The impact was devastating—there was a terrible stigma to getting divorced back then—and money became precious. Odette's mother had to go back to work, at the US Postal Service. Odette was unable to afford the rent at the Delta Gamma sorority that she had joined after matriculating at Wisconsin. Instead she and her brother and her mother moved to an apartment on Hoyt Street, near the school campus. It was an obvious change in lifestyle but they made the best of it. Every Sunday afternoon they held an open house where Odette's friends flocked, including football players and sorority sisters. Schreiner was among them. They did not start dating right away, but it was easy to see why he became so smitten with her.

Odette did not suffer fools gladly. She corrected you

if you used the wrong word. Sometimes with mock exasperation she chastised in French. She majored in art and English at Wisconsin and because of the institutional sexism that existed back then, it was assumed that her only professional choice after graduation would be as a teacher. But she had a strong sense of duty—she wanted to make a difference in the war—and enlisted in the WAVES as an officer candidate after graduation, going east for the first time in her life at the end of 1943.

She and Schreiner had started dating the previous spring. She knew Schreiner was a big deal on campus, the Big Deal, but Odette could not have cared less: truth be told, she did not even like football that much. He hung a pin on her. He took her to see *Life with Father* with her mother, row 19, the tickets $2.75 *each*, a sure sign of love.

He told his parents about her and then ever so lightly admonished them not to tell anyone because they were "loudmouths." He went over one night to play bridge at the home of a Wisconsin teammate, Pat Lyons, and his wife, and he helped change the diapers of the Lyonses' baby. He teasingly wrote to his parents that it was good training for marriage with Odette. But their relationship was dead serious; they got engaged within months of going out with each other. With help from his aunt

Emma, he gave Odette a diamond ring in a platinum setting, one diamond in the middle and three smaller ones on either side. It wasn't ostentatious—neither Schreiner nor Odette would have tolerated that—but it was beautiful in its modesty. She drew him out, helping him to overcome his shyness. He felt a sense of comfort with her that he had never felt before with a woman. They laughed together, traded playful quips with each other, talked about the books they had read. They thought about getting married before Schreiner shipped out to war. But he decided against it because of the reality of making Odette wait for someone who might never come back.

There was a possibility that he would not enter Marine Corps Officer Candidates School until the summer of 1943, which gave him more time with Odette and his own family, but he hoped it would not happen. "I have no desire to stay around awaiting my call when the rest of my friends are in there really accomplishing something," he wrote to his parents. "Please don't try and change my mind as it won't do any good as I know I'm right."

He took his physical in May of 1943. He had 20/20 vision, could hear a coin click at twenty feet away and a whispered voice at fifteen feet; his temperature was 98.6 degrees, his height 73 inches, his weight 197 pounds, his blood pressure 116/62, his resting pulse 70 beats per minute, and he did not have a single hemorrhoid. The only thing that wasn't perfect were his teeth, which were riddled with fillings from cavities, with number 16 missing. "He is physically qualified to perform all his duties on the sea and in the field," concluded his examiners. On May 24th of 1943, he officially entered the marines as an officer candidate.

Within days of his arrival at Parris Island for basic training, he wrote to Odette's mother, Lula, or Mrs. Hendrickson as he addressed her. They had played a great deal of bridge together and Schreiner was impressed with her acumen. If nothing else, he believed that the marines would help him rise to the challenge. "[K]eep your bridge game sharpened up because when I leave here my mind will be so analytical that I'll want some shark like you to tangle with." There was also this:

"I'm depending on you to keep my little girl just as sweet as she was the day I left, but I'm really not worried at all." Even though he worried all the time.

10
Football Is War

As in every other small town in America, the sons and daughters of St. David and the surroundings went off to war in 1943, thousands of miles away that felt like millions after growing up in the small scrap of a place. Many were the children of immigrants, the path their fathers and mothers had excavated out of nothing opening the way for an America that was their own. Citizenship for them was a birthright and not something they were forced to apply for before the court as their parents had done. They went off to war with pride as first-generation Americans in their crisp uniforms before fear set into the bones. The sons and daughters of St. David served in the army, the navy, the marines, the air corps, and the signal corps. They did stateside training at Great Lakes, Quantico, Childers,

Pendleton, Drew, and Sheridan. They went overseas to French Morocco, Anzio, Luzon, New Guinea, the Ardennes, Normandy, Iwo Jima, and Okinawa. They won Purple Hearts and Bronze Stars; lived for their country and in a few instances died for it; came back whole and came back irreparably damaged from visions that became nightmares.

Lawrence Grubisich, a first cousin of Tony Butkovich, enlisted in the air corps in June of 1942 and became a bombardier. Niles Ayres entered the navy in June of 1943. Joseph Cirilli joined the air corps on January 1st of 1943 and trained as a radio operator and machine gunner on a B-24 Liberator. Paul Crnkovich entered the marines in July of 1943. John Lidwell joined the army in May of 1943. Six Kumer brothers served: Casimer, Charles, Edward, Emil, Joseph, and Rudy. So did two Radosevich brothers: Isadore and Joseph. And the Maxwell brother and sister, Richard and Rosa. And the Skender brothers from the extended family: two Joes and Johns and one Donald. And six Starcevich brothers: two Josephs, Albert, Chester, Peter, and Robert.

The best-known son of St. David, Tony Butkovich, knew he would serve, but he was unsure when. He had enrolled in the Navy ROTC program when he had gone to Illinois in 1940 and then joined the Marine Reserves in 1942. He had registered for the draft but had yet to be called. He was a Big Ten running back, hoping to squeeze out one final year of football in 1943, a last-chance opportunity. As a player in the Big Ten, he knew of the accomplishments of his future Mosquito Bowl opponent Dave Schreiner in 1942. He had seen his future Mosquito Bowl teammate George Murphy face-to-face when Illinois had lost to Notre Dame the same season. Butkovich had shown flashes of greatness, as in the game against Ohio State the previous year, when he had returned a kickoff eighty yards in the snow and would have scored a touchdown had he not stepped out of bounds on the three-yard line because he'd thought it was the goal line (he did score on the next play). In one of the greatest wins in Illinois history, he had been part of a double lateral for a touchdown that had beat Minnesota, 20–13, and ended its two-year Big Ten winning streak. He'd stayed in the locker room for an hour after the game, still in uniform, disheveled and dirty, his lips swollen and bloody and his face caked with tears. "I don't want to get dressed," he'd said. "I never want to leave." The win had been made even sweeter by the play of his best friend, Alex Agase, who as a lineman had scored two touchdowns on recovered fumbles.

"Who said they're tough!?" Butkovich had yelled. "Who said they're tough!?"

It had been the best of football and the best of Butkovich, the greatest moment of his career, perhaps because it had little to do with individual performance and more with the euphoria of eternal boyhood.

His total offense per game in 1942 ranked twenty-third in the Big Ten. His yards per carry was below three, disappointing for someone who could run the hundred-yard dash in ten seconds.

The 1943 season would be his final season of greatness—assuming that there would be a 1943 season; no one knew with so many current and prospective players having gone to war between the ages of eighteen and twenty-one.

Football coaches simply presumed that there would not be enough talent to go around to sustain a season. They gained a glimmer of hope when the army announced that it would start a specialized training program on campuses around the country. To the coaches that meant that a flood of young men who had played football previously would be available: since they were on college campuses, they would presumably be treated as college students. Which presumably meant that they would participate in all extracurricular activities for as long as they were there. Which presumably meant football. There was one impediment: the army considered that idea hogwash.

The program was called specialized training because it *was* specialized training. The army dictated that those enrolled would not have time for anything else. They were being prepared for war, not football. Campuses were useful because of their facilities. Coaches everywhere were furious that the game was not being given its due place in the American soul. How dare the war interfere?

The US Army saw no parallel between calling plays in the huddle and leading a group of men through muddy gruel after it had rained for ten straight days or up the claw of an exposed hill with enemy fire engulfing them. No one could possibly argue that football was vital to the military interest.

Except the US Navy.

II

The navy didn't just believe in football; it worshipped it, convinced that the core of football—discipline, teamwork, physical sacrifice, pain, and violence—was also the core of war and therefore the single best form of training.

"We are fighting in one of the most desperate wars

in which man has ever engaged," said Secretary of the Navy William F. Knox in a memorable speech before the Touchdown Club in Washington, DC, in January of 1944. "This is a war where you kill or get killed! And I don't know anything that better prepares a man in peace for bodily contact, including war, and especially the kind of war we have got to fight in the Pacific, than the kind of training we get on the football field."

The navy saved college football from decimation during the war years, deliberately keeping the game alive through a series of decisions that supplied both players and competition. It wasn't just Knox who was such a proponent of football in the vital interest of the war. Other top commanders, many of whom had played football and considered it a seminal part of their lives, felt the same way. As Wilbur D. Jones, Jr., wrote in his comprehensive book *Football! Navy! War!: How Military "Lend-Lease" Players Saved the College Game and Helped Win World War II*, "The Department of the Navy's vision, organization, and drive truly proved to be the engine of wartime football. After early and serious evaluation, emboldened by vocal leadership from the president and naval officials, the altered sport persevered as well as possible under exceptionally extenuating circumstances."

On July 1st of 1943, Butkovich was sent from Illinois to Purdue University to attend the new V-12 Navy College Training Program. The program took place on 131 college and university campuses across the country, 40 of which offered marine officer training. Many players lasted at their schools for only a few months before they were called up to active duty but were still able to squeeze in seven or eight games.

The 1943 season became the most bizarre in college history, players moving from school to school in the middle of the season depending on which ones participated in the V-12 program and the liberalization of transfer rules. As a guard from Wisconsin who moved to Northwestern University put it, he "got traded for a halfback."

Not everyone agreed with the navy's embrace of football, including some within the navy itself. Joseph "Gene" Tunney, the great former heavyweight champion serving as the director of physical training for the navy, felt that the link between football and combat training was silly. "We have got to get down to the fact that we are in a war," he said. "You can't train a man to be a fighter by having him play football or baseball. It has to be done the hard way—with special calisthenics and road work to build stamina and with bayonet drill and handling of weapons to develop a warrior psychology." To Tunney, the navy's football programs on its bases were simply a way to give "fat football coaches" a job.

Elmer Burnham did not like being a major college football coach. He had an almost hippie-esque approach to it in an era when the best practice sessions were correlated with the amount of blood left on the field. He limited scrimmages because of their propensity to cause injury. Instead, team members often traded positions with one another and played touch football.

In 1943, he was the head football coach at Purdue University, in his second year. The season before had been lousy, a 1–8 record, and there was no reason to think that 1943 would be better with so many men off to war and only one starter returning. To maintain the program, Burnham felt, he would have to cobble together a team with a combination of players under the age of eighteen coming out of high school and ones classified as 4-Fs. Though declared physically unfit for military duty because of such conditions as asthma, trick knees, a bad back, or poor hearing, they were still able to play football for sixty minutes.

The most creative use of 4-Fs was at the University of Tulsa in Oklahoma, which fielded a football team on which twenty-four of the forty-one players had been either classified as physically unfit or medically discharged from the military. They may not have been good enough for the armed forces, but they were good enough on the field to go undefeated until losing to Georgia Tech in the Sugar Bowl. It reached the point that Army Chief of Staff George C. Marshall, Jr., expressed great concern over the draft status of professional football players; he was so upset by the issue that he ruminated over it during a military conference in Cairo, Egypt. "There has been no doubt in my mind for a long time . . . that the physical exemption business has reached the point in some cases of almost a racket," he wrote in a memorandum to his staff in 1944. Under Secretary of War Patterson was more emphatic, noting that the parents of men fighting overseas "cannot understand how a professional football player, who takes grueling punishment before thousands of spectators, evades military service by the excuse of a punctured ear drum, wetting the bed, or some other trifling blemish." A directive was eventually issued that professional athletes would not be rejected for military service until each case was reviewed individually by the War Department's personnel section.

Burnham did not end up taking the 4-F route. Once Purdue was designated as a V-12 campus, his fortunes expanded without his having to do anything. Six players from the University of Illinois were sent to Purdue in the summer of 1943 for marine officer training, including Butkovich and future Mosquito Bowl player John Genis. Burnham sat back and waited for more riches: a record 151 players showed up for fall practice. The final squad included twenty-six marine trainees and nine navy trainees. Burnham went from having no one to having a team potentially locked and loaded with experienced players, none of whom had been at Purdue the previous season.

The V-12 program did gain many young men one final season of football before the war, Butkovich among them. There was potentially another way to continue playing in college, one that would have guaranteed him not just one more season but *three* without any worries about being drafted.

Become a service academy draft dodger.

III

The Selective Service System liked to make the point during the war that virtually no one aged eighteen or over was exempt from being drafted. There were deferments, but they were temporary. No one got a free pass. But that wasn't true.

The US Military Academy and the US Naval Academy *were exempt*. Though institutions dedicated to war, they provided insulation from war. They both shortened their requirements because of the war, but Army still required three years of matriculation and Navy required two. No other schools in the country could provide such protection except for students majoring in science, engineering, mathematics, and a few other fields considered essential to the war effort.

West Point in particular was a football safe house during World War II, a place for the greatest players in the country to put any fear of combat aside and continue playing football without interruption for three years. A pitch like that—play for Army or go to war—was hard to resist. Which was also why Army had its best teams in history in 1944 and 1945, both undefeated and national champions.

One would have assumed that individuals attending the service academies would have been among the first to go overseas as commissioned officers once the war started, particularly since there was a shortage. If the assembly line of war was pushing out officers in as little as ninety days, how could West Point cadets and naval midshipmen not be subject to the same limitations on training? Not enough time to train? Everybody entering the services during the war had insufficient time, and many officers died or were wounded because of it. "[T]he U.S. Military Academy was literally a gated haven and sanctuary from the outside world during the war," wrote Jack Cavanaugh in his book on Army football. "[S]o long as players kept up to speed on their studies, players at West Point were exempt from active duty."

Given that the army had forbidden officer candidates being trained on college campuses from playing football, why was it allowed at West Point? It stemmed from the conviction that exemplary Army and Navy football teams were essential for morale domestically and overseas, proof of US strength and power; as the going went on the football fields of Navy and Army, so the going went of the navy and army in the Pacific and Europe.

For those who started at Army in the fall of 1943, the war would be over by the time they graduated in June of 1946. With the war no longer a threat, some avoided the compulsory service requirement by flunking out of the military academy before graduation and going to other colleges or to the pros to continue playing football. That prompted President Harry Truman's military aide, Major General Harry H. Vaughan, to respond to the issue, after receiving letters from upset mothers wondering why their sons had been drafted when service academy players had not. Vaughan wrote back the following make-no-bones-about-it response:

> My reply was—and the President agreed with me—that they certainly look like draft dodgers. They have spent two or three years being educated at government expense at the academies where they were draft exempt.
>
> Now, when the shooting is over, they resign. Doesn't it look as if the only reason they went to Annapolis or West Point in the first place was to avoid the draft?

Even as the war raged, the subject of football in the service academies went to the highest echelons of the administration and the military establishment. Secretary of War Henry L. Stimson discovered that much to his shock: as a way of introducing a little comic relief into the usual intensity of cabinet meetings where life-and-death decisions were constant, he raised with Roosevelt the future of the Army-Navy game for 1943. Stimson said he had previously written Secretary of Navy Knox that in deference to public opinion the game should simply be canceled because of travel restrictions in place. Knox had replied that football was of too much inspirational value to the Naval Academy to give up. With tongue firmly in cheek, Stimson noted that he had sent the correspondence over to Roosevelt and there had been no answer to an issue of such "very serious importance." This elicited great laughter from the cabinet just as Stimson hoped, whereupon the issue of athletes and sports was then debated for eighty minutes without resolution. Roosevelt tried to slough off a decision on the game to a committee so as not to offend anybody, but reluctantly agreed with the cabinet that only the commander in chief could make such a call. He had the 1943 game played at Michie Stadium at West Point instead of Philadelphia's Municipal Stadium and a typical crowd of 100,000.

Although there was no definitive proof, it was likely that General Douglas MacArthur, the supreme commander of the Southwest Pacific War and the media darling of the war despite having fled the Philippines and leaving his men and the Filipinos to be decimated and tortured by the Japanese, was in the midst of it all. He held great sway with West Point, having graduated first in his class in 1903. Later as superintendent he made it a priority to increase the level of its sports programs. Given his popularity and pain-in-the-ass prickliness and flash-flood indignance when he perceived phantom insult and his presidential aspirations, the top command and administration were terrified of MacArthur, Roosevelt most of all. Whatever MacArthur wanted MacArthur got, and he wanted a great Army football team as essential fiber for the fighting man. He essentially recruited Earl "Red" Blaik, the successful Dartmouth coach and West Point graduate, to take over the program.

In 1944, the game was played in Baltimore, near the Navy campus at Annapolis. Army won 23–7, to take the national championship and achieve its first undefeated season in twenty-eight years, a feat so important that MacArthur dashed off a telegram to Blaik:

> The Greatest of all Army Teams. Stop.
> We have stopped the war to celebrate
> your magnificent success. MacArthur.

Of all the malarkey pumped out in World War II, this may have been the greatest of all.

World War II was a boon for Army football. It had not only the finest teams in its history but some of the finest teams in the history of football, led by the Heisman Trophy tandem in the backfield of Felix "Doc" Blanchard and Glenn Davis, Mr. Inside and

Mr. Outside, featured on the cover of *Time*. Between 1944 and 1946, Army had an aggregate record of 27–0–1. As everyone else scrambled, and waited for the inevitable call-up of players, and had no idea of who would be on the roster from one week to the next, Army luxuriated in its player riches. It wasn't simply the three-year draft exemption that made West Point unbeatable, but liberal eligibility and transfer rules during the war to encourage participation.

George Barney Poole, the All-American end from Army, played college football for *eight years* from the age of seventeen to twenty-five between 1941 and 1948 while millions served in the war. Poole attended the University of Mississippi in 1941 and 1942, then transferred to the University of North Carolina in 1943 on the V-12 program. He should have been called up, but instead he received a commission to West Point and played there in 1944, 1945, and 1946. He flunked out in 1947 and therefore compulsory service was not required because he had not graduated even though he had been at the academy until a month before graduation. He returned to Mississippi for two more seasons since his time at West Point was considered military service and was therefore exempt from the eligibility rules. He subsequently played end with the New York Giants.

DeWitt "Tex" Coulter, a six-foot-four, 230-pound

tackle, enlisted in the army and was there for less than a year before he went to the Military Academy in 1944, making it through the rest of the war playing football there. He flunked out in 1946 with a deficiency in mathematics before he would have graduated. It seemed clear that, like other players, the only interest he had in West Point was football. Like Poole, he did his duty with the New York Giants after becoming the seventh overall pick in the NFL draft.

Men overseas resented that players were safe from harm, playing football, while they smelled like shit and looked like shit and drank water like shit and coffee like shit and shit into little cans and thought like shit because they were tired as shit and scared as shit trying to stay alive in spite of all the shit unless you died because of all the shit and most definitely did not give a flying shit about the Army football team. Hometown and statewide teams, yes. But not the players at West Point, whom many considered draft dodgers. As John McLaughry put it, "It doesn't seem right, all these apparently healthy football players being exempt, and many of these men out here eighteen and twenty months all worn down with malaria and still working like hell."

Tony Butkovich was going to serve in the war. By electing the marines, just like the sixty-four others who would play in the Mosquito Bowl, he was selecting a service with almost double the casualty rate of the other branches. His aspiration to be a marine was the same as that of many great college football players: to be a member of the corps aligned with their self-image as macho, fearless athletes for whom combat was the only choice, the football field as prelude.

There was consolation for Butkovich: by joining the marine officer training program, he did get that final season in 1943 before hell. Starting at fullback, he played behind an offensive line that included three of his teammates from Illinois. The style of running that he had learned in high school was distinctive, almost curled into a ball with his back and butt raised and his knees toward his chin. It made him hard to tackle; he bounced off other players and then relied on his speed once he found open space.

Purdue played his former team, Illinois, early in the season; it was basically Illinois playing Illinois, given the number of Illinois players who had transferred to Purdue. The combination of Illinois players and so-called Purdue Illini combined for 50 points in a 40–21 Purdue win. Despite being tackled by his younger brother, Bill, prompting the public address announcer to irresistibly say "Butkovich tackle by Butkovich," Tony Butkovich was unstoppable. He gained 207 yards on twelve carries, an average of 17.2 yards per attempt. He also scored four touchdowns of 80, 25, 7, and 2 yards.

Butkovich began to get nationwide attention, the whispers turning to murmurs and then to routine plugs in the sports columns that the kid could be an All-American. As Russ Needham put it in the *Columbus Dispatch*, "Butkovich would hit and Appleby would hit him. Butkovich would continue for a yard or two or three, carrying Appleby and his weight along with him." He scored three touchdowns that game, giving him seven in two conference games. Against Iowa he scored three more times, giving him ten. His name began to creep from the lower half of the sports page in one column to the top half of the sports page in two columns and sometimes three. The snob boys back east at the *New York Times* were following him.

He had a steady girlfriend before he went overseas, the daughter of a doctor from the East. They apparently thought about marriage, but Butkovich said no. He didn't want to be forced into the terrible decision of having to choose; in the event that he was killed in action, the $10,000 government-guaranteed life insurance policy would go to his mother.

11

Separate and Unequal

In 1943, John McLaughry was learning how to kill.

It was rewarding but exhausting.

After his bitter experience with the disorganization of the army air corps, where he had begun to question his own patriotism, he now felt purpose, Marine Corps purpose. The Japanese would ultimately conclude that the United States had emptied out its jails and insane asylums and put the prisoners and patients into the corps. A Japanese soldier taken prisoner told interrogators he wondered if it was true that marines ate their grandmothers. Marine headquarters, if asked the question, most likely would have neither confirmed nor denied.

McLaughry's typical day started at 5:45 a.m. and lasted until 8:00 or sometimes 9:00 p.m. No sitting around the stove waiting for orders as in the air corps. "We never spend a lot of useless time standing in lines waiting for things, going places where we aren't expected, and doing things the 'Army' way," he wrote to his father. "Every minute is accounted for, and we really have to be on the ball. There is so much to learn and absorb in a short time, that it fairly leaves you spinning."

On the shooting range he did well. He qualified as an expert on the .45-caliber automatic pistol with an 88.9 percent average and also on the M1 Garand rifle. He shot the Browning machine gun at 200, 300, and 500 yards. It had a kick, and one of his eyebrows split open on the first shot, gushing blood. McLaughry found the field problems fun but intense. His "patrol" was ambushed, and he managed to escape only by diving into some underbrush and lying as still as death for twenty minutes. On the way back through the "lines" he spent half an hour stalking an "enemy" who turned out to be one of the men on his own patrol. The "enemy" thought he was an enemy, and they were quite surprised to see each other.

In wet, sleety snow in northern Virginia with the temperature 15 degrees and a twenty-five-mile-an-hour wind, they went on an eighteen-mile trek. They had to push their way through heavy underbrush and brambles and ford a stream and then a river with frigid water up to their knees. McLaughry alternately froze and sweated underneath his clothes because of the physical exertion, which only made him feel even more frozen when they stopped to rest. Two men had to be taken back to Quantico because of exhaustion, one of them after he had fallen into the river. As they waited two hours for chow, they built little fires to stay warm, and one doofus got so close that his pants caught fire. Which made everyone else laugh their ass off because everything in the Marine Corps was funny except for death, and that depended on who died. It only got better when the doofus rolled in the snow to put the fire out and then even better when his trouser leg peeled off and he was down to his long underwear. It was a test to see who could not take it and would quit. No one did, probably because those who knew what was coming had gone to sick bay that morning.

McLaughry was commissioned as a second lieutenant on February 10th of 1943. He wanted combat, his first choice to become part of the Marine Raiders, a special commando-style unit that had served during the victory at Guadalcanal in 1942 and early 1943. If that was not available, he hoped to become a line officer in a heavy-weapons company that included 81 mm mortars, heavy machine guns, and antitank guns. He was drawn to their destructive power. His final choice was a rifle platoon on the front lines, where he would be in the shit pretty much all the time and wars were won and lost.

His actual assignment was shocking, puzzling, and disappointing, more undesirable than any other in the Marine Corps, the "gulag," where the worst officers got dumped, the ones with no common sense and even less respect, who whined and complained and drove everyone else batshit. It made no sense to McLaughry, who had been near the top of his class. In all probability he got the assignment because he was levelheaded, clear-eyed, and enlightened, the Marine Corps back then not known for its educational advancement.

The place was Montford Point in Jacksonville, North Carolina, as far away as you could get from the nexus of Camp Lejeune and still be within its confines, in the northwest corner, thick with underbrush, brambles, poison ivy, insects, and poisonous snakes.

Montford was where Black marines trained. Ostensibly they were preparing for combat, but they would almost certainly never see it because the command had decided that white marines on the line did not trust them, much less want to be anywhere near them. The Marine Corps did not want Black marines; they had been forced upon it, and it did everything in its power to make sure they were never heard from again except as grunts in service and supply. So they were herded into Montford Point. Virtually every Black who enlisted in the marines went to Montford Point, segregated just as virtually every other unit in the US military was.

"I bet you'll never guess where I was assigned," he wrote to his parents in a series of letters from Montford Point in early May of 1943. "Ten of us were assigned to negro troops here. . . . I have no idea what we're in for, but I am disappointed that I didn't get with the 23rd Marines which pulls out soon. Why we were assigned to this I don't know. . . . I still can't get over it."

II

The incident could have happened in 1942 in Missouri, where a twenty-six-year-old cotton mill worker, Cleo Wright, was taken by a mob from the city jail. He was in detention for allegedly stabbing a white woman to death, although he had already been shot three times by the arresting officer, dragged behind a car through the Black section of Sikestown at speeds of up to seventy miles an hour, and then set afire. It could have happened the same year in Mississippi, where Ernest Green and Charlie Lang, both fourteen, after supposedly attempting to attack a thirteen-year-old white girl,* were taken from the county jail in Quitman and hanged from the same railroad bridge that had been the scene of four previous lynchings.† It could have happened in Detroit, where, during a racial riot, police were responsible for killing seventeen individuals, all of them Blacks.

A separate incident, which received no attention, took place across the Atlantic, the English welcoming their American allies not having realized that many of them believed that the Jim Crow laws of the South could and should be transported to a foreign country. No Black soldiers in the pubs. No Black soldiers in the restaurants. No Black soldiers having any contact with white women. The English, appalled by the conduct of American soldiers in general, their coarseness, bombast, and racial hatred, refused to comply. It was their country, and Black soldiers were welcomed in a way they had never been in the United States, where

---

* Their actual crime may have been using profanity, according to one press account.

† Lynching was not deemed a federal crime by the US Senate until 2018. The House of Representatives passed a revised version of the legislation in 2020. Congressional efforts up until then had repeatedly failed. In 1936 Roosevelt refused to support an anti-lynching bill because of a fear he would lose southern votes in the upcoming presidential election.

they had been segregated into shithole facilities, poorly trained, and with rare exceptions given the shit jobs, like McLaughry's men at Montford.

Two privates from Georgia, one twenty and the other twenty-six, in the army for a little over a year and part of a military police unit, saw two Black soldiers in the same public houses they had been in in the town of Rugeley, Staffordshire. The two soldiers were Robert Stafford and William Walton. They were technicians in Company D of the 390th Engineer General Service Regiment and were on their way back to camp at around 10:30 p.m.

William Forester and Tracey Bryant were both privates. They told the two soldiers to stop, suspecting that they had been flirting with white women. Stafford and Walton knew they were in trouble. They started to run but were overtaken. Stafford tried to reason:

"Don't hit me. Don't hit me. Let me talk to you."

Walton managed to free himself and went for help, leaving Stafford behind.

Forester started punching first. Bryant had gone ahead but came back. He heard Stafford pleading to be left alone and reacted by hitting him two or three times with his left fist. Forester punched him at the same time. Stafford went down. Bryant was on top of him and hit him three more times in the face. Forester kicked him in the head, face, and shoulder.

Some English soldiers tried to intervene and were told to mind their own business.

"Let's kill this fucking Black bastard."

A British civilian was walking home when he heard the disturbance and saw Stafford lying in the road. He told Bryant and Forester that they could not just leave him there.

One of them answered back.

"Leave him alone. I put this damn nigger in the middle of the road for the goddamn truck to run over him as he is no good. He has been out with a white girl, and out in the States we don't have anything to do with them. We treat them like dogs."

They dragged Stafford to the side of the road. Then they strangled him to death with his own tie, pulled so tight that the only way to get it off afterward was to cut it off, the fifteen-inch circumference of his neck reduced to twelve inches. Forester and Bryant, who had had as many as twelve pints of beer, went back to camp whistling. They were arrested that night and in March of 1944 were tried by the Office of the Judge Advocate General and sentenced to life in prison. It was justice of a kind, although it wasn't.

In figures not released until after the war, it was

revealed that seventy soldiers had been put to death in the European theater by either hanging or firing squad between July of 1942 and November of 1945. Fifteen were white and fifty Black, 79 percent of the total even though Blacks made up roughly 9 percent of the army.

The Rugeley case was shocking and likely isolated, although there is no way of knowing since incidents of this type were almost certainly not reported to the authorities. But it was emblematic of the way too many whites from every region of the country viewed Blacks during the war, the blatantly racist shift that had taken place in the military since the founding of the country.

III

Some five thousand Blacks had fought in the Revolutionary War. The number rose to three hundred thousand in the Civil War, with many serving with distinction in the Union army. The military's attitude toward Blacks had shifted during World War I. A total of 404,348 African Americans had served, all of them segregated from whites. Most had been in services and supply—the lowly work of quartermaster, stevedore, and pioneer units—and there were only 1,353 Black commissioned officers.

There were notable exceptions. The all-Black 92nd

and 93rd Infantry Divisions of the army were sent into combat in France in World War I. They had a casualty rate of 35 percent, with 584 men killed. About 550 received decorations from the Americans and the French. But in what would become a pattern, public praise was followed by private condemnation by the military establishment. A study by the Army War College in 1925 concluded that the Black soldier overall had failed in combat in World War I because of "his mental inferiority and the inherent weaknesses of his character." The reasons given were from the eugenicist pseudo-science template: "The cranial cavity of the negro is smaller than the white, his brain weighing 35 ounces contrasted with 45 for the white"; "in the process of evolution the American negro has not progressed as far as the other sub-species of the human family"; "such negroes as have shown marked mental attainments also show a heavy strain of white blood." The study was not considered some scurrilous racist screed; it became the basis of how Black soldiers would be treated in World War II.

There were fewer than four thousand enlisted Blacks in the army in 1939 and only two Black combat officers. The several thousand in the navy were mess men in white uniforms, paid less than their white counterparts. At the outset of the war, there were no Blacks in the Marine Corps. "If it were a question of having a Marine Corps of 5,000 whites or 250,000 Negroes, I would rather have the whites," Marine Commandant Thomas Holcomb told the Navy General Board.

The passage of the Selective Training and Service Act in September of 1940 and its vow that "there shall be no discrimination against any person on account of race or color" seemingly marked a huge step forward in increasing the number of Blacks in the armed services and gaining them at least some measure of fair treatment.

Unofficial policy became that African Americans should make up roughly 10 percent of the overall armed forces, reflecting their proportion within the US population—except that it was up to the War Department to decide when that would happen, and the easy out for it was that there was no place to put Blacks because, after all, separate facilities would have to be built to ensure that Blacks and whites would virtually never come into contact with each other during training.

It was only after the threat of a massive march on Washington that Roosevelt did something definitive. On June 25th of 1941, he issued Executive Order 8802, banning racial discrimination in the military. But segregation under the *Plessy v. Ferguson* doctrine of "separate but equal" remained the policy. Though "separate" was strictly enforced, "equal" was not.

African Americans began to enter the services, although at the beginning of the war all sorts of pretexts were found to reject them: illiteracy, venereal disease, urethritis, psychoneurosis, whatever else came in handy. As of 1943, the rejection rate for Blacks was 53 percent versus 33 percent for whites. Lack of education was a legitimate issue since many Blacks, particularly those in the South, had received virtually none.

By the end of 1942, despite serious obstacles to enlisting,* more than 467,000 Black troops were serving in the army, nearly a fivefold increase from the previous year. The army ultimately came close to the promised 10 percent quota. But the conditions and atmosphere did not change. It wasn't just the shame of inadequate facilities at bases, forts, posts, airfields, and camps around the country for Blacks in the military. It wasn't just the self-perpetuating cycle of insufficient training of Black officers, which led to poor leadership in the field, which was used by white military and War Department leaders as proof that Black officers were incapable of command. It wasn't just Secretary of War Henry Stimson saying that Black men

---

* In Mississippi, a favored tactic to bar Blacks from enlistment was to claim that, based on the physical examination, they had syphilis when there was no proof.

weren't capable of handling modern weaponry. It wasn't just Roosevelt citing racial progress in the navy by noting that "colored boys" had replaced Filipinos as mess men and could certainly play in "colored bands" on board ships because, after all, they were "darn good" at it. It wasn't just the fact that college-educated Blacks, instead of being coveted as officers and utilized by the military for needed skills, were often dumped into units where the only requirement was physical strength and subservience. It wasn't just the Red Cross separating Black blood from white in its blood donor program. It wasn't just military installations adopting Jim Crow laws to keep the locals in surrounding towns happy, which meant that Black American soldiers serving their country had to sit in the back of the bus behind white American soldiers if the bus driver let them on at all. It wasn't just making sure that no Black officer could give orders to a white one regardless of their respective ranks. It wasn't just the false promises of being allowed to fight in a combat role.

It was the way in which virtually all of the roughly 1 million Blacks who served were institutionalized into inferiority from the very beginning of the war, with daily degradations small and large. They were there to serve white troops in the capacities of stewards, truck drivers. They staffed supply depots, ammo dumps, bakeries, laundries, medical sanitation, and polished the oak of the officers' club after they passed the tests of being light-skinned and having clean fingernails.

In his 1941 State of the Union address, Roosevelt listed the four freedoms that every individual in the world had a right to enjoy: freedom from want, freedom from fear, freedom of speech, freedom of religion. It was a stirring speech, both memorable and inspirational. There would be freedom for Jews liberated from concentration camps. There would be freedom for the Chinese after more than 15 million had died at the hands of the Japanese. There would be freedom for the people of Germany and Japan from fascism and military dictatorship. There would be freedom for much of occupied Europe. But there would not be freedom for the 13 million Blacks living in the United States of America.

More opportunities for combat for Blacks did emerge at the end of the war. The navy, under the leadership of Secretary of the Navy James Forrestal, made strides to put Blacks and whites together on ships. The army became the nation's largest employer of Black Americans.

Roughly 2,500 Black volunteers—privates already serving in Europe in support units—were integrated into the army as replacement troops in 1944 and 1945, including on D-Day and during the Battle of the Bulge. In a subsequent survey of 250 white officers, 80 percent felt the Black troops had performed "very well" in combat and that integration of the military worked. In the same survey, three-quarters of 1,700 enlisted men reported that their experience had made them feel more respect and friendship toward their fellow Black soldiers. Of all the reports and studies written on the issue of race, that may well have been the most revealing, reflecting not the suppositions of the high echelon but the realities of the men on the front line, where there wasn't a lot of time to worry about skin color if you wanted to keep your ass in one piece. Not that the public would ever know. The survey was never released; the War Department suppressed it so as not to give ammunition to civil rights leaders who were pushing for integration in the society as a whole.

John McLaughry wasn't a politician; he was a marine preoccupied with learning how to kill and survive, not with civil rights. All he had was his ground zero perspective, which virtually no one actually making policy could claim. He was aware of the stereotype of Blacks, but based on his interactions with them, he didn't see it. "There are a lot of good boys here," he wrote home from Montford, "smart and ambitious who if they had a decent chance in civilian life would go a long way." The Black recruits were eager to learn and devoured all the military manuals they could get their hands on.

McLaughry was assigned to the 6th Depot Company as one of three commissioned officers overseeing about 125 men. It wasn't a combat unit, but word was that they were going to be shipped out overseas. The company left North Carolina at the end of July of 1943. Their destination was Naval Station Treasure Island in San Francisco Bay,* but it was full, so they ended up at a barren, shabby naval replacement center forty miles east of Oakland. Their surroundings did not matter. After the slog of Montford Point, McLaughry's men understood what it was to be a marine, so special that even white navy sailors were in awe of them. McLaughry and the other officers worked them hard, and no one complained or dropped out. They strutted and "put on the dog" even more than usual to show the navy boys just what it took. One afternoon they did a three-hour hike over the hills and back in heat and dust, then marched into camp with as much snap as

---

* The navy base became known for its psychiatric ward, where gay seamen, rather than being punished, as homosexuality was illegal in the military, were treated with understanding and then discharged. The innovative policy was one of the reasons San Francisco became a haven for gays.

McLaughry had ever seen. He knew they were tired, but they reacted to every command he gave like clockwork. He also knew that most marines would not want to hear about Blacks' potential. He worried about what might happen overseas if they were actually in an active war zone.

"I know that as a whole most of the white Marines resent the negroes very much," he wrote his family. ". . . [T]hey would just as soon shoot them as look at them and it'll be even worse in the war zone where killing is an everyday occurrence and men are taught to do it."

12

Remember the *McKean*

McLaughry finally got his wish. He left Treasure Island and went overseas in the summer of 1943. The trip to Noumea in New Caledonia, a key stopping point for troops and the naval fleet, took twenty-five days. It was miserable in its snail's pace, punctuated by training classes for McLaughry's men during the day. At night in the all-white wardroom he played cards or chess or read or wrote letters. He played poker the first week, losing all the money he had, eight dollars. He also grew a mustache that, much to his surprise, was both red and thick. The ship passed through submarine-infested waters, so there was the constant fear of being torpedoed, "getting the 'fish,'" as McLaughry called it in letters home.

They arrived on August 31st to see rugged mountains

rising out of the sea into the cloud cover. McLaughry
drew an insignia for the 6th, an eight ball at the top, a
pair of dice within the crest below, and the company's
motto, IN "DICE" SPERAMUS, at the bottom. Everybody
loved it. To his surprise, the 6th Depot Company was
disbanded, leaving him once again without a command
and just floating. He put in for a transfer. In the interim
he was placed in charge of the motor pool of about fifteen hundred vehicles, ranging from jeeps to bulldoz-
ers. It was another bullshit assignment, and he was so
weary of the bullshit. He *wanted* combat, so why not
put him *into* combat? No wonder the war could take
years; those who actually wanted to fight were doing
everything else but.

Noumea was teeming with troops, as many as fifty
thousand during the war. He and other officers lived in
huts on a hilltop, fearful that the high winds would blow
all of them away, which at that point seemed prophetic,
given his military career thus far. The one bit of good
news was that although the mosquitoes conducted daily
raids, it was with less propulsion than the North Carolina varieties at Montford Point. He found refuge in the
officers' club, plentiful beer and every now and then the
gods' nectar of hard liquor. Typical of his quiet obser-
vance, he watched the slot machine one night. Officer
after officer had put in a quarter and lost.

He slid in a few quarters of his own and lost them. He had just one quarter left . . .

Jackpot!!

Twenty-two dollars.

Maybe it meant something.

On September 22nd of 1943, a year to the day since he had left the army air corps, he received word that his transfer request had been approved. He was going into the Marine Raiders.

As batshit as the marines were, the Raiders were even more batshit. They were a fast-moving and handpicked unit designed for going behind enemy lines and conducting quick-strike guerrilla warfare. They carried two knives, one the classic nine-inch bowie and the other a raider stiletto for close-in combat. They had rifles, of course, but rifles made noise and revealed location; the preferred method of killing was with the stiletto into the neck, shoved straight through, quiet and precise. The previous year at Guadalcanal, the 1st and 2nd Raider Battalions had become legendary under Lieutenant Colonels Evans Carlson and Merritt Edson, defying all the odds at Tulagi and Bloody Ridge, ruthless, no longer taking prisoners after one of their own was found on a stake and castrated in a typical example of Japanese sadism that had literally been beaten into their soldiers since the first day of training.

It was only because of the brotherhood of football that McLaughry had been approved. The commanding officer of the 2nd Raider Battalion, Lieutenant Colonel Alan Shapley, had been not just a football star at the Naval Academy in the 1920s but perhaps the best athlete in the school's history, with twelve letters in football, basketball, and track. He knew that McLaughry had played football and done so exceptionally well, and that was enough. When McLaughry sailed on the USS *President Hayes* from Noumea for the next stop, Guadalcanal, he shared a berth with the chaplain who in turn was next to the berth shared by Shapley and Lieutenant Colonel Joseph McCaffery. Shapley and McCaffery liked arguing over football—who beat whom, who had played where, who was better than whom. McCaffery had been a football star at Pennsylvania Military College, so he knew his stuff. They were formidable opponents. When there was an impasse, McLaughry was brought in as the closer, due to his pedigree at Brown and the New York Giants and his coaching lineage. It was flattering. But as a lowly second lieutenant, he was slightly terrified at arbitrating between two senior officers.

Finally, *finally*, he had expectorated the bitter experience of the air corps, from which he had washed out. Now he felt even with his brother, Bob, his *younger brother*, Bob, who *had* become a fighter pilot. His greatest fear was how to break it to his mom that he had joined the Raiders. So he asked his father, Tuss, to play blocking back: "Give her the good word, will you?"

By early October of 1943, McLaughry was on Guadalcanal. One night in mid-October, almost nine thousand miles from Providence, he watched the most beautiful sunset he had ever seen, whispery slicks of gold and red and purple across the sky. Whether you believed in Heaven or had your doubts, you just knew it was up there on a night like this.

Until two weeks later, when death and casualties came in from the front at Bougainville, an island within the Solomons chain about 430 miles from Guadalcanal. One of them was McCaffery. He was a raider, in the thick at Guadalcanal and then as the commanding officer of the 2nd Raider Battalion at Bougainville. He was beloved because he was tough but also because he was decent. He led his men onto the beach at Bougainville on All Saints' Day, November 1st of 1943, forging ahead until machine-gun fire ripped from a bunker so well concealed he couldn't have seen it and if he couldn't see it, how was he going to return fire? He jumped into a trench and kept moving. Then fire from a Nambu light machine gun got him four times in the chest. The corpsman and battalion surgeon tried to save him. It was futile.

His mother, Marion, a widow who lived in Chester, Pennsylvania, had already suffered through the death of one son: Hugh McCaffery had died shortly after Pearl Harbor in an air corps plane crash in the mountains of California. She was recovering from a severe cold when she received notification that her remaining child, Joseph, was now gone. The family, which had owned a hotel in Chester, had been inseparable. Now everyone she loved had been taken. She went into shock and died twelve days later, ostensibly of pneumonia, but everybody knew that wasn't the only cause.

It was at the moment McLaughry heard of McCaffery's death that he realized what all men going into combat realize, no longer abstraction, no longer sucked in by the purple streak of the sunset. "Up 'til now," he wrote to his parents, "the war has been just something I read of, heard of, and talked about, back in a nice safe base. It all seemed very objective, but now it is just really beginning to come home to me just what it all means. I'm not there as yet, but it is very near and my friends are there, and many of them will never come back."

Then he did what all servicemen must: "Enough of that."

II

On November 15th of 1943, McLaughry left Guadalcanal for Bougainville. Along with roughly 180 other marines, he was assigned to the high-speed transport USS *McKean*, hull number APD-5, part of a twenty-three-ship convoy. Navy ships, just like the men on board, had distinct personalities. Some ran like clockwork; others ran counterclockwise. Some were blessed, some were cursed. Some had swagger and wanted to be out front. Some were shy and only wanted to be in back. Some were easier to love than others. Some were mule stubborn. The *McKean* was a plodder, a four-stack destroyer built in 1919, what the crew called a "piddle-diddle." As the Allies made their offensive up the Solomon Islands chain, the *McKean* was dependable and uncomplaining. But she was tired, brittle, and weak, with no strength left in the metal of her hull. She needed a nursing home, but the exigencies of war prevented it.

The destination was Bougainville. The Japanese had garrisoned a force of somewhere around fifty thousand there to build naval and air bases as a launch point to destroy the lines of communication among the United

States, Australia, and the southwest Pacific. They also wanted to protect their key base of Rabaul. The Americans wanted to neutralize Rabaul by building airfields on Bougainville to launch their own attack.

The weather was clear and the moon was bright as the *McKean* and its convoy made its way to Cape Torokina on the coast of Bougainville in the early hours before dawn on November 17th of 1943. There were 153 officers and enlisted men on board from the navy and 185 troops from the marines. The ship's speed was thirteen knots.

At 0300, radar sighted three enemy torpedo planes and eventually as many as eight from a distance of about twenty miles. One of the planes appeared to be going after the USS *Talbot*. Then suddenly it turned sharply to the right and headed directly for the *McKean*. Four 20 mm guns on the starboard side began firing, but the bigger guns could not be used because the USS *Talbot* was in the line of fire.

The plane banked to the right and paralleled the *McKean* at a distance of about two thousand yards, almost skimming the water at an altitude of fifty feet. The plane approached to about three hundred yards and fired. The torpedo exploded on the starboard side at 0350. Fifty-two marines and sixty-four naval officers and crewmen died.

But not McLaughry.

The truck taking him to the embarkation site had broken down. He and fourteen other marines arrived an hour late, and the *McKean* was full. They were transferred to the USS *Ward* in the same convoy. McLaughry heard a series of enormous explosions as they neared the Empress Augusta Bay and knew the convoy had been attacked. All the marines were ordered belowdecks, but, irresistibly drawn to the action, he sneaked out and found a spot near the bow. It was only later he found out that it was the *McKean* that had been torpedoed. He wondered if it was luck that had made him an hour late—or maybe fate or something else entirely.

Later that morning, just after dawn, McLaughry and the other marines disembarked from the *Ward* and arrived at the beachhead on Bougainville. They were greeted by the explosion and whistle of aerial bombs. They took off into the jungle along the Piva Trail and had been hiking for about a mile when a Japanese Zero just above the treetops started firing away. The target was actually a few hundred yards ahead of them, but they jumped into the bushes as an extra precaution. Unfortunately, the spot they picked was quite near where the war dog platoon was bivouacked.

He and another guy landed in a pile of dog shit.

It was still his first day of combat.

13
Sunday Sheet

Anne Schreiner became the family ballast after her son went into the Marine Corps in 1943, her ceaseless cheer an antidote to the dread that every mother and father had of the Western Union telegram. On Sunday nights she sat down at the typewriter at the home on Tyler Street to write what she called "The Schreiner Sunday Sheet."

It was a two-page, single-spaced feast of comings and goings in Lancaster, no detail too small, because the flow of a small town was always in the small details: who was doing what, who had gotten sick, how the bridge games were going, the status of the local Red Cross drive, the hard truth that Schreiner's father, Herb, referred to as the "Old Man," had gained so much weight that the new suit he had bought a few months before no longer fit.

Reading it felt like Sunday pot roast or ice-cold milk or chocolate chip cookies fresh out of the oven in the Wisconsin winter. She wrote with grace, sweet humor, and wryness, conveying the feeling to her son that life went on in their town as it always had and would go on exactly the same after he came home. He would return changed—every man who went to war came back changed—but the beauty of Lancaster was that nothing had really changed at all.

"The Schreiner Sunday Sheet" was distributed to David, Odette, his sister, Betty, his brother-in-law, Hal, and a few chosen others. It usually began with family news, then continued with news of locals now in the service. Interspersed was the news of Lancaster: Margaret Schmidt had been operated on for a tumor in her abdomen, Mr. Stoneman of Platteville had been elected national president of the Rural Electric Association, a game of bridge with the Carthews had been followed by coffee cake at midnight.

She tried to be upbeat, light, and breezy, but there were times where it became impossible. Nobody knew if Mark Hoskins, her son's adored friend from childhood, was still alive after he had been shot down over Hungary. The hope was that he had made it out of the plane and been taken prisoner, a better fate than crashing or landing in the ocean. Then came news that his brother Charles, an army private with the 5th Infantry Division fighting in France, had stopped writing home. That wasn't unusual, since men moved quickly while in combat. But then his parents received a telegram stating that he was missing in action. Anne knew that her son, already grappling with the news about Mark, would be horribly upset. But she could not ignore it. The Hoskins and Schreiner families were inseparable, and she knew their boys just about as well as she knew her own children.

> Charles is that fine type, not fitted by nature to either be a part of a fighting army nor to ward off the scars to his sensitive soul of the horrible sights of war and filth. Nor did he have sufficient training in bloody fighting such as that was on the Western Front. But let it be said to his everlasting credit that he wanted to be a part of it with every fiber of his being. . . .
>
> Let us hope that Charles is safe, as a prisoner, as a hide-out, as one cared for perhaps by the peasants—that Charles is alive. And let us cling to that hope with all courage, and perhaps a bright day may come when we hear that he did not have to give all in such a tragic way.

Charles Hoskins is buried in the Luxembourg American Cemetery near Hamm.

II

If Anne Schreiner was determined to supply the oxygen of optimism to her son, he was determined to supply the oxygen of optimism to his parents about life in the Marine Corps. Little complaints seeped out about life in boot camp on Parris Island as a member of Platoon 380. Drill instructors left an indelible impression, maybe the most of anyone in the Marine Corps. They certainly made for the best stories. They were iconic and iconoclastic, severe and stern, total shits filled with bullshit, pushing you beyond any limit you ever imagined to what felt like death and then pulling you back in spite of your shitbird sorry shitbird self that deserved to be left in the swamp with the other shitbirds. They were master psychiatrists in breaking kids into nothing and then building them up into marines, teaching them that the only person they could ever truly depend on in their entire life would be the guy next to them in the foxhole, and if they didn't do everything in their power to protect one another, they were the worst thing they could ever be called in the Marine Corps, which was a coward. Normally DIs had three months to train a shitbird, but because of the war the period had been shortened to eight weeks. It wasn't a lot of time to take recruits, many of whom had never been away from home and had been insulated from any adversity, plunge them into the most alienating situation they had ever been in, teach them to take every order big and small without question and love their rifle more than their dick.

DIs yelled, punished, harassed, belittled, and saw everything even when they weren't there. They were a royal pain-in-the-ass: "Make the fucking bed again, shitbird. . . . Use your toothbrush to clean the piss-hole and the shithole, shitbird. . . . Wear this pail over your head, shitbird, so I can clang it like a dinner bell, shitbird. . . . Polish the floor with sand, shitbird."

Someone turned his head in drill and then somebody else did, and suddenly they were hunting the grounds for five hundred cigarette butts. One guy tried to cheat—he collected only 268, but he figured the DI would never check the pile. Wrong. The DI did check the pile, and the guy had to start over and not only collect the five hundred butts but string them together.

The ones who were trim and in good shape made it through. The ones who were overweight and out of shape disappeared, gone without a trace. The worst thing was for a DI to know your name or make up one for you to ride you mercilessly, such as Fuck-Off Number One and Fuck-Off Number Two, the Marine Corps's version of Dr. Seuss. Those two were twins, which made them stick out even more. They had blisters all over their feet from marching every day. They were overweight. They went into the sick bay, and once a marine went into the sick bay for more than a couple of days, he was gone. There were others who were dead set on becoming marines until they got to Parris Island and realized they had made the worst mistake of their lives. Like the recruit who got out by climbing to the top of the barracks with fire cans of sand in each hand and jumped, breaking both his legs. But an instant bond of family developed for those who did make it:

> I'm a shitbird, I'm a shitbird, I'm a shitbird
> 'til I die.
> But I'd rather be a shitbird than a fucked-
> up DI.

Schreiner went through it just as every other recruit went through it. He left a piece of butter on his plate in the mess hall one day and was forced to eat it, not as disgusting as it was humiliating. His drill instructor was fond of holding boxing matches with his opponent blindfolded. The making of one's bed in the barracks became the definition of infinity, the mattress tossed over and the recruit forced to start over even though it was wrinkle-free. A recruit who brushed off a bug that was biting him while he was standing at attention was told by the corporal, "Don't brush off these bugs—they've got to eat—and down here they eat off the boots."

"The things that are hard to take is everybody riding you all the time but it is just part of learning to be subordinate," Schreiner told his parents. "This is wonderful training and is doing me lots of good."

That was the sanitized version. In a letter written shortly afterward to Betty and Hal, he was far more honest: "I keep telling the folks that I'm crazy about the Marines and the truth is that I like it but you sure go thru a lot of hell and many times I have been ready to quit." The lectures on military nomenclature and courtesy were far more complex than he had ever imagined, and he was having trouble catching on, as was mostly true for him in any new course of study. The menial chores drove him crazy. But he was confident that when he finished the eight weeks of boot camp he would "not only be a 1st class housewife with my washing, bed making, sewing etc. but a 1st class fighting man."

He was lucky in that he and several Wisconsin teammates had entered boot camp at the same time and could engage in mutual commiseration. Among them was the onion eater.

14

Bauman

The Bauman brothers had grown up too quickly, struggling in the Depression in a working-class town south of Chicago where the soot from the steel mills coated the sills of the windows. Bob was thirteen. His brother, Frank, or Frankie, as he liked to be called, was ten. Their father, Frank, had been a sergeant on the Harvey police force in Illinois. He was beloved, but then his heart began to go. He died in 1934 at the age of forty-one.

He left behind those two boys and his wife, Bertha. There was a wake with an open casket at the family home on Center Avenue in Harvey. It was bewildering to Frank as a little boy, having to sit there. He went outside and started playing with some other kids. He was simply acting his age when his mother came out of the house and sternly told him to get back inside. He never forgot that. From that moment his goal was to please his mother, never disappoint her.

There was after that something melancholic about Bertha, trudging through life. She had been married to Frank for eighteen years and was a housewife, and now he was gone. His sister Emma, red-haired and lively, moved in to give the boys some permanence and inject some life into the household. They could laugh with her. She provided them with a warmth that was difficult for Bertha to show. Emma also helped financially, working for a period of time as a stenographer for an insurance company in Harvey.

The town of sixteen thousand, twenty-five miles south of Chicago and twenty-two miles east of the towering steel mills of Gary, Indiana, had been hit hard by the Depression like everywhere else in America. Even before Frank Bauman died, the family had been forced to drop two life insurance policies, receiving a cash surrender check of $146.87 from the Federal Union Life Insurance Company in Cincinnati.

Bertha presumably had some type of police survivor's pension, but it wasn't enough. To make ends meet, she took in boarders on the first and part of the second floor of their home on Center Street. They lived by the railroad tracks. Men—hoboes, as they were called back then—often came off the freight trains hungry and desperate. Bertha took them in and fed them a meal for free. The boys started working, Bob shortly after his father died and then Frank—a quarter there, a dollar here, anything.

They toiled in the onion fields of South Holland, taking home the bruised ones so they could at least have onion sandwiches, following them with a stick of Wrigley's gum to disguise the odor. Bertha baked the bread to save money. Every week they had Sunday dinner around the table, where they ate delicious homemade sauerkraut and talked and laughed. The boys were big as young teenagers and would only get bigger—much bigger. As a treat they would share one of those small prepackaged apple pies. Bob would cut them neatly in half and scoop out all the apple filling when Frank wasn't paying attention. Frank could not understand why his half always tasted dry until he figured it out. He hated those pies for the rest of his life.

They were often hungry, but they never complained. They were always concerned about their mother, tried to help her to make ends meet so it would be one less thing to worry her.

Bertha loved her boys. You can tell from a picture taken of her in which they are arm in arm, her proud smile. Nobody liked to say it, but Bob was her favorite, with a twinkle in his eye to suggest a little mischief, an early lover of beer and smokes until he vowed to quit and always started up again. They were both alpha males, Frank more of a reluctant one when his brother was around. Frank got a nickname as he grew older, Dudley Do-Right.

They both went to Thornton Township High School, the jewel in the Harvey crown, formidable academically with 2,900 students. Bob was named third-team all-state in football his senior year in 1938. He played end, but what made him legendary was his punting, averaging sixty-two yards per kick in a 7–6 win over Chicago's Pullman Technical High School to preserve an undefeated season. He lettered in football, basketball, and track at Thornton. Frank, three years younger, also lettered in football, basketball, and track at Thornton and was all-state in football, as well as honorable mention all-state in basketball. His moniker was "Big Blond Frank, the Human Tank."

Bob would never be known for his academics. It was often a matter of doing just enough to skate by. In his sophomore year at Thornton High, he got three C's, one B, and one D. His only A came in physical education. Frank studied in high school. He liked to study. He was meticulous in everything he did. He was a member of the National Honor Society. He was active in the school beyond just sports: class president his sophomore year and treasurer as a senior. He was later honored for outstanding scholarship as a freshman at the University of Illinois.

Bob went to Wisconsin, where he started at tackle and did the punting in Wisconsin's best season in history in 1942: two years later he played in the Mosquito Bowl alongside Schreiner. At Illinois in 1942, Frank played with Tony Butkovich. Like Butkovich, he then went to Purdue and started on the offensive line on the 1943 team. Bob was listed as six foot two and 210 pounds. Frank was listed as six foot three and 211 pounds. In 1943, Bob was drafted in the twenty-fourth round by the Chicago Bears. In 1946, Frank was drafted in the twelfth round by the Chicago Bears after being named an All-American by several prestigious outlets. Bob became an officer in the Marine Corps. Frank became an officer in the Marine Corps.

Bob was obsessed with getting a tan regardless of the weather. Frank was just a hunk. Working shirtless in the Chicago subway system one summer while still in college, he took a break, went aboveground, and discovered that he was being followed by someone. He pinned the man up against a wall in an alleyway and wanted to know what the hell was going on. It turned out that the man was a talent scout, had seen Frank's physique, and wondered if he might do a screen test for the film role of Tarzan in which Donna Reed would be playing Jane. Frank went ahead with it, hated the pictures that were taken, and knew that of all the aspirations in his life, playing Tarzan was not on the list.

Bob would have grabbed it and never looked back.

15
Forget Me Not

When Odette and Schreiner got engaged at the end of May in 1943, the announcement in the *Wisconsin State Journal* described him, undoubtedly to his chagrin, as the "famous U.W. Football Star." He was concerned that his sister had said little about his engagement in a letter she had written to him and took it as a sign that maybe she thought he was being impulsive. He promised her he had not jumped into it. Less than two weeks later, he mused to his parents that maybe he and Odette should get married once he received his commission as a second lieutenant in September of 1943.

Married?

Of course you may not think this is the
proper time to think about it but I can't

help it. You may feel that I want to jump into it without knowing what lies before me.

I know that Odette is the girl for me and she wants to get married. I *know*. Don't think I'll run off half-cocked. I just want to know what you think.

He wasn't the only one to wonder about getting married, one of the most important questions of life that had been put under a magnifying glass by the war. In every man:

Will I return? Will I be the same? Will she be the same?

In every woman:

Will he return? Will I be the same? Will he be the same?

The echoes that overlapped:

I barely know her.

I barely know him.

We are strangers.

‖

After receiving his private first class stripes and six sets of khakis, Schreiner left Parris Island in the middle of July for Quantico, Virginia, to begin officer training as a member of the thirty-third candidates class, together with Bauman. Quantico was a grand resort compared to Parris Island: brick barracks, better food, sleeping in until 5:30 a.m. instead of 5:00. Most of all, he liked being treated like an adult and not a shitbird.

There was a great deal of classroom work for Schreiner, far more than he had been given at Parris Island, and he was intimidated by it. He felt lost at the beginning. On many days there were four one-hour lectures with ten-minute breaks in between, accompanied by remarkably dense and complicated training manuals that took away all instinct and would kill you in combat if you followed them precisely.

Schreiner took detailed notes in a 10-by-61/2-inch notebook with a spiral binding at the top: the differences between the Wildcat, the Corsair, the Seagull, and the Helldiver; how to read airplane identification; the fundamental Marine Corps structure in which a division of roughly twenty thousand was divided into smaller and smaller parts.* He was expected to know inside and out

---

* There were three rifle regiments below the division; three battalions beneath each of the regiments; three companies below each of the battalions; three platoons below each of the companies; three squads of thirteen below each of the platoons; three fire teams of four each below each squad, with a sergeant or a corporal in charge. In other words, a division at full strength of roughly twenty thousand men was ultimately broken down into units of four.

the use of the mortar, scouting and patrolling, antiaircraft defense, and close-order drill, among other sub-
jects. Perhaps the greatest thrill so far was seeing the
actor Tyrone Power, a fellow Quantico trainee, spiffed
out in his marine uniform.

Schreiner was now twenty-two and a college graduate. He was engaged to get married. He would ultimately
be responsible for more than a hundred men in some of
the worst conditions known to humankind. But he was
still the boy far away from home, asking his mother to
send him T-shirts and shorts and a coupon for brown
mahogany dress shoes that cost $8.50. Then an iron and
an overnight bag. Unsolicited, she sent him fudge, and
by consensus it was the best fudge of any of the moms,
certainly the creamiest.

He found time to write an unsolicited letter to
eleven-year-old Dick Singleton, whose family knew
Odette. He was bedridden and idolized Schreiner,
prompting the Wisconsin star to contact him to bol-
ster his spirits.

> I understand you have been in bed for a
> while so take good care of yourself now
> so that you you'll be strong enough to

play football. Write and tell me about yourself, Dick, and what you like to do.

Your friend,
Dave Schreiner

On September 8th of 1943, at 10:30 a.m. in the post theater of the Recreation Building of the Marine Barracks at Quantico, he graduated as a member of the thirty-third candidates' class and became a second lieutenant. It was a blip for Schreiner compared to the planned upcoming weekend in Washington with Odette: rooms at the Hotel Statler, the Army Navy Country Club in Arlington, Virginia, for dinner and dancing. A handsome young man made a hundred times more handsome by the uniform. A smart, vibrant woman with him on the hourglass of time. A swank hotel room. The swirl of a perfect dance, the repeated romance of the war and one that broke too many hearts.

About two months later, he saw Odette again. In between finishing up at Quantico and shipping out to Camp Elliott in San Diego, he had a ten-day furlough in Lancaster in mid-November of 1943. It was his first time home since he had joined the Marine Corps six months earlier, and all he wanted was to be with his family and Odette in simplicity: bridge games, taking care of his sister, Betty's, new dog with promises to walk and exercise and wash her. He gently admonished his parents not to plan anything special, although he did suggest that they go one night to East Dubuque across the border in Iowa and let their hair down a little bit. He knew it would be his last time home for several years, and he worried that by that time he would be an old bachelor with a gray beard. His parents did not want him to marry Odette, at least not now. They had written him a long letter about war marriages and how they often did not work. They had sent it several months earlier, and it had taken him a while to agree with it, but based on what he had later seen firsthand, he now believed it was true. He told them that he had no intention of getting married for a long time to come. Several weeks later, after seeing Odette, he thought he should marry her before shipping out—before he changed his mind again.

On November 17th of 1943, he caught a 4:10 p.m. American Airlines plane from Washington, DC, to

Chicago, then a train. He sent his parents a telegram to let them know what time he would be arriving so they could pick him up:

ARRIVING EAST DUBUQUE AT 1144 ON NOV. 18TH THURSDAY. CAN'T WAIT TO SEE YOU ALL LOVE. DAVE

Three days later, Anne Schreiner held a combination Easter egg hunt, Thanksgiving dinner, and Christmas to take full advantage of her son's time home. Odette was among those at the table, the hollow helplessness within both her and her fiancé of having no idea when they would see each other again.

The same day, 6,530 miles away in the Central Pacific, the first amphibious assault by the marines on a defended beachhead in World War II began just after dawn. What happened would define the Marine Corps in the rest of the war, a precursor of the destiny of Schreiner, McLaughry, Butkovich, Bauman, Murphy, and every other player in the Mosquito Bowl and of course every other member of the corps going into combat on Peleliu, Saipan, Guam, Iwo Jima, and ultimately Okinawa, the inherent death trap of amphibious assault on contested land no matter how much advanced planning. Although they had been indoctrinated into what it meant to be a marine in World War II, they did not truly understand it yet. Nobody in the Marine Corps truly understood it yet. Not just sacrifice and bravery but their own expendability. Men would die and sometimes they would die for no reason except expediency, innocents to be slaughtered, no glory except for the tripe put out by reporters writing from the safety of a tent.

16

Committed to the Deep

The logbook was single spaced, handwritten by navy chaplain W. Wyeth Willard* in small and scripted letters. You could read the entries in the logbook line by line across or as a series of columns up and down. On the first page were serial number, name, rank, date, and cause of death, with "GSW" indicating "gunshot wound." There were forty-seven entries down the column:

GSW Head and Neck
GSW Abdomen
GSW Neck
GSW Neck
GSW RT Side

---

* Chaplain Willard was attached to the marines.

GSW RT SIDE of chest

GSW chest

GSW Head

GSW chest

GSW chest

GSW RT Thigh

GSW Head

GSW Head

GSW RT shoulder

GSW RT Leg

Type of wound Unknown

Type of wound Unknown

GSW Multiple

GSW Shoulder and head

GSW LT Cheek

Type of wound Unknown

Type of wound Unknown

Type of wound Unknown

Type of wound Unknown

Type of wound Unknown

GSW Forehead

GSW Forehead

GSW Neck

GSW Head

GSW Multiple

GSW Multiple

GSW RT Groin

GSW head

Type of wound Unknown

GSW chest

GSW chest

GSW chest

Gunshot wound Multiple

GSW Head

GSW Side

Shrapnel Multiple

GSW Head

Shrapnel Head

GSW Abdomen

GST RT side and Chest

GSW Mult Head and Chest

GSW RT Hip

Page after page after page of tidy strokes, describing how men in war had died in the battle of Tarawa. Each one unadorned, a line in a ledger.

There was one final category the chaplain had entered: the details of burial. In many instances he had written "Burial Details Unknown." Everybody would be interred. It was a marine credo to leave no man behind. But nobody had been ready for the shocking number who had died from November 20th to 24th of 1943 on a tiny islet in the Tarawa atoll, maybe eight hundred yards in depth and two miles across, the worst loss of life in a single battle in Marine Corps history up to that point. Sorting out the dead, some of them found in the water or strewn on the shore with the waves nudging them back and forth like pebbles, would take time.

Willard and other chaplains divvied up the islet to make sure that as many of the dead as possible would be properly laid to rest. His logbook listed 705 of the 1,143 men who had died in roughly seventy-six hours, most of those in the first horrific day.

Forty-one different cemeteries eventually ringed the islet, most in the area of what had been designated Red Beach 1, where the fighting had been particularly intense. Several were on the other side of the islet on Black Beach 1. Some contained only a single grave. At Cemetery 33, the biggest site, 153 men had been buried side by side in three different trenches labeled Rows A, B, and C. Graves registration personnel consolidated the forty-one gravesites into one cemetery called Lone Palm, each body dug up, wrapped in a blanket, and then placed in a wooden casket. The ones who could not be identified—and there were several hundred—had their skulls photographed from three different angles in the hope of one day discovering who they were. Their headstones read UNKNOWN along with a sequential number in the upper right-hand corner.

Some of those found on the shoreline after the attack had been facedown with their legs apart, unable to save themselves from the machine-gun fire, blocked by a seawall of thick coconut logs on the lip of the beach that had kept them caged in. Others, forced to wade a half mile to shore, had been mowed down after the landing boats they were in had gotten stuck on the coral reef rimming the islet.

It was no surprise.

The navy and marine command had been concerned for months about the tide being too low to allow sufficient clearance above the coral for the boats to land. The marine officer in charge of the troops thought the chances were fifty-fifty, but he wasn't in overall command, his job being only to implement orders. Those in command hoped for the best, tried not to assume the worst, and went ahead with the invasion. The Joint Chiefs of Staff, 7,214 miles away in Washington, had set a strict timetable for the war, and the attack could not be postponed, no matter how many men might die (although attacks were postponed including Guam and Okinawa). Some battle had to be the first to test the essential strategy of amphibious assault in World War

II against a defended beachhead, and Tarawa got the call. That was just the way it went, the luck of the draw for those struggling to shore. Better luck next time—if you were still around.

> *GSW Head and Neck*
> *GSW Abdomen*
> *GSW Neck*
> *GSW Neck*
> *GSW RT Side*
> *GSW RT Side*
> *GSW Chest*
> *GSW Head*
> *GSW Chest*
> *GSW Chest*
> *GSW Rt Thigh*
> *GSW Head*
> *GSW Head*
> *GSW Rt Shoulder*
> *GSW Rt Leg*
> *Type of wound Unknown*
> *Unknown*
> *GSW Multiple*
> *GSW Shoulder and head*
> *GSW Lt Cheek*
> *Type of wound Unknown*

Type of wound Unknown
Type of wound Unknown
Type of wound Unknown
Type of wound Unknown
GSW Forehead
GSW Forehead
GSW Neck
GSW Head
GSW Multiple
GSW Multiple
GSW Rt Groin
GSW Head
Type of wound Unknown
GSW Chest
GSW Chest
GSW Chest

After World War I, the Marine Corps had pinned its existence on the doctrine of amphibious assault to gain a unique combat specialty and remain relevant. Though it had originated as a seaborne force, the Great War had turned marines into infantry troops, a combat role the army felt it could and should do. The army had also grown tired of the marines getting all the attention and credit even when their contribution in comparison had been negligible, albeit noble. The resentment had reached its height after the Battle of Belleau Wood in 1918. A war correspondent for the *Chicago Tribune* named Floyd Gibbons, who had been in the battle and lost an eye there and wore a black eye patch like a swashbuckling pirate, wrote a testimonial to the Marine Corps that forever cemented its reputation as the country's greatest and bravest fighting force. The marines had been valiant; roughly a thousand of them had died during the siege. But it was the army that had done the vast bulk of the United States' fighting in World War I. Gibbons made it seem as if the army had been nonexistent.

The army could not wait to get its hands on the marine budget and be done with all that Semper Fi swagger hotdog bullshit, how the next time they bathed would be the first and that screwy tilt in their eyes as though they hated everyone except themselves and didn't much like themselves, either. The navy wasn't so crazy about the Marine Corps, either. Its original mission, to board enemy vessels and enforce peace among wild-eyed sailors, had become obsolete in modern warfare. Maybe it could defend a base or a supply or ammo depot. That was about it. The navy existed to sink other ships. It did not exist to play second fiddle and provide endless bombardment cover to the marines when they landed on some island in the middle of nowhere. Nor did it want its ships in a holding pattern offshore with the constant threat of Japanese attack by air and sea. Sorting out the priorities was a constant dilemma throughout the Pacific war, and there was no easy solution.

The corps forecasted its own obsolescence if it did not do something to emphasize its importance. The problem with amphibious assault as a combat specialty was that it had been roundly rejected by the military establishment. Ever since the disastrous Gallipoli campaign in 1915 in World War I, experts had felt that the strategy could no longer work. Men landing on a beach against an entrenched force were simply too vulnerable, as the British had been shown by the Turkish on the Dardanelles.* Modern warfare, with its bigger weaponry and the advent of aerial bombing and strafing, made such attacks impossible.

If the marines foresaw their own obsolescence, they also foresaw the future war with Japan and the way in

---

* The marines determined that the reason for the failure at Gallipoli was that the British had done virtually everything wrong: poor leadership, being outmaneuvered, haphazard planning, the failure of landing craft to get troops and artillery onto shore quickly, the lack of surprise, landing in the wrong place. The idea had come from First Lord of the Admiralty Winston Churchill in what was his worst hour. He was forced to resign.

which amphibious assault must play a major role. In 1921, *twenty years* before Pearl Harbor, a very strange and brilliant marine major named Earl "Pete" Ellis wrote a paper for the Marine Corps in which he said that Japan was the United States' greatest enemy and the two would ultimately engage in war. He based his hypothesis on the tactical movements of Japan in the Pacific after World War I and on what he interpreted as its clear goals of expansion under the cloak of secrecy. He predicted with uncanny prescience that the initial strategy of a Japanese attack would be to destroy a great portion of the US fleet. He further predicted that the United States, in declaring war in retaliation, would adopt an island-hopping strategy across the Pacific, building up advance bases and airstrips until the Japanese homeland was close enough to be easily attacked. The only way to fend off the Japanese would be by adopting an amphibious assault doctrine as a new kind of military strategy.

Ellis may have been the most brilliant marine in history and also the most tragic. Suspected to be bipolar and hospitalized several times for alcoholism, he never went above the rank of major because of his emotional instability. He died in 1923 at the age of forty-two on the Japanese-controlled island of Palau in the western Pacific while supposedly on a spy mission. No one knows quite how he died. But his amphibious assault theory, now considered one of the greatest in the modern history of military strategy, was thoroughly embraced by Marine Commandant John Lejeune.

In 1933, the Fleet Marine Force was established. Marine Major General Holland M. Smith, known as "Howlin' Mad" for getting into fights with the army and navy whenever he thought the marines were being slighted (which was often), became the father of the amphibious assault doctrine. He pushed it relentlessly, convinced that it could work with meticulous planning in which every facet was delineated. It required rigorous training; down-to-the-minute coordination among land, sea, and air forces; the establishment of a big enough beachhead for both troops and immediate supplies such as water, food, and ammunition to enable a quick advance; the invention of a troop-carrying vehicle that could get over any obstacle from sea to beach and then drive inland. If you could not figure out how to land troops, amphibious assault was useless.

In 1937, the amphibious assault doctrine was issued by the Marine Corps and ultimately adopted by the navy. But a study was a study and a manual was a manual and tests in the field were tests in the field. The only way to see if the theory worked was to attack an entrenched enemy with real action, real bodies, and real ammunition. Tarawa became that battle, marking in earnest the start of the island-hopping campaign through the central Pacific that would ultimately lead to Okinawa on the doorstep of the Japanese homeland. The great victory at Guadalcanal in the Solomon Islands, northeast of Australia, had been epic for the Marine Corps. But the initial landing there in August of 1942, the largest in the Solomon Islands chain, had been largely unopposed.

The landing on Tarawa would not be.

A string of twenty-five small islets in the umbrella of the Gilbert Islands, the Tarawa atoll was roughly 2,400 miles southwest of Pearl Harbor. The Japanese had seized it from the British shortly after the surprise attack on Pearl Harbor. It felt essential to get Tarawa and nearby Makin back under Allied control, as they were considered by the Joint Chiefs of Staff to be pivotal launching pads for aerial bombing of the Marshall Islands, which would enable a push 550 miles closer to Japan. According to the strict timetable the JCS set, the attack on the Marshalls had to begin no later than January of 1944.

The attack on the islet of Betio, the main islet within the Tarawa atoll, would take place on November 20th of 1943, even though the tidal conditions during that time frame were known by the top command to be notoriously uncertain and could make the coral reef, which extended all the way to the beach in certain places, a deadly snag.

The Japanese, well aware that it would be the site of the attack, had assigned to Betio some of their best and most experienced soldiers, the Imperial Marines. Using enslaved Korean conscripts, they had spent almost a year digging by hand to build weapon installations, some of them almost entirely buried in the sand and fortified with thick concrete walls. Then they lay in wait, counting on American forces to be totally unprepared for this style of defense and clinging to the clichés that the Japanese were nothing but bespectacled, beaver-toothed banzai maniacs incapable of actual strategy.

The assault infantry of the 2nd Marine Division, which would land several hours after dawn, didn't know where they were going until the day before. The ones with the most to lose, they were also the ones told the least. They had learned how to take orders in boot camp. They accepted the act of killing. Their rifle *was* more important than their dick. They were willing to die, or at least many of them were. That was what was expected of them. There was no vote taken on whether they should delay the attack, given the possibility of some of them getting killed before they hit a single grain of sand.

Three thousand tons of naval projectiles were fired upon Betio in the early-morning hours before the marines landed. It was the greatest bombardment in the history of warfare per square foot up to that time. The navy was confident that it would eradicate all Japanese resistance on the islet. So were the marines, chortling and joking that nobody could possibly survive.

Most of the landing boats carrying several waves of marines to shore from transports were officially designated Landing Craft, Vehicle, Personnel, or LCVPs. They were called "Higgins boats" after the man who had designed and built them, Andrew J. Higgins, a boisterous, booming-voiced New Orleans shipbuilder who loved his bourbon almost as much as he loved his country. He could be loud and difficult and argumentative, but he was also a boatbuilding genius. The Higgins boat was thirty-six feet long and had a shallow draft of four feet. It could both get up onshore and get back off it; it carried thirty-six troops and had a recessed propeller that enabled it to plow right up onto a beach. His inspiration had come from a boat he had originally designed for Louisiana bayou trappers and rumrunners. The Higgins boats changed the course of the war, particularly after they were redesigned with a ramp in the bow so the men did not have to jump over the side. General Dwight D. Eisenhower, with some hyperbole, referred to Higgins as "the man who changed the war for us." But in the Pacific, they still had to get over the coral reefs rimming many of the islands.

The margin at Betio was going to be razor thin. The best-case scenario, with a five-foot tide: roughly twelve inches of clearance over the coral, just enough for a Higgins boat to float over. The medium-case scenario, with a four-foot tide: enough to get relatively close to shore so the marines would not have to wade in from too far a distance. The disaster-case scenario, with a three-foot tide: dead in the water.

The latest tide tables for the atoll of Tarawa had been done 102 years before and were unreliable anyway. The navy worked up new tide tables based on observations at Apia in Samoa, even though it was a thousand miles away. Reconnaissance photography from the submarine USS *Nautilus* was helpful but still inconclusive. The top command rounded up Australian and New Zealand naval reserve officers familiar with the tides of Tarawa and the Gilbert Islands. The consensus was that the tide would rise to five feet. One of them was Major Frank Holland, who had lived on Tarawa for fifteen years. But he changed his assessment and said it would not approach three feet. If the admirals paid attention to his warning, they would have to delay the attack.

Conditions were lousy and the admirals knew it.

The target date of November 20th coincided with a neap tide, one of two days each month when the high tide is at its lowest. Waiting for a full moon or a new moon to get a strong high tide would have been far safer. But Rear Admiral Richmond K. Turner, the overall commander of Operation Galvanic,* did not favor the optimal periods of attack that a higher tide would provide, in either early morning or late afternoon. An early-morning attack would not leave enough daylight for naval bombardment beforehand, and a late-afternoon assault would mean that some waves of marines and reinforcements would land in darkness. To be assured of a high enough tide that would allow bombardment with sufficient daylight would mean waiting too long for the timetable that had been set. To make matters worse, the tide advisers warned that there was a condition known as a "dodging" tide in which high tide never occurred at all. There was yet another phenomenon, depending on the moon's position from the earth, when the tide would be even more weakened. It

---

* Turner's nickname was "Terrible Turner." It was only fitting that he got along well with Howlin' Mad Smith, proving that cantankerousness often cancels out cantankerousness.

happened only twice a year, and one of those would be on the day the attack was scheduled to begin.

It was a tidal mess. There was no way of accurately predicting how high the tide would be; there were too many variables; they could only go on hope and a prayer, the educated guesses of war that too often turned out to be fatal ones.

The attack went ahead.

The tide was three feet.

Dead in the water.

A large group of infantry marines was forced to leave the Higgins boats and wade as much as eight hundred yards across the waters of the lagoon to shore. The equipment they had been given to carry was more suitable for a picnic. Their blankets became as heavy as anvils when wet. The men were waist-deep in the water and in some cases neck-deep. They held their rifles aloft to keep them dry. Artillery, which could have been set up on a nearby islet to neutralize the Japanese defenses, was considered and rejected. The men tried to avoid the bullets from Japanese light and heavy machine guns that skimmed and hissed. The coral had potholes, and some marines slipped into them.

The exact number of those killed and wounded

trying to get to the beach that first day was never determined. One hundred? Two hundred? Twice that
many? The estimates varied. It was undoubtedly fewer
than those who made it to shore and were then killed
by machine-gun fire as they tried to surmount the seawall and move inland. But at least the marines onshore
could do something—crouch, lie flat, try to find cover at
a nearby pier. The men in the water had no place to go.

GSW chest
Type of wound Unknown
GSW back
GSW abdomen
Type of wound Unknown
GSW chest
GSW head multiple
GSW head
GSW LT Side
GSW head and abdomen
Type of wound Unknown
Type of wound Unknown
GSW forehead
Type of wound Unknown
GSW abdomen
GSW multiple head
GSW rt side and chest

GSW head and rt arm
Type of wound Unknown
On beach
On beach
In the water
On beach
Making his way toward beach
Headed for beach
Disembarking from LVT
Standing in the water
Headed toward beach
GSW head, throat
GSW head, face
Cause Unknown
Cause Unknown
Cause Unknown
GSW chest

It never should have happened the way it did. The coral could have been beaten.

The marine commanders knew it before the battle. There was another landing craft available besides the Higgins boats to get ashore. It had been specifically designed to overcome obstacles such as coral. It looked strange and ridiculous and it was relatively new, but it could work. The marines were convinced of that; the navy not so much, most likely because the navy had not designed it. The craft bore the military name Landing Vehicle Tracked, or LVT. It was also called by other more readily accessible names: amphibious tractor, amtrac, the Alligator. But not even those names did justice to the improbable origins of that remarkable *weird-assed thing*, neither man nor beast, boat nor vehicle, which revolutionized amphibious assault in the Pacific.

Its father was a man named Donald Roebling, eccentric, quirkily brilliant, undeniably odd-looking at around three hundred pounds with much of it in his buttocks. He came from one of the greatest industrial and engineering families of the nineteenth and twentieth centuries. His great-grandfather John A. Roebling had designed the Brooklyn Bridge, and his grandfather and grandmother had guided the project to completion in 1883. Donald Roebling's father became the largest shareholder in the immensely successful John A. Roebling's Sons Company, which invented cable wire for the building of suspension bridges.

Donald Roebling wasn't interested in any of that. After receiving a $5 million inheritance upon his twenty-first birthday in 1929, he moved from the family mansion in Bernardsville, New Jersey, to Clearwater, Florida, and built a fifteen-room Tudor mansion known as Spottiswood that was perhaps the most beautiful on the west coast of Florida. It was a source of intrigue to locals: they wanted to know what he was doing inside one of the buildings on the estate, a fully equipped machine shop outfitted to satiate his love of tinkering. He was a secretive mad scientist, perhaps because he was attempting to design and build something outlandish and crazy, a vehicle suitable for hurricane rescue that could travel on both sea and land and would be rugged enough to negotiate treacherous terrain. It was an enormous engineering challenge; the vehicle had to be light enough to run at a decent speed over water and land but also tough. Donald Roebling worked for four years with three assistants, using aluminum to reduce the vehicle's weight and equipping the bottom with tanklike treads with little paddles sticking out of them.

In 1937, he unveiled what he had been working on, his fourth prototype. Dubbed "the Alligator," it was a svelte 8,700 pounds, and tests showed that it could go 8.6 miles an hour at sea and 18 miles an hour on land. It looked a little bit like a tractor because of its treads; a little bit like a Flash Gordon–style spacecraft. It had a wheelhouse in the front and a sunken space in the back to carry rescuers or supplies. It captured nationwide attention mostly because of its appearance. In October of 1937, *Life* magazine ran a two-page photo spread on the Alligator and what it could do: traverse mangrove swamps, grind through fallen trees, get over gnarled hills, cruise the water at a steady speed.

Several high-ranking marines, including the corps commandant, anticipating the war to come, had a eureka moment when they saw the article. They believed that the *weird-assed thing* could, with modifications, solve the enormous dilemma of amphibious assaults in the Pacific: how to get men and supplies over the obstacles that rimmed many islands, whether nature-made, such as a coral reef, or man-made by the Japanese, and onto land.

The navy reluctantly conceded that the Alligator might be of some limited use. It ordered two hundred, constructed in steel rather than soft aluminum. Its initial effectiveness was proven at Guadalcanal in the transport of supplies. On the eve of Tarawa, Holland Smith was convinced that the Alligator could be used to transport personnel to land over the coral reef rimming Betio. Admiral Turner did not like the idea. He felt that the Alligators available from Guadalcanal were too slow and had sluggish steering. They also did not have enough armor plating in the right places. Turner and other naval officers were supremely confident that the three hours of bombardment the morning of the assault at Betio would shatter the Japanese defenses.

Holland Smith, given that it was his marines who would be doing the assaulting on Tarawa, made it clear to Turner:

"No LVTs, no operation."

Turner relented. Seventy-five Alligators that had seen service at Guadalcanal were refurbished. Smith located another hundred sitting in San Diego that had been remodeled and were brand-new. Fifty of the LVT-2s were transported to the marines waiting off Tarawa. The other fifty went to the landing on the Makin atoll. The split was strange, given that the top command knew well beforehand from aerial photographs that the landing at Tarawa would be far more fiercely contested.

The number of LVTs wasn't enough; three times that many were needed.

The first three waves of marines, riding in LVTs, got over the coral and up onto the beach despite the withering Japanese fire. The succeeding waves, without the benefit of the LVTs and going ashore in Higgins boats, did not. Instead, too many hung there, only to die.

GSW throat
GSW chest

GSW head

GSW head

GSW multiple

GSW abdomen

GSW head, abdomen

Cause Unknown

GSW head

GSW head

GSW abdomen

Cause Unknown

GSW head

Cause Unknown

Cause Unknown

Cause Unknown

Cause Unknown

GSW chest

GSW multiple

GSW multiple

GSW face

Cause Unknown

GSW chest

Cause Unknown

Cause Unknown

Cause Unknown

Cause Unknown

Cause Unknown

Cause Unknown

Cause Unknown

GSW multiple

Cause Unknown

GSW head

Cause Unknown

Cause Unknown

Cause Unknown

Thirty-seven casualties were taken aboard the USS *Harry Lee* the first day. The *Harry Lee* was a combat transport, not a hospital ship. It wasn't prepared. Neither was the USS *Doyen*, the USS *La Salle*, or the USS *Sheridan*. Nobody was prepared for the stunning number of wounded in seventy-six hours, more than two thousand. Ninety-three more were taken onto the *Harry Lee* on November 21st, three on November 23rd, four on November 24th—a total of 137 from the 2nd Marine Division.

The wounded come alongside the *Harry Lee* in boats and have to be hoisted up to the ship's deck on individual litters. Moving them adds to the agony, the syrettes of morphine wearing off, the wails of men with intestines shredded by shrapnel, femur bones shattered. The best method is to hoist the entire boat to the top, which is far easier on the patient and enables doctors to get on board and quickly do triage. But that is impractical with any kind of a sea running, so the procedure is limited.

Sailors rubberneck at the rail.

Because of the fierceness of the fighting, many of the injured have received no treatment from medical officers or corpsmen for twenty-four hours or longer before evacuation to the transport ships. Their wounds are filled with jags of coral and sand. Hemorrhaging has gone on uncontrolled. Some have been stranded on the edge of the coral reef for hours. Abdominal wounds, the worst of all, have gone untreated, not that there is much that can be done anyway except douse them with sulfanilamide and stuff the pipes back in.

The sick bay is totally inadequate. The operating room isn't much better; the heat is oppressive with the ports closed. A secondary holding area is set up in the junior officers' quarters but is largely useless for the seriously injured, its passageway so narrow that men have to be lifted from litters and carried to bunks slumped in blankets, causing even more pain.

The casualties in bunches add to the confusion and chaos. Boresha has a blast injury to both eyes. Houtz has multiple wounds in the face and scalp and shoulder. Lynn has an amputated thumb and a wound in the right shoulder. Harris has crushing injuries of the extremities.

FROM THE LOGBOOK OF THE *HARRY LEE*:

NOVEMBER 21, 1943

0045 MARSHALL, E., 276113 U.S. Marine Corps, committed to the deep.

0845 BOZARTH, David B. Jr., 308950 U.S. Marine Corps, committed to the deep.

1545 MAHONEY, J. W., 360699 U.S. Marine Corps, committed to the deep.

1817 GILBERT, W. E., 308796 U.S. Marine Corps, committed to the deep.

NOVEMBER 22, 1943

0817 PRICE, Thoron E., 516585 U. S. Marine Corps, committed to the deep.

1437 FREDERICK W. E., 813120 U.S. Marine Corps,
committed to the deep.

NOVEMBER 23, 1943

0738 NORRIS, Joseph, 434484 U.S. Marine Corps,
committed to the deep.

NOVEMBER 1943

0840 COLLINS S. E., 390677 U.S. Marine Corps committed
to the deep.

The assault on Tarawa did result in a US victory,
the United States ultimately overwhelming the Japanese, as it would in every land battle to the end of the
war with its far superior troop numbers, weaponry,
equipment, food, medical supplies, naval bombardment, and aerial bombing. There were only 146 survivors out of a Japanese garrison that had numbered
more than 4,800 men. Of that number, 129 were Korean conscripts. The rest had been killed or committed
suicide. The islet of Betio was taken and its airstrip secured for attacking the Marshalls. It was a collective act
of bravery that would go down in the annals of the Marine Corps. As Major General Smith put it, the reason

for victory was actually simple: "It was willingness to die." But it was more than just willingness.

Over a thousand pages of after-action reports written shortly afterward, when the campaign was still raw and not filtered through the lens of revisionism and hindsight, made clear that numerous other miscalculations and mistakes had been made. Some were bigger than others, but the litany was overwhelming. The attack wasn't ready:

- The period allotted for rehearsal, November 7th through 12th, was insufficient.

- Major General Julian Smith, the commander of the 2nd Marine Division, had designed an attack plan to make the best use of the three infantry regiments available, but for reasons never fully understood, his superior, Holland Smith, decided to pull out one of the regiments and hold it in reserve. That neutered Julian Smith's plan of attack. With roughly six thousand men available for the initial landing—far too few to conduct diversions or flanking maneuvers—he had to change his tactics to a straight-on frontal assault. It also meant going into battle with less than the three-to-one ratio of marines to defenders that was a linchpin of amphibious assault doctrine when attacking a fortified beachhead.

• Transport ships carrying supplies were sloppily loaded and then unloaded in a frantic rush, so that the troops on the beach had piles of nonessential gear and not enough hand grenades, ammo, fuel, and water.

• The concussions from salvos fired by the command ship USS *Maryland* the morning of the attack knocked out its communications equipment for a period of time, creating crucial gaps when the commanders on board overseeing Operation Galvanic could not get in touch with personnel onshore.

• The army-designed TBY radio used onshore wasn't waterproof, had a limited range, and was therefore useless. The marines utilized it because better models were not available to them.

• Many radio operators were insufficiently trained, to the degree that the local time zone became confused with Greenwich Mean Time.

• Coordination of air and naval support, crucial for a beach landing, broke down. The navy pilots assigned to provide brief and intense bombing on the morning of the attack inexplicably showed up twenty-five minutes late.

• The delay held up the beginning of naval bombardment, which prevented what was supposed to have been three nonstop hours of bombing and bombardment before the marines' landing to keep the Japanese constantly on the defensive. Continuous bombardment before landing was another linchpin of amphibious assault doctrine.

• The navy battleships and cruisers fired off three thousand tons of shells with the goal of blanketing the island, not targeting specific targets. The method was ineffective in getting at many of the Japanese installations, as was the ammunition used for the bombardment.

• Numerous supposed sightings of periscopes of enemy submarines in the water resulted in a dangerous spray of friendly fire. The periscopes were actually powder cases and other loose gear that had been thrown overboard during bombardment. As a result automatic weapons were fired wildly without any regard for other US ships in the vicinity.

• D-Hour, the time of the assault, was delayed twice, first to 8:30 and then to 9:00 a.m., which led to another snafu in air strikes because no one bothered to radio the pilots in the carrier planes of the change. Sticking to the original timetable, they dropped their bombs and strafed too early, which gave the Japanese twenty-two minutes free from bombardment, enough time to regroup and make ready for the marine landing.

• Close air support just after landing became difficult because the pilots were partially blinded by clouds of smoke and dust from the naval bombardment of the island. The pilots had problems locating the targets that had been called in and seeing the exact location of the marines.

• The impact of bombardment was gravely overestimated by the naval commanders, and the quality of the Japanese emplacements was gravely underestimated. Intelligence and mapping beforehand had shown precisely the location of Japanese fortifications. But the most crucial factor, their physical sturdiness and concealment, had not been determined. The weapons fortifications were constructed of steel-reinforced concrete up to six feet thick, buried under mounds of coral sand camouflaged with palm fronds. Almost five hundred pillboxes had been built half-submerged below ground level with little more visible than the eye slits used for firing machine guns. The pillboxes were also connected by a series of interlocking trenches so that soldiers could move among them without exposing themselves to gunfire. Fourteen coastal guns were protected by concrete, and forty pieces of artillery were sunk into the ground. A few of the bigger emplacements received direct hits from five-hundred-pound bombs and huge shells from the navy's sixteen-inch guns but were unscathed. That only provided further proof that bombardments needed to be longer and better targeted.

• The hulks of the abandoned LVTs and Higgins boats became nests for Japanese snipers.

At night they swam out to them, waited until morning, and shot marines in the back. In some cases they manned machine guns left on the boats, and for a short time, the marines thought they were shooting each other. The marines killed the snipers once they figured out what was happening, but the process began anew the following night. The hulks of the ruined craft should have been destroyed or guarded. They were not.

• On the afternoon of the attack, requests were made from the beach for ammunition, water, and rations. The material was sitting in boats already in the lagoon. But the obstacle of the coral reef and the inability to secure the beachhead had created a massive traffic jam offshore, with about two hundred craft milling about, unable to land. More LVTs would have at least partially solved the problem, but there were none available to ferry supplies to shore because they were either already in service or destroyed by the enemy.

Tarawa raised the unspoken questions of World War II: To what degree are those in command responsible for saving the lives of as many men in combat as they can, versus achieving the strategic objective regardless of how many men may die? What is the line between the duty to serve and the duty to be killed?

Tarawa proved that there wasn't one.

The top command at Tarawa—along with most war correspondents and military historians—considered the battle to have been a painful but necessary experiment that had led to numerous improvements in amphibious assault as the war continued. The period of naval bombardment became significantly longer, underwater demolition teams were heavily utilized, the LVT was further modified and became indispensable although hardly perfect. It is also true there were subsequent assaults that were strategically questionable and adversely affected by poor intelligence and repeated underestimation of the Japanese. The number of US casualties in later battles only increased exponentially compared to those on Tarawa as the war continued and the targets got bigger: Saipan, Peleliu, Iwo Jima, Okinawa. As amphibious assault techniques improved, so did the Japanese defenses.

The marines forced to wade ashore at Tarawa on November 20th were cannon fodder, their only armor, as General Julian Smith had feared before the battle, their khaki shirts.

The bravery was incomparable. But at what price? The logbook of the dead held no answers.

Cause Unknown
Cause Unknown
Cause Unknown
Cause Unknown
GSW head, abdomen
GSW face
Cause Unknown
Cause Unknown
Cause Unknown
Cause Unknown
Cause Unknown
GSW chest
Cause Unknown
Cause Unknown
Cause Unknown
Cause Unknown
Cause Unknown
Cause Unknown
Cause Unknown
Cause Unknown
Cause Unknown
Cause Unknown

GSW head

Cause Unknown

Cause Unknown

GSW chest

Cause Unknown

Cause Unknown

GSW chest

Cause Unknown

GSW chest

Cause Unknown

Cause Unknown

Cause Unknown

GSW stomach

Cause Unknown

Part Two

17
The Patrol

It was now 0400.

Everyone going out was already awake.

McLaughry, appointed to second lieutenant and the leader of the 3rd Platoon of Company G of the 2nd Raider Battalion, was in charge. A corporal and two PFCs from his platoon had volunteered: Hugh Vogel from Washington, twenty; Gilbert Crum, Jr., from Alabama and Keith Neault from Michigan, both nineteen—none of them old enough to vote but old enough to kill and be killed. At twenty-seven years of age, McLaughry was responsible for their lives.

They needed to travel as quickly and as quietly as possible on the patrol. They wore caps instead of helmets and carried canteens with padded covers. The only items in their packs were food, a change of socks, an extra pair of shorts, and a poncho. Their C rations were cans of hash, beans with crackers, and powdered coffee and cocoa. An extra D ration chocolate bar or two was thrown in that tasted like chalk. The men would eat them. At a certain point in combat they would eat anything. But what they really cared about was having enough cigarettes. The cans were wrapped in the socks and poncho to avoid making noise. They carried semi-automatic M1 rifles, with the exception of Neault, who had a tommy gun. Their ammo was limited to one eight-round clip in the weapon and four spare clips. That made forty rounds per man—a supply hardly fit for self-defense in the blind jungle, so God help them if they were spotted and got into a firefight.

They were going into Japanese-held territory for two and a half days to locate possible troop movement in some of the worst jungle in the Pacific, on the island of Bougainville in the Solomons—a mix of mangrove swamp and marsh, lowlands and hills surrounding a 7,500-foot volcanic mountain from which lava still ran and smoke billowed at night. The jungle could make you feel as though you were going mad, pressing in, on your hands and knees searching for a hole in the undergrowth, looking up to see nothing but black because of the tree cover, strings of thorny vines a massive spider's web, knotted roots of trees crawling over one another like snakes, sharp blades of kunai grass up to your shoulders, young vegetation strangling old, the simultaneous smell of birth and death. Crocodiles hung around the edges of the stream beds. Malaria-carrying mosquitoes were everywhere in the morning and then, after taking the afternoon off, back out at night. Fatted leeches waited for the next blood feast. Yet there was something about the jungle that went deep, the most alone you had ever felt in the world but not lonely, maybe what it felt like to listen to the inside of your soul, or God. There were noises, strange noises, close and far away. Everything echoed. Then silence.

The fight for Bougainville was winding down, as far as the marines' involvement was concerned. Airstrips were up and running. Key portions of the island, the last essential piece in controlling the Solomon chain, were under Allied control. The Japanese were still there but had largely gone into hiding. The I Marine Amphibious Corps, made up largely of the 3rd Marine Division and two Raider battalions, was in the process of being relieved by the army.

The date was January 9th of 1944, seven weeks after Tarawa, or Another Tarawa as marines called it when they went into subsequent battles: God forbid they turn out to be as FUBAR.

McLaughry had only three days left before his

battalion would be replaced. It should have cut him a break, given that thousands of soldiers from the army's American Division had already arrived. Why not let them go on patrol? They loved telling the marines what to do anyway, whenever they had the chance. It wasn't as though McLaughry was familiar with the terrain where the patrol was headed. He knew where he was supposed to go, or at least he thought he did, but the aerial photography had been worthless because the jungle was virtually impenetrable. He had no map. His guides were a compass and the sun, assuming that he could even see the sun through the rain forest canopy. But Major General John Hodge, the commander of the American Division, had decided that no one in his outfit was sufficiently acclimated for a patrol as difficult as this.

With the army out, the two Raider battalions became the prime candidates for the patrol: the 3rd Raider Battalion was due to be relieved on the day the patrol was scheduled to begin, so it was out. That left the 2nd Battalion, but McLaughry still thought he was safe from the assignment; the battalion had close to a thousand men when it was at full strength, and McLaughry's forty-five-man platoon had already done its duty by going out on two daylong patrols in the past three weeks.

Five raiders from a platoon in Company F started out before dawn. But one had a recurrence of malaria, and another could not handle the jungle rot on his feet—gaping ulcerations in the skin and competitions held at night to see who could squirt a jet of milky pus and blood closest to the top of the tent. They came back quickly—which raised the question in McLaughry's mind of why those particular guys had been chosen in the first place, if two of them would obviously never make it. Actually, you had to hand it to the platoon leader: it was a first-class way of getting out of the assignment without it looking too much like getting out of it.

The fair thing to do would have been to send out men who were fit from that same platoon. But that didn't happen, for reasons that were never explained— just as almost all decisions handed down from above were never explained. Military protocol dictated that the more unfair something was, the more it became inevitable. In military math, $1 + 1 = 3$. Pointing out that it actually equaled two was fruitless and stupid, unless you wanted to get dressed down or serve a sojourn in the brig.

The battalion commander ordered a draw of straws, and ultimately it came down to Kone, from the weapons platoon, and McLaughry.

McLaughry wasn't good when it came to straws.

He looked for volunteers from his 3rd Platoon. Crum, Neault, and Vogel stepped forward. Major Washburn offered up First Lieutenant Eric Pedersen; he had recently joined the battalion as a replacement officer, and Washburn thought the patrol experience would be good for him. Washburn assigned him to go as an acting PFC under McLaughry.

Lucky Pedersen.

Two others from outside McLaughry's platoon were selected to collect intelligence.

There were seven of them in all.

The route was basically an elongated triangle, going out perpendicularly from the Torokina River for roughly eight miles to the Sava* River, where they would bivouac for the night. There was a mini-island on the river, little more than a sandbar, covered by vegetation. A major trail was suspected to be in the area, potentially serving as a primary route for the Japanese. They had to hit the exact spot—not only to gather intel and try to pinpoint enemy activity there but also to avoid friendly fire. Several of the 155 mm field guns known as "long Toms" would be dropping rounds about a mile up the river. They would bivouac for another night on

---

* The Sava river is also known as the Sawa.

the second side of the triangle, then head back on the third.

It was now around 0500.

It was an unusually dark night in the jungle. They wanted to cover as much ground as they could before daylight. They had to clear their own protective perimeter first. Crum was in the lead, with McLaughry next and the others behind him. Crum took a light hold on the telephone wire that snaked down from their position and guided them down the steep hill. McLaughry held on to a strap on Crum's pack because it was so dark. They managed to stay on the steps cut into the trail and avoided sliding down into the thickets on either side.

They followed the wire to the Company E command post, Vogel calling out the password to alert the watch. Which wasn't so easy. Sometimes the password was so complex that the marine approaching got it wrong or forgot it, then had to scramble to avoid getting shot, since those were the orders. Giving the name of someone inside the wire was usually enough. But the Japanese had become adept at mimicking English. They called marines by their first names after overhearing chatter, which became a way of getting around the password.

McLaughry's men got through and hustled past Company E's firing pits. Seventy-five yards up ahead were the river and a double perimeter of barbed wire. An opening had been made for them. They went through. They were on their own.

Their goal of crossing the Torokina before dawn turned out to be overly ambitious; the sky was already showing the first hint of light. But there was a low mist covering the river, and they hoped it would hold for six hundred yards until they got to the jungle on the other side. If they ran into a Japanese outpost along the river, they would be decimated. Feeling exposed, they crossed as fast as they could, slipping on the fist-sized smooth stones at the bottom. They fell to their knees in the water, and one of them went onto all fours and got soaked. The crossing seemed to take forever, but finally they reached a low bank with bushes overhanging the water.

They scrambled into the heavy undergrowth. For the first few yards, the terrain was a marshy tangle of ferns, roots, small trees, bushes, and vines. After about fifty yards, the ground became more solid. They were in the jungle now, and they stopped to rest because they were already exhausted. The only noise they heard was silence, except for the hum of some insects. The only way to tell it was daylight was by looking up through the crevices between the trees. No smoking was allowed, no matter how satisfying it might be, since smells, particularly smoke, seemed to hang in the jungle air and could alert roving Japanese on the lookout for a patrol like this one.

The men took their shoes off and replaced wet socks with dry ones to ward off the affliction known by the finely euphemistic term *immersion-foot*. Wet socks caused wet feet, which could stay wet for days if they weren't careful—which would cause ulcers that rubbed against one's boots, which would cause the feet to go numb and then turn purple. Gangrene could set in and raise the dreaded possibility of amputation of toes or feet. McLaughry loved dry socks. They were more important to him than any other piece of clothing. He hung his wet pair from his haversack in the hope that they would dry. Between the humidity and likely afternoon rainstorm, it was doubtful.

They set their course by compass, with an azimuth of 110 degrees. Later, as it became lighter, they would navigate using the sun.

They started off in the same order as before, at five-yard intervals from one another. But as the undergrowth became thicker, they had to close up to maintain visual contact. They moved onto ground with larger trees than before, more hanging vines, and undergrowth so heavy they practically had to crawl. They found a trail and saw no indication that it had been used within the last forty-eight hours.

They took another five-minute break.

As they prepared to move out, they became aware of somebody or something coming down the trail from the rear. They had already scattered off to the sides of the trail to rest; now they edged farther back and dropped to crouched or prone positions. They brought their weapons to the ready. There was the *click-click-click* of the safeties being released.

Five seconds. Ten. Fifteen.

A figure, hidden in deep shadow and foliage, broke into view. The noise made it obvious that a large detachment was following him. He wore a visored cap, which could indicate a member of a friendly unit. But his face was tanned and resembled that of a Japanese soldier, who were not above wearing American helmets as a form of ambush.

Ten yards away. Then five.

Pedersen, previously in the rear, was now the closest to the men approaching. He could see something and yelled:

"We're marines!"

The group approached closer and closer.

They were startled.

Being startled was bad. Being startled was when the shooting started.

Somehow everyone held off—which was a huge relief and probably saved some lives but did little to explain why two different groups of marines had run into each other in the most impenetrable jungle in the Pacific.

It turned out that the marine in front was a Navajo. Members of the Navajo Nation served in the war with distinction and exemplary success as radio communicators because their language was indecipherable to anyone except themselves and could not be understood by the Japanese. With a "code talker" on either end of a transmission, they spoke to each other in code based on their own language and then translated into English for their fellow marines. It was a brilliant system. But even if the resemblance between a Navajo and a Japanese soldier was remote, the Navajo should not have been at point on a jungle patrol. That was too risky. Decisions were split second. Considered debate was not in the lexicon of combat in World War II. His platoon leader should have taken that into account.

Their patrol had been expected to last a day, but they had bivouacked the night before and were now on their way back. In addition, McLaughry had slightly changed the route of his patrol to avoid the enemy.

Neither knew of the other's change in plans. It could have been a catastrophe.

The patrols separated. There were constant jitters after that. Unlike smoke, sound did not carry far in the jungle; the incident showed how easy it would be for an enemy to approach within a few yards and not be heard until it was too late.

It was now 0700.

The overcast had cleared, and it was beginning to warm up. The combination of the temperature, the 100 percent humidity, the suffocating embrace of the jungle, and the physical exertion made every step exhausting.

The ground was still relatively flat, but they could see no more than fifteen to twenty yards in front of them. The trees, mangrove and banyan, were huge, some more than a hundred feet tall. The biggest problem was the "wait-a-minute" vines. They were long and slender with a few scattered leaves and thorns like sharp fishhooks. It was possible not even to know that you had been hooked for ten or fifteen feet, until the vine reached its length and dug into you, causing lacerations and torn clothing. Then you had to walk back to unhook yourself.

They came to the first sizable stream, about twenty-five feet across. The bank was exposed so they checked up and down before crossing. Vogel slid down the bank first and scrambled across on a fallen tree and a few dry rocks. McLaughry went next but slid down too quickly. His pants got snagged on a sharp root, ripping them from just below the fly, right along the crotch seam, almost all the way up to his belt in the rear. It looked as though he was wearing two separate pant legs.

The other men laughed their asses off. Something good had finally happened.

The water in the stream flowed fast enough to be drinkable. Military regulation was to use chlorine tablets in the canteen and wait roughly an hour before drinking. But McLaughry knew from growing up in New England that the water, coming from a stream with its origins in the mountains, was safe to drink. It was one of those regulations that was well-intentioned but utterly impractical on a patrol like this, waiting an hour when you were perspiring like a pig and exhausted and had several miles to go over some of the worst terrain in the world.

They made it another quarter mile to a relatively clear spot with four huge trees. Neault shinnied partway up one of the trees to get some bearings. He could see Mount Bagana, an active volcano spewing its smoke by day and fire at night. They were a quarter of the way to the Sava.

About two hundred yards later, they hit another stream, whose water was reddish in color from the volcanic lava fields. But once again, it ran fast and clear. McLaughry replenished his canteen, as much for the color of the water as from any pressing need. He hoped it would bring him good luck. Once again, he did not use a chlorine tablet.

It was now 1000.

They were in the marshes. Mud and rotten vegetation rose to their ankles. They were in full sunlight, and the heat was oppressive. They took a rest break, and this time McLaughry allowed them to smoke. Even he had a cigarette.

They moved out of the marshes into low hills. The sun was gone now. The sky had started to cloud over in preparation for a rainstorm. It rained an average of eleven inches a month in Bougainville. They tumbled out of heavy undergrowth into a small clearing. There was a native hut that had fallen apart. The garden was overgrown and looked as though it hadn't been touched in at least six months.

Suddenly from their rear they heard the purr of a small plane approaching. It was an army observation plane, likely looking for a target of opportunity for the artillery. The marines jumped back into the scrub growth to make sure they were not spotted and mistaken for the enemy. That happened more than anyone liked to admit, an estimated 2 percent of all casualties in the war caused by so-called amicides due to miscalculated fire or shells falling short.

The plane circled once and flew on in a northeasterly direction.

They came across a barely perceptible trail that showed no signs of recent use. They followed it through towering trees with a canopy of leaves and vines as heavy as McLaughry had ever seen. The shoulder-high grass on the trail alternated with the broad leaves of banana trees. Because of the lack of scrub undergrowth, the going wasn't too difficult.

They went off the trail to keep to their compass course and immediately ran into dense vegetation. Vogel had to fight through thickets or edge around them, in detours of ten to fifteen yards. At the same time, it started to pour rain, but they barely got wet under the thick jungle canopy. They found shelter under a banana tree and waited out the storm. They ate some cold C rations or bit into the chocolate bars. Nobody had an appetite.

Not long after the rain stopped, they found another trail, closely parallel to the direction in which they were heading. The grass on either side had been disturbed, and they could tell it had been recently, since grass in the jungle takes twenty-four hours to bounce back. A little farther along they found some footprints on the soft ground, which they thought were also recent. Another two hundred yards on, the dirt carried clearer prints—they were split-toed, in the style of footwear the Japanese sometimes wore. They also noticed two dry spots on a log. They indicated that at least two people had been sitting there during the recent rainstorm. Which meant they were extremely close ahead. The McLaughry patrol veered off into the steep foothills.

It was now 1330.

They had covered about five miles with about three more to go for the day, which was enormously ambitious and maybe unrealistic. The going was uneventful for more than an hour, apart from a moment when they heard something or someone running off to the right. They stayed motionless in the heavy brush for five minutes. The jungle was once again silent except for the occasional parrot or parakeet call. They heard nothing more.

It was now about 1740.

They had located a major trail, four to five feet wide,

which had obviously seen a lot of use. They were on high alert, inching forward, listening. Soon the trail widened and they found the remains of a fire with empty cans and banana fronds lying around it. They poked through the burned sticks and saw that the ashes underneath were not yet caked by the rain. Crum found a red cloth patch with two stars, the insignia of the Japanese equivalent of a PFC. They decided that as many as a dozen Japanese soldiers had bivouacked there overnight.

They got out of there in a hurry. Around the next bend in the trail, Vogel signaled back to McLaughry. He had spotted the Sava River, just visible through the trees. The path swung through another curve and edged down to the water, and there were the ford and the sandbar covered with vegetation—their target.

It was now 1800.

They made camp in an area about ten yards in from the river that was well hidden on all sides. McLaughry posted sentries at the water's edge, in a series of one-hour watches. The light was rapidly falling. Once again there was silence except for the soft sound of the flowing water of the Sava and the buzz of mosquitoes. It was perfect in its own way. How could anything be so serene when it could explode at any moment?

It was now 1930.

They heard about a dozen explosions in rapid succession upriver, then another burst five minutes later. It was the "long Tom" field guns.

McLaughry took the first watch. When Pedersen replaced him, McLaughry fell asleep on his poncho with his pack for a pillow, leaning up against a shallow mound for comfort. He became aware of a prickly itch underneath his jacket and then on his arms. But he managed to sleep until Pedersen woke him to the sound of distant rifle and machine-gun fire. Pedersen asked McLaughry what he thought it was. He had no idea.

It stopped.

He tried to fall back asleep.

He still itched, which was a distressing sign given that the islands of the Pacific were rife with disease. Malaria from the anopheles mosquito was the most prevalent. During the campaign of Guadalcanal no precautions had been taken at all, resulting in 90 percent of the men getting it. It wasn't fatal but it was miserable, one's temperature spiking up to 106 degrees and then back down in an unpredictable cycle. Because of the need for manpower, men were required to stay on duty unless their temperature was over 104 degrees. The main treatment for malaria, quinine, had been shut off by the Japanese seizure of Java. Atabrine had been invented back in 1930, but it only suppressed the symptoms. The men who took it hated it, not only because it made them nauseous or turned their skin yellow but also because they believed it caused them to go impotent.

Another great fear was filariasis, also known as *mumu,* or "big leg." A swelling of the lymph glands, it often affected the scrotum and genitals, causing them to enlarge and ache and, like Atabrine, aroused fears of impotence. According to one rumor, too good to be true and too good not to be true, some island natives carried their balls around in a wheelbarrow because they had grown so big. Although the disease occurred mostly in Polynesia, men stationed everywhere in the Pacific were afraid of it.

McLaughry still itched.

It was now 0500 the following day.

The sky began to lighten. Everyone woke up and got ready. McLaughry was feeling stressed and ate a few biscuits and drank some cocoa in cold water. He picked up his poncho and saw the source of the itching: he had been sleeping on an anthill.

He had no idea why he had not seen it the night

before except that he had been exhausted. There were bites on his torso, arms, and upper back. He would survive with his scrotum intact and no need for a wheelbarrow.

It was now around 0730.

They were in semiopen marsh, ankle deep in the muck, with scattered bushes and trees poking up from mounds of spongy ground. McLaughry was about five yards behind Crum. McLaughry shot a quick glance at the river, and when he turned back around, he saw Crum's pack bobbing up and down in the water. Crum had stepped into a hole hidden beneath the thin covering of roots and grass and had plunged in over his head. McLaughry dropped his rifle. He and Neault grabbed the pack and pulled Crum out of the hole. He could easily have drowned. What likely saved him was that it had happened so quickly that he hadn't had time to flail or panic. He was completely soaked and covered in muck from his knees down. That caused as much laughter as McLaughry splitting his pants.

It was now 0800.

They had covered about two miles in the past two and a half hours. The river wandered basically southward and they had no problem following its course, but the terrain became progressively worse. They were slogging through deeper water now, and the treacherous marsh cover was pocked with holes like the one that had almost swallowed Crum. They were coated in muck from the knees down. The heat and humidity climbed by the minute, and everybody was drenched in sweat.

The next several hours were uneventful except for seeing spotter planes again—two this time instead of just one. It meant that they were seriously looking for the enemy. McLaughry and the rest of the patrol rushed for cover, as they had the previous day. Getting shot by your own would make you as dead as getting shot by the Japanese.

The terrain turned from marsh into genuine swamp. Vogel was in the lead, and they were going in a north-westerly direction, heading back toward home but still with roughly eight miles to go to their destination for the night. Soon the water was up over their knees—and often up to their thighs or waists. It felt as though their boots were going to be sucked off by the mud at the bottom. Where they could find footing, the tangle of roots and other vegetation was waiting to trip them up. Clumps of trees grew right out of the slop. In spots, large tracts of reeds went to head height or even higher and were difficult to penetrate. They needed a machete, but all they had was a single bowie-style knife.

They struggled for more than an hour to make less than a quarter of a mile of progress. The sun was directly overhead, and the temperature was hovering at about 90 degrees with nearly 100 percent humidity. It put them into the position of being cool from the waist down in the swamp water while broiling from the waist up because of the temperature and humidity. The mercy of an afternoon rainstorm did not seem likely, given the clear skies.

It was now 1400.

The terrain got easier, becoming more marshland than swamp. They adjusted the azimuth to nearly due west. The terrain changed once again to semimarsh and heavy jungle with a few high trees. For a period of time they even had solid ground underfoot, and soon they stumbled across a substantial trail. It must have been one that they had already encountered farther north, possibly the one where they had found the tracks of the Japanese the day before. Here there were no signs of recent usage, so they moved on. They had gone barely two hundred yards when they heard noise in the jungle off to the right of them. McLaughry signaled an immediate halt.

The noise stopped.

They stood still for five minutes and didn't hear anything more. McLaughry worried that they had gotten careless from their miserable hours of wading through swamp water, so now they moved with extreme care and kept their noise to a minimum. Within minutes they heard something again, what sounded like someone running, behind them and off to their right. Pedersen heard it first and passed the word in a loud whisper. They froze in place and listened. All they heard was silence. They waited for more than five minutes, and then McLaughry also thought he heard something.

They speculated that they had nearly run into a small enemy patrol and that the Japanese had thought they were outnumbered by McLaughry's patrol and fallen back to a safer distance. Or it could have been the jungle just having a laugh.

It was now 1630.

They moved onto higher ground and crossed several of the streams they had crossed the day before.

It was now 1800.

They needed a place to bivouac. In the middle of a small river, they found a gravel bar about fifteen yards long and ten yards wide, covered with small trees and undergrowth. It provided good protection, with its natural moat and an unobstructed view for about thirty yards up and down the river. McLaughry scheduled the watches. He was totally exhausted and too tired to eat when he bedded down for the night. The ground was hard and since he was wet he felt cold, but he fell asleep easily.

It was now 2230.

McLaughry was shaken awake by Vogel, who whispered that he and Pedersen thought someone might be snooping around. They all went to their guard post at the northern point of the island. It was pitch black, with the sky barely a shade lighter than the land. Vogel whispered something, but Pedersen told him to be quiet. McLaughry heard nothing, but Vogel and Pedersen insisted that they had heard the sound of someone wading in the water. McLaughry still heard nothing but the river current and finally went back to sleep.

It was now 0445, day three of the patrol.

Pedersen awoke McLaughry and the others since it was starting to get light out. He was still tense, and he and Vogel went back to the watch lookout. The others prepared to move out.

It was now 0515.

Vogel came back with a big grin on his face.

Pedersen had definitely heard something in the vicinity of some fallen trees by the bank of the river. The sound had started and then stopped, always in the same location. Vogel had heard it, too. Pedersen had taken Vogel's bowie knife and crawled out onto the trunk of one of the fallen trees as far as he could go.

The sound had stopped.

On his second watch, Pedersen had once again crawled out on the fallen tree with the knife in hand. The sound hadn't returned, but it was only when it got light that he knew for sure that nobody was there.

The noise had been made by a broken branch from one of the fallen trees. The branch swished in the water, making a noise, until it got caught in the undergrowth and the noise stopped. Then the current would dislodge the branch and the noise would start again. When Pedersen had crawled out onto the tree the first time, the branch had become permanently stuck and the noise had stopped for good.

It was now 0520.

They had about four miles left before reaching the starting point of their patrol, at the Torokina. The last leg was in the lowlands, a combination of dense jungle, bog, marsh, and swamp. Vogel was in the lead because he was by far the best at keeping on course and finding the best route through heavy undergrowth. Every now and then they ran into jungle growth so heavy they had to detour around it. The knife had been fairly effective in the swamps but not here, where masses of thick vegetation intertwined with hanging vines. Their progress was painfully slow. They were already hot and drenched and exhausted. Their footwear, either the distinctive raider lumberjack-style boots or field shoes, was starting to disintegrate from being constantly wet. McLaughry's pant legs had completely separated. Fortunately he had brought an extra pair of skivvies, so he didn't look too crazy. Everyone was caked with mud from the waist down. They were hollow-eyed from lack of sleep.

It was now 0700.

They stopped to rest. They had progressed about three-quarters of a mile in roughly an hour and a half. They could see the peak of Mount Bagana, above the cloud cover. They spent the next hour and a half slogging through mud and water about a foot deep, getting tangled up in the roots and undergrowth beneath the water. They occasionally sank into the ooze up to their knees. They eventually reached dry land and came upon a north-south trail. There were no signs of recent use, but it had definitely been used in the last few weeks, and almost certainly not by US troops. If it really was a Japanese jungle route, just a few miles from the US lines, it was a substantial find. They crossed another river that was reddish in color. McLaughry once again refilled his canteen for luck.

It was now 1000.

They rested and figured they were less than three miles from the Torokina and should reach it around noon. The sky was clouding up for a rainstorm. The terrain still oozed. A downpour started. After about two and a half hours, they broke onto a narrow trail running along the banks of the Torokina. It was a welcome sight, but their relief was short-lived. They heard a series of explosions about a quarter mile south. McLaughry could tell from the *whoosh* sound they made that they were high-caliber mortar shells. They worried that they had been spotted and mistaken for Japanese. Or that a detachment of Japanese had been discovered and would run into them. They took off down the trail almost at a run. They considered moving off the trail back into the jungle, but that would have slowed their progress down. It had ceased raining, but the heat and humidity were still stifling.

It was now 1330.

They traversed the Torokina just below the 2nd Raider Battalion outpost.

The marines on duty were surprised to see them. McLaughry figured it was because they looked so tattered and bedraggled, with mud caked all over them.

Back at their position, their whole platoon was there to greet them. They were welcomed like lost brothers. Even Captain Jacobsen from battalion headquarters. It seemed like a lot of fuss, until McLaughry figured it out:

It had been assumed that they were dead.

A patrol made up of Fiji islanders, expert at traversing the jungle, had heard rifle and machine-gun fire two nights before in an area where the McLaughry patrol was supposed to have been. The two scout planes that had been sent out the following day were not looking for the enemy; they were looking for McLaughry's patrol. When they could not be found, there was fear that they had been killed. The fear became conviction when they did not return by midmorning.

Now that it had been conclusively established that McLaughry was not dead, he washed as much mud off as he could. He changed to dungarees and borrowed a jacket and shoes to give a debrief to the intelligence section of the Americal Division. He went to division quarters and was ushered into the office of a full colonel. He was pleasant enough but formal. McLaughry was forced to stand during the half-hour meeting even though he had just been through the most physically demanding three days of his life. He had taken notes during the patrol and gave as much information as he could about possible enemy movements, the terrain, the precautions the men had taken to keep safe, the equipment they had carried, the food they had eaten. He had also made a rough map of their route. He offered to leave the notes but all the colonel wanted was the map. There was a sergeant there as well, taking his own notes.

The colonel asked a lot of questions, and McLaughry tried to answer all of them. The colonel seemed satisfied except for one thing that really upset him: the failure to follow the regulation on the use of chlorine tablets.

McLaughry tried to explain that water from mountain streams was bound to be pure enough. He also pointed out that because of the heat and physical exertion, it just didn't seem practical to wait an hour for the chlorine tablets to work. He had needed water then and there to continue onward.

McLaughry was dismissed. He was told he would

have to wait around until a jeep was available to make the fifteen-minute trip back to his sector. As far as McLaughry could tell just by looking, there were plenty of jeeps and one-ton trucks around that weren't going anywhere. McLaughry thanked him and walked more than halfway before he got a ride with a warrant officer.

He was still totally exhausted, but he had more work to do, ensuring that Company G was packed up and ready to go, since it was about to be relieved. It was a time-consuming task, and then something unexpected came up. The army officer taking over did not like Company G's positions and defenses. He said the company would not be relieved until it had reinforced the dugouts and firing pits and strengthened the lines. That seemed like something the army personnel should be doing since they were the ones moving in, but McLaughry and the others worked until dark filling sandbags and digging so they could get out the next morning.

One good thing did happen: his battalion command post got a call from one of the airstrips, saying that McLaughry's brother, Bob, would be flying in the next day for a refueling stop after making a bombing run on Rabaul.

The following afternoon at 1600, John McLaughry was at an airstrip waiting for his brother, Bob. Because the army was late taking over, McLaughry would have missed him altogether had his marine commanding officer not allowed him to be dismissed from his duties early.

He went into the first tent he saw, which appeared to be an operations center. There were half a dozen pilots sitting around talking, another pilot on the phone, and some clerks at field desks. McLaughry asked if anyone knew Bob or his squadron, but nobody did. On his way out he took another glance at the pilot on the telephone. He had a reddish beard and mustache. He glanced at McLaughry, who was sporting his Kaiser Wilhelm–style mustache and was twenty-five pounds lighter than usual. It dawned on them where they had seen each other: back home in the States, when they had been wearing shoulder pads and not facial hair.

Bob could stay for only half an hour before he had to fly back to his base in the New Georgia Islands. McLaughry walked with Bob to see his plane. It was a dive-bomber, a battered SBD-2 Dauntless. McLaughry was a little concerned when his brother started it up and it coughed and sputtered. Bob eventually got off the ground and back to his war. John McLaughry went back to his, back on Guadalcanal in February of 1944, to train for what would ultimately be the assault on Guam.

After he left Bougainville, he heard that the army had discontinued extended reconnaissance patrols. Vigilance was being relaxed—which also meant that there was no longer any decent intelligence on enemy troop movements.

In early March, some fifteen thousand Japanese soldiers launched a desperate attack on the army perimeter, not far from where the 2nd Raider Battalion had been posted. The defensive line was broken, and the US Army Air Force briefly evacuated most of its aircraft from the vital airstrips after losing a number of planes to Japanese artillery shells. The army quickly regained the lost ground, but it took three weeks to crush the attacks and push the Japanese out of artillery range of the airfields.

By McLaughry's count, his patrol had been the only one of seven to fulfill its given mission.

Even without the chlorine tablets.

$1 + 1 = 3$.

18
Pen Pal

Touchdown Tony, Rugged Buck Tony, Bronc Butkovich, the St. David Scourge, the Chunky Illinois Express, the Battering Ram. The mighty Butkovich had run out of nicknames.

At the end of October in 1943, he had received notice that he was to report for basic training at Parris Island on November 1st. Purdue was 6–0 at the time, and Butkovich was having arguably the best season of any running back in the country.* He had already gained 686 yards on 114 carries and scored thirteen touchdowns. He had become the darling, shaking the curse of "great potential." With three games left, a season of twenty touchdowns and a thousand yards rushing was

---

* The argument could also be made for Bill Daley of Michigan, Bob Odell of Penn, and Creighton Miller of Notre Dame.

well within grasp for the son of an immigrant from the coal village of St. David.

With three games left, nothing could stop him. Except the marines.

There would be no more football for Butkovich except for one final game against Wisconsin on October 30th of 1943, no degree as a physical education major taking such courses as intercollegiate athletics administration, health and education, and botany. His abrupt departure before the end of the season was a big deal in college football, covered in the *New York Times*, the *Chicago Tribune*, and the *Baltimore Sun*. Purdue was ranked fourth in the country and possibly on its way to not only an undefeated season but a national championship, the first in its history. Butkovich had gotten Purdue there but he would not see his team to the end. All over the country, college players in the V-12 program were being called into marine service.

The Wisconsin game was in Madison that year of 1943. The great season of 1942 under Schreiner and Bauman had devolved into a sour mess with their absence. The team had lost five of six games and could not score. The Wisconsin defense wasn't much better, giving Butkovich a chance to break the Big Ten scoring record of 72 points set by Gordon Locke of Iowa in 1922. He needed 13 points and was backed by a fine offensive line that included the sophomore wunderkind Frank Bauman, who was bigger and tougher than his brother, Bob (although there would never be any admission of it).

Butkovich scored in the first quarter on a thirty-three-yard run. He scored again on a one-yard plunge in the second quarter to tie the record. Purdue scored again in the third quarter: Butkovich was given a chance to break the record with the point after. It wasn't his specialty, and the kick went wide. Purdue scored again. Butkovich was given another shot to kick the extra point. Wide again.

In the fourth quarter, with roughly three minutes left, Sam Vacanti intercepted a pass and returned it to the Wisconsin four-yard line. Purdue was leading 25–0, and gentlemanly sportsmanship dictated running out the clock. But Purdue was determined to give Butkovich a parting gift to take into the corps.

He got down to the one-foot line on first down. The Wisconsin defense stiffened, and Butkovich was stopped on second down.

Third down . . .

He scored on the last carry of his college career to break the Big Ten conference scoring record with 78 points. He had broken the conference scoring record in only four games, an average of slightly more than three touchdowns per game. He had scored sixteen touch-downs for the entire season in *seven* games, 96 points. He had gained 833 yards overall with an average per carry of six yards. Despite his truncated season, he was named first-team All-American by the United Press and second-team by the Associated Press. Purdue somehow won its last two games without him to finish the season undefeated, with a 9–0 record. But by that time Butkovich could only hear about it at Parris Island.*

Boot camp was boot camp, no different than it was for McLaughry or Schreiner or Murphy or Bauman or anyone else, hold your nose and deal with it.

While Butkovich was in boot camp, he received a letter from a nine-year-old named Tom Milligan. He was from Richmond, Indiana, a town of about thirty-five thousand seventy miles east of Indianapolis. Even in the farmlands of cattle, hogs, and 4-H fairs, Richmond bustled with industry, factories, and the pride

---

* As the only undefeated major college team, Purdue should have been named national champion, but the oligarchy of Notre Dame was too intimidating. Notre Dame lost its final game of the season to Naval Station Great Lakes, 20–14, on a last-second Hail Mary pass in what was perhaps the greatest upset up to that point in college football history and certainly the least remembered. To make the insult even deeper, Purdue had also beaten Naval Station Great Lakes.

of creating, of making instead of servicing. To be in an America coming out of the Depression and into the war was to be in a land pulsating with the great gristle of production. The rest of the world was shattering into rubble, innocents in Leningrad licking the glue of wallpaper to stay alive during blockades, hiding in attics until the thud of Nazi jackboots found them, jumping into Tokyo Bay, which was literally boiling because of incendiary bombing by the Americans. The only deaths in the mainland United States during the entire war would be a family of picnickers in Oregon, killed by a Japanese weapon as strange as it was desperate called the balloon bomb.*

The United States in the war was no longer isolationist, but it was insulated. For all the editorial page and politician paeans to sacrifice, the war was far away and would remain far away except for those directly affected by it, the mothers, fathers, sisters, and brothers of sons and siblings in combat. As the historian Paul Fussell wrote in the *Atlantic*, "The real war was tragic and ironic beyond the power of any literary or philosophical analysis to suggest, but in unbombed America

---

* Fundamentally it was a giant balloon, almost like a parachute, with a small bomb attached that utilized the aerodynamics of the jet stream to get across the Pacific. Thousands of them actually did make it to the West Coast; the intent wasn't to kill but to set fire to croplands, and in that regard, they failed miserably.

especially, the meaning of war seemed inaccessible. Thus, as experience, the suffering was wasted."

The economy of every other major combatant was crumbling. The United States' was growing, actually *booming*, during the war as it supplied planes, tanks, bombs, guns, bullets, and everything else needed for a war being fought across *two oceans* five thousand miles apart while also providing billions of dollars in aid to Great Britain and Russia for their own military buildup. With a 65 percent increase in wages during the war and a low inflation rate of roughly 3.5 percent annually, the standard of living went up for most Americans. Unemployment was at a historic low of 1.2 percent. Incomes rose for everyone regardless of gender, color, or skill level. Manufacturing workers' income grew by 25 percent during the war. The economic boom spread throughout the country, with about 15 million civilians relocating to places where there were jobs. Roughly 700,000 Blacks left the South and established themselves in manufacturing jobs in Los Angeles and Detroit, regardless of the endemic racism in those cities. The war was a boon for racetracks. Department store sales went up. The gross national product increased by roughly 50 percent. The idea of great American sacrifice was largely a myth.

Richmond, Indiana, was emblematic of the country's economic underpinnings. Few in the country had ever heard of Richmond unless they were Quaker and went to Earlham College. Yet it was likely that almost every American had bought something that had been made there. It made two-thirds of the world's push lawn mowers and was one of the world's largest manufacturers of pianos. It had been the birthplace of recorded jazz in the 1920s, Hoagy Carmichael, Louis Armstrong, and Jelly Roll Morton coming to town to do sessions. All that in a town of thirty-five thousand.

Richmond also produced families such as the Milligans, Dad the Wayne County agricultural agent; Tom and his twin brother attending Baxter Elementary School and picking milkweed pods so the fibers could be used in the making of life jackets; an older sister in high school; Mom holding the fort whatever her exhaustion. Not exciting, maybe; just the dependable rhythm of an America that thrived across the country with opportunity and commerce.

Tom wasn't into jazz. As a Cub Scout he undoubtedly pushed a lawn mower or two, but it wasn't the kind of thing he could fall for either. What he really loved was college football players, and the one he loved the most was Tony Butkovich. He had clipped out every story he could find on Tony from the 1943 season. The number 25 that Butkovich wore became the nine-year-old's favorite, and he began wearing it during his own basketball games. He had a cousin who was at Purdue at the same time Butkovich was there. When he had first visited the campus with his mom, Butkovich had opened the door of a building for them. His mom did not have a clue who the guy was, but the cousin did: "That's the most famous guy at Purdue."

Tom wrote to several players asking for their autograph: Butkovich, Heisman Trophy winner Angelo Bertelli of Notre Dame, University of Georgia halfback Charley Trippi. They all wrote back. Butkovich went a step further: he asked Tom if they could begin a correspondence.

So it started, letters back and forth between the two during the war, whether Butkovich was stateside or overseas. The letters were sweet and simple. Tom wrote to him about his family, the Cub Scouts, and the success and failures of the elementary school basketball team. Butkovich wrote back asking about Tom's sister in high school and was particularly concerned to hear that his twin brother had been sick.

Much later, while stationed at Guadalcanal, Butkovich met a naval coxswain named Gene Keesling. He told Butkovich he was from Richmond and on his way home on leave.

"Do you know the Milligans?" Butkovich asked.

Keesling said he did; Tom Milligan's father, S.W.,

was known throughout the county. So Butkovich wrote a letter for Keesling to hand deliver: the seaman carried it in his shirt pocket over 7,956 miles. The letter wasn't long, just a few sentences. But Butkovich knew he had been remiss in not writing to Tom, and he just wanted to apologize.

When the NFL draft was held in April of 1944 at the Warwick Hotel in Philadelphia, the Cleveland Rams made Butkovich their first-round pick and eleventh overall. He desperately wanted to play pro football, and it was more than just an idle dream, given his final college season. But he was at Camp Lejeune by then and would be in the marines until the war was over, and nobody knew when that would be. The US high command had concluded that the war would stop only after an all-out assault on the Japanese homeland in the fall of 1945 at the earliest. The Japanese people's will was too strong, and their devotion to the emperor an essential part of their character and culture. The soonest Butkovich could play for the Rams would be the fall of 1946 after a two-year layoff from football, not to mention the accretion of physical rust and the inevitable psychological scars from fighting in total war.

As part of the V-12 program, he was in the officer

candidate program. In a letter of recommendation, his former University of Illinois coach Ray Eliot wrote of Butkovich, "He has great tenacity of purpose and is a fearless, dynamic individual. He is a boy of high moral character and fine personality and is one who will gain the respect of all that come in contact with him." He qualified in officer training in the bayonet, swimming, and the M1 rifle, although his score on the range, 272 out of 400, was pedestrian. The academic and intelligence portions were not going to be easy: he failed to make the grade, which meant he would not become a second lieutenant. He was a private first class until May 16th of 1944, when he was promoted to corporal while still in the United States, still waiting to go overseas.

But he was useful to the marines in their ceaseless public relations machine and love of football players as the ultimate infantry weapon. In a memorable picture taken at Parris Island in January of 1944, while he was still in basic training, with the headline "Grid Greats on Uncle Sam's Team," eleven college football stars, now in uniform and holding rifles, formed an offensive line and backfield. Butkovich was among them. It was a strange picture, recruits in the supposed hell of basic training being plucked out to pose as a football starting team while some of their brethren in basic training were walking around with pails over their heads and being told to lick the shit stains off their underwear. But the marketing strategy was unmistakable: college football was a way of life, at least a way of military life, if you wanted to be one of the strongest, the toughest, and the bravest.

19
Not a Damn Thing

While Butkovich was still in boot camp, Schreiner and Bauman left the United States on January 23rd of 1944 for New Caledonia on the Dutch ship the *Sommelsdijk*. The weather on the trip across the Pacific was calm except for two days when many on board got seasick. Vomit was an essential feature of overseas transport life in general, not just the act itself but the physics. Many tried to do it over the side. But some didn't make it, and as a result the deck became rather slippery. Helmets proved useful for dire emergencies. For enlisted men, the accommodations were canvas bunks in stacks of four, which required a certain consideration of which one to get depending on one's tastes and preferences. The top bunk was generally considered the best: vomit traveled downhill, which was a plus; if a guy got sick, he had to worry only about doing a disservice to himself. Since the cots tended to sag, a top bunker also did not have to worry about the sinking-ass problem. The major impediment was the utility pipe above the top bunk; it made getting in and out a little difficult, and invariably the men forgot about the pipe and clanged their head on it. At least in the bottom bunk a guy could get out the quickest.

There was little or no ventilation, so many of the men slept on deck. That was definitely more comfortable, unless a guy fell asleep underneath one of the guns and did not receive the warning that it was about to shoot off a practice round. Then he awoke quickly. Schreiner and Bauman were served meals in the tranquillity of the officers' mess. The enlisted of course ate in a separate area and the chow was pretty good, but once again there was the pervasive upchuck problem. Some could not get through a meal without launching, the smell of which caused a chain reaction among the men waiting on the ladder to get into the always crowded mess area, which in turn caused a chain reaction among those waiting outside. The military supplied a tablet for seasickness, containing sodium amytal, scopolamine, and atropine, the good news being that the men who took it might not be vomiting anymore but the bad news being that they were now walking around in a drugged stupor. Those who didn't like the pills could always use bags supplied by the War Department ingeniously marked VOMIT, FOR THE USE OF.

There were saltwater showers that only made them feel sticky instead of clean. Doing laundry was a disaster: some tied their dungarees with rope, threw them off the stern, and dragged them through the water in the hope that the turbulence would act like a washing machine, which it sort of did unless the rope loosened and the dungarees drowned at sea. Fresh water* for enlisted men was confined to the scuttlebutts at specified times during the day. Their use was limited, and more than once an unsuspecting marine took a swig only to realize that it was salt water.

The highlight of the trip, or maybe the lowlight, was the hundreds-of-years-old King Neptune ceremony in which those crossing the equator for the first time, known as "pollywogs," went through a series of initiations to become full-fledged seafarers, known as "shellbacks." Everybody went through it, not just the ship's crew but also anyone else on board, including marines. It was a ritual practiced by navies around the world. In the nineteenth century, pollywogs in some cases had been beaten with boards and wet ropes and thrown overboard or dragged in the water from the

---

*   It was produced by the evaporation of salt water.

stern. Deaths did occur, so the ceremony had been cleaned up to some degree; in World War II the ritual involved various tests; a pollywog's mouth might be stuffed with a "truth serum" made up of hot sauce, aftershave, and uncooked eggs; or they might be made to crawl on hands and knees on slippery decks while being swatted with short lengths of fire hose; prodded with an electrified piece of metal; shorn of hair; and of course made to kiss the axle-greased stomach of the de facto master of ceremonies known to all as the Royal Baby, even though few could remotely explain why he was called the Royal Baby.

II

Schreiner and Bauman disembarked at Noumea on February 9th of 1944. The setting and accommodations were embarrassingly good, the equivalent of today's ecotourism. Their tent was floored and came equipped with electric lights and mosquito nets over the cots. The site was high on a hill with a mountain range on one side and the Pacific on the other. The food was excellent. There was plenty of water for drinking and showers. Schreiner developed a suntan and played lots of horseshoes and bridge, and he and Bauman went swimming in a mountain stream.

It was all good fun, but Schreiner increasingly began to question why he was there. He did not think it was in the expectation of his getting better at horseshoes and bridge. "Everything continues here as usual with the chow excellent, the water cold, and with nothing at all to do," he wrote to his parents. "It appears to some people that we are making a huge sacrifice but Lord knows we're not. We have excellent facilities, the climate is good, we don't work hard and my only complaint is that we're not accomplishing a darn thing."

A month later it was getting to him even more—too much leisure and loafing and the hyperfocus that would be required in combat waning. "As of yet we have not done one thing for the good of the old U.S.A. Not one damn thing! We've been out of the states approximately two months now and they have been entirely wasted as far as the war effort is concerned."

The problem was that you daydreamed in between the boredom. You thought about past regrets and missed opportunities. You wondered if the best years of your life were spinning by. You saw what others had back home, marriage and children. You felt old in your early twenties because you were old, responsible for the lives and deaths of the teenage men below you who were as clueless about life as they were gung ho, not that you knew much more but acted like you did.

You thought about the future when you should have been thinking only about the near future, about the coming battle because there would eventually be one. As Schreiner reluctantly pondered over what he would do with his life when he got home from the war, he received a wise letter from his old Wisconsin coach, Harry Stuhldreher, who was able to say things to him that others could not.

Although Schreiner had been the second-round draft pick of the Detroit Lions, Stuhldreher dissuaded him from even considering it. Pro ball was good for a little quick money, maybe, but players hung on too long and after that could not adjust to other fields. He spoke from experience, having played professionally for three years, watching men unable to cope with the inevitable diminishment of their physical skills, their bodies breaking down from too many hits, too much viciousness, and too much disregard for injuries. "They are not a credit to anyone," he wrote, the one thing they were good at being of no use in the real world. He bluntly told Schreiner that he would never top the laurels he had already received in college football, so there was no point in going pro anyway. He urged him instead to continue to pursue medical school even though his "grades were not what they should have been." Schreiner took the advice to heart. Mostly.

In a letter to his parents he said he was now considering two options, both of which involved marrying Odette as soon as he got back. The first was to return to Madison and go to medical school there, which he said to appease his mother. The second, which he had never mentioned before, was to take several courses in agriculture and become a dairy farmer. "Farming is the best life one can lead and I'm seriously considering it." Since no one in his family had been a farmer since his great-grandfather in the 1800s—and that hadn't lasted very long—it seemed a strange notion. Schreiners were merchants and investment counselors. But something was changing within him.

One of the few times he got mad at his parents was when there was a small item about him in one of the Milwaukee papers. The source was obvious: they had given out information only because their son was still a star and reporters kept calling and they were sympathetic to journalists just trying to do their job. There was no malice. But Schreiner was livid. "Do I have to keep asking you nicely not to give out stuff on me. I don't like publicity, particularly when it comes from my family. If this doesn't stop I'm not going to like it one bit. I don't care if anyone knows where I am or what I'm doing." It made sense then that farming, at least momentarily, appealed to him: the solitary quiet, the focus on the earth and what it could yield, being away from it all without any responsibility except for raising a family with Odette, the privacy that was so antithetical to the military, where everything he did, shitting, pissing, sleeping, eating, was out in the open.

Almost as soon as he mentioned the idea to his parents, though, he called it all "baloney," too far away and "indistinct to really plan." It almost seemed he was scared to look ahead, as if the best way to jinx the future was to think you might have one.

20
Temptation

John McLaughry had quickly been thrown into the shit when he first arrived on Bougainville, trying to establish himself with a platoon of marines more suspicious, ornery, and contemptuous of authority than the typical marine, if that was possible—and it was. In the minds of the raiders, all shit did not stink the same; theirs stunk better.

They were not inclined to like him even if he was a raider, this interloper into the corps, slithering in from some officer training program, a *rental* marine with no prior combat experience in the previous campaign of Guadalcanal and a traitor anyway since he first enlisted in the army air corps. He probably didn't even know enough to put toilet paper underneath the top of his helmet to keep it dry, and he likely blushed when he saw one of the porno pictures the navy boys had gotten ahold of and bartered for souvenirs. His idea of a pinup was probably a Pembroke coed with saddle shoes.

Their best hope for McLaughry was that he would not overcompensate for his insecurity and self-doubt by acting as though he knew what he was doing, based on the manuals he had read in the great hot zone of Quantico in northern Virginia, where you slept on a bed, got three meals a day and leaves to Washington, went to dance parties, and drank fine whiskey instead of being slipped an overpriced bottle by a stevedore for forty bucks or finding one left behind by the Japanese that was actually poisoned. There were strategies you needed to know, and they were important to learn, but so much of combat was human instinct and prior experience. You had to feel the situation, not read about it.

Without any warning, McLaughry had replaced a well-liked second lieutenant who had cracked up a few days earlier. When the former New York Giant dug a foxhole for the first time, half of the men in the platoon sat on their haunches, not saying a word. It wasn't as though it was complicated: you and your foxhole buddy used the entrenching tool that was essential gear to build a hole big enough to hold the two of you and deep enough to give you cover. There was often a little hole in the corner from which to kick out an enemy grenade or take a dump. As one foxhole buddy slept, the other took watch, and they alternated during the night. But the raiders in McLaughry's platoon were like buzzards, waiting for him to screw it up. He felt raw and embarrassed.

After he settled in a little bit, a PFC actually introduced himself and said he was from the same area of Pennsylvania as McLaughry's family. It made him feel a little more wanted, that maybe somehow this would work itself out—until a week later, when they were on the line and two mortar shells landed back-to-back within five yards of the PFC's foxhole. The kid went batshit and tried to leave, and McLaughry and a corpsman had to wrestle him back before several other shells hit. He was evacuated to the beach, and McLaughry could not say for sure what had happened to him after that.

Bit by bit he gained the respect of his men. They could see he was quiet and steady, made careful and deliberate decisions, wasn't some rules-and-regs fetishist who carried six changes of underwear in his combat pack but knew the value of dry socks to prevent your feet from turning raw and festering and rotting. He quickly picked up that the best thing about a training manual was often to do the opposite. Gaining his men's trust was the most difficult task he had faced in his life, but he had done it by depending largely on his intuition. Every facet of military life was spelled out, except perhaps for common sense.

Now, in the early part of 1944, he returned to Guadalcanal from Bougainville, no longer a raider. The group was being disbanded, the feeling among top marine commanders being that an elite fighting unit was redundant since all marines were elite fighters. There was also the unspoken problem that elite units sometimes went rogue and stopped listening to anyone except themselves.

As he waited to see where he would be attached next, Guadalcanal was *sort of* delightful now that the island was in US hands. It was being turned into a military staging area for the central Pacific campaign. McLaughry's tent was only twenty yards from the Pacific Ocean, and he loved the sound of the surf pounding on the beach—until it started raining and rained some more, Guadalcanal back to its evil ways. A wind blew up the likes of which he hadn't seen since the Great New England Hurricane of 1938. Some of the tents in his camp went flying, and a young marine was killed when the top of a coconut tree sheared off and fell on him.

The men spent two weeks lying around on Guadalcanal before training started. McLaughry read *The Robe* by Lloyd C. Douglas. He also took in *Star Spangled Rhythm* with Bob Hope and Bing Crosby and thought it was quite funny: American troops might not be the best fighters during the war but no one could touch them when it came to movies.

Once again McLaughry had no idea where he would be reassigned, a recurring theme in his military life. But then he caught a stretch of luck when he was assigned the newly constituted 4th Regiment;* his specific assignment was to lead a weapons company under the command of Major Bernard W. "Barney" Green, a seasoned hand from the Raiders. McLaughry was temporarily placed in the sick bay tent until permanent officers' quarters were built for the company, patients running over him to be treated for malaria and those cursed tropical ulcers caused by being constantly wet at Bougainville. Some men had marched mile after mile with open sores the size of half dollars covering their legs and feet. They were impossible to treat in action, and some never went away, even after treatment. McLaughry, of course, had staved them off with both his extra-socks routine and what he called "the useful and the superfluous"; for the first two and a half months on Guadalcanal, he kept all his necessary possessions in the upper half of his pack in a bundle about thirteen inches square: a pair of dunga-

---

* It replaced the old 4th Regiment, which had been part of the surrender to the Japanese in the Philippines in 1942 and the subsequent
Bataan Death March. It had been the first regiment in the history of
the Marine Corps to surrender.

rees, a dozen pairs of socks, a bar of soap, a razor, and a toothbrush, with a poncho strapped to the outside.

A club and mess were built for the officers. There were the Saturday-night fights. The boys in the ring could fight, but the best part was watching Shapley, now the commander of the new 4th Regiment, as the referee. In addition to winning all those letters at Annapolis, he had been a great fighter there. He was still in superb shape, and it was clear that nobody in the ring, however good, wanted to screw with him.

Somewhere around May of 1944, McLaughry began training for the invasion of Guam, the largest and southernmost of the Mariana Islands. He also got a new tentmate, everybody's All-American.

Dave Schreiner.

He could not wait to tell Tuss.

"Did I ever tell you about the football team we could get up in this regiment from the officers—it sure would be a power house and bigger than the Chicago Bears in its prime."

He rattled off for his father the size of a hypothetical front seven on offense: a center who weighed 230 pounds and had been an All-American; two tackles coming in at 245 and 255 with experience at Ohio Northern and Northwestern; two guards at 210 who had played in college and the pros; both ends at 200 pounds, including

Schreiner. Not that anything would come of it; Guadalcanal obviously was not known for football. But it was
fun to dream, to take an edge off the gruel of training
and the military cycle of hurry up and wait.

II

Guam was another piece in the island-hopping puzzle
as US forces moved ever closer to the Japanese homeland. The establishment of air bases there would, for
the first time, give the newly minted B-29 bomber access to bombing both the Philippines and the Japanese
home islands. It would also give the armed forces the
opportunity to recapture Guam, a longtime American
possession, won in the Spanish-American War of 1898.
Guam had been taken by the Japanese the same month
as Pearl Harbor, leaving the local populace at the whim
of their captors' authority.

McLaughry's platoon would operate a variety of
heavy weapons: 75 mm antitank guns set on movable
half-tracks, .50- and .30-caliber machine guns. The
work was easier than being in an infantry platoon at Bougainville. Yet he missed it. There had been something
alluring about marching through impenetrable jungle,
trudging through a neck-high swamp, and crawling
through a labyrinth of brush. He had found it fascinat-

ing, the intoxication of exhaustion and adrenaline, fear and fearlessness, man as primal beast looking for other human primal beasts.

As he waited to go into his second round of combat, he dwelled on the disparities and inequities of military life in wartime: medals given out like candy as morale boosters for acts that had never happened the way they were described, the flawed missions turned into great acts of heroism and fed to the American public as successes, the nagging suspicion that an excellent officer he had worked with at Montford Point had not been able to get into the Raiders because he was Jewish.

He expressed to Tuss what he felt was the hypocrisy of a nation that, for all its alleged sacrifice, was filled with draft dodgers finding loopholes through the political sieve of the Selective Service System, for example, claiming that their wife and kids would suffer economic hardship if they went overseas. He knew one classmate at Brown who had done just that, even though his own father was a wealthy business executive. "It sure doesn't seem right, especially when I have boys in the company who are PFCs making $60.00 + month, from poor families, who have kids and yet volunteered. . . . [T]here is a lot of resentment about service men with easy jobs, staying in the states. I guess you and I know plenty of them."

Tuss, who had volunteered for the Marine Corps and

been appointed a major in charge of recreation at Parris Island (he was too old for combat), had firsthand experience with what his son was saying. He had received roughly a dozen letters asking for a favor of one kind or another—an assignment to a noncombatant position as a physical instructor, a father asking him to keep tabs on his son who shortly after entering the military had seemed determined to marry a young woman that the father did not approve of. Because of the high regard he was held in by the sports community, he was even asked to intercede on behalf of Brooklyn Dodgers player/manager Leo Durocher after he had been drafted and was looking for a possible way to fulfill his military obligation and still be able to run the club.*

III

Schreiner anguished over Odette while at Guadalcanal. "Sometimes I think it's unfair to have her wait for me," he wrote to his parents. "After all there's a chance I won't come back and then where'll she be? And I do think of how old she'll be—nearly 25. We should have

---

* Durocher was ultimately ruled ineligible for service with a punctured eardrum, although his hearing problem didn't seem to prevent him from loudly arguing with any umpire whose call infuriated him. His nickname was "Leo the Lip."

gotten married before I left and had one in the oven. If she'll wait for me I'll be plenty happy but I can't blame her if she doesn't." Odette had definitely wanted to get married before Schreiner went overseas. She loved him madly and wanted him to experience the feeling of being a married man. But she understood that the timing just wasn't right, although it was hard to know whether it was Schreiner who wasn't ready, or his mother, Anne, who had decided that he wasn't ready.

Odette was hardly idle, initially housed at Smith College in Northampton in Massachusetts for training with the WAVES as part of the officer candidate program. Those enrolled understandably resented the false image being created; as one publication put it, they were nothing but a "cream-puff women's organization whose members just look glamorous in uniform and do easy, quiet jobs in the most decorative way." They were being trained to do jobs left open by Navy men who had gone off to combat.[*] They served at nine hundred different shore stations across the United States not simply in clerical roles but as aviation machinists, control tower

---

[*] Navy Secretary Frank Knox said he would only admit Blacks into the WAVES "over his dead body." After his death, successor James Forrestal changed the policy by a sliver: of roughly 85,000 WAVES during the war, seventy-two were Black, a percentage of .0008. It was yet another example of the disenfranchisement of Blacks from American society.

operators, statisticians, cryptographers, and weather forecasters. Predictably Congress was initially opposed to the idea of women serving in the navy, but thanks to the efforts of First Lady of the United States, Eleanor Roosevelt, a bill establishing a women's reserve as a branch of the Naval Reserve was enacted in 1942.

As indoctrination into navy life, Odette and other candidates took courses while stationed at Smith in naval history and organization, ships and aircraft, and law and communications. An hour and a half was spent each day either in military drill or in the gymnasium. Women who were not up to standards were quickly billeted out. Subsequent to graduation in February of 1943, Odette was sent to US Naval Training School on the campus of Hunter College in the Bronx, dubbed the USS Hunter, where she ultimately reached the rank of lieutenant and became responsible for the training of eight thousand women enlistees.

The helplessness of being apart from her fiancé led to inevitable tension at times. A phone conversation between the two of them when Odette was still at Smith and Schreiner on the West Coast preparing to ship out disintegrated into yelling. "I hope I never yell at you that way again!" he wrote to her. As Schreiner continued to train for combat, Odette took advantage of New York with the little downtime she had—a concert at Carnegie Hall featuring Vladimir Horowitz, meals at Nick's in Greenwich Village and Keen's English Chop House on West Thirty-sixth Street near the theater district. Eating out for Schreiner was when a fellow marine captured a pig and butchered it.

"You are subject to more temptations than I—I know that," he wrote her. ". . . But darling we have faith in each other and in things always coming out right side up—don't we . . . but I want you to go out and have fun—you deserve it and there's no reason why you shouldn't. But don't make me jealous by talking about it because I am a very jealous person as you probably know. And the reason it's okay with me is that faith in you again."

Odette worried that Schreiner was putting her on a pedestal, his image colored by longing and loneliness, which in turn made his expectations for marriage unrealistic once he returned. He wrote back:

"Just remember that all I'm existing for is you and that you are really all that counts. I'm not putting you on a pedestal one bit. I fully expect we'll have our little arguments and differences but our love will be stronger than any little things like that. As you always say to me 'I love you for your faults.'

"Keep sweet like you were when I left and keep

healthy so you can mow the lawn and shovel the side-walks! I love you dear. I love you oh so much. And how I need you!"

He made arrangements through his parents to send her a dozen roses each month when he was away in combat and incommunicado, to let her know that she was the "swellest girl in the world" and that he was always thinking of her. He knew his father might think he was crazy to spend that much money (itemizing expenses was something of an obsession for Bert). But it was *his* money and a way of trying to maintain a lifeline to someone he would not see or talk to for several years. Said a card accompanying one of the deliveries:

> "Hoping these flowers don't detract from your beauty—Love, Dave."

21
Millimeter

McLaughry, Schreiner, and Bauman left Guadalcanal on June 4th of 1944, ostensibly bound for
Guam. The battle was supposed to start on June 18th of
1944, but the campaign for Saipan in the Marianas was
taking much longer than expected.

Saipan had become the pivotal battle of the war for
the Japanese. Its ultimate fall, on July 9th of 1944, combined with the decisive Battle of the Philippine Sea the
previous month, made a Japanese victory in the war
impossible. They lost three carriers, which depleted
the Imperial Japanese Navy to virtually nothing and
rendered it useless. As many as 600 carrier- and land-
based planes were destroyed, resulting in the death of
Japan's most experienced pilots, who were impossible

to replace. Saipan, described as impregnable by Prime Minister Tojo, was the opposite.

The Tojo-led government resigned. Two high-ranking naval officers, Admirals Soemu Toyoda and Mitsumasa Yonai, in interrogations with US officials after the war, described the defeat at Saipan as "the end" of all Japanese hopes. The daily food intake of the Japanese population after the battle dropped below the minimum standard to about 1,800 calories. Coal and steel output had significantly dropped, iron ore stockpiles had plummeted by two-thirds, imports had dwindled. "After Saipan was lost no miracle could have helped the empire of the Rising Sun," wrote the United States Strategic Bombing Survey.

Had the Japanese surrendered after Saipan and not sought concessions, there would have been no bombing of Tokyo in which roughly 97,000 people died; nor the firebombings of sixty-five other cities in which as many as 500,000 died. There would have been no battles on Iwo Jima or Okinawa. They would have saved themselves from the dropping of the atom bombs.

Unconditional surrender would have made Japan dependent earlier on US benevolence, which, as it turned out, was enormous during the postwar reconstruction of the country into a democratic society, with the emperor retained as a ceremonial figure despite those who believed he was a war criminal because of his obvious knowledge of the war and pivotal decision-making.* But the Japanese people's pride, sense of honor, and conviction of destiny as the chosen people of the world were too deeply embedded in them. They had a proud warrior code that was noble, but it had become perverted by the militarists, who endlessly glorified death as long as it wasn't their own. As the US Strategic Bo mbing Survey pointed out, "While defeat in war is a military event, the recognition of the defeat is a political act."

The Japanese engaged in a futile banzai attack on July 7th of 1944 at Saipan. Beer and sake provided their drunken courage, crazed screams at 4:45 in the morning against eight-round M1s and water-cooled .30-caliber machine guns. A total of 4,311 Japanese troops were killed in thirteen hours.

Several days later, civilians who lived on Saipan, many of them Japanese working in the sugarcane fields on the island, began to congregate at the north-ern end of the island atop an eight-hundred-foot cliff at Marpi Point. As bone-exhausted marines dressed

---

* For all his supposed cluelessness and impotence at the hands of his military inner circle, it was the emperor who elected to end the war with the Imperial Rescript of surrender on August 15th of 1945, after the dropping of the atom bombs and the declaration of war on the Japanese by the Soviet Union.

in a composite of rags stood on jutting crags of rock and watched with their helmets tilted low, several civilians jumped off the cliff onto the knife-sharp coral. Then several more. Then more and more. Children who begged their parents not to force them to die were pushed off. A woman in labor jumped. Another ran through the bushes near the cliff as if escaping a fanged predator. She stopped to make sure the coast was clear, then made a final dash for the edge and jumped, an oddly banal occurrence, like a lumpy sack flung overboard from a ship, with a marine there to photograph it. A father walked back and forth on the crest of the cliff with his family, unsure of what to do until an impatient Japanese sniper shot and killed him. Then the rest of the family plunged to their deaths.

The marines mounted a loudspeaker, using a civilian to beg those still at the edge not to jump, vowing to supply them with food and shelter as they had to those who had surrendered. But few on the edge believed it, having been convinced by Japanese soldiers that Americans would torture, rape, and kill them. A young boy lay crumpled on the coral in the fetal position, as though he were sleeping, a woman lay with her head turned to the side as if ashamed, a man lay with his slippers loosely hanging off his feet. Some jumped into the ocean, making little splashes of water like the breaking of an icy pond. Some died immediately upon impact. Some were overcome by the current. Some eventually drowned and were carried out by the sea to navy ships, where sailors shot them, supposedly so the bodies would sink.

Hundreds jumped over the cliffs at Marpi Point in Saipan, maybe thousands. Nobody will ever know how many for sure. *Time* and *Life* magazines ran stories on the suicides with unflinching pictures. Their intent was to shock, and the event did shock, except for the Japanese authorities, who seized upon it as a good public relations moment and extolled the dead as the embodiment of the fighting spirit of the Japanese people. The subtext was obvious: if every Japanese citizen followed the example of those civilians, who had given up their lives, then the war could still be won. Even if there was no one left.

II

The 4th Regiment remained at sea because of the possible need for reinforcements at Saipan, McLaughry for fifty-six days until the middle of July. The ship, the USS *Zeilin,* was a large passenger and cargo vessel built in 1921 that still had wooden decks and steam-powered winches. The ship was overcrowded. The men got off

the boat only once, on what was essentially a desert island with no trees. One marine died of heat prostration.

Schreiner's transport fared a bit better, being sent
to Eniwetok, where working parties were established
to help move food to the appropriate storage areas on
board. Cases of food were "accidentally" dropped, one
marine lifting a crate with the tip-off "Heads up, falling cargo" before tossing it and a jackpot of delicious
oranges spilling onto the deck. After another several
days back at sea, another marine was smart enough to
befriend a navy sailor who had a key to the beer locker.
There are certain secrets in the military that never
remain secret for long—where the beer is stored chief
among them. A healthy mix of marines and sailors
showed up and kept showing up, which led to the military equivalent of $E = mc^2$:

> More beer = singing
>> More beer and more singing = fighting

Navy crewmen had to use high-pressure hoses to
break up what became a near riot.

Marine morale was getting there.

After the postponement of nearly a month and a half
of the Guam campaign because of the slowness of

Saipan, McLaughry and Schreiner and Bauman's regiment, now part of the 1st Provisional Marine Brigade, invaded Guam on July 21st of 1944. The execution of the amphibious assault doctrine on the island was the best of the war, with seamless coordination among the sea, air, and land forces. Prelanding naval bombardment was sustained for the appropriate length of time and moved inland as the troops first hit the beach to provide further cover. Planes came in on time with rockets. McLaughry could not believe that any enemy could possibly still be alive as he neared the shore— the oft-repeated refrain that no one could survive. But many did, including a dazed water buffalo tied to a coconut tree.

Only one member of McLaughry's platoon was hit during the landing, shell fragments in the butt. He apologized profusely when he was evacuated since the exact same thing had happened to him at Bougainville. Many marines considered him inordinately lucky. Butt wounds were good, very good, benign as wounds went, and therefore excellent for ridicule. The only thing better was getting shot in the butt while shitting. McLaughry did not see much action the first day and hunkered down in a foxhole for the night. On the second day the Japanese briefly overran Hill 40 and broke the line in two places. McLaughry's company burned out the barrels of four of their machine guns in covering the front. Roughly 350 Japanese were killed.

In the latter stages of fighting on a patrol near Ritidian Point, after several Japanese had been killed, a marine decided to behead one of them and place the head on a wall overlooking a road as if keeping watch. A different patrol came through the next day, mistook the severed head for a living Japanese soldier, and dived for cover to guard against ambush. The patrol thought it had purposely been made fools of and came back into camp livid. The company chaplain was also displeased, offering the standard lecture that it was fine to kill Japanese soldiers but not to desecrate the dead. The words had little impact.

Guam was declared secure on August 10th of 1944. The Americans suffered roughly 1,700 killed and 6,000 wounded. The number of Japanese deaths was about 20,000, including isolated pockets of Japanese still on the island after defeat and eventually killed. Guam became one of the world's busiest ports in the last year of the war, with 1,700 ships entering and leaving every month.

Schreiner, his baptism of fire coming fourteen months after entering the Marine Corps, did well. McLaughry was impressed. He acted as an assistant platoon leader on the 75 mm half-tracks, vehicles capable of going forty miles an hour with a self-propelled gun. They had never been popular and had initially been dubbed "Purple Heart boxes," meaning that whoever manned them had a good chance of being wounded.

Schreiner found that out when the back of his head was creased by a bullet. He spent a few days in the hospital, protesting that the wound wasn't serious and seeming almost embarrassed about it, even though another inch in any direction could have killed him. The worst part was the pro forma telegram sent to his parents: "When information is received regarding nature or intent of wounds you will be informed." It would have been better not to send any word at all.

Schreiner himself sent several letters telling them what had happened, but the mail was slow. They waited and waited until they finally received the first letter from him saying the wound had been "just a singe."

"Hair will cover it up so that you will never know I once went to war!"

He was much more concerned with his parents' anniversary and their making sure to take some of his money and buy themselves a present.

After the battle they still had to mop up the Japanese stragglers, some of whom liked to attack at night with the words "Babe Ruth must die!" To which a marine would respond, "The emperor eats shit!" The orders were to shoot from their foxholes at anything they thought was moving, although they were expected to exercise fire discipline so all hell didn't break loose and they ended up killing some of their own. Hubbard was standing watch at about 10:30 p.m. when he claimed he had heard something move out in the bush despite a wretched downpour. Hubbard started shooting with his .45, awakening McLaughry next to him. Pedersen joined with his .45. They ran out into the pitch black of the night and got so fouled up that they almost ended up shooting each other. There was nothing there. The next morning they got a rash of shit from the other veterans for making the kind of rookie mistake a green replacement might make, shooting at noises and shadows.

On August 21st of 1944, memorial services were held at the brigade cemetery in the village of Agat. Each platoon was allowed to send a truckload of fifteen men, about a third of its complement. McLaughry wanted to go, but he deferred to other members who had lost comrades and friends. The Seabees cut pieces of aluminum from downed airplanes, engraved the names and serial numbers of the boys killed on them, and put them on crosses to afford them greater dignity than a painted name.

McLaughry wrote to his parents:

> Just to think a month and one day ago, all those boys were alive, and waiting to go ashore; you'd have thought they didn't have a care in the world laughing, joking, etc. none of this grim stuff you read of. Even coming in and just a few hundred yards off shore, everyone was thoroughly enjoying the show—it was a magnificent one I'll never forget, with everything from Battleships to destroyers opening up at point blank range, and the dive bombers diving in dropping their loads. It wasn't 'til the mortars started dropping around us, and we left the landing boat to haul out our guns and hitch them to the half-tracks that we came down to earth and realized that the shooting wasn't all one way.

22

March of the Crabs

By mid-September of 1944, McLaughry, Schreiner, and Bauman were back on Guadalcanal from the 4th Regiment. Butkovich and Murphy arrived from the 29th. Another change in structure took place when the 6th Marine Division came into existence on the island: the 4th, 22nd, and 29th Regiments and the 15th Artillery Regiment became part of it. The formation was a complement of roughly twenty thousand men designated for what would become the Battle of Okinawa.

Schreiner was reassigned to the 1st Battalion of the 4th Regiment, in charge of the 3rd Platoon of Company A. He had wanted to be in a rifle company, regardless of the inherent dangers of combat on the line, controlling the life and death of the men in his platoon. His intent was not to make everyone happy, which was impossible anyway given the inherent nature of the military, in which everyone was obligated to bitch and moan about *something* or it would not be the military. The only thing he felt he could do was to be "fair and square," as he put it, make decisions based on what was best for the platoon, create a hard-hitting outfit capable of attacking and advancing. He knew that his men, "the boys," as he called them, as if he were a wise man instead of a twenty-four-year-old, would come around once they accepted training instead of hating it. He took pleasure in having among his men not just the son of a colonel but the son of a man who had been a prisoner on a Georgia chain gang. He also wanted to command a platoon in Company A so he could be in the same company with Bauman, who was the leader of the 1st Platoon. They took a few hits of Japanese wine to celebrate the occasion.

Within the 4th Regiment of several thousand, the two were thick as thieves, interlocked to the degree where they became known as "Bob and Dave"; it was automatic that Bob would do anything for Dave and Dave would do anything for Bob: fight for each other, save each other. They were more than simply war buddies. They went back to the best moments of their lives on the playing fields of Wisconsin.

Like Alfred E. Neuman, Bauman had a kind of "What, me worry?" attitude. He was brave and loyal in combat, but he could also be irreverent and accessible.

"The Halls of Montezuma" was, of course, the sacred marine hymn. Bauman carried his own version on a piece of paper:

> From the Streets of San Diego
> To the Shores of the Salton Sea
> Where the desert winds are blowing
> And the women all love me.
> Where we spend our time on liberty
> Pitching woo with sweet sixteen's
> We're the wolf pack of the service
> The United States Marines . . .
> We can laugh and love from dark 'til dawn
> When the soldiers are in bed.
> We will laugh and love when they are gone
> And the Sailors all are dead.
> If the Army or the Navy ever gaze
> On heaven's scenes
> They'll find the Angels in the arms
> Of United States Marines.

He was good for Schreiner, loosening him up a little bit and getting him to go on beer runs and to parties, including one where he and Schreiner threw a colonel outside a tent and somehow managed not to get disciplined. On the occasion of his birthday on May 13th of 1944, he and Schreiner and the other platoon leader of the company, John "Punchie" Clark, tied one on together.

Beer was always a major preoccupation in his letters home. He facetiously told his cousin Dorothy that he would give pretty much everything he owned in the world, or at least twenty-five bucks (equivalent to almost $390 today), for five bottles of Budweiser. In truth, he had plenty of it.

He told younger brother Frank that a friend had mercifully left him a case of beer after not having been issued any for a month. He loved to tease his future sister-in-law, Dale, and Dale loved to tease him, trading "bullshit" with each other, as he put it. "You can send me a dozen cases of Bud," he wrote to her. "They will be greatly appreciated." In another letter: "I haven't been doing anything of interest lately although I drank 2 cases of beer myself last night. I felt a little thirsty and there wasn't enough to have a party so I figured I might as well have some."

"What a vacation I'm having," he wrote a couple of months later, when there was little to do except sleep. "Now don't you wish you were here—we could have so much fun. You could help me drink this case of beer I have in front of me. Do you think you could hold 12 bottles?" He confided to Dale in the same letter that he had been writing to other women besides his fiancée, Arlene Bahr, and that his conscience was bothering him, even though it was all casual.

Maybe his conscience was bothering him . . .

It was always hard to tell with Bauman how much he said with clear eyes and how much he said with a silent wink.

He continued to take care of his mother from afar, giving her money so she could get a winter coat and making sure that a monthly allotment of a hundred dollars be sent to her, just as Butkovich was doing with his mother.

He heard only sporadically from Frank in the fall of 1944, not because of any lack of devotion on his brother's part but because Frank was busy. In football he was named second-team All-American for Purdue by the Football Writers' Association of America—all the more impressive because he had played only roughly half the season before being called up to the Marine Corps's officer training program. Taking Bob's advice, he approached basic training at the end of 1944 on Parris Island in the "proper spirit" of not taking it personally when he and the other recruits were called shit-birds morning, noon, and night.

Most marines felt pride when pinned with the Purple Heart for having been wounded in action. Schreiner, in a letter to his parents, called it "a big medal and a lot of baloney. You get it for just a scratch nowadays." He also asked that he no longer be referred to in letters as "lieutenant," in part because it sounded imperious and drew unwanted attention to himself.

As September turned into October in 1944, fall was in the air, or at least the memory of it. Schreiner in his mind traveled back to Wisconsin. It had always been the time of year he liked best—the crisp air that with each breath felt like starting over, the turning of the leaves to blushing red and soft yellow, the bluish haze over the hills like a halo, the Friday-night bonfire before the Saturday football game against Notre Dame or Ohio State or Iowa.

Now he and the others were on Shit Island to form the 6th Marine Division. Guadalcanal was roughly 8,500 miles from New York Harbor on the southern end of the Solomon Islands, not that that would have meant anything to most Americans: shown a map, they would have had enough trouble even picking out

Japan. From several miles out at sea the island looked carpeted in green all the way to the 7,661-foot peak of Mount Popomanaseu. It was picture-postcard perfect, what many imagined a Pacific island to be until, as one marine put it, you discovered what a "putrefying shit-hole it really is."

The island changed from a fantasy into something so horrible it was still fantastic: the razor-sharp kunai grass, the rain forest covering much of the island impenetrable. It was a good hiding place for the Japanese stragglers still there since the end of the Guadalcanal campaign in 1943.

An injection of painkiller was sometimes required to dull the pain of a centipede bite. The march of the crabs to spawn in the ocean filled the men's tents, and they, too, left calling cards if the men didn't dump out their boots and inspect their cot before going to bed. One Sunday afternoon after church, Melvin Heckt and several of his tentmates went on a crab attack: they swept out about fifty that had set up their own camp underneath the wooden platforms. Then they massacred them with machetes, blowtorches, and everything in between, leaving a horrible stench but the great satisfaction of no more crabs. Until the crabs gathered all over again.

Rats infested the tents as well, and although

McLaughry may have been a great blocking back, he was a better rat killer, earning an unofficial commendation from his tentmates. One marine saw the opportunity of playing an extreme prank: he took a bunch of rat pups, sneaked them underneath the covers of an unsuspecting tentmate before he got into his fart sack, and watched the ensuing insanity when the guy woke up. Boys will be boys, but nothing compared to marines being marines. They would put cornflakes into a bed or remove the springs, or they would pour water on those who were sleeping.

The island improved vastly as construction battalions built facilities, neat rows of encampments for the regiments of the 6th Division near Henderson Field, mess halls, officers' clubs, a sick bay, a library, showers, a chapel, a radio station, a clothing store, a soda fountain, walkways to keep the mud off people's feet, a multiline telephone switchboard, an infrastructure of roads and underground pipes, a head for one of the generals like an oversized doll house, and the one place on the island where a man could have what he began to wish for more than anything else in life: an immaculate shit.

Rivers were fished with dynamite. Wild hogs and goats were captured for feasts. Under the supervision of expert "brewmasters" from the Ozarks, hooch was created from fermented fruit. The secret sauce of "torpedo juice," 190-proof alcohol extracted from the fuel used by the navy for torpedo motors, was mixed with grapefruit or orange juice. The navy had put poison into it to make it undrinkable, but the ever-enterprising marines figured out a way to extract the poison. Except when they got poisoned.

It was a good place to take care of minor medical needs. Briscoe sent a marine to sick bay to deal with his painful ingrown toenails. While he was there, he was given a bonus circumcision, leading him to spread the word: "Don't let Briscoe send you to sick bay." Training was sometimes brutal, twenty-mile treks into the unyielding terrain. A mock village called Bonegiville was built with forty different structures (including an *okiya*, or geisha house).

When they had time off, the marines engaged in the singular American troop fetish of souvenir hunting. As an Australian soldier put it, "They'll shoot a Jap and he'll jump in the air and before he hits the ground, they'll be all over him frisking him for souvenirs." Out at the front, men with pliers or KA-BAR knives pulled the gold fillings of dead Japanese soldiers with the bodies still warm, stashing teeth in their wallet as keepsakes or fashioning necklaces from them. The ears of dead soldiers were strung together, and rings made out of leg bones were considered Tiffanyesque pieces.* Souvenir stands popped up on Guadalcanal like swap meets, according to Judith A. Bennett's book on the Pacific war, *Natives and Exotics*. Some sold Japanese skulls found on corpses and marked them with "Made in Japan." Soon enough, there was a lively trade in counterfeit goods: an entrepreneurial marine found some sewing machines and started churning out fake Imperial Japanese Marines battle flags for sale. It was the same with swords, honed to perfection from vehicle springs by former blacksmiths. Marines were not the only ones who knew that there was a sucker born every minute. The natives on Guadalcanal were generally assumed to be dim-witted, but often they were not. Realizing the demand for straw skirts, they started a minifactory and sold them at PRICES TOO GOOD TO BE TRUE!!, using yellow dye from Atabrine tablets dissolved in water to add color.

In campaign after campaign, after-action reports by intelligence officers bemoaned the pilfering of potentially valuable documents from dead Japanese officers by enlisted men. "The desire for souvenirs . . . led to

---

* The practice of collecting teeth, ears, and skulls was ultimately banned by the military and subject to court-martial—good in theory but enforced only sporadically.

needless inexcusable loss of life, time and effort," said a report on amphibious operations on the capture of the Marianas. But the men didn't take just documents; during the capture of Guam, eight enemy field chests containing valuable medical equipment and supplies were stolen by navy medical officers "seeing a private windfall," said an after-action report by the III Amphibious Corps.

But by the end of 1944, it all got boring. Something had to happen.

Even if it meant beating the shit out of each other.

23

The Mosquito Bowl

Before McLaughry had left for the Guam campaign, he had made the boast to his dad that the 4th Regiment could go toe-to-toe with the NFL champion Chicago Bears. That was crazy—but maybe not so crazy if the football talents of the 4th and the 29th Regiments together were combined. With a coach such as Notre Dame's Frank Leahy and time to practice, they almost certainly would have defeated any other team playing college football in 1944—except perhaps the West Point draft dodgers.

Of the sixty-five men listed on the rosters of the two regimental teams for the Mosquito Bowl:

Fifty-six had played college football. Most of the rest had played in high school. The remaining handful just wanted in on the mayhem.

Twenty-two had been starters at such schools as Purdue (3), Notre Dame (2), Wisconsin (2), Duquesne (2), Michigan State, Fordham, Brown, Cornell, Colgate, Texas Christian, Tulsa, California, Northern Illinois, Colorado State, St. Mary's, Mississippi State, and Wake Forest.*

Sixteen had either been drafted by the pros or received offers.

Five had been team captains.

Three were All-Americans.

FROM THE 29TH:

Saxon Judd, end at the University of Tulsa: All-Missouri Valley Conference 1941 and 1942 as Tulsa went undefeated and won the Sun and Sugar Bowls. Caught nine touchdown passes in 1942 on only thirty-five catches, unheard of back then. Drafted in the third round by the Chicago Cardinals.

Charles Behan, captain and end at Northern Illinois State

---

* All of those schools played major college football in the 1940s.

Teachers College:* Played with the Detroit Lions. One of
the nation's top decathletes.

Mendle Earl "Big John" Bond, running back from Texas
Christian University and North Texas Agricultural College:
All Southwest Conference honorable mention. Drafted by
the Boston Yankees.

Walter "Bus" Bergman, quarterback from Colorado A&M
University:† Winner of ten letters in football, basketball,
baseball. Student body president. Turned down contract
offer from the Philadelphia Eagles.

John Genis, tackle from the University of Illinois and
Purdue University and captain of the respective teams in
1942 and 1943: Teammate of Butkovich and Frank Bauman
at both Illinois and Purdue. Drafted by the Brooklyn
Dodgers football team.

Wayne "Rusty" Johnston, all-everything back from
Marquette University: Starred as sophomore. Drafted by
the Chicago Bears.

---

*   Now Northern Illinois University.
†   Now Colorado State University.

*Hank Maliszewski, starting end from Duquesne University.**

Frank Callen, starting quarterback from St. Mary's College.

Jennings Moates, starting running back from Mississippi State University as a sophomore: Scored the winning and only touchdown against Ole Miss in 1941 to give Mississippi State its first Southeastern Conference championship in history.

John Perry, All-Southern Conference tailback at Wake Forest University and later Duke University: One of the most promising sophomore running backs in the country.

Edmund Van Order, Jr., starting tackle on number one–ranked Cornell University in 1939 as a sophomore.

---

* Maliszewski was named to one All-American team, the All-Polish Surname, chosen in 1940 by Zygmunt Kaminski, sports editor of the Polish-language newspaper *Nowiny Polskie* in Milwaukee: Czekalski at tackle from Manhattan College; Filipowicz, fullback from Fordham; Garbinski, guard from Penn State; Juzwik, halfback from Notre Dame; Knolla, halfback from Creighton University; Kuczynski, end from Penn; Maliszewski, end from Duquesne; Matuszczak, quarterback from Cornell; Mocha, center from Washington; Molinski, guard from Tennessee; and Zajkowski, tackle from Temple. Such team listings were common in foreign-language newspapers as a source of ethnic pride and assimilation into the most American of games. There were also All-Croatian, All-Italian, and All-Jewish teams.

Robert Neff, starting tackle from the University of Notre
Dame.

Murphy, the captain, from the University of Notre Dame.

Butkovich, All-American from Purdue University: Drafted
in the first round by the Cleveland Rams.

FROM THE 4TH:

Paul Szakash, fullback from the University of Montana:
Played four seasons with the Detroit Lions.

Lee Bennett, tackle from Michigan State College of
Agriculture and Applied Science:* Played with the Detroit
Lions.

Willard "Bill" Hofer, quarterback and letter winner from
the University of Notre Dame: Drafted by the Green Bay
Packers.

William Vlademere "Bill" Lazetich, wingback from the
University of Montana: Played with the Cleveland Rams.

Stanley Ritinski, starting end from Fordham University

---

* Now called Michigan State University.

team that won the Sugar Bowl in 1941: Drafted by the New York Giants.

Hugh Semple, starting tackle from Ohio Northern University.

Ted Stawicki, starting center from American University.

Robert Herwig, All-American center from the University of California and a starter on the basketball team.

Bauman, from the University of Wisconsin: Drafted by the Chicago Bears.

McLaughry, from Brown University and the New York Giants.

Schreiner, All-American from the University of Wisconsin: Drafted by the Detroit Lions in the second round.

‖

The well-organized 29th challenged the unprepared 4th to a warm-up in early December, a likely psych job to make the 4th think it did not have a chance.

McLaughry, the unofficial organizer for the 4th, had hoped to get in a few practices. But 105 mm artillery school got in the way with its requirements of learning cosines, the use of a slide rule, and fixing angles. The 4th managed to cobble together a team of enlisted men and officers. The rules were the same as for regulation football except that there were only five men on the offensive line instead of seven. It was also two-handed touch above the waist, which was ridiculous since everyone tackled anyway. The 4th tied the 29th, 0–0, considered a great upset given the 29th's prior preparation. In another warm-up a week before the Mosquito Bowl, McLaughry's 4th Regimental Weapons Company played an all-star team made up mostly of officers from the entire 4th Regiment. McLaughry drew up five passing and four running plays and did get a practice in. The 4th all-stars were heavily favored. They had practiced twice the previous week and outweighed the weapons company by thirty pounds on the offensive line and twenty pounds in the backfield. The game was scoreless after three periods. In the fourth quarter the regimental weapons team scored a safety, and that was that for a 2–0 win. The all-stars were so shocked that they asked five members of the weapons company to join the 4th's roster for the Mosquito Bowl.

The expectations for the game only grew. The Mosquito Network decided to broadcast it live, a big deal since the network had radio stations on military bases throughout the Pacific as part of the Armed Forces Radio Service (AFRS). It had been established on Guadalcanal by a group of marines with broadcasting experience from the United States. The shacklike studio they were housed in was dubbed "Radio City," a reference to NBC headquarters in New York. The first broadcast was on March 13th of 1944. The programming was eclectic and ranged from news to Saturday-night boxing matches to church services to music and entertainment that included *The Bob Hope Show*, *The Jack Benny Program*, and the Boston and NBC Symphony Orchestras. Perhaps the most popular show was Hy Averback's *Atabrine Cocktail Hour*:

> From the fungus-festooned Fern Room, high atop the elegant Hotel DeGink in downtown Guadalcanal, we bring you the dance music of the Quinine Quartet.

There was no Quinine Quartet. Nor was there any Hotel DeGink, although one marine with dead seriousness wanted to know its location. Averback also had a "swap shop" segment to facilitate the sale or exchange of war souvenirs. As was prevalent, the navy Seabees flooded the program with fake Japanese flags (made of American parachute cloth) and so-called war clubs whose ebony was actually pinewood stained with shoe polish.

The station began live broadcasts, which made the Mosquito Bowl a natural. The announcer, Keith Topping, had impressive football credentials; he had been a star player at Stanford in the 1930s and the winner of the most valuable player award on defense in the 1936 Rose Bowl. The game was originally called the All-Star Classic, but whether it was the brainchild of the Mosquito Network or a correspondent covering the game for the papers back in the States, it became known as the Mosquito Bowl.

The network whipped up ample hype the week of the game by issuing a program with full rosters, projected starters, and a detailed schedule of events:*

1330–1400: Music by Regimental Bands.
1400: Reception of Major General Lemuel C.
SHEPHERD, USMC, Commanding General,
6th Marine Division. Honors by 29th Marines
Band.

---

* The time of the game may have been moved up to the morning to lessen the heat and humidity.

> 1405: Colonel Victor F. BLEASDALE, USMC, Commanding, 29th Marines, and Colonel Alan SHAPLEY, USMC, Commanding, 4th Marines, meet in center of gridiron and exchange greetings.
>
> 1415: Kickoff.
>
> Half: (1) Music and ceremony by 4th Marines Band.
>
> (2) General SHEPHERD changes to opposite side of field.
>
> (3) Music and ceremony by 29th Marines Band and 29th Marines Drum and Bugle Corps.
>
> End of game: Band music.

The 29th typically had its act together, its program roster containing position, number, first and last names, rank, school, years played, and football honors. The 4th managed to list position, number, last name, and school; several of the names were spelled wrong and several schools incorrectly listed. The 4th's roster had roughly ten players coming out of high school, which indicated a potentially fatal lack of depth given that virtually everyone on the 29th's roster had played college football. But the 4th was no patsy. McLaughry was slated to start in the backfield, and so was Jack Brennan, a high school kid out of Yonkers who could *fling* it, so much so that McLaughry wrote to Tuss suggesting that he recruit him.

The tentative front five of the 4th—Schreiner and Ritinski at ends, Herwig at center,* and Semple and Bennett at tackle—averaged six foot one and 220 pounds, enormous for a line back then. The 4th was *still* the underdog, but it had a strategy with McLaughry's fingerprints all over it, to shuttle three different teams in and out during the game to keep the players fresh and defeat the heat and humidity that presumably could wear down the older players from the 29th. It was a risky strategy: Tuss, of course, had made his career doing exactly the opposite by playing the same eleven "iron men" in almost three consecutive games. His theory was: play your best guys until they drop.

The tentative starting backfield for the 29th featured Butkovich at fullback, Bergman and Bud Seelinger from Wisconsin at halfback, and Callen at quarterback. The tentative starters on the offense line were Murphy and Maliszewski at ends, Neff and Genis at tackle, and center to be a game day decision. They averaged about 6 feet and 195 pounds, smaller than the 4th, but all of them had started in college: at Notre Dame (2), Purdue,

---

* Herwig was one of the coaches of the 4th Regiment, but as the game progressed he could not help himself and created havoc on the field.

and Duquesne. What was most remarkable in the 29th was its depth. Five of the players who did not make the starting lineup had been major college starters.

The Las Vegas consensus: the 29th should blow out the 4th.

The day before the "big game," as McLaughry called it, he wrote to his parents and said with typical understatement, "It'll probably be the biggest sports event that has ever taken place out here." As far as anyone knew, there had never been an organized sports event played "out here."

It was a *big game*, not simply because of bragging rights but because of the betting: officers from the 4th alone had collectively put $3,000 on the outcome. Before the game, enlisted men wagered a day's pay, a week's pay, a month's pay. The likely presence of beer probably had a significant influence.

In his letter home, McLaughry sounded confident but not cocky. He had once again drawn up most of the plays, using as examples what Tuss had run at Brown. Actually, he sounded excited; a part of his life he'd presumed was long past was once again at hand. From start to finish the game would take about two hours. That was nothing compared to the purgatory of waiting day after day and knowing that the next campaign would be his third and that was when the luck ran out. But it was two hours not to think about it, not to think about anything besides playing football and hoping that Brennan would show off his rocket arm and Herwig would still be an All-American monster despite not having played competitively for seven years. As for himself, he felt in the best shape of his life except for getting a little winded, up to his playing weight of 200 pounds.

"It ought to be quite a brawl."

At least fifteen hundred marines ringed the Pritchard Field parade ground. The game had the atmosphere of a big-time college contest, with pregame starting player introductions over a loudspeaker system, the live broadcast on the Mosquito Network, regulation fifteen-minute quarters, two officials. As the home team, the 29th had removed as many shards of coral as possible from the parade ground, but many still remained and would become a significant hazard.

But it was a game, a *real* football game in 1944, the day before Christmas, one that got stateside publicity and mentions in the *Chicago Tribune*, *Wisconsin State Journal*, and *Salt Lake Tribune*. The broadcaster Ted Husing, the father of the play-by-play, talked about it on his nationally syndicated radio show on CBS.

The crowd was boisterous, but there was an under-current of tension because of the betting. There were no bleachers; the only ones who got to sit were the two regimental commanders and Major General Lemuel Shepherd, the commanding officer of the 6th Marine Division.

Melvin Heckt watched from the sidelines, amazed by the pomp of it all: the marching bands, the regimental commanders shaking hands at midfield before the game, everybody standing at attention before General Shepherd sat down. It was like Army v. Navy, only it was marines v. marines, and these guys were a lot tougher. PFC Neal McCallum of Fox Company of the 29th Regiment could tell from the atmosphere how starved the marines on Shit Island were for some respite from the monotony.

Many of the details of the game have been lost after nearly eighty years, but what was supposed to be two-handed touch devolved into tackling or at least semi-tackling. It got rough and a little nasty. Spicer claimed it was the roughest game in which he had ever played. Genis likened it to an alley fight back home in Chicago, Pickarts went wobbly and woozy with stars. Castignola had to have stitches. Cerise thought they were crazy. Schreiner hurt his arm. McLaughry said the hitting and hard playing were as rough as he had ever seen without being dirty. His dungarees were torn all to hell in no time. The players' knees and elbows were a bloody mess from cuts inflicted by the coral on the field that in some cases later blew into infections even with proper first aid. The game seesawed back and forth with near touchdowns and field goals, but nobody could score.

The final was 0–0—a perfect score really, no winners or losers.

Just the two hours of life that turned into death several months later when more than a dozen of the sixty-five who played were killed at Okinawa.

There was a Christmas Eve service after the Mosquito Bowl. A program was printed, featuring on the front an illustration by Lieutenant Thompson of a kneeling marine, his dog tags looped around his neck, laying down his rifle and pack and helmet at the foot of Mary and the baby Jesus. "The savior is born," Thompson had written at the bottom. You did not have to be religious to be moved by it. Forsythe the chaplain had written what appeared to be a letter with a serviceman's reflection on the meaning of Christmas:

What our loved ones have always done before, I see them doing again for Christmas. The decorated tree is by the window, the light is in the door. Perhaps some may even have the starry bulbs on the evergreen lawn. It makes us glad to know that you at home can enjoy a measure of Christmas spirit in peace and beauty. The greetings we have all read, the boxes of good things we have opened have also helped to bring Christmas to this Island of Palms. Not only for tonight but for the New Year before us, do we hope that the love that asks, and gives, and prays will help to sustain us all our days.

A Christmas feast followed the next day; then it was back to training until New Year's Eve. McLaughry, sufficiently recovered from a charley horse sustained during the game, knew that the night would be memorable. The officers' club bar was scheduled to open from 2:30 p.m. until 5:30 p.m., then reopen from 10:00 p.m. until 2:00 a.m. The enlisted men had saved up ample amounts of Stump Juice, Raisin Jack, and Sick Bay Alky, along with issued beer and stateside whiskey.

"Should be a wild night."

It was the last New Year's Eve that 1,622 members of the 6th Division and corpsmen would ever have.

Part Three

24
Bound for Hell

The 6th Marine Division left Guadalcanal for the planned invasion of Okinawa somewhere around March 15th of 1944. McLaughry and Schreiner were on board the *Marvin McIntyre*, Butkovich on the *Clay*, Murphy on the *George Clymer*. Combat transports were not known for their spas, heated rock massages, and reminders to hydrate. But they were a cushy joy compared to Bauman's mode of transportation, LST 794. The acronym stood for Landing Ship, Tank: those confined had another name for it, Large Slow Target.

The men had left Guadalcanal with quartets crooning a parody of "Goodbye Mama (I'm Off to Yokohama)" that they called "Goodbye Mama (I'm Off to Okinawa)." They loafed, played poker, and read and wrote letters on board even though there was a temporary ban on outgoing mail. There were movies, boxing matches, good food, and fresh water.

It was en route that the enlisted men were finally filled in on where they were going after the months of training and waiting around. The briefings included maps, relief models, and lectures on enemy dispositions, health conditions, the native population, weather, and the dreaded habu snake, which scared the living shit out of most everybody to the degree that some preferred death by enemy to death by snakebite. They handed out casualty lists from the Battle of Iwo Jima, which had taken place roughly a month earlier, the only battle in which there had been more US casualties than Japanese killed. Neal McCallum looked at the lists and wondered what he had gotten into. He had wanted an adventure far from the street corners of Candor, North Carolina, and so had joined the marines. He now realized that there was probably a much better way to have an adventure.

Okinawa was the largest island in the Ryukyu group, sixty miles long north to south and between two and eighteen miles wide. It had a significant civilian population of roughly 450,000, most of whom were farmers cultivating tiny plots of sugarcane, sweet potatoes, rice, and soybeans. It was four thousand miles away from Pearl Harbor but only 476 nautical miles from the home islands of Japan. It was actually a protectorate of Japan, which implied that the islanders would have allegiance to that country, but the Japanese government treated the Okinawans as subhuman, as it did everyone else in the region who wasn't Japanese. Natives of the island were used in servitude and as construction laborers, military conscripts, and teenage nurses. Women forced into sex slavery as comfort women were housed in decrepit shacks where snaking lines of filthy Japanese soldiers in slovenly uniforms waited their turn.

With its natural anchorages and airfields, Okinawa would serve as the perfect launching point for the final invasion of the war, the siege of the Japanese homeland. For the Japanese, the goal would be to string out the battle as long as possible to gain time to prepare for the defense of Kyushu, the southernmost homeland island, and the other main Japanese islands, and to increase the opportunities for the kamikaze suicide planes to try to destroy the US fleet. They were also convinced—yet another criminal delusion—that the Americans would drop their demand for unconditional surrender and agree to a conditional one if enough US troops were killed. The horrific casualties at Okinawa resulted in the complete opposite, the dropping of the atom bombs.

————————

The 6th Division convoy arrived at the atoll of Ulithi on March 25th of 1945 for a couple of days of rest and relaxation before the final leg to Okinawa. The men descended to the beautifully named island of Mogmog, which looked like a place named Mogmog should, replete with ball fields, beer gardens, a tavern, and an ice cream barge, missing only Dorothy Lamour dressed as a mermaid. The allotment was two beers each for enlisted men and unlimited for officers, so McLaughry made sure that his boys got several extra cases. They played baseball and horseshoes and ate fried chicken and ham sandwiches and topped it all off with thoroughly enjoyable fights with the navy.

Some marines stayed on board ship to listen to a live jazz band made up of other marines. Others went for the beer onshore and got so stinking drunk they could not make it up the landing nets to get back on board ship. The captain ordered the ladder to be lowered so that nobody would fall into the ocean. The next day he got onto the loudspeaker and said he had never seen such a spectacle in his life and Company I should be ashamed of itself. Nobody gave a shit; they were far too hungover to comprehend anything remotely verbal.

Plus, he was navy.

Fuck you.

John and Tuss McLaughry

McLaughry leading the Brown University
commencement, 1940

McLaughry

Dave Schreiner

Schreiner in uniform, November 1943

Schreiner and his fiancée, Odette Hendrickson, at Quantico with another officer and his date

Odette and Schreiner at Thanksgiving, 1943

Odette in the WAVES

Roses to Odette from Schreiner on the
first anniversary of their engagement

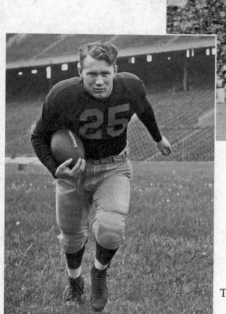

Schreiner making a catch

Tony Butkovich

Butkovich (*third from left*) with other marine football players as part of a public relations campaign

George Murphy

Murphy with Notre Dame coach Frank Leahy

Bob and Frank Bauman playing horseshoes

Frank, Bertha, and Bob Bauman

Bauman on Guadalcanal

McLaughry on Guadalcanal

The handshake: Schreiner and
Butkovich at the Mosquito Bowl

FOOTBALL CLASSIC!
29th MARINES vs. 4th MARINES
- AT PRICHARD FIELD -
Sunday, 24 December 1944 at 1400

SCHEDULE OF EVENTS

1330–1400   -   Music by Regimental Bands.

1400   -   Reception of Major General Lemuel C. SHEPHERD, USMC,
Commanding General, Sixth Marine Division. Honors by
29th Marines Band.

1405   -   Colonel Victor F. BLEASDALE, USMC, Commanding, 29th
Marines, and Colonel Alan SHAPLEY, USMC, Commanding,
4th Marines, meet in center of gridiron and exchange
greetings.

1415   -   Kick-off.

Half   -   (1) Music and ceremony by 4th Marines Band.
(2) General SHEPHERD changes to opposite side of
field.
(3) Music and ceremony by 29th Marines Band and
29th Marines Drum and Bugle Corps.

End of Game   -   Band Music.

* * * * * * * * *

The Mosquito Bowl program

Marines landing at Tarawa

The beach after the invasion of Okinawa

Major General Lemuel C. Shepherd, Jr. (*left*), and General Simon Bolivar Buckner, Jr. (*right*), on Okinawa

Lieutenant General Mitsuru Ushijima

Marines on Okinawa

They left Ulithi on March 27 for the final four-day journey to Okinawa. They took showers, water never feeling more glorious, as it would be the last shower for a while, whether the water was gritty with salt or not. Some worried about getting down the landing net with all that gear on their back and a gas mask and rifle and falling into the ocean, where they could barely swim even when they weren't carrying anything. Others thought about how they could get out of all of it; two marines agreed to shoot each other and claim it had been enemy fire.

Schreiner wrote to his parents. He said he knew that people back home in the States were upset over the casualties at Iwo Jima but told his parents it had been "the wrong steer," a small island in which a slugging match had been unavoidable. He had gotten his hair cut so short that he looked "like a real German Heine." But he thought the look was neat, and he didn't have to bother with it. He had been playing a lot of bridge and couldn't help brag that he and his partner had made "3 little slams, two of them in a row!" He ended the letter with this:

I have a little copy of the New Testament which I've been looking thru lately.

Last night I read Christ's sermon on the
mount. The Bible certainly gives one
faith in everything—knowing that with
faith everything is bound to come out al-
right.

Much love to a couple of grand people—
Dave

He also wrote a lengthy letter to Odette:

I've been dreaming of you at night and
last night you talked to me in your apartment and your voice was just as natural
as it could be. It made me very lonesome
for you.

He told her he carried with him the Saint Christopher medal she had given him. McLaughry thought
about how he would take care of the weaponry under
his control. Murphy couldn't help but think about the
baby daughter he had never seen, born in South Bend
the day before he had shipped overseas from the West
Coast. Butkovich still had the pen pal relationship with
Tom Milligan from Indiana: he knew that Tom would

continue to write to him and that it might be hard to respond. Bauman most likely dreamed of beer.

They had all placed their fate at Okinawa into the hands of a general previously consigned to the gulag of the Aleutians, the most thankless assignment in the Pacific war, who, for all his baths in the icy cold water of the Alaska territory, testing sleeping bags in sixty-below temperatures and all the other acts of being a military macho man, lacked the attribute that mattered the most in a battle of this magnitude with nearly two hundred thousand army and marine ground forces under his command, the largest ever assembled in the Pacific: combat experience.

25
Buckner

His name was Simon Bolivar Buckner, Jr., the longest mouthful of a name in the army and all that it implied.* His father was Simon Bolivar Buckner, named after Simón Bolívar, the Venezuelan revolutionary known as "El Libertador," who had led several South American countries to independence from Spanish rule. Simon Bolivar Buckner had been a Confederate general in the Civil War who, despite unconditionally surrendering to General Ulysses S. Grant in 1862 at Fort Donelson, had become a hero of the South. He had gone on to become governor of Kentucky and later a vice presidential candidate on

_____

* Some would argue that army General Lucian King Truscott, Jr., was just as much of a mouthful.

BUCKNER · 341

the Gold Democrat ticket in 1896. The Confederacy
was still alive and well after the Civil War, Buckner
cheered by twenty thousand attendees at the convention of the United Confederate Veterans association
in 1905 in Louisville. He became the oldest surviving
lieutenant of the Civil War, the South's greatest gentleman soldier. His shadow was mammoth. He was
sixty-three and in his second marriage when his son
was born, making him more of a grandfather figure
than a father.

The son liked to portray himself as a barefoot urchin
in the Kentucky bluegrass. But he grew up on the an-
cestral estate of Glen Lily, a pilgrimage site where surviving members of the Confederacy visited his father. He
accompanied his father on the campaign trail and to the
Gold Democrats' nominating convention. The family
went on a grand tour of Europe together. The father
made a direct appeal to President Theodore Roosevelt to
recommend the son for appointment to West Point, and
Roosevelt quickly agreed. When the son was stationed
in the Philippines as a young man, the father shipped
him a twenty-five-foot motor launch so he could tour
the islands in style. It was an entitled life that continued as the son grew older: there was a live-in maid for
his family while he was an instructor at the Army War

College, and his wife, Adele, was from southern aristocracy and frequently graced the society pages of the *Washington Post.*

Buckner Jr. was known for his wit and grandiloquent writing style and leadership skills at West Point. He was average in terms of performance, 58th in order of general merit out of 108, near the bottom in ordinance and gunnery (94th) and in the lower half in drill regulations (68th) but in the top fifth in military efficiency (13th), soldiery deportment and discipline (20th), and military engineering (19th). He excelled in English and military hygiene but was poor in mathematics and philosophy. He played football but was a substitute on the substitute team, in other words fourth string. He did far better in wrestling and was on the board of the governors of the First Class Club.

His ensuing military career up until World War II was hardly bound for glory. He was promoted to captain during World War I but did not see combat. He was known largely as an instructor and expert in the crucial area of tactics, which became paramount in the Pacific war when the supply line sometimes stretched to six thousand miles. He returned to West Point and ultimately became the commandant of cadets, banning aftershave on the grounds that men were supposed to smell like men based on his own definition, the bouquet of body odor.

He was fond of taking plebes on thirty-mile hikes and then carrying the gear of several who collapsed. While at the military academy, he created a drink recipe that would ultimately become an enduring legacy, still written about decades after his death.

On June 12th of 1935, President Franklin D. Roosevelt went to West Point to give the graduation address, accompanied by his then army chief of staff, Douglas MacArthur. West Point superintendent Major General William D. Connor, knowing that FDR enjoyed a good cocktail, decided that Buckner should use his Kentucky expertise to make mint juleps, a singular skill that no one else in the military could match. The results were so successful that FDR asked for a second one, although the waiter serving him thought he should be cut off. MacArthur, according to legend, knew his limits and had only one, with the explanation "I think I will stop now while I still know who is President."

Two years later, General Connor, who was sponsoring a luncheon for the fortieth reunion of the class of 1897, wrote to Buckner that "the fame of the mint juleps that you served the day The President was with us has travelled far and wide." Buckner wrote back that the mint julep "is not the product of a FORMULA. It is a CEREMONY and must be performed by a gentleman possessing a true sense of the artistic. . . . It is a rite that must not be entrusted to a novice, a statistician, nor a Yankee. It is a heritage of the old South, an emblem of hospitality."

He then delineated no fewer than eleven steps:

1. Go to a spring where cool, crystal-clear water bubbles from under a bank of dew-washed ferns . . .

2. Follow the stream through its banks of green moss and wildflowers until it broadens and trickles through beds of mint growing in aromatic profusion and waving softly in the summer breezes. Gather the sweetest and tenderest shoots and gently carry them home.

3. Go to the sideboard and select a decanter of Kentucky Bourbon, distilled by a master hand, mellowed with age yet still vigorous and inspiring . . .

4. In a canvas bag, pound twice as much ice as you think you will need. Make it fine as snow keep it dry and do not allow it to degenerate into slush.

5. Into each goblet, put a slightly heaping tea-spoonful of granulated sugar, barely cover this with spring water, and slightly bruise one mint leaf into this, leaving the spoon in the goblet.

6. Then pour elixir from the decanter until the goblets are about one-fourth full.

7. Fill the goblets with snowy ice, sprinkling in a small amount of sugar as you fill.

8. Wipe the outsides of the goblets dry and em-bellish copiously with mint.

9. By proper manipulation of the spoon, the in-gredients are circulated and blended until Nature, wishing to take a further hand and add another of its beautiful phenomena, en-crusts the whole in a glittering coat of white frost. Thus harmoniously blended by the deft touches of a skilled hand, you have a beverage eminently appropriate for honorable men and beautiful women.

10. When all is ready, assemble your guests on the porch or in the garden, where the aroma of the

juleps will rise Heavenward and make the birds sing.

11. Propose a worthy toast, raise the goblet to your lips, bury your nose in the mint, inhale a deep breath of its fragrance, and sip the nectar of the gods.

Never has a drink sounded so beautiful, infused with so many of the qualities Buckner cared about in his life: tradition, ritual, chivalry; the sublimity of nature; vocabulary, wit, and a strong whiff of grandiose bullshit.

II

Buckner was still a colonel at the age of fifty-four, the suspicion he fought too much with generals to be promoted. He was assigned to Alaska in 1940 after the Joint Chiefs of Staff felt it necessary to strengthen the US defenses there, given the possible outbreak of war and the territory's proximity to Japan. Buckner distinguished himself over the next three years as a genius of logistics. He showed a remarkable capacity to get facilities built: barracks, landing strips. Under his watch the army presence went from 2,300 to 94,000 men as the United States became determined, once the war began, to oust the Japanese from their toehold on the Aleutian Islands, which jutted out west of Alaska. They were the shortest distance from US territory to Japan, roughly 1,400 miles as opposed to 3,350 from Pearl Harbor, giving the islands for a moment a strategic significance. Buckner reveled in hardship, teaching himself to read without glasses by squinting, sleeping on a cot with a single sheet as a covering, taking a morning shower of melted Alaskan ice. While he was stationed there, he made a trip to Washington to give a personal update to FDR, always with friends in high places because of his father.

In one of the all-too-typical banishments of Blacks in the war, more than three thousand soldiers, many of them from small southern towns, were sent into the subzero weather of Alaska without proper equipment to help build the Alcan highway. Buckner did not want them. "The very high wages offered to unskilled labor here would attract a large number of them and cause them to remain and settle after the war with the natural result that they would interbreed with the Indians and the Eskimos and produce an astonishingly objectionable race of mongrels which would be a problem here from now on," he wrote in a letter to Brigadier General Clarence Sturdevant, who was in charge of the highway project for the Army Corps of Engineers. If

Black troops did come to work in the ports, Buckner wanted them "kept far enough from the settlements and kept busy and then sent home as soon as possible." Similarly, Buckner barred Aleut and Inuit women from service clubs until Alaska Territory governor Ernest Gruening complained to FDR.

Buckner's penchant for condescending doggerel almost got him recalled. As was typical of the US military during the Pacific war, there was no single commander in Alaska. Instead, the territory was divided between the army and the navy, with neither having the authority for ultimate decision-making. Buckner commanded the ground forces. Rear Admiral Robert A. Theobald commanded the navy and naval air forces. Buckner considered Theobald too cautious and composed a poem mocking him that he read out loud at a meeting of top officers that included Theobald. In the ten commandments of the military, number one was never to criticize a senior commander of the opposing service publicly; in this case the sin was all the more egregious because Buckner had virtually been ordered to get along with Theobald. The admiral was understandably incensed, and he wasn't the only top commander to find Buckner insufferable during his career. Army Chief of Staff Marshall felt that Buckner should be recalled until he was talked out of it, perhaps because they shared the bond of having attended the Virginia Military Institute.*

Ultimately the strategic importance of the Aleutians faded. The weather was miserable, a 112-mile-per-hour wind once blowing Buckner's headquarters building down when he wasn't there. In one of the great embarrassments of the war, the Americans attacked the island of Kiska in 1943 with thirty-four thousand troops only to discover that the Japanese had left the island without detection. Buckner himself described it as a "great big, juicy, expensive mistake." The eminent historian Samuel Eliot Morison, whose fifteen-volume account of naval operations during the war is considered one of the great military histories of all time, called the Aleutians the "Theater of Military Frustration," in which nothing of any appreciable value during the Pacific war was achieved, and where being stationed was regarded as "little better than penal servitude."

The only one who definitely seemed to enjoy it was Buckner, whose enthusiasm, vigor, and ability to get things done helped put him in charge of organizing the Tenth Army, which would become the massive Okinawa landing force.

---

* Marshall had graduated from there in 1901. Buckner had gone there for two years, from 1902 to 1904, until he reached the minimum age of eighteen to attend West Point.

If combat experience was a necessary criterion—and it is mind-boggling to think it would not have been, given the scope of the Okinawa campaign and the increasing ingenuity of the Japanese—Buckner was a poor choice for a leader. But that obviously was not the criterion. He was measured by other criteria that often counted for more: he had gone to West Point while George S. Patton was there, he was known to two presidents, the lore of his father connected him to Ulysses S. Grant and Robert E. Lee, and he was a member in good standing in the service academy back-scratcher network.

He was a beneficiary of the interservice rivalry infighting among the three services (four if the army air corps is counted as a separate entity) that was rife during the Pacific war, in which grown men acted like feudal warlords, engaging in pettiness, turf protectionism, and discredit campaigns by running to their favored organs of Henry R. Luce's *Time* and *Life* magazines (pro-marine) or the Hearst papers (pro-army and pro-MacArthur). The army hated the navy. The navy hated the army. Everybody hated the marines. The marines hated everybody else—not all the time but too much of the time, and too many lives were jeopardized and lost as a result.

There was no supreme commander in the Pacific,

although everyone agreed in principle that there should be. Instead, in an effort to mollify the army and the navy, an inherently unworkable structure was put into place in March of 1942, splitting the Pacific zone so that MacArthur was made commander in chief of the Southwest Pacific Area and Nimitz was in charge of virtually all of the remainder. The reason for a lack of unified command "was evident," wrote the World War II historian Louis Morton.

> There was no available candidate who would be acceptable to everyone concerned. The outstanding officer in the Pacific was General MacArthur, but he did not have the confidence of the Navy. Certainly the Navy would never have entrusted the fleet to MacArthur, or to any other Army officer. Admiral Chester W. Nimitz, the chief naval candidate for the post, had not yet acquired the popularity and prestige he later enjoyed, and he was, moreover, considerably junior to MacArthur.

At one point Brigadier General St. Clair Streett suggested that the only way to achieve unified command would be to remove MacArthur and buy him off with the ambassadorship to the Soviet Union. MacArthur spent much of the war criticizing the navy leadership and arguing through the conduit of the Hearst papers that he should be placed in command of the entire Pacific Theater. More than just a power play, it was something he truly believed, and he argued the point well:

> Of all the faulty decisions of the war perhaps the most unexplainable one was the failure to unify the command in the Pacific. The principle involved is perhaps the most fundamental one in the doctrine and tradition of command. . . . The failure to do so in the Pacific cannot be defended in logic, in theory or even in common sense. Other motives must be ascribed. It resulted in divided effort, the waste of diffusion and duplication of force and the consequent extension of the war with added casualties and cost.

Marshall was often placed into the role of referee, trying to get commanders to work with one another in the common goal of winning the war as quickly as possible. It seemed inarguable and elemental, except to the men involved, for whom the idea of accommodation could be considered a fatal leadership weakness.

The presence of the marines only made the situation more volatile and fractious. The navy and the marines got off to a terrible start at Guadalcanal in 1942. The marines believed that the navy had left them high and dry without sufficient supplies, rations, or ammo, pointing to the actions of Admiral Frank Fletcher in pulling out the three carriers under his command to refuel them.* The marines had a point; they had been left high and dry. The navy had a point; the longer its ships waited around, the greater chance that they would be attacked by the Japanese. The two services worked relatively well together after Guadalcanal.

Not so with the army.

It wasn't just mere name-calling.

The marines thought the army strategy of softening up the enemy with extensive artillery bombardment was both slow and excessively cautious. The army felt that the marine command was reckless and got men killed unnecessarily.

The army also resented the credit the marines received in the Pacific, in part the result of an ingenious public relations strategy in which working newspaper reporters were recruited into the marines, went through

---

* As with everything else military-related, there are differing versions. John B. Lundstrom offered a sympathetic treatment of Fletcher's decision in an article in the September 1992 issue of *Naval History* magazine.

basic training, and then embedded as combat correspondents with great reportorial latitude. The marines
believed in giving broad access to reporters and went
out of their way to make sure that copy passed quickly
through censors and film footage was promptly sent
back to the States. They knew that reporters, ever appreciative of not being treated like pond scum, would,
as a matter of human nature, reflect that gratitude in
more favorable coverage. They did not try to hide the
carnage: war was brutal. They wanted the public to
know what was happening, most famously in allowing
marine cameramen to take footage of Tarawa, including the bodies of dead marines in the water.*

The historian Morton believed that true unity of
command was achieved only on the battlefield, when
life and death were at stake. It was then that the jealou-
sies and misplaced pride were put away. But that wasn't
always true.

At the Battle of Peleliu in September of 1944, Major
General William H. Rupertus, the commander of the
1st Marine Division, repeatedly declined reinforcements from an available army regiment because he

---

* The footage was taken by Marine Staff Sergeant Norman T.
Hatch. Risking his life, Hatch used a hand-cranked 35 mm Bell &
Howell camera. The footage was made into an eighteen-minute documentary titled *With the Marines at Tarawa* that won the 1945 Academy Award for Best Documentary (Short Subject).

had a low opinion of their combat skill. Instead, he reportedly allowed his division's 1st Marine Regiment to suffer high casualties before he was overruled and the regiment was replaced by an army infantry regiment. Lives hung on his decision: the 1st Marine Regiment alone suffered 1,672 casualties, including a shocking casualty rate of 71 percent in its hardest-hit battalion. Rupertus should have been replaced. He had severely fractured his ankle in a training exercise two weeks before the invasion and was determined to hide the injury by staying in his headquarters virtually the entire time, barking out increasingly irrational orders over the phone until he reportedly cupped his head in his hands and seemingly gave up. He was quietly shunted aside to become the commandant of the Marine Corps Schools in Quantico, Virginia. He died of a heart attack a few months later in March of 1945 at the age of fifty-five.

In the Saipan campaign the previous June, Marine Lieutenant General Holland Smith, fed up with what he perceived was the slowness of the problematic 27th Infantry Division, had relieved its commander, Army Major General Ralph Smith. That had led to a media shitstorm known as "Smith versus Smith," the Hearst newspapers pounding on Holland Smith and the marines for perceived recklessness and the brilliant war

correspondent Robert Sherrod, in a rare moment of ir-
responsibility, using a marine source to claim in *Time*
magazine that the 27th had been cowardly. Nobody
had been cowardly. But the leaders of the 27th were
woefully flawed.

An army board of inquiry chaired by none other
than Buckner himself concluded that Holland Smith
had acted within his authority to relieve Ralph Smith
but had had no grounds to do so, given the facts.

Given his prior experience on the battlefield, Holland
Smith should have been the commander of the ground
forces at Okinawa. He *was* the father of the amphibious assault doctrine. But it was never going to happen
in light of Smith v. Smith. Lieutenant General Robert
C. Richardson, Jr., the commander of army forces in
the Pacific, told Holland Smith that the marines were
incapable of leading troops of any significant size and
called the corps a "bunch of beach runners." Holland
Smith was later kicked upstairs to a job that kept him
off the battlefield, making Buckner the clear winner.
His handling of the Smith v. Smith controversy, as the
chairman of the inquiry board, apparently convinced
Nimitz that Buckner could lead a combined ground
operation without there being constant fighting among
the services. Buckner's complete lack of combat expe-

rience did not seem to bother him at all, despite the massive size of the assault forces at Okinawa.

Buckner's role as peacemaker became an important qualification, maybe enough to overcome his inflexibility in a campaign that would go on for double the predicted number of forty days.* There is no doubt that he was badly and embarrassingly outmaneuvered by a Japanese defense that was virtually hidden. At one point or another his tactics were questioned by some of the best combat minds of the Pacific war: Nimitz, MacArthur, Turner, Marine Commandant Alexander A. Vandegrift, the commander of the army ground forces, General Joseph W. "Vinegar Joe" Stilwell, 6th Marine Division Commander Shepherd, and Army Major General Andrew D. Bruce. Nimitz, the most senior among them and the most important, was not one to question the decisions of the commanders under him. He was the opposite, keeping his ego in check when volcanoes exploded. But less than a month into the Okinawa campaign, he publicly threatened to replace Buckner. The style of the Japanese defense had given Buckner a formidable task, one so difficult that MacArthur, who wanted to be everywhere at all times

---

* This is based on a forty-day supply of ammunition on Okinawa, before more had to be shipped in.

doing everything but ever mindful of bad publicity, was glad he wasn't there. He had known that there would be significant casualties. But Buckner was still painfully slow and cautious, matched only by his stubbornness and penchant for oration.

In his diary entry for March 31st of 1945, on the eve of the Battle of Okinawa, Buckner wrote in his diary, "Tomorrow is Easter Sunday, my father's birthday and the day of my first battle. I hope that I shall be able to look back upon it with the same degree of enthusiasm with which I anticipate it."

He forgot to mention that it would also be April Fool's Day.

26
April Fool

The call to the armada waiting offshore, the "Typhoon of Steel," as the Japanese called it as they watched mesmerized through their binoculars from higher ground, came at 0406 on April 1st of 1945 from Admiral Richmond Kelly Turner:

Land the landing force!

It was four hours and twenty-four minutes before the first wave of marines was scheduled to land: H-hour.

Men were already up, fastidiously fiddling to make sure that all their equipment was in perfect condition, even though they knew it was: the compulsive cleaning of the innards of the M1 rifle with a small brush, the oiling of the machine gun, the sharpening of the KA-BAR knife. McLaughry had spent the night working on preparations for unloading and just before dawn supervised the swinging of the M7 tanks from the attack transport into a landing craft known as the Landing Craft, Mechanized, or LCM.* The fit was tight, but the placid sea cooperated, so there wasn't a lot of rocking. Debts were settled, such as "I want to pay you back the pack of cigarettes before I get killed." There was the traditional steak-and-eggs breakfast before battle for at least some of the marines. The medical surgeons understood the tradition but weren't so crazy about the prospect of operating on men with abdominal wounds and finding undigested meat inside their stomachs. The thick spew of fumes from the revving up of the vehicles inside the ship holds made some men sick before they even hit the water.

Bill Pierce, with the weapons company of the 29th Regiment that had played in the Mosquito Bowl, attended Mass and took Communion as he and others waited for the order.

Away all boats!

Ammo was handed out, the men told to take as much as they wanted. Pierce carried an M1 rifle, so he took only one bandolier containing roughly ten clips of preloaded ammo. There were no grenades because too

---

* Roughly fifty feet in length, it could carry eighty troops or one tank. There were several different models.

many accidents could happen on the way to the beach and they could presumably get all they wanted once ashore. There was the useless gas mask, which the men resented because it meant one more piece of equipment, and they threw it away at the first opportunity. They already had about sixty pounds of equipment to carry.

The weapons company was called over the speaker system of the ship. It was their turn. A chill went through Pierce. His mouth was already dry. Everyone just looked at one another. Pierce watched as a crane swung the 37 mm gun over the rail to the landing craft below. He and the others were given an additional belt containing two carbon dioxide cylinders that could be inflated into a flotation device if anyone fell into the water while using the rope ladder hanging over the side of the ship. Of course there was no way to test if the cylinders actually worked, so Pierce hoped that everyone knew how to swim, which some did not.

Jim White, a rifleman with Company G of the 29th, thought about fear. He had grown up in old houses in Oklahoma that expanded with heat and contracted with cold. They had creaked and made unexplained groans, and sometimes he had been afraid to go into the darkened rooms upstairs. The fear had peaked and then gone away. Over time it got easier to bear. But the fear he felt in combat was different and far more intense, rising and falling but always there when he went to bed at night and got up in the morning, an underlying apprehension no matter how much laughter and jokes and downtime there might be. He knew the fear would only multiply when he was moving forward on attack out into the open, totally exposed, with no foxhole to take along with him, so *fucking* naked, feeling like the only person on the face of the earth with all those blasts of smoke and fire and shrapnel that had somehow not already obliterated him or made him stark raving crazy because you should be stark raving crazy, saved by the adrenaline rush that kept you moving. He would realize that his dread of enemy weaponry was a measure of its impersonality. He feared bullets, but there was something expected about them, *they were aiming at him*. Air bursts from shells were tracked mostly by sound, the *sound* of knowing that something is coming but not knowing when it was coming, where it was coming from, and who specifically it was coming for. It was the land mines that he feared the most, stepping on something concealed beneath the ground that, if you were lucky, killed you instantly or, if you were unlucky, severed off a leg and threw it into the air.

The weather was 75 degrees with clear to moderate skies, a breeze from the east-northeast, and negligible surf off the East China Sea. The transports were generally about ten thousand yards northwest of the assembly area, which in turn was about thirty-five hundred yards from the line of departure. After the troops were loaded onto LCMs, McLaughry and the others circled for about half an hour. The only enemy fire during the landing came from coastal artillery emplacements, and the shells landed far off the mark. Planes were everywhere, including one near McLaughry's transport, suddenly breaking out of the sky and flying low. Antiaircraft fire opened up from nearby transports. So did a .50-caliber machine gun from McLaughry's LCM. On the run to shore, the marines' LCMs were supervised by the navy and had navy gunners. The gunners were supervised by an ensign. They were keyed up, nervous, shooting at everything. The ensign on McLaughry's landing vehicle did not have a clue. McLaughry outranked him and had his men take over since they had been in combat.

It was too late. The plane was a friendly and went down. The marines squinted to see if the pilot had been able to escape. They saw no movement.

The ensign continued on a southerly course, convinced he was on the correct azimuth. Instead he headed the LCM right into the pathway of fire coming from ships farther offshore. McLaughry took over once again, ordering the ensign to reverse course. They arrived at the destination only a few minutes late.

II

Black smoke from the naval shelling filled the sky as Pierce and the others made their way to shore. They could not see.

Where's the beach? Are we in the right place? Will we be killed?

Their landing craft moved with greater speed, and they could see hundreds of smaller boats ahead of them near the shoreline. The boat ground to a halt. The navy coxswain lowered the front ramp. The men pushed the 37 mm gun off, only for it to land in almost three feet of water. The boat was hung up on coral about a hundred yards away from the beach. The coxswain, no dummy, had already gotten the fuck out of there. An LVT heading back to the unloading area after dropping off troops went to their aid. Somehow, among eight of them, they managed to push the gun back on board.

The bombardment by the naval guns had begun just before dawn at 0530, and eventually numbered 44,825 shells five inches or larger. It was the final crescendo of a Wagnerian opera of destruction that had begun on

March 25th of 1945 with harassing fire by fast-moving battleships. A day later, fire support ships had moved in for the destruction of weapons and fortifications both on Okinawa and on the island chain of Kerama Retto, about fifteen miles west of Okinawa in the Ryukyus.

The Japanese had decided not to defend Kerama Retto, leaving behind about 350 suicide boats, one-man craft with a top speed of fifteen to twenty knots propelled by a Chevrolet car engine and carrying two depth charges of 264 pounds each. They were to be armed by well-educated high school graduates in their teens, ordered to sail smoothly up to US ships before unloading the depth charges as close as a meter away. The operators had five seconds to escape before the igniters went off, meaning that there was no escape. There was consolation in the Japanese tradition of a posthumous promotion to second lieutenant and a slightly larger pension for the surviving family.

Roughly 560 civilians living on the islands, convinced by their government's relentless propaganda that the Americans would rape, rob, and murder them if they surrendered, had committed suicide, fathers killing their families before disemboweling themselves. On the largest island, army troops from the 77th Infantry Division heard screams and explosions in the night.

After the mass suicides by civilians on the cliffs of Saipan, no one was terribly surprised at Japanese soldiers driving innocents into a suicidal frenzy.

The preliminary bombardment had continued until April 1st; then there was the bombardment on the day of the landing, almost 45,000 shells and 33,000 rockets and 22,500 mortar rounds. The rockets dazzled, *pfft-pfft-pfft*, as they were automatically launched row by row, *pfft-pfft-pfft* as they shot out in thin arcs of light, *pfft-pfft-pfft* one after the other after the other.

General Buckner had awakened at 0430; he wrote in his diary that he had eaten hotcakes as a way of "getting fortified for a day of fighting." He watched from what he called "the fifty-yard line," in the command room on the flag deck of the *Eldorado*, satisfied with what he called "a magnificent spectacle." During the campaign he considered taking pictures, given that photography was a passionate hobby of his, but he thought it might not be appropriate when thousands of lives were at stake. Men prayed as the Roebling's LVTs,* which had changed the course of amphibious assault in the Pacific, took them to shore. There were more than a thousand

---

* Since the Roebling invention, there had been many iterations of the LVT and different models. They were not perfect and had been a disaster at Saipan.

of those craft, the line extending for eight miles. The Japanese, from high ground, continued to watch, still mesmerized but also calm, the binoculars focusing on a marine chomping on chewing gum—*gum!*

Some, such as Bob McGowan of How Company of the 29th, were convinced that they were going to die; others, such as Jim Whitaker of Fox Company, were convinced that they were going to live. It was so often the opposite; those who were pessimistic were often the ones who made it and those who scoffed at death the ones who did not. Some on the LVTs felt for the triggers of their rifles, only to feel the hand of the gunnery sergeant holding them back.

One marine played "Give My Regards to Broadway" on the harmonica to the singing accompaniment of several of his buddies. Another wondered how he would feel when he killed his first Japanese: shocked, vengeful, or simply as though he were doing a job on an assembly line.

The entire 4th Regiment, which included roughly twenty-five Mosquito Bowl players in addition to McLaughry and Schreiner and Bauman, was in the first wave scheduled to land on the western shore of Hagushi Bay on the west coast of Okinawa at 8:30 a.m. They loved their commander, Colonel Shapley, which not only gave them greater faith in themselves but the desire to fight for him. Back on Guadalcanal, Lieutenant Dick Baumhardt had once decked a sergeant who had constantly picked and pecked at him and had been told to report to Shapley at 0700 for disciplinary action. Shapley at the age of forty-two still looked like the halfback he had been at the Naval Academy, still in top shape. He had wanted to play in the Mosquito Bowl and could definitely have handled himself, but everyone would have been afraid to hit him and maybe hurt him, given his rank. Or maybe it was vice versa. He was the son of an admiral, which explained his officers' abundant liquor supply. He was a hero of Pearl Harbor, having been blown into the water by the huge explosions that had sunk the USS *Arizona* and still able to save the life of a marine who was near drowning.

Shapley was outside his tent, working the shit out of a punching bag. Baumhardt stood at attention under guard when Shapley handed down his disciplinary action: "Lieutenant, when you throw your goddamn right, keep your elbow in because you're dissipating too much of the blow. Now, if you have to hit him again, follow up with an equally good left. Dismissed."

Butkovich, Murphy, roughly thirty other players from the Mosquito Bowl, and the entire 29th Regiment were being held in reserve offshore. They did not share a similar love of their commander, Colonel

Victor F. Bleasdale, who at Guadalcanal had confined them to the brig for three days if they weren't buttoned up properly or did not cross the street of the encampment at the designated intersection. He was forty-nine years old and had served with great distinction in World War I, but that war was over and nobody shed a tear when he was replaced during the battle.

Butkovich had been switched into headquarters company of the 3rd Battalion of the 29th Regiment. Some felt that he had been transferred to gain some peace and quiet, headquarters being a little farther back from the front lines. He was affable and friendly, but it was hard enough mentally preparing for combat without being constantly asked if he was going to turn pro after the war. Given their football mania, the marines wanted a piece of Butkovich that he could not afford to give.

After an hour of shelling and air bombardment, Okinawa was obscured by dirt, dust, debris, and smoke. Those watching from the ships thought it must be impossible for anyone to have survived. But they were wrong, just as they had been wrong in past battles when they had said the exact same thing. The Japanese had learned to survive. As the war ground on, they had only gotten better at using terrain for protection against bombardment.

The 4th Regiment landed at 8:39 a.m., the 1st Battalion, including Schreiner and Bauman, on beaches two and three. So did the 22nd Regiment of the 6th Division at roughly the same time. The 1st Marine Division and two army divisions landed as well—close to sixty thousand men by the time the day was done.

Wading in off the surf, they braced for the worst.

April Fool.

III

Bewilderment, confusion, relief. The hope against hope that the Japanese had said to hell with it and decided instead to prepare for the invasion of their homeland and left Okinawa altogether. Jubilant cries of "Happy Easter!" Communications personnel laying down telephone wires without having to duck fire. Surgeons mentally prepared for months for horrific casualties standing around bored, smoking cigarettes. The mortar boys singing "Little Brown Jug." Several marines holding an Easter picnic. One flipping through a comic book. Another hoping to get a tan on the beach.

There was virtually not a speck of resistance from the Japanese except for a few mortar rounds and sporadic small fire. Nobody expected it, although strong intelligence and analysis of previous Japanese defenses should have predicted that the Japanese would now resort to a new and improved strategy. As far back as the campaign of Tarawa, roughly sixteen months earlier, they had begun to make effective use of concealed fortifications and emplacements. At Peleliu they had made great use of caves and tunnels and had taken every advantage of the island's rugged terrain to the point of making the marines virtually defenseless. At Iwo Jima the brilliant lieutenant general Tadamichi Kuribayashi had made even greater use of cave and tunnel warfare to hide troops and weaponry. He had made a careful strategic decision not to immediately oppose the landing of the marines but to wait until the beachhead was crowded with men and equipment. It should have been anticipated that the Japanese would go a step farther into total concealment and not defend the beaches, where they had no hope of withstanding the firepower of the US forces.

Buckner and his command knew that the Japanese would utilize the Okinawan terrain to its fullest. The command knew that the Japanese would use an elaborate network of underground caves impervious to bombardment, just as they had in the past. But they did not know the true extent of their defenses, and they couldn't let go of the stereotype of the Japanese as death-loving maniacs rather than shrewd defenders with admirable fire discipline. "The American commanders had made the mistake of believing that the Japanese had learned nothing in the course of the war," wrote senior marine officer Jon T. Hoffman, in an article for the *Marine Corps Gazette*. "Instead, the enemy was now skillfully conducting a defense in depth designed to minimize his exposure."

Intelligence about Okinawa was lacking, as it was throughout much of the Pacific war. Initial aerial photography had done a poor job of exposing enemy fortifications before the battle. Because the nearest Allied airfield was fourteen hundred miles away, only B-29s had sufficient range to reach it; the weather in the Ryukyus was so poor that only two of the nineteen days scheduled were suitable for photography. Carrier-based planes were also used, but there had always been a question of how well trained their pilots and navigators were in aerial photography or, for that matter, how much it interested them. The US military's initial invasion map of Okinawa had left large areas lacking topographical detail areas because of inadequate photo coverage.

Faulty intelligence had led to the great failing of drastically underestimating enemy troop strength. In January of 1945, the total number of Japanese troops on

Okinawa was estimated to be roughly 55,000, with the expectation that the number would increase to 66,000. The lack of resistance on the beaches seemed to confirm that there was a relatively small number of troops present. Nor did intelligence consider the Okinawans who had been conscripted to aid the Japanese forces—more than 20,000 of them. The actual troop strength of the Japanese thus was more than 100,000, a glaring underestimate of 34,000.

For all the months of planning, the Americans had no idea that the key objectives of Yontan and Kadena Airfields had been virtually abandoned except for dummy planes made of straw and fake antiaircraft guns made of bamboo poles in the hope of inducing wasteful bombing. They were unprepared for the Japanese strategic use of artillery on Okinawa, their best deployment of the war, in which they seemed to have every inch of the island registered for pinpoint targeting. The Americans knew by now that no amount of naval bombardment would be effective in penetrating caves, from which artillery concealed by steel doors was pushed out on railroad tracks and then pushed back in like a lethal jack-in-the-box. Massive naval and aerial bombardment did kill thousands of Japanese troops, restricted their movement, and destroyed essential lines of communication. All of that was vital to ultimate victory.

But the concealed emplacements, the ones that would kill Americans throughout the months that followed, went largely untouched.

Buckner's lack of war experience showed glaringly when the decision was later made to attack the island of Ie Shima, just west of Okinawa. Drawing on the embarrassing disaster of Kiska in the Aleutians, which the Japanese had evacuated before it was attacked, to the utter surprise of US forces, Buckner pointed to the photo intelligence on Ie Shima: it showed that the Japanese had dug trenches across the airfield on the island to deny immediate use of it to the Americans, just as they had on Kiska. He concluded from that that the enemy had left Ie Shima and suggested to Major General Bruce, the commander of the 77th Army Division, that an initial landing be made with just two companies to see if there were any Japanese left on the island.

Bruce responded quickly, "That plan would work out fine if there were only a few Japs on the island, but if they are just hiding there, and in a larger force, we could lose every man in the two companies. So General Buckner, if you are asking me what to do, I prefer to land not just a couple of companies, but two entire regimental combat teams."

Buckner's strategy would have been a disaster. There

were roughly *three thousand* Japanese on the island.*
Many of the Japanese were hiding in caves, which at
that point in the Okinawa campaign in mid-April was
the obvious enemy strategy.

Even when there was good intelligence, it was ignored.

Aerial photography had shown as many as *five
thousand* Japanese troops on Ie Shima, based on interpretation of aerial photos by naval officer Robert N.
Colwell, the chief of photo intelligence. Colwell was
prepared to give that information to Admiral Turner
at a meeting until Turner abruptly ended it, perhaps
because he felt that still more intelligence was needed
or because Buckner had just been one-upped and embarrassed by an officer serving underneath him.

It was simple: the success of the Battle of Okinawa
would hinge on the personal bravery of the marine,
army, and navy men who were there.

Like every other battle in the course of human
history.

When Buckner discovered that the Japanese had
elected not to defend the beaches, he concluded that his
counterpart, Lieutenant General Mitsuru Ushijima, the

---

* The legendary war correspondent Ernie Pyle was killed at Ie
Shima on April 18th of 1945.

commander of the Thirty-second Army of the Imperial Japanese Army, had made a grave tactical error. "Everything is going well and so far my opposing general has not displayed any noticeable degree of military brilliance. At least, he has not yet done [any] of the things that I hoped he would not think of," Buckner wrote to his wife, Adele. Except that neither he nor anyone else on the command staff had thought that the Japanese would not defend the beaches.

Ushijima, deferring to his brilliant senior staff officer Colonel Hiromichi Yahara, outfoxed Buckner at every turn. The Japanese had amassed concentric circles of defense in the southern part of the island that were unseen by the Americans when they landed. The strongest defensive position was known as the Shuri Line, which ran across the island and was named after the ancient Shuri Castle. Yahara knew it was only a matter of time before the Japanese troops would be destroyed by the Americans, but that was the point. He was trying to buy time, to conduct a battle of attrition in which the goal of killing as many US troops as possible could be carried out. The Americans would have to come to the Japanese, and the only way to do it on the ground would be through frontal assault into a catacomb of hills and caves.

The best way to get at the Japanese in the caves and

concealments was through what Buckner referred to as the "blowtorch and corkscrew" technique. Utilizing napalm, a so-called jellied incendiary was invented and configured for use not just at Okinawa with portable flamethrowers but with flame-throwing tanks.*

The spray of gasoline infused with napalm could travel three hundred feet from a tank, much farther than a portable flamethrower could throw it, and with uncanny accuracy. Because it stuck to the skin (imagine having jelly smeared all over your body, only it is burning at a temperature of 1,000 degrees Celsius), the instinctive method of rolling on the ground to put out flames became useless. If people used their hand to wipe the jellied gobs away, they got the gobs all over their hands. The tiniest speck caused excruciating third-degree burns. A larger amount caused fourth- and fifth-degree burns, which went through fat, muscle, and bone. Just as lethal as its flames, the napalm infusion sucked out oxygen in enclosed spaces

---

* Napalm was a collaborative discovery piloted by the Harvard chemist Louis Fieser in 1942. He had coined the word *napalm* using the beginning letters *nap*, from "napthenate," and *palm*, from "palmitate." He once said he had believed it would be used only on buildings and to get rid of crabgrass. Fieser later repudiated the use of napalm during the Vietnam War and removed any association with it from his official biography. Its use was officially banned by the US Army in 1977 on moral grounds.

that had been sealed shut and replaced it with toxic levels of carbon monoxide that poisoned their occupants to death. The Japanese were terrified of nothing except the flamethrowers. Over and over, the possibility of its use was the only thing that caused enemy soldiers to surrender.

US infantry accompanied the flame-throwing tanks at Okinawa, providing fire support and gaining positions at cave openings. Their use in the battle was unprecedented and enormously effective in getting at the caves. Because of the compound's jelly consistency, it could bounce off a wall and go around corners. Some people it hit were instantly burned to death. Others fled from caves in terror and were instantly picked off by infantry stationed above, what the Japanese referred to as the "horse-mounting" technique. Another favored American technique was known as "basting before baking": in the basting phase a portable flamethrower operator gave two shots of thickened gasoline to ensure that the target was "wetted down"; in the baking phase he fired a third shot to ignite the gasoline and envelop the target in fire.

Jellied incendiaries made of napalm and gasoline changed the Pacific war more than any other invention, which had come courtesy of Harvard University in a chemistry laboratory. Napalm bombs dropped on

Tokyo killed nearly ninety thousand people during two nights in March of 1945, the flames they caused rising thousands of feet high, and many people were killed when they jumped into Tokyo Bay, not knowing that the heat had caused it to boil. It was also used on nearly seventy other Japanese cities.

No combatant in World War II used the flame-thrower more than the United States, in particular in the Pacific war. Some felt that it was too barbarous and horrifying even for total war. President Roosevelt had banned the use of chemical warfare, but this *was* chemical warfare because of its poisoning impact. Military personnel and the Chemical Warfare Service argued that the deaths were mercy killings, far quicker than being shot or blasted by high explosives. They claimed it wasn't the burns that killed a person but the instantaneous systemic shock to the nervous respiratory systems in combination with the searing of the lungs and the carbon monoxide poisoning.

It was only late in the war that comprehensive studies were conducted in which pigs and dogs were anesthetized, fastened to an iron frame in a so-called conflagration room, and then burned to death with gasoline for subsequent autopsy. The studies showed that far from being an instantaneous mercy killing, death by an instrument such as a flamethrower could take several minutes as the body and internal organs were consumed by flames.

Marines and soldiers could sometimes hear screams from inside a cave after the jelly of flame had been sprayed, screams like they had never heard and would never hear again—except for the ones inside their heads for the rest of their lives.

IV

The distance from the beaches to Yontan Airfield was about a mile uphill. Ceremonial Okinawan burial tombs made of concrete, perfect for conversion into pillboxes, were empty. The edge of the airfield was seized by Schreiner and Bauman's 1st Battalion at 10:30 a.m. They went across *standing up*; it was a ghost field. The US command once again thought the Japanese had made a tactical blunder in not defending such an important objective. But the Japanese thinking was that there was no point in defending the airfield if the Americans were going to take it anyway, as they had with virtually every other airfield during the Pacific war.

Yontan Airfield was taken without resistance by the 4th Regiment. They had reached their L + 3 line, meaning that the regiment was three days ahead of schedule. At 1800, the 4th dug in for the night; all was quiet except for a Japanese plane that landed on the airstrip hoping to refuel and taxied directly into the 1st Battalion command post. The pilot exited with some papers, realized that the airfield was no longer in the possession of his compatriots, reached for his pistol in a good-to-the-last-drop gesture, and was riddled with bullets.

"There's always ten percent that don't get the word," said a marine.

"The Japs have missed their best opportunity on the ground and in the air," Buckner confidently wrote in his diary that first day.

April Fool.

The total number of those from the 4th killed in action that first day was five, including a corporal from the 3rd Battalion nicknamed "Red" for his hair color. His name was John Henry Anderson, and he had enlisted in the Marine Corps when he was eighteen. He had fought in the Battle of Guam, where he had received a shrapnel wound in the hip and been awarded the Purple Heart. He had also played in the Mosquito Bowl.

He was going over a rise near the airfield when his friend Gallagher lost sight of him.

"Hey, Gallagher, they got your buddy. I saw him

lying on the ground." Gallagher rushed up to a body and flipped it over. Anderson had died of a gunshot wound.

A Japanese sniper was firing, so Gallagher had to crouch down and go for cover. Another marine was able to get to Anderson. He retrieved his wallet and gave it to Gallagher, the threadbare details of a life that was over.

John Henry "Red" Anderson was the first player from the Mosquito Bowl to die.

He was buried on Okinawa in 6th Marine Division Cemetery No. 1, Grave 6, Row 1, Plot A.

He was twenty-two years old.

27
Abandon Ship

April 2nd of 1945 started much like the day before as the 6th Marine Division prepared to move north. It was still far ahead of schedule, moving so quickly that valuable captured material was left behind and scarfed up by the souvenir vultures. They were not directly assigned to combat but were all too willing to approach the front lines in pursuit of documents that meant nothing to them because of the language barrier, unaware that some of them contained crucial intelligence on Japanese troop strength and should have been handed over to their superiors. Most likely they couldn't have cared less anyway as long as they hit their booty quota.

There was slightly more resistance that second day on Okinawa. A Japanese soldier hidden in a ditch in camouflage beside a road rose into a sitting position and shot First Lieutenant Thad Dodds, the commander of Company B of the 1st Battalion of the 4th Regiment, in the head. He was the first of hundreds of officers who would ultimately die in combat on Okinawa. The officers were targeted by the Japanese as prizes. The enemy looked for telltale signs: map cases, an enlisted man careless enough to address his superior by rank in the hearing of the Japanese, undue commotion around someone that indicated his importance, body language.

Hofer, the former quarterback from Notre Dame who had played in the Mosquito Bowl for the 4th Regiment, took over after Dodds was killed. He wore a red bandanna to match his red hair and had won a Silver Star for "gallantry and intrepidity" on Guam as a platoon leader, deploying his men to hold their ground against a superior enemy force until help arrived. Known for his ceaseless aggressiveness, he was wounded shortly after replacing Dodds. Baumhardt in turn replaced Hofer and had a different philosophy: "I am not Mr. Hofer. I am not going to roar 'Follow me.' I'm going to keep you alive long enough to keep me alive. I'll get you back, and you get me back." It wasn't movie glamorous, but it worked. He survived the war.

Advent and Hays from Schreiner's Able company died. Twelve were killed from Company L: Platoon Sergeant Hojnacki; corporals Karr, Rhinow, and

Wright; PFCs French, Gonzales, Grassi, McDermott, Parker, Phillips, and Suttle; and Private Sleeper.

On April 2nd of 1945, Pethick was found dead by himself in a foxhole. As there had been no Japanese opposition, it was first thought that he had been killed by shrapnel from the navy guns firing offshore. Instead, it turned out that he had been stabbed to death. Some believed it had been done by the hands of a fellow marine who was after the .38 Pearl Grip revolver he carried. Pierce preferred to believe that he had been killed by Japanese fire even if it wasn't possible. It felt better that way.

"Everything is now going well," Buckner wrote to his wife, Adele. "Thoughts of my responsibility for so many lives are always sobering, but the fine fighting qualities of my men fill me with enthusiasm in my present task."

Everything was not going well. Two divisions of his army were turning south into what would be a bloody shitstorm, unknowingly moving into the mass of the Japanese resistance, falling for the trap.

Then there was the sea . . .

It became an afternoon, twilight, and nightly spectacle for McLaughry and Schreiner and Bauman and

Butkovich and Murphy and the rest of the Mosquito Bowl players from the 4th and the 29th, as they headed north, cheering when a kamikaze plane was shot down by antiaircraft fire and landed in the water and booing when one of them scored a hit on a naval ship. It was a thrill to watch, the streams of tracers overlapping the sky, Fourth of July in the Pacific even though it was April. It was hard to believe that any act of war could be so exciting and beautiful and so deadly. Whitaker thought it was even better than a Betty Grable movie.

The first kamikaze operation had taken place on October 25th of 1944 off Leyte Island in the Philippines. Of the 650 suicide missions conducted in the islands, 27 percent were deemed a success. The Japanese were besides themselves over the new weapon they blindly thought would turn the course of the war.

II

April 6th, 1415*

Cregut is in the CIC room of the USS *Bush* operating the SC-2 Air Search radar when he picks up an echo blip about ninety miles northwest. Sometimes a blip like this is just storm clouds, but this one is differ-

---

* Times are best estimates, based on "U.S.S. *Bush*(DD529) S-e-c-r-e-t Action Report" at http://www.ussbush.com/far2.htm.

ent, large, very large. He can't believe it, and he calls Lieutenant West over to look at the scope; he, too, is puzzled. They track it on the air plotting table, recording the course and speed every one to two minutes. The blip has an estimated speed of 145 knots, fast, too fucking fast. West looks at the images on the radar as they multiply. "There must be hundreds."

West informs the bridge. Call to general quarters.

April 6th, 1430

An estimated 230 kamikaze planes have taken off from several islands in the Ryukyus to the north and southwest of Okinawa to try to destroy as much of the naval fleet as possible. The pilots open their canopies and signal to others with their scarves when they have sighted a US ship. They are doomed, but they have left behind a remembrance of themselves for cremation in the family shrine: a lock of hair, fingernail clippings. Contrary to popular perception, the kamikaze are not the lunatic dregs of Japanese society, mad bombers—at least at first. Many of them are recent college graduates and brilliant, well versed in American, French, and Russian literature. Some look forward to dying for their emperor. Some go with reluctance; there are claims that blocks of concrete have been tied around their waists so they will not bail out. Some are drunk on sake when they take off. Some reek of perfume to feel pure. A group of enemy planes thirty-five miles to the north, closing rapidly. Another group and another and another. Raids one, two, three, four.

April 6th, 1455

Raid 1: Bush shoots down two Vals.

Raid 2: The kamikaze are driven off to the west.

Raid 3: The kamikaze are controlled from the east.

Raid 4: A plane sighted low on the water, heading straight for the *Bush*. Full rudder by the *Bush* to the left to bring the ship abeam to starboard and gain greater insulation from attack. The ship's speed increased to twenty-seven knots. A five-inch battery opens fire at a range of seven thousand to eight thousand yards. The plane employs roller-coaster tactics—climbing, dipping, weaving—its altitude from ten to thirty-five feet. All batteries firing at the maximum rate, on target. The plane keeps coming and coming. The range is now two thousand yards. The rudder shifts hard right to swing the stern clear and minimize exposure. The plane changes course. Most of its wings shot off. Still coming.

April 6th, 1515

The plane somehow gets through. Crashes at deck level on the starboard side between stacks 1 and 2. A bomb, or maybe it is a torpedo, explodes in the forward engine room.

Cowherd is in the plot room when the range of the plane goes down to zero. The only thing that saves him is a bulkhead separating the engine room. A six-foot section of the engine room blower weighing 3,500 pounds flies into the air, knocks off the SC-2 antenna, and lands on the port wing of the bridge. Aguilar is frantically busy in number 5 handling room feeding five-inch rounds to Northcutt on the number 5 gun. When the plane hits, it feels to Aguilar as though the *Bush* has run into a stone wall. All forward motion stops. The lights go out. Aguilar and others have to feel their way through the rear compartments and somehow get up the ladder to the fantail. Men have gathered, some of them badly injured. Peterson climbs out of the aft firearm to escape the killing hiss of steam. Borroz is on the phones near the torpedo shack. He is knocked down by the explosion and loses the phones but somehow doesn't have a scratch. Soo Hoo and Anderson are stationed in the blast shield of the after-torpedo tubes. After the hit, Anderson opens the hatch, shoves Soo Hoo out, and then exits himself. A French Canadian seaman works belowdecks. He is Errol Flynn handsome and has a thin mustache that is the subject of gentle teasing by Northcutt. He is badly burned.

He looks up at Northcutt, gives a little smile, and says, "I suppose my mustache is frazzled, too?" He doesn't make it.

The ship lists ten degrees to port. Four men escape from the forward fire room with severe burns and eight from the after fire room. Grigsby and others start for the open hatch on the starboard side. They have to go up three decks on a ladder with water coming in. He runs into steam on the second deck. He can't see or breathe, so he waits for the water level to catch up to him before advancing up the ladder. Men below are being scalded to death by the steam. He makes it topside knowing there is horrible burning going on belowdecks. All personnel in the forward engine room are believed to have been killed immediately. The galley, sick bay, supply office, midship repair locker, battery locker, radio number 2, and laundry all destroyed. The five torpedoes in tube 2 are fired to prevent explosions. Detonators are removed from depth charges and rolled over the side.

Blakely and others start tossing food, supplies, and equipment over the side to lighten the *Bush* and maybe forestall its sinking. Aguilar and McFarland go forward in an effort to salvage pay records and currency that were placed into mail bags before the battle as a precaution. Empty five-inch powder cans are affixed to the bags to keep them afloat, and they are tossed into the water. Attebury makes sure that the maps and charts are secured and will go down with the ship. It is sinking and then settles. Life rafts are dropped but not secured together, and some float away.

Carney is blown into the deck below and breaks his pelvis, although it feels as though his back is broken. A Black steward named Jackson lifts Carney and puts him in a raft. Jackson keeps going down into the engine spaces to pull up men who have been burned. He is big, and Lubin has no idea how he squeezes himself through the deck hatches. He is shoeless, and his feet are bloody. He doesn't make it.

Wysocki has been shot in the left shoulder. He dives into the water to save a sailor who has been blinded. Northcutt and Serviolo help Wysocki change into dry clothes after he is back on board. It is then they realize the seriousness of his wound; the bullet exited underneath his right armpit. He doesn't make it.

April 6th, 1715

Three Zekes circle the ship at a range of about ten miles, going into and out of the clouds.

April 6th, 1725

One of them peels off straight into the sun, positioned straight ahead of the ship, almost impossible to locate. It does a wingover and commences a 25- to 30-degree dive while strafing.

April 6th, 1730

It dips its left wing and crashes into the ship, once again between stacks 1 and 2. A large fire starts. The ship virtually cut in two, held together only by the bottom and keel. The wounded are put into float nets tied off the stern. Pieces of wood are tied around some of them to help them stay above the water.

Westholm tells his men to abandon ship and swim far enough away to protect themselves from strafing. Butler tries to stay underwater as long as possible to avoid the spray of fire. Shirey removes a small plaque from the bridge with a St. Christopher medal on it. No one else is there. He grabs a can of V-8 juice and one of the captain's cigars and starts shooting at the Japanese planes.

April 6th, 1745

A Zeke peels off and starts a shallow dive on the starboard beam. It is weaving. It pulls out at the last moment, gains altitude, and does a tight turn. Butler can see the pilot's face. It feels as though they are looking at each other. The twin 40 mm guns fire into the cockpit of the plane. The pilot is now dead and slumped over.

The plane crashes on the port side just above the main deck in the vicinity of gun number 2 and the wardroom. Flaming gasoline starts to spray everywhere. The casualties being treated there are either killed or burned to death. The fire is impossible to put out as ammunition starts to explode. The entire forecastle is enveloped in flame. Tontz and West go to the coding room to remove the equipment. They put it into a weighted canvas bag and throw it over the side. Brody is badly burned, and fellow seamen are trying to apply ointment. The skin comes off in their hands. "Thanks for trying to help me," he says and jumps into the ocean to drown. The whole ship seems afire. Cross gives his life jacket to an older sailor who cannot swim. Cross doesn't make it. Gerriets goes over the starboard side in a ball of fire.

The light is starting to fade.

April 6th, 1830

An unusually heavy swell rocks the ship. Tearing and crunching sounds are heard. The *Bush* starts to cave in amidships. The bow is inclined about 15 degrees above the stern. The ship folds in two. Westholm is the last to leave and has to be coaxed by the ship's doctor, Johnson. "If you don't get off, I'll shoot you!" Johnson shouts. Shirey jumps into the ocean wearing a life belt inflated by CO_2 tubes. One side has a hole in it, so he inserts his lucky silver dollar in it. He swims for a life raft and watches the pictures painted on the five-inch gun mounts of the *Bush* dissolve into flames. The CO_2 tubes on McManus's life belt don't work because he has been using the belt as a pillow. He is picked up. Butler looks back, sees the bow and stern rising out of the water at a 90-degree angle, then watches it disappear beneath the waves. He doesn't feel fear or panic but an overwhelming sense of loss. Reeder watches the flag on the bow go under. He starts to cry. The ship sinks in about 350 fathoms of water in the approximate location latitude 27° 16′ N, longitude 127° 48′ E.

Survivors are spread all over because of the strong current and breeze and the medium sea. The water is getting choppy. The waves are running five to six feet. Northey and Libassi cling to a piece of wood. Northey is injured. "I can't make it, but you can." He floats off forever. Shirey grabs onto a double ring on the side of the raft. He moves up a notch to a safer position every time a seaman drops off because he can't take it anymore.

Willis, the division commander, is in the center of the float net. Stanley is injured and hanging from the side. Men try to get Stanley up onto the net, but there is too much weight already. One of the men says that Willis appears to be dead and asks others if it is permissible to move him. Homer, the pharmacist's mate, confirms that he is gone. He is placed into the water so Stanley can get on top of the float net. A young officer is unable to control himself and keeps trying to swim away in the darkness. Johnson, the doctor, keeps going after him until he can't anymore. The young officer swims away for good. Men begin to swim for shore, seventy miles away, and are never seen again.

It is dark now. Men are exhausted by the pounding of the sea and try to keep their heads above water as they await rescue hour after hour. Water temperature dropping to 52 degrees. The only time Youngren feels any warmth is when he urinates in his pants. Some of the men swallow salt water and start to retch. One positions a picture of his family inside his life jacket so he can see them until he dies. Another has his wallet in his hand with a photo of his wife and young son. Some men who can't bear any more become violent and hysterical. They slip out of their life jackets and drown. There is no moon or stars. Japanese planes arrive in the night, looking to strafe those in the water. Some men have small one-cell flashlights. There are strict orders not to use them, but they are the only way to draw the attention of the rescue ships. The men get excited as they approach. Some start swimming and smash against the hull or are caught up in the propeller screws. The rescue ships do all they can. Those on board hear pleas for help from men who know there is no hope and that the sea will take them.

Eighty-eight men from the USS *Bush* dead or missing:

Akers, Anderson H, Anderson R, Baker, Baldwin, Barrich, Bartnick, Batchelor, Baykowski, Beals, Blair, Bray, Bresnahan, Brody, Cechal, Chaplinski, Copp, Crenshaw, Cross, Davey, Day, Dillard, Dolgas, Drew, Duncan, Eskola, Foster, Frankenberg, Futrell, Gerriets, Greenberg, Gunn, Hagerty, Hall, Hay, Huard, Jackson, Johnson, Jones D, Jones O, Kenner, Kirby, Koebbe, Kosty, Kowalski, Krygier, Kulis, Ladner, Leffler, Long, MacKnight, Mart, Martin, McCarty, McFarland, Meisetschlager, Merrick, Mills, Moclair, Moffit, Montour, Northey, Pace, Parker A, Parker H, Phillips, Pomerance, Rush, Schwarzin, Scott, Sprague, Stewart, Swindell, Szczech, Tetak, Tillman,

Tinan, Trella, Vertz, Weithman, Welch, Weth-
erbee, Willis, Wood, Woodhurst, Wysocki,
Yates, Youtsey.

The USS *Colhoun* is attacked at 1714 when it comes to the rescue of the *Bush*. The flaming fuselage of the kamikaze plane skitters across the deck. The engine and bomb penetrate the main deck and explode in the after fire room. Fragments pierce both the forward and after bulkheads. There is a four-foot-square hole on the port side below the waterline. The gun crews of 40 mm mounts numbers 3 and 4 are killed or badly burned by the crash and ammunition that has caught fire. The gun crews of the 20 mm guns numbers 1 and 3 are severely burned. Several are badly burned by steam from number 1 engine room and number 2 fire room while fighting the fire.

A Zeke and two Vals approach. Guns numbers 4, 5, 25, 26, 27, and 45 open up. One of the Vals crashes. The other plows into the forward fire room and its bomb explodes, breaking the keel and making a hole about twenty feet long and four feet wide in the starboard side below the waterline. The IC room, diesel engine room, and ship's office bulkheads are pierced, starting oil and electrical fires. The *Colhoun* is dead in the water. There is another attack by a Zeke and two Vals.

The gas tank of one of the Vals bounces off the main deck, where the bomb explodes, and there is another hole below the waterline three feet square in compartment C-205. Thirty-five men are killed or missing in action. The ship is impossible to save. It is sunk intentionally by gunfire from the USS *Cassin Young* commencing just before midnight.

The Battle of Okinawa is less than a week old.

28
The Tortoise

Twenty-six ships were sunk or damaged in the kamikaze attack of April 6 and 7, the first of ten group attacks in what became known as the Ten Go campaign. After several other attacks resulted in the deaths of about six hundred naval personnel, Admiral Nimitz flew to Okinawa from his headquarters in Guam to visit Buckner on April 23rd of 1945. He was cordial—Nimitz's style was always to be cordial. But he was not pleased by the slow movement of the ground forces and the obvious implication that the loss of navy lives and ships was secondary: "I'm losing a ship and a half a day so if this line isn't moving in five days, we'll get someone to move it so we can all get out from under these damn kamikaze attacks."

In his diary Buckner briefly referred to the visit of

Nimitz and said he had left "apparently well-pleased." But he knew he had to do something and changed his original plan. He decided he had no choice but to better utilize the marines. There was a suspicion that he had consigned them to a secondary role, not even calling up a superbly trained division in reserve when the situation became dire, because he wanted Okinawa to be an army show and an army win and not allow the marines to take all the credit as they usually did.

For the marines of the Mosquito Bowl and the rest of the 4th and 29th Regiments, the initial weeks of April had continued to be easy, the push north into the Motobu Peninsula unopposed, the atmosphere still strange and surreal, mostly waiting for an enemy that seemed determined to never reveal itself. The greatest obstacle to safety at one point wasn't the Japanese but American friendlies. Strafed accidentally by a Vought F4U Corsair, Major Robert Fowler of Fox Company of the 29th and a player in the Mosquito Bowl, stood up. He frantically waved to the plane and yelled to anyone within earshot to give him their white underwear to hold up: a strip of white visible from the sky designated the front of the US lines.

Everybody was in green.

Three men from the 2nd Battalion died from rocket fire from the Corsair.

It was only in mid-April of 1945 that the 4th and 29th Regiments began to experience combat on the Motobu Peninsula. The going had been easy up until then. But it was also strange, eerie. Where was the enemy? Nobody thought they had simply up and left. But that did not stop them from believing it.

The Japanese had been there all along, as usual well concealed. Photographs of the peninsula, about seven miles long and five miles wide, had been inadequate. The failure was blamed on cloud cover; when in doubt in war, blame the clouds, but subsequent photos, even without them, did not show the enemy's trails underneath the trees.

The Japanese were under the command of Takehido Udo. He had chosen as his command post a ravine on Mount Yaetake, replete with an extremely sophisticated telephone and radio communications system to receive reports and send out orders. The Japanese were far better equipped for mountain fighting than the Americans were. They were familiar with the trails and used horses as transportation, building paddocks and corrals in concealed spaces and stocking them with veterinary supplies. Udo knew that the marines would ultimately prevail, but his goal was to drag the skirmish out as long as possible, and he had the necessary weaponry to do it: 25 mm guns originally used by the navy set inside the hills with camouflage; 13.2 mm mortars; a battery of field artillery.

The Japanese style of defense was a glimpse of what would only magnify during the Battle of Okinawa into a storm of blood for the marines of the 6th Division. The first objective on the peninsula was a seven-hundred-foot ridge, then Hills 230 and 210 and Mount Yaetake. The Japanese were hard to spot as they let go with Nambus. Once the marines located the source of the fire and neutralized it, they did not find any dead Japanese soldiers, only bloodstains on the ground. It was clear that the Japanese had hidden their dead in the rocks and rocky terrain to make themselves even more invisible, a phantom enemy. The best method of attack was to pin the Japanese down with supporting fire until the marines could blast the caves with explosives and grenades and then pick off the Japanese soldiers trying to escape. Some Japanese, knowing that the cause was hopeless, blew themselves up with grenades rather than surrender.

Twenty-five men of the 6th Division were killed on April 12th of 1945, eight on April 13th, nineteen on April 14th, thirty-five on April 15th.

It was on April 15th, as Mount Yaetake was in the process of being taken, that Major Bernard W. Green, known as Barney, the commander of the 1st Battalion, which Schreiner and Bauman served in, was in an observation post supervising his men. A group of Japanese hiding in the tall grass let the marines pass by, then opened up and shot Green in the head.

It was a terrible loss not just to the battalion but to McLaughry in particular. The son of a chauffeur from Philadelphia, Green had joined the raiders out of Officer Candidates School, and McLaughry had served under him. It was almost impossible for McLaughry to accept that not only Green but also several others he had known well were gone. The hard reality was that McLaughry's heavy weapons, designed to protect and give support, had not done much good. They were useless because of the rugged terrain of mountain and rock and undergrowth to the point where McLaughry and his men had stopped using them and served as riflemen on the line.

Rusty Johnston was a corporal in Company E of the 2nd Battalion of the 29th Regiment on the same day Green was killed during the siege of Mount Yaetake. He was from Lubbock in west Texas, the son of William and Annie Johnston. He knew how to take hard knocks and had worked his way through high school at a Piggly Wiggly grocery store in Lubbock. He had been a great athlete in high school in both football and

404 · THE MOSQUITO BOWL

basketball and for a period of time had attended Texas Tech University. He had gone on to Marquette University in Milwaukee and was a rising star on the football team at running back. He had moved to Notre Dame's V-12 program but had not played, leaving the school in November of 1943 to attend the Marine Corps Officer Candidates School. He had earned the qualification of sharpshooter on the firing range on Parris Island. But he had not made it as an officer and had been returned to the enlisted ranks.

He was fatally hit by shrapnel during the siege of Mount Yaetake.

Wayne Horton "Rusty" Johnston was the second player from the Mosquito Bowl to die.

He was buried on Okinawa in 6th Marine Division Cemetery No. 1, Grave 164, Row 7, Plot A.

He was twenty-four years old.

29
The Little Girl

A day later, April 16th of 1945, as the siege of Mount Yaetake continued, Bauman was badly injured in his arms and legs by grenade fragments. He refused to be evacuated or receive medical treatment until all the other wounded in his platoon had been safely removed. Then he slid down the mountain and was sent to a hospital in Guam. He received the Bronze Star with a citation that read:

> His unwavering fortitude, self-sacrificing devotion to duty and grave concern for others reflect the highest credit upon himself and the United States Naval Service.

Frank had had a hunch that his brother would get hit. When the news came, he thought it was a blessing, as the wounds were potentially serious enough to get Bob sent back to the States for further treatment. "I am certainly glad he left Okinawa when he did for it's a rugged place now," he wrote in a letter to his aunt Emma. He knew that the only obstacles would be Bob himself and his loyalty to his platoon, the conviction that he had to go back. But surely Bob would realize the stakes. He had a fiancée. He had a mother who would always need his help. He had a brother who would need constant reminding he was the younger brother.

Schreiner got through unscathed. The next day, April 17th of 1945, his platoon and the 1st Battalion attacked the crest of Mount Yaetake but were pushed back. The Japanese and the marines tossed grenades at each other over the crest. The 1st Battalion then conducted a full-scale siege, letting loose with their Browning Automatics, screaming in a technique borrowed from the Japanese in a banzai attack, and taking Mount Yaetake for good.

McLaughry had celebrated his twenty-eighth birthday on April 8th of 1945 during a lull in the northward push, one of his men swiping the great delicacy of a can of boned turkey. An even more beautiful present, a half pint of sick bay brandy normally used to relieve shock and battle fatigue, also materialized. As he looked back over his life, he realized that it had been five years since he had led the procession through the Van Wickle Gates on commencement day at Brown, a real future ahead instead of one predicated on not getting blown up. "It hardly seems possible," he wrote to his parents.

McLaughry listened to the English-language propaganda broadcasts from Tokyo describe the battle as if it were a parallel universe, the Japanese claim of their having sunk so many ships at Okinawa that the United States would have been without a single ship. According to the broadcasts, some must have been sunk two or three times. Tokyo Rose and her propaganda show, *Zero Hour*,* became must-hear radio. Her voice was alluring and teasingly taunting and she knew more about troop movements than most marines did (the best source for Japanese intelligence was US newspapers). It was tongue-in-cheek farcical and McLaughry loved it.

---

* In one of the more bizarre stories of the war, Iva Toguri was born in the United States and was a graduate of UCLA when she visited Japan and was stranded there after Pearl Harbor. She was forced to renounce her US citizenship (she initially refused) and ultimately found work on the radio. The nickname "Tokyo Rose" was given to her by servicemen. She returned to the United States after the war, was convicted of treason, and served six years in prison. She was later pardoned by President Gerald Ford.

Some marines, the so-called roosters, took great delight in using the mail to inflict cruelty. A marine from Alabama kept talking about how he had a wife and two mistresses. The roosters got sick of it. When he left unsealed letters on his bunk waiting to be mailed and was off doing something else, the roosters went to work like cat burglars. They switched the envelopes so his wife got the letter addressed to one of the mistresses and the mistress got the one addressed to his wife. After replies arrived telling the Alabama kid in general terms that they were going to cut his privates off, he assumed that he was the one who had somehow screwed up.

Bored with rations, the marines hunted alternative sources of food as a pastime. As a group of them patrolled in the vicinity of Mount Yaetake, one pointed to a small field where a cow and a bull stood side by side.

"There's our chow!" a sergeant shouted.

He pulled out his .45 pistol, whereupon a marine from Kansas protested that it was just wrong not to let the bull and cow consummate what had always been their intent. The sergeant put away his .45. The marines gathered on a stone fence and cheered and booed as the bull kept missing the mark. It was clear that the bull was a novice, or maybe just not very good. The Kansas marine went up to the bull and guided him into the right position. The act was done to climactic cheering, a fifteen-minute respite from the war. The cow seemed happy, the bull not so much as he was killed for what some said was the best meal of their lives that night.

||

It was in the north in the area of Mount Yaetake that Sergeant Raymond Gillespie of Company K positioned his squad on a hill, with two men protecting the rear. He was in the 22nd Regiment, the third infantry regiment in the 6th Division along with the 4th and the 29th. They were a superb outfit, although clearly lacking in football players: hence no participation in the Mosquito Bowl.

He could hear civilian chatter, then yelling and screaming. Two Japanese soldiers came running down a stream and were killed. The stream was red with blood. The shooting continued, which was when Gillespie saw her.

There were roughly three hundred thousand native Okinawans still on the island after more than a hundred thousand had been removed to safety. Most of the able-bodied, including high school girls, had been forced into service by the Japanese. The high schoolers were used as nurses' aides in underground caves and field hospitals, treating wounds teeming with enough maggots to fill a small bucket, cleaning maggot-infested and pus-smeared bandages so they could be used again on soldiers who would inevitably die anyway, helping to hold down those whose limbs were being amputated without anesthetic, cleaning up feces and diarrhea, preventing soldiers from drinking their own urine, holding the cocks of amputees so at least they could piss straight.

As the battle progressed the tragedy of the Okinawans only got worse. As many as 150,000 died in the battle, 80 percent in the last three weeks. The total number of deaths of children fourteen and under was roughly 11,500, nearly 90 percent of whom had been pushed out of their shelters by Japanese soldiers. Infants were not spared, and 1,170 under the age of two were killed.

She was a little girl making her way to the hill Gillespie's squad was on, her face dirty and her body shaking with sobs. She was about seven years old.

"Cease fire!" Gillespie yelled.

Out of the corner of his eye he saw the platoon sergeant come up to the line and prepare to fire.

"Don't you dare, you prick. I'll take that goddamn rifle away from you!"

The platoon sergeant missed the first time.

He hit the little girl the second time just above the groin, and she fell.

American troops went out on "pussy patrols" to find natives. A group of marines found two women with their pants pulled down; obviously they had been raped. There were indications that members of the 29th had started a paid brothel using a local woman. Authorities reported nine arrests for rape on Okinawa, undoubtedly an undercount. On a patrol into the hills in the Mount Yaetake region, a platoon from the 29th came upon a family of Okinawans sitting by their home. A corporal claimed that the man in the group was a Japanese soldier posing as a civilian. Several marines told him that he was too young, but that didn't stop the corporal from pulling out his .45 and shooting the man in the head. The family went crazy with disbelief and grief. The corporal just shrugged. "Let's go."

American troops were tacitly discouraged from taking surrendering Japanese soldiers alive at the beginning of the war, until their value as sources of intelligence was fully realized. Whatever unspeakable acts by Americans, their behavior was nothing compared to the organized atrocities committed by the Japanese against Allied troops, prisoners of war, and natives of countries in the surrounding region. They killed an estimated 30 million troops and civilians, roughly half the total killed in World War II, although few realize it, the Pacific and Asia-Pacific wars* always in the shadow of the Atlantic conflict. The number most likely is higher since the estimates of Chinese killed in war ranges from 12 million to 50 million.

Among the Japanese methods of killing and torture used—chemical warfare; injection of prisoners with bacteria; forced drinking of a liquid form of mustard gas; starvation; live vivisections; amputations; mass burnings; cutting off of breasts; being placed in pressure chambers until the eyes popped out of their sockets; beheadings; forcing the son of a Chinese family to have intercourse with his mother, the father with his daughter, and the brother with his sister, before killing them all; forcing women who were menstruating to

---

*   Some scholars date 1931 as the beginning of what would be a fourteen-year war against China. The Japanese referred to it only as the "China Incident" and not "war" so that rules of engagement regarding prisoners of war did not apply because it was an incident. Of course in the Pacific war, the Japanese refused to follow rules of engagement regarding the treatment of prisoners of war anyway.

sit over heated charcoal stoves; tying soldiers to stakes with their legs spread and dynamited so their bones shattered and their feet severed and then being choked to death.*

The Japanese exhibited homicidal contempt in the treatment of Okinawans. Mothers who had fled into caves were forced to suffocate their babies if they made too much noise. Sometimes the babies were thrown out of the caves at night in the hope that US forces would kill them, as the US forces had been given strict orders to shoot at anything that moved because of the constant reality of Japanese infiltration.

Japanese soldiers hoping to escape or penetrate the lines would dress in civilian clothes and use civilians as human shields. Civilians were terrified into committing suicide because of Japanese soldiers telling them over and over that American troops would savage them.

The American senior command at Okinawa was exemplary in planning and trying to save as many civilian lives as possible; in many ways that was its finest hour. They urged them with leaflets to stay on the main road and not attempt to come through the lines at night. They begged them to surrender and promised

* According to an exhaustive study by R. J. Rummel from the University of Hawaii, roughly 3 million were killed alone in massacres and atrocities.

that, contrary to Japanese propaganda, nobody would be killed or sexually assaulted. They got them off the battlefield into supervised areas, where they were fed and medically treated. They protected women against sexual assault with extra guards and made it clear that any forcible act of sex would be subject to execution. Tens of thousands took up the American offer of protection.

Gillespie could not simply be a bystander. He reported to the lieutenant of the platoon what had just happened. "That son of a bitch just shot a little girl."

The lieutenant wanted none of it. "Keep your mouth shut, Gillespie, or you'll be court-martialed."

"Bullshit. I'm not here to kill children."

There were tender mercies.

Cans of peaches were spooned into the mouths of grandmothers. Candy bars were handed out to little children, and some were adopted as mascots by infantry companies. Always looking for an opportunity to fuck with the army, marines taught kids to say "Doggies eat shit!" A young boy fell into a beautiful sleep sandwiched in between two marines. It made for a beautiful picture. But there were other ones not taken.

Corporal Charles Pugh of Company K of the 22nd had been warned by intelligence of a possible Japanese counterattack. The machine gunners in his company thought they heard the voices of soldiers in the night and opened up per their instructions.

The next morning they discovered their targets: a woman, an elderly man, and two small children. They had gone to receive their rice rations and had been carrying them back in a bucket that made the noise. It was filled with .30-caliber machine-gun bullet holes, and the rice had trailed out in a line, as if tracing the direction of the bullets. It only became more difficult for Pugh, the perfection of that straight and steady arrow pointing to death. He had a ten-month-old son back in the States, and his wife was pregnant with their second child. But all he could see in that moment was one of the fingers of the mother atop a child's head. She must have been trying to protect him.

The little girl was still alive. Gillespie walked over to her and cut off the clothing around the wound. He dressed her wound with sulfa powder and a bandage as best he could. He picked her up and carried her along a trail in between the hills. The platoon had gone ahead. Corporal Franklin Coomer had stayed with Gillespie, but Gillespie told him to catch up to the unit: he knew he was in trouble and did not want Coomer swept into it.

The little girl got heavy after a while, and Gillespie went down on one knee to rest her weight against his legs. She reached over and touched his hand.

They did not speak the same language, but they understood each other. "You're all right, dear." He had said it before; this time he did so with tears in his eyes.

He carried her to the main road and waved down a jeep that took her to the regimental field hospital. When he returned to the platoon, the lieutenant never mentioned what had happened. Which, in the way of the military, meant that it had never taken place.

30

Return to Sender

Shortly before the the taking of Mount Yaetake, during language period at Baxter Elementary School, Tom Milligan wrote his pen pal Butkovich a letter: "I am just fine. How are you? How are the Marines and you coming?"

The letter contained the musings of a nine-year-old boy—Evansville Bosse taking the state high school basketball championship in Indiana for the second time in a row; everybody in the family, including the dog, Ginger, all fine and good; a happy Easter. Butkovich had just arrived on Okinawa, where the writing and mailing of letters wasn't feasible. But several months earlier, he had written Tom to tell him that he had played in the Mosquito Bowl and promised to look him up once the war was over.

Tom mailed the letter on April 9th of 1945. That same day, Butkovich and the rest of the 29th Regiment were making their way north. He was a mortar man in the headquarters company of the 3rd Battalion. After the difficulties of Officer Candidates School, where he had washed out, his most recent assessment evaluations had been excellent, a 4.83 aggregate in five different categories out of five. He had become a fine marine.

In February of 1945, while still at Guadalcanal, Butkovich had written to his parents. He had told them everything was okay and thanked his mother profusely for the care package. The fruit cake had been a huge hit, and the peanuts had been a great gesture, although, as he gently pointed out, they had gone bad by the time they arrived and next time she should send only nuts in cans. He worried about his brother Bill, telling his parents to push him to leave Illinois and get a defense job or otherwise he would be drafted. He told his mom that there had been "some swell movies lately," two of which he thought she would particularly enjoy because they dealt with Catholicism: *Song of Bernadette* and *Going My Way.* Perhaps best of all, it looked as though he and John Genis, his college football and Mosquito Bowl teammate, would be together for the duration of the war. "He's my best buddy," he wrote.

During the early-morning hours of April 18th, a day before the north of the island was secured, Butkovich and the marines he was with were ordered to move up from the foxholes they had dug for the night. He was bone tired, and, given that resistance was light, he apparently did not see the point of digging yet another foxhole. Most of the men felt that way. Daybreak would come soon enough anyway.

He wrapped himself in a poncho. In his exhaustion, he shifted around. The poncho rustled.

Japanese snipers always listened and always watched . . .

It wasn't until fourteen days later, or maybe it was fifteen or sixteen, it was hard to know exactly, that his parents were notified by telegram back in St. David that their son was dead. Because of his prowess as a great college football player who had once captivated the nation for a brief moment in time, there were a few write-ups. "Former Star Falls at Okinawa" read the headline in the *Illinois State Journal* out of Springfield, difficult to find unless you really wanted to find it. Then, except to his family and men who knew and had served with him, he disappeared, and after the war, as those men grew into careers and families, he would disappear from them, Touchdown Tony all he was and would ever be.

He left behind the things he had carried to war: a knife, a map of the world, a prayer book, a civilian tie, three pencils, six handkerchiefs, a lighter, a box containing letters and newspaper clippings. The possessions were sent to his parents in St. David, which also included a chain with an identification tag on it. Ana Butkovich wrote to the Marine Corps that the chain and tag belonged to someone else and asked to receive the ones belonging to her son. The Marine Corps wrote back that dog tags were government property issued for the express purpose of identifying the dead and she could not have them, even if she did have the dog tags of a fallen marine completely unknown to her.

Tom Milligan waited for a response to his letter. It came back to him on May 24th of 1945 with a notice stamped on the envelope:

"USMC Reports Undeliverable. Return to Sender."

Anthony James Butkovich was the third player from the Mosquito Bowl to die.

He was buried on Okinawa in 6th Marine Division Cemetery No. 1, Grave 215, Row 19, Plot A.

He was twenty-four years old.

31
A Thousand Ants

The day before he knew he would die on Okinawa, Bob McGowan did everything right in the foxhole he shared with Soper. Pinned down by enemy fire on May 13th of 1945 in the early stages of what became known as the horror campaign of Sugar Loaf, he rolled on his side, took out his carrot, and peed into the C ration can in a fluid motion worthy of at least a Silver Star. But when he went to throw the contents out, presumably the easy part, his sleeve got caught on his cartridge belt and Soper got drenched with piss. Mc-Gowan thought that Soper would be upset, but he just laughed it off. Which was why he loved Soper: he was always there for him, unflustered, understanding that if you got a little piss all over you in war, then you had done all right.

McGowan was a sergeant and squad leader with How Company of the 3rd battalion of the 29th. He had grown up in the small town of Meridian in western Pennsylvania, helping to augment the income of the family of four during the Depression by hunting, fishing, and trapping. His father was an electrician but, like everyone else in those hard and unforgiving years, held odd jobs and was badly burned in a gas well explosion. His mother took in sewing to help the family get by, and they grew their own vegetables. McGowan went to college to study engineering but dropped out when the war came, hitched a ride home, and after Pearl Harbor was the first in line at the regional recruiting office to enlist in the army. A marine recruiter who happened to be in the office got to him first.

On the ship over to Okinawa, he and a fellow squad leader, Slover, had read news sheets showing the casualty figures at Iwo Jima—almost seven thousand were killed—and they couldn't help but wonder about Okinawa. Slover had won five hundred bucks playing craps. He did not seem worried about getting killed as much as he was trying to figure out how to get the money back to his wife and kid. McGowan hadn't worked the exact timing out yet of his demise, but he knew it was coming. Which also made him do things that otherwise he never would have done. Once he accepted the fact, he just did his best to support his brothers and not think about being a hero or a coward and just have it come quickly when it did come. But if his legs went airborne when he stepped on a mine, he hoped somebody would just shoot him.

McGowan had been at the Mosquito Bowl, impressed by the impunity with which the participants had beaten the crap out of each other. He was in the same company as corporal Eli Kaluger, a player for the 29th. But company distinctions became moot in the Sugar Loaf campaign because of the killing and savagery and marines being blown away. What McGowan experienced was the same as what George Murphy went through in Dog Company of the 29th and the same as McLaughry and Schreiner and Bauman would ultimately experience in the 4th. There would be no mercy granted. If there had been, Tony Butkovich would still have been alive.

McGowan was a sergeant and the squad leader of the 3rd Platoon of Company H, a complement of thirteen men including himself and Soper. It was the squad leader who carried the syrettes of morphine in his breast pockets to kill off the pain—three in one and two in the other as a fail-safe in case one pocket was crushed. Nothing was more valuable than morphine. The syrettes were hard to get, and you had to be careful not to dole them out too easily. You gave it to one guy, and before you knew it someone else had a wound twice as severe. It meant making horrible decisions, judging one agony against the other.

They had been at the siege of Mount Yaetake in April, and McGowan's squad had pretty much gotten through it unscathed, although there had been some bad moments. There was a 75 mm artillery piece that the Japanese had hidden in a cave—sliding out on those railroad tracks to fire and then sliding back in behind a steel door. There was a sizable rock in front of the cave, and as McGowan went around it, Landry killed a Japanese soldier who was there. The cave entrance was covered with camouflage netting. Martin, who was a fire team leader, threw a white phosphorous grenade into the mouth of the cave. But it got caught in the netting, which flung the grenade straight up like a baseball. McGowan, Martin, and everyone else who was close by made it the hell out of there.

The biggest excitement up north came when McGowan took point with a machete to cut through thick vegetation. They were on a narrow path, trying to maintain silence, when a dreaded habu snake lay right in front of him. It was a cool morning, so the habu was slow, and McGowan lopped its head off. He went a few yards more and could hear First Lieutenant Hank Johnson blasting away at the writhing corpse with his .45. It kind of blew their cover, but it was also funny. The men loved Johnson as their platoon leader and called him by his first name, which was unusual for an officer. They were still up north when they were rocked by mortars. Everyone dived for the nearest hole, Johnson jumping into a pit where Okinawan farmers kept human dung for future use as fertilizer. He flew up out of the hole and found some water to clean himself off, and everybody thought that was pretty funny, too, even in the midst of getting shelled. Without shit the marines would have had a lot less to laugh at. So thank God for it.

Now the 29th was headed south toward the defensive position known as the Shuri Line, where the Japanese had amassed. The marines were convinced that they knew the reason: the army.

Both the 4th and 29th Regiments and the entire 6th Division had thought their mission would be over once they took the northern end of Okinawa. In twenty days from the landing on April 1st, the division had covered 84 miles and secured 436 square miles of Japanese territory. More than 2,500 bodies of dead Japanese soldiers* had been counted, as compared to the division's own losses of 236 killed and 1,061 wounded. They had done everything they were supposed to do. But now, in early May, they were headed south into withering Japanese fire. The army divisions in the south were on their heels.

Three of the army infantry divisions—the 7th, 77th, and 96th—achieved results. But the 27th infantry got into terrible trouble at the outset and should have perhaps been replaced by the 2nd Marine Division, which had distinguished itself at Guadalcanal and Tarawa and was a designated reserve force for the Okinawa campaign. But after a brief feint maneuver at the beginning of the invasion, the 2nd had been ordered back to the area of Saipan, ostensibly to prepare for a different campaign.

Before the 27th Division had been inducted into service in the army in 1940, it was a division of the New York National Guard. It had performed well in World War I but was suspected of cronyism and favoritism among its officers, with promotions going to the most politically connected, those that Marine General Holland Smith scoffed at as coming from "a gentleman's

---

* Body counts of the enemy are notoriously unscientific in war and are sometimes inflated to show success. They must be taken with a grain of salt.

club . . . New York's silk stocking outfit." Like much of what Smith said, there were his truth and the truth and the actual truth somewhere in between. But serious questions had been raised about the 27th's performance in each of its three previous combat assignments: Makin in 1943, Saipan and Eniwetok in 1944. Among the criticisms: being trigger happy, lacking aggressive spirit and discipline, and in one instance the truly unforgivable sin of not burying their own dead. Most of the criticisms came from marines, but other army officers were also contemptuous. Dick Thom, a battalion operations officer in the 96th Division, said of the 27th, "They were nasty; morale was awful. . . . Fuckups of the Pacific. Never had a successful campaign." It was not the men on the line who were to be blamed, virtually everyone concluded, but the woeful senior leadership, who were often over the hill or inexperienced.

Initially, the 27th Division had not been intended for combat on Okinawa. It was meant to be a "floating reserve," to be used for garrison duty after the island was secured. When the other army divisions ran up against the strength of the Japanese defenses, Buckner moved the 27th forward into the line. Its men were thrown deep into the shit. Buckner should have foreseen the result, given the division's past performance.

On April 19th of 1945, the division lost twenty-two of its tanks in a single failed advance, an astronomical number. On April 20th, pinned down on a steep escarpment, one of its companies broke and ran, and the division suffered 506 total casualties, the single worst day of any army division in the entire battle and probably the only instance on Okinawa in which American forces had more wounded and killed than the number inflicted on the enemy. The situation was becoming critical, and Buckner's hope for an army-only show in the south was no longer viable.

A trade-off took place: the 27th went into the northern sector, which had been secured by the 6th Marine Division, to do garrison duty, and the 6th Division went south into the heat of the conflict with no more illusions that it would be only a matter of days before they would head to R and R on Guam.

It was psychologically punishing to go from the belief that their battle duty was done to being told to get ready to move out again. "A man has to argue with himself," wrote then captain Philips D. Carleton in *The Conquest of Okinawa: An Account of the Sixth Marine Division* as an eyewitness observer for the Marine Corps History Division. "He has to discount to himself his chances of being killed or wounded, and finally, tired of his own internal wrangling, he has to adopt impatiently a sort of fatalism."

In comparison to what the army had gone through in the first month on Okinawa, the marines had lived a privileged life. The casualty rates of the four army divisions had been seven times those of the two marine divisions. The number of casualties suffered by the 27th during its two weeks in combat was almost equal to the number of casualties of *both* marine divisions in the entire month of April.

The trucks transporting the marines to the south in early May of 1945 were on one side of the road. The trucks transporting the 27th Division to the north were on the other.

The sign some marines had put up on their side, pointing south into the shit: "WAR . . . BLOOD . . . DIRT."

The signs they had put up on the army side, pointing north away from the shit: "USO . . . HOT DOUGH-NUTS . . . WARM BED."

They passed each other.

This is because of your fucking ineptitude, your fucking lousy leadership, your constant fucking fuck-ups that we're bailing your asses out.

The army threw energy-boosting snacks such as candy bars to the marines' side to help fortify them.

The marines threw them back and made barking sounds at the "doggies."

The 27th had had enough. *Go ahead and bark. You bastards live like dogs anyway.* They mimicked the motion of a movie camera. *You care about publicity so much you're fucking willing to let yourself get killed for it.* The hatred was real. It would not be forgiven by either side.

All for one and one for all . . .

‖

On the morning of May 14th of 1945, Lieutenant Johnson was told to take his 3rd Platoon, attack across a draw, and take grid 7671 on the left flank of Sugar Loaf Hill. It was a suicide mission, but Johnson was taking orders from above, and that was it. He and McGowan just blinked at each other and knew it was going to be a slaughter with their flank exposed, shot at from virtually every direction.

They could call in artillery, but they'd better have the coordinates right, otherwise it would end up on their asses. They were petrified and tired and sick from dysentery, so much shitting and trying to shit your anus turned inside out and the shit filling your pants and sometimes leaves sticking out as you ran for your life. The thick cotton uniforms they wore in the heat meant they were constantly chafed. Fortunately, there were enough rations, and McGowan was the only one who liked the canned lima beans and ham.

McGowan always wondered if Johnson had gotten the orders confused, but later he spoke to Captain Gamble, who said no, "that was the game plan." Johnson was immediately shot through both shoulders. He stood up and said he had to find McGowan so he could take over the platoon. They rolled grenades toward the Japanese to try to get by them and run across a valley to a small hill. Johnson was shot in the head with a machine gun, the Nambu that pumped out eight hundred rounds a minute and was much lighter than the cumbersome American-model 30-cal. machine guns lugged around like anvils.

Slover was maybe twenty feet up the slope of the little hill when he was shot. He yelled to Rafferty to catch his wallet and threw it to him. The Japanese finished him off. Rafferty never got the wallet. It lay there until Slover's body was picked up. Rafferty got a hole in each shoulder.

McGowan was lying on top of an Okinawan burial tomb lobbing grenades. He threw all he had, and

Martin tossed up some more from inside the tomb, where he could just see over the edge. McGowan had to cover his eyes because machine-gun fire from two sides was throwing shit up all over the place and he was afraid of getting fragments in them. He held one arm over his eyes as Martin rolled him the grenades. It was really the only way to neutralize the Japanese, lob grenades into their pillboxes or foxholes and take them inch by inch.

He felt something hit his shoulder. He looked down, and a grenade was rolling down his right leg. It fell over the lip of the tomb and blew up in Martin's face. It killed Martin instantly.

McGowan hopped off the tomb to help Martin, but it was useless. He moved off to his left to another tomb and took out his last grenade, white phosphorous. As he was about to pull the pin, he stepped too far around the side of the hill he was behind, and the Japanese got him in their sights from another hill. The grenade dropped to the ground. His right arm turned around in its socket from a bullet he took. His pack and cartridge belt were shot off. There was no pain or noise. He did not even know he had been shot through the biceps. Another bullet just missed his spine by an inch and went through his lung. That one he did feel, as though he were standing against a brick wall and the strongest man he knew had just hit him with a ten-pound sledgehammer. The bullet went all the way through. Somehow, he did not fall down. He staggered against the entrance of the tomb. He was bleeding from his mouth. He figured from watching cowboy movies that once you started bleeding from your mouth, you were dead. That was it. So get your shit together and act with final duty.

He stripped his rifle and threw it away as instructed during training so the Japanese could not use it. He called Knoss over and told him to administer one of the remaining morphine syrettes that he carried in his shirt pocket to him. Knoss shot him up in the calf. He told him to find Soper and that Soper was now in charge of the squad. The last he had seen of Soper was when he and Judge had taken the top of the hill. He crawled into the tomb for protection. He said the Lord's Prayer and the Twenty-third Psalm and lost consciousness. Sometime later somebody threw a grenade into the tomb, or maybe it was a mortar shell, and exploded the burial urns that the Okinawans kept inside. He did not awaken.

What woke him up were the inch-long ants that covered him. Ants? *Ants!* Now he was mad and said to himself that if he was going to die he was not going to be covered by a thousand ants.

"Fuck this fucking place."

He had to go back through the valley, filled with marine dead and dying, sitting ducks because the Japanese had been shooting machine guns from three sides. He had the two bullet wounds. He found a little depression where Tyree and Ruddy and Rafferty from his squad were lying wounded, next to Johnson, who was dead. He dived in with them. They lay there flat all day. Japanese snipers knew their location, so they could not move. They were lying partially in water, and McGowan could hear his lungs sucking in liquid. The others tried to stop his bleeding, but they could not get a patch on. A marine holding his rifle above his head at high port came running, most likely looking for McGowan. He was blown away. In midafternoon, the Japanese started walking mortars six feet this way and six feet that way to cover as much area as possible before hitting the precise mark. Ruddy and Tyree lay there, knowing it was coming. McGowan was spread-eagled on his back—they all were—with his helmet over his nuts. He still knew his priorities.

A mortar shell landed beside his right foot and blew half of his boot off. Shrapnel shot into his right foot. A piece of shrapnel got stuck in Tyree's forehead, and McGowan reached over and pulled it out. Another mortar landed next to McGowan's head and didn't go off because of the mud. McGowan couldn't drink any water because he thought he was gut shot. It didn't matter anyway because the canteens were full of bullet holes. Another runner came in, and everyone screamed at him:

"Get down! Get down!"

"The lieutenant says to tell you—"

He was shot through the head and fell on top of the three of them. He was dead, but his body was still thrashing and kicking McGowan: he used his last syrette of morphine to put a stop to it. They pushed the body out to use as a shield.

Around 4:00 p.m., three tanks and a platoon of marines came roaring in. The tank started firing a machine gun. The three men still in the ditch were holding their heads down because of the ricochet, and a bullet landed in the middle of McGowan's back and burned like hell. McGowan put a helmet on Ruddy's rifle and stuck it up as high as he could without getting shot.

"There's marines in here! There's marines in here!"

The tank commander popped through the hatch. McGowan told him to get the hell out of there. The Japanese had eight-inch artillery shells registered on the exact spot. The tank commander didn't believe him. Right then shells started falling, blasting up two-foot clumps of earth that fell all around them. A marine supporting the tanks was standing over McGowan. He was big, about 200 pounds.

He was disemboweled.

He fell on top of the three of them. The tank driver did a 180 to get out. Rafferty, Ruddy, and Tyree made their move and climbed onto the tank in the hope of reaching safety. McGowan thought there was too much flying shrapnel and decided to wait until twilight: he hoped the Japanese might relax a little bit because of the time of day and not get a good bead on him. Around nightfall, he went. He had a hundred yards to go to relative safety, which felt like a hundred miles. Somehow, despite his wounds, he was able to run; he didn't know how he did it, the adrenaline rush of the body trying to save itself. He didn't want the aid of corpsmen. The two attached to the platoon had both lost their legs anyway.

He was taken to an aid station, where the doctor asked if he wanted a Coke.

"I always heard you got brandy." He gulped down a hit and passed out.

When he woke up, there was a corpsman next to him.

"We thought we lost you a couple of times last night."

McGowan did not have any personal possessions, but he wanted to thank the corpsman, so he gave him his leather belt. He was still partially in shock. They loaded him onto a jeep in the prone position to another aid station. The jeep was ambushed. The driver took off running.

McGowan lay there watching bullets go through the back of the jeep. He didn't think much about them; they were more of a curiosity, just some more bullets, big deal, let's see where they land. Other marines saw what the driver had done and screamed at him to get back into the jeep. He did.

McGowan was taken to a field hospital that was being shelled, and he could hear someone screaming that his arm had just been blown off, but he was stiff as a board and could not roll under his cot for protection.

A few days later, he was flown to a hospital in Guam. As he was about to be airlifted from Guam to Hawaii a nurse asked him, "Would you like a cigarette, soldier?"

"I'm not a soldier. I'm a marine!"

Don't ever fucking forget it.

After Guam, he was sent to Hawaii, then to a hospital in San Diego. He didn't want his parents to know how seriously he had been injured. So he got Staff Sergeant Sam Regal, his best friend from home, who had also been with the marines on Okinawa, to write a letter for McGowan saying that he had only been wounded in the arm, little more than a scratch, even though he was being evacuated. Regal had visited McGowan in the field hospital and knew he had almost died. Seeing him shook him up to the point of tears—but he wrote the letter anyway and never mentioned the second bullet that had nicked his lung. A few days later, McGowan wrote to his father, one of the few letters he ever wrote to him, and told him what had really happened. Then he wrote his mother, "Guess I'll be back with company in five or six weeks. . . . Today they pinned a Purple Heart on me. I'll send it home as soon as I can get around. Don't know if I'll ever look at it again when I get home. I'm just another vet who's been there now."

He grieved over the obliteration of his squad: four killed—Martin, Soper, Laney, Judge; nine wounded—McGowan, Lancer, Huber, Thibodeau, Rafferty, Nuzzi, LaFountain, Novitski, Knoss.

He wondered, as all men in combat wonder, what else he could have done, if he had abandoned Soper and Judge on that little hill, if they had made it to the top knowing that they were going to get killed but hoping to draw enough fire to save him. McGowan had been closest to Soper in the platoon, but he had also had a soft spot for Josephus Judge. He was eighteen years old and had grown up in rural West Virginia. McGowan wondered if he had ever worn shoes before he got into the Marine Corps. He was small and wiry, hardly a hunk, except that he had been an ornery little turd and liked going across the street in Pine Grove to try to beat up the neighborhood kid, just as the neighborhood kid liked to try to do the same to him.

When they found him, his head had been impaled on a stake.

He was gone, and so was Soper, and McGowan, despite his serious injuries, was still alive. It was no accident that after the war he developed a serious drinking problem that lasted for more than twenty years until he righted himself. He began to speak and write about what had happened to him, and it was only in the catharsis of doing so that he found a semblance of peace.

He remained in the Marine Reserves after Okinawa. He was called up for the Korean War. He had to stand there naked for a physical inspection by some staff sergeant who did not have a single campaign ribbon and told him to bend over and saw where one of the bullets had entered and said in a loud voice that everyone could hear:

"Birthmark, middle of the back."

"Birthmark? That's a bullet hole, you stateside son of a bitch! Here's another one! Here's two more!"

That made the point. Somebody along the line realized that taking bullets, coughing up blood from a nicked lung, getting hit with shrapnel in the foot, crawling out from a mass of ants, and finding his best buddies all dead was enough service to the country.

Fifty-five men from the 6th Marine Division died the same day, May 14th, on which McGowan was wounded, twenty-nine from the 29th Regiment.

The regiment would soon join the 22nd Marines in their siege of the hill roughly three hundred yards wide and fifty feet high, so small it did not show up on standard military contour maps. It was named Sugar Loaf because of its resemblance to a sugarloaf cake. In the landscape of Okinawa, it was pathetic-looking, a pimple on the ruined earth.

Taken retreat retaken, taken retreat retaken, taken retreat retaken a third time and a fifth time and a seventh time and a ninth time and still not taken against an enemy in one of its strongest defensive positions of the entire war, concealed within a warren of caves and connecting tunnels with camouflaged machine-gun nests, unseen mortar pits, and superb use of artillery. Most deadly of all was the mutually supporting fire not just from Sugar Loaf itself but from Horseshoe and Half Moon,* those three inconsequential hills a triangular arrowhead of death, now of pivotal strategic

---

* Half Moon was also known as Crescent.

significance for the entire Okinawa campaign. Attack Sugar Loaf, and a blizzard of fire came from Horseshoe to the right and Half Moon to the left. Attack Half Moon, and a blizzard of fire came from Sugar Loaf and Horseshoe. Attack Horseshoe, and a blizzard of fire came from Half Moon and Sugar Loaf. The surrounding area was skinned of life by artillery and mortar shells, so there was little cover. You had to keep moving, get to the top of the hills and stay there, even though the Japanese had the reverse slopes expertly covered and could fire accurately from below.

So many officers and rank and file were killed and wounded that companies were depleted. Replacements came up, did not have a clue about what to do, and were scorned by the vets because they were taking over for men loved and gone. They were thrown into battle to fulfill manpower requirements—essentially alone, sometimes shooting wildly, pulling a pin on a grenade and then trying to shove it back in, perhaps their best use as dead bodies shielding foxholes.

None of the players of the Mosquito Bowl, virtually the entire sixty-five-man roster from the 29th and 4th Regiments, would ever be the same after the fighting on that sugary sweet hill and the surrounding area.

32

At All Costs

George Murphy never talked much with his Mosquito Bowl teammate David Mears about the daughter he had never seen. Murphy was so modest that Mears was surprised to find out that he had not simply been a starting end on the Notre Dame football team in 1942 but the captain. Murphy took a drink at the officers' club but never to excess. Contrary to Bauman, he did not brag of his benders, real or imagined. He had no discernible idiosyncrasies, unlike their other tentmate, Bus Bergman, who loved the feel of a cigar in his mouth although he never smoked them. Mears was a little different as well, improbably nicknamed "The Beast," given that he had been a journeyman offensive tackle at Boston University and wasn't that big at six feet and 185 pounds. He did not have a big temper. He did not get into fights. The only thing Mears could figure was that he acted *beastly*, whatever exactly that meant. Both Mears and Bergman had played for the 29th in the Mosquito Bowl, and so of course did Murphy.

Three days before Murphy landed on Okinawa, he wrote a letter to his wife, Mary Catherine, following afternoon Mass on board ship. He had been going to Mass and taking Communion every day during Holy Week, "asking the Lord to take care of me. I feel confident that he will, he always has so I'm not too much afraid."

Murphy had shipped out overseas the day after Mary Grace had been born. She turned eight months old the same day he wrote the letter: March 29th of 1945. Guadalcanal, where he had first arrived in the fall of 1944, had kept him busy with training. He had no time to dwell on morbid thoughts. But on the eve of battle . . .

"I would give everything to see you and Mary Grace right now. I don't think I've ever been as lonesome for anybody in my whole life."

Murphy and his men were told to take Sugar Loaf on May 15th of 1945, so they took the top of the hill and held on. But even before they went in, it was clear that the marines had come into disaster; the siege would take seven days to gain 520 yards, an average of 74.286 yards a day.

From the initial approach to Sugar Loaf to the end, at the start of a major southward push on General Buckner's orders, the 6th Marine Division would suffer 2,662 killed, wounded, or missing in action.

Sugar Loaf was misnamed. It should have been called Suicide Hill. Instead, it was given another name by the marines: "This piece of shit."

The three hills stood about a mile from the centuries-old Shuri Castle. They formed the western anchor of the Shuri Line, and their defenses were incredibly well manned and fortified. Underneath the castle were the headquarters of the Thirty-second Army of the Imperial Japanese Army, 160 feet beneath the surface at its deepest point. Its main tunnel ran 1,280 feet in length, housing as many as a thousand men in a combination of primitive squalor and incongruous luxury. The pantry of Commander Ushijima had been stocked with fine food and decent scotch whiskey, unlike that of the soldiers, who ate balls of rice. The second in command, Lieutenant General Isamu Cho, had brought along a chef and a pastry chef to make afternoon tea. There were bunks, a dispensary, a makeshift hospital, a telegraph section, an air intelligence section, a weather section, and a kitchen. The smoke from cooking was diverted through exhaust shafts screened from the view of US troops.

The temperature inside was often 90 degrees with

100 percent humidity. The innards were never dry, and men developed rashes. There were shafts and fans to provide fresh air, but they were ineffective; the smell of feces and blood and piss and pus was pervasive once wounded started coming in. The lights were never turned off. Night became day and day became night, as the command staff could work only after dark, when it was safe for messengers to go back and forth between the headquarters and the troops. They toiled until just before dawn and tried to fall asleep as the daily bombardment began, rattling the walls lined with thick planks of wood, the sounds of explosion after explosion causing psychological terror but the bombs never penetrating the complex.

As horrible as the conditions in the tunnels could be, the Japanese defense was working far better than anyone on the American side had imagined it could. Japan had no navy left. The vast majority of its planes were used for kamikaze attacks, and they were rapidly being whittled down. Their firepower came nowhere close to the Americans'. Yet the Japanese military was stringing the battle out just as they had hoped.

The main Japanese defensive position, the Shuri Line, ran from a little north of Naha, Okinawa's largest town, through Shuri Castle, in the center, to Yonabaru. It was about eight miles long and fundamentally a system of bunkers and tunnels cut into the sides of ravines and hills, with no elevation over five hundred feet. Sixty miles of tunnels had been dug by hand, with their entrances shielded on reverse slopes: the backs of the hillsides, away from the enemy's expected approach. Outside, slit trenches allowed for safe movement between positions. Antitank guns, machine guns, mortars, and artillery pieces poked out through narrow slits. Altogether, the system of pillboxes and caves was vast enough to conceal virtually the entire Japanese force of more than a hundred thousand men.

To force the collapse of the Shuri Line, the marines would have to hack their way through one powerfully fortified position after another, and Sugar Loaf was the worst of them all. To take and hold Sugar Loaf meant simultaneously moving against the other two hills that supported it with deadly interlocking fire. They would need to conquer not just Sugar Loaf but the two other hills as well. In conquering those hills, men were forced to witness what no man should ever have to.

Splintered bones. Open abdominal wounds with glistening intestines. Legs blown off at the knee and arms blown off at the socket. There were so many worsts, but men talked most of all about the maggots, what seemed like millions cramming the dead flesh of a wound so you couldn't even see the wound anymore, frantic and frenzied and fighting down to the last scrap black or greasy. The long sigh of a man before he died, maybe at the absurdity of how that was the way it all ended, in the middle of fucking nowhere. A marine with stumps where his legs had once been trying to stand. A man trying to run back to his trench after a shell reduced him to a little bit here and a little bit there. Stepping on a mine where a split second before you had seen a body and the second later there was only a vapor of bloody mist. Dying of a single bullet hole in the helmet and a picture of Mom slipping out from inside the crown. A marine with his brain neatly scooped out like an ice cream cone. Making sure that you approached the hulks of tanks from upwind to minimize the smell of the bodies that had burned to death inside. Blood spray in an operating room hitting the ceiling of the tent and the doctor covering the wound he was operating on with a sterile towel so it would not become contaminated with drippings from the top of the canvas. Men slipping and falling on the spilled innards of dead Japanese soldiers. Eating rations a few feet away from the arm of a Japanese soldier sticking out. Ho hum. Big deal.

Morell's 6th Tank Battalion was threading its way carefully through the minefields near Sugar Loaf when one of the tanks hit an antitank mine stacked with two five-hundred-pound bombs. The tank flew upward, flipped over, and landed on its turret. The warped metal made it impossible for the five men inside to use the escape hatch, and the metal was too hot for anyone else to touch it. All they could do was listen to the screams.

On the afternoon of May 14th, the 22nd Regiment's 2nd Battalion, cursed with a good idea of what awaited them, launched a combined tank and infantry assault on Sugar Loaf. Tanks leading the men across the flat ground toward the base of the hill were quickly disabled or driven off by severe 47 mm fire. By 1500, the 2nd Battalion's Fox Company was pinned down and taking heavy losses. They tried another push, again supported by tanks, and again they were cut down by devastating machine-gun and mortar fire. With dusk approaching, Major Henry A. Courtney, Jr., the executive officer of the 2nd Battalion, gathered the remaining seventeen marines from Fox Company and another twenty-seven from George Company, who had survived their units' own disastrous attack on Sugar Loaf two days previously. His plan was to have his men move up the slope in a line, under cover of darkness, then dig in and hold the top of the hill. That was what they did—but spread thin and pinned down for hours just below the crest, their position was untenable.

The marines and the Japanese were lobbing grenades at each other over the crest of the hill, each side unable to see the other. Bullets, mortar shells, heavy artillery. To break the stalemate, Courtney instructed his marines to fix their bayonets, creep up to the crest, throw two grenades each, then charge over the top. It seemed to work—but only for a moment. Soon the south slope of the hill was swarming with Japanese again, and a furious mortar barrage ripped across the marines' thin line. Courtney was killed, a fragment of shrapnel slashing across his neck. All night, the marines faced a merciless barrage of shelling and shooting, even from behind them, where Japanese had infiltrated by tunnel or crept around the sides of the hill. They were getting massacred. At dawn, they were down to one officer and nineteen exhausted men. There was no way they were going to keep the foothold on the hill without help.

The 22nd had been decimated in trying to capture Sugar Loaf and the surrounding terrain. The regiment's commander, Colonel Merlin Schneider, was relieved on the orders of the 6th Marine Division commander, Major General Shepherd. He later said he had believed that Schneider was simply worn out. But there was scuttlebutt that he had been relieved for his refusal to send his men to assault the hill again until they had a day of rest to regroup.

In the midst of the assault on the Sugar Loaf complex, five players serving in the 29th who had played in the Mosquito Bowl were wounded: John Genis, Eli Kaluger, David Mears, Jennings Moates, Robert Neff.

At all costs.

||

On the morning of May 15th, Lieutenant Colonel Horatio Woodhouse of the 22nd Regiment was convinced that his Company K could hold the hill with the help of the 29th. The task went to Dog Company, and the first to go forward was George Murphy's 3rd Platoon. It was clear that there was barely a toehold left on Sugar Loaf and the marines who had been there all night were about to be overrun. Murphy's platoon of about sixty men pushed up the hill and found themselves facing a concentrated counterattack. The hilltop was still held by marines, but the Japanese were about to take over its topmost ridge, and Murphy needed to hold it. He ordered an assault with fixed bayonets. His men reached the crest. Soon they had gone through all of the 350 grenades they carried.

Nothing worked. The attack was doomed from the beginning. Mortar shells were coming down so thickly it seemed as though the whole hilltop was exploding.

Captain Howard Mabie, the commanding officer of Company D and Murphy's superior, asked Lieutenant Colonel Woodhouse for permission to withdraw. Woodhouse refused.

At all costs.

Murphy himself radioed Mabie for permission to get the fuck out of there. The US forces were overwhelmed. Mabie said he would have to hold, on orders from Woodhouse. Murphy ordered his men to fall back anyway. Those who were left, he felt, must have a chance of staying alive, not required to commit suicide in a cause that was hopeless.

Murphy covered his men as they scurried down Sugar Loaf. He and a new recruit, Wilmot, started dragging the machine gunner, Curnutte, both of whose legs had been mangled by a grenade. Wilmot was shot in the chest. He died without a word.

In his letter to his wife Murphy had written:

Mary Grace is 8 months old today it hardly seems possible. Wish her a happy birthday for me and give her a big kiss. Be careful my darling and please don't

worry too much because I'll be home
with you before you know it. I love you
more than I can ever tell you honey and
always remember it. Good bye dear and
I'll write the first chance I get. I love you.

A mortar shell landed a few feet in front of Murphy.
Or, as it seemed to Curnutte, he was shot in the face
with a bullet.

At all costs.

George Edward Murphy was the fourth player from
the Mosquito Bowl to die.

He was buried on Okinawa in 6th Marine Division
Cemetery No. 1, Grave 208, Row 9, Plot B.

He was twenty-four years old.

33
Crazy for Revenge

Neal McCallum, a mortar man in Fox Company of the 2nd Battalion of the 29th, left the staging area of Machinato Airfield on the same day that George Murphy died. He was on his way to the battlefield with fellow members of Fox Company when they passed two trucks piled high with dead marines. They were wrapped in camouflage ponchos. He saw blotches of blood, and as he knew that the men were recent victims, it struck him how quickly blood dries, the unceremonious bleaching out of life. He saw contorted and twisted legs. He could see the agony of the men's last moments on Earth on their faces. It scared the hell out of him and everyone else. Later that day, around dusk, he and Goodman were pinned down in a shallow gulley near a bloated Japanese soldier who had been dead for two or three days, stinking as all the dead do when they are rotting away, filled with maggots. Goodman, from North Carolina, was next to him, and he kept repeating over and over, "They won't believe me. When I get back home, they will not believe this." They spent the night there, and they could see marines from the 22nd running to the rear. McCallum was thinking about the dead marines wrapped in their camouflage ponchos. He would soon go to the front line, and he couldn't understand why no one had told the 22nd to turn around and go back on the attack. He was young and inexperienced and knew nothing about combat yet, and it was only later he learned that the marines of the 22nd had been ordered to fall back. They had been up on the line fighting for three days, and they had been obliterated. The job of tackling Sugar Loaf and its two adjacent hills now fell to the 29th.

The fallen on May 16th of 1945 was worse than on May 15th.

Berg, Bruno, Cullen, Davis, Dorn, Eck, Fithian, Fox, Green, Guin, Harry, Hoffman, Hope, Hughes, John, Johnson, Keller, Lamb, Lane, Lanier, LeVine, Ludwig, Marentette,

Meyer, O'Leary, Ours, Owens, Parson, Porter,
Rowe, Shinn, Shoemaker, Slonski, Smith,
Sutton, Taylor, Trook, White, Winchester.

On May 17th of 1945, the 2nd Battalion of the 29th
moved up on Sugar Loaf. Second Lieutenant Behan,
the commander of the 2nd Platoon of Fox Company,
had been hit in the mouth with shrapnel. He was
bleeding and awkwardly bandaged and had great difficulty speaking. He should have been taken off the
line for medical attention, but he refused to go. He
was upset, angry, irrational in his fury. Murphy had
been one of his best friends. They had both been on
the 29th Regiment team in the Mosquito Bowl.

"Follow me," he mumbled, hard to understand because of his wound.

He stood up and was running almost as though he
was charging. It wasn't tactically sound. He should
have been crouching, and the need for caution was now
greater than ever. That did not matter to Behan. He
started shooting randomly with his .45-caliber pistol
in the direction of the Japanese, firing into his sadness
and hatred.

It was a gift for the Japanese.

His runner, Hulek, saw the bullets coming out

through the back of Behan's dungarees. He was shot three times in the chest by machine-gun fire.

Behan received the Navy Cross for his actions, the second highest honor a marine could receive. He had acted with bravery. He had acted with tragedy, revenge too often the refuge of the dead.

Charles Edwin Behan was the fifth player from the Mosquito Bowl to die.

He was buried on Okinawa in 6th Marine Division Cemetery No. 1, Grave 339, Row 14, Plot B.

He was twenty-four years old.

Ed Van Order had received a degree in civil engineering from Cornell University in 1942 with courses in calculus, physics, chemistry, bridge building, and drafting. He had started as a sophomore on the Cornell football team in 1939, which had gone unbeaten and been named national champion by several outlets, its most notable achievement turning down the Rose Bowl so players could catch up on their schoolwork. He had worked as a structural engineer for Curtiss-Wright, designing parts of military aircraft before enlisting in the marines in September of 1943. He was the son of a professor from Cornell and had a wife named Carolyn. He had been assigned to the Marine

Corps's air wing after boot camp but had chosen the infantry instead.

He was from the same company as Behan and died the same day of either multiple shrapnel wounds or a gunshot blast in the chest.

His mother later wrote a letter to Marine Corps headquarters asking for specific details regarding her son's death. "He is our only child sir and it is truly hard to be patient. We would appreciate any information you can give us." She also noted something else that upset her: "please note that his first name is spelled EDMUND."

Her request for information was denied. The spelling of his first name was corrected in future correspondence.

Edmund Van Order, Jr., was the sixth player from the Mosquito Bowl to die.

He was buried on Okinawa in 6th Marine Division Cemetery No. 1, Grave 149, Row 6, Plot B.

He was twenty-four years old.

34
Carry On

The day after Charlie Behan and Edmund Van Order died, there was another sustained attack on Sugar Loaf, the tenth or maybe the eleventh in a week.

The attack of the 29th Regiment went off at 8:30 a.m. on May 18th of 1945. Tanks tried to work their way through minefields and heavy fire. Six were disabled. An hour and a half later, another tactic was orchestrated at the suggestion of Captain Mabie, a joint tank-infantry advance in which half of his Company D went around the right flank of Sugar Loaf to draw the attention of the Japanese while the other half went around the left flank. With the Japanese severely weakened after a week of fighting, Mabie had been right in thinking that the flanks of Sugar Loaf would be exposed.

One tank got through on the right and one on the left.

Dog Company now controlled Sugar Loaf. But could they keep it?

Continuous mortar fire poured in from Horseshoe. Fox Company took part of the ridgeline of Horseshoe but bogged down in a grenade battle with the Japanese entrenched in a deep ravine. The fighting was close in, like the worst of trench warfare in World War I, and the fighting raged through the afternoon and dusk. The three companies of the 2nd Battalion of the 29th, Dog and Echo and Fox, each had three mortars. They fired candle flares into the night at one- or two-minute intervals in order to see Japanese troops pounding them with machine-gun fire and sneaking close with grenades. Star shell bursts were fired by ships offshore, men fighting for their lives under false stars and fake moonlight.

The main Japanese counterattack came at 0230 and it was conducted with lethal expertise. They fed reinforcements up through the ravine and hit the marines on Horseshoe with mortars lobbing white phosphorous shells and machine-gun fire that raked through Fox Company from the side. Horseshoe was temporarily lost but on Sugar Loaf, the marine lines held.

Sugar Loaf was forever theirs. The western flank of the Shuri Line was now irreparably exposed. It was only a matter of time before it would be overrun by the army's 7th and 96th Divisions and the 1st Marine Division.

The Japanese themselves were surprised at their effectiveness in keeping the Americans from taking Sugar Loaf for so long. From their vantage point on Shuri Heights, the command of the Thirty-second Army had had a perfect view of the enemy maneuvers: virtually every time the Americans attacked up until the end, they successfully counterattacked. Their mortar pits were impossible to pinpoint. The Japanese troops fought brilliantly and heroically in the triangular hills of death. They remained in their caves withstanding American artillery and tank barrages, then ran outside when the fire stopped and engaged in close-in fighting. Colonel Yahara, the chief operations officer, believed that his forces could have won the campaign of Sugar Loaf had they not run out of ammunition. There is no question that the Americans had been taken by surprise by the strength of the Japanese defense and it was only through sheer willpower, sacrifice, and bravery that the marines finally took it. It ranked with the greatest campaigns ever fought by the Marine Corps, although Buckner in his diaries made only oblique reference to it and never mentioned Sugar Loaf by name.

The once serene countryside of the Amekudai Plateau, as the Japanese called the rolling plain above the capital city of Naha, had become soaked and steeped in blood.

Yahara and Ushijima had once ridden horses together over the plateau amid the splendor of the hillocks, but now it was filled with dead bodies. War was the ultimate scavenger, stripping trees until only blackened branches were left like hanging bones, turning any reminder of life into scorched ruin, the little that was left, blown-out hulks of tanks and spent shell cases, spilling down a hill, the garbage dump of death.

The underground headquarters of the Thirty-second Army shook and echoed with blasts from US naval shells and tanks. The sweat stink of fear only got worse, the thick smell of blood only thicker, the screams and groans of the fatally wounded only louder. Ushijima sent a message to Imperial Japanese Army headquarters asking for more air support to destroy the navy ships just offshore. "We have lost many elite troops but still believe in the immortality of the Empire," he said.

But headquarters had given up on Okinawa to prepare for the invasion of the Japanese homelands. Hang in there, boys. Die for the emperor astride his white horse.

Thirty-four men from the 6th Division were pronounced dead on May 18th of 1945:

Aikens, Arndt, Berry, Bolash, Brewer, Carson, Fields, Gillespie, Haughey, Hofolter, Hood,

Irish, Johnson, Lengyel, Mannino, Marcom, Marcos, Myers, Palermo, Ragen, Rogers, Rose, Rowe, Rudy, Sabine, Sacca, Schleicher, Schrock, Schumacher, Shaughnessy, Smith, Tauss, Violette, Wier.

Seventy-eight the following day, May 19th of 1945:

Albright, Allen, Bailey, Bishop, Bogdan, Bolden, Bornheim, Boyette, Bradley, Brazleton, Brennan, Brown, Cacciofi, Carles, Carnevale, Chase, Connelly, Dancause, Dixon, Eccleston, Ellison, Everett, Exstrom, Farner, Feimster, Finn, Fischer, Freeman, Freudenstein, Gardner, Garrity, Hanson, Henderson, Hodgin, Hunt, Kalish, Kawecki, King B, King M, Kohler, Kreiner, Madigan, March, Maritato, Marshall, Mellor, Molloy, Monroe, Mullins J, Mullins J, Myers, Nesnick, Nishanian, Ortlof, O'Toole, Parsons, Petroski, Phinney, Pickard, Powell, Prpich, Rebel, Reilly, Rudsten, Ryan, Sanders, Santini, Segroves, Sloan, Sorenson, Stowinsky, Sullivan, Tennury, Van Arsdale, Vazquez, Welch, Wooler, Yester.

||

John Hebrank was a corporal in Fox Company of the 29th.

The son of a Baltimore architect, he had graduated from Charlotte Hall Military Academy in Charlotte Hall, Maryland, where he had been captain of the football team, class president for four years, and winner of the Burr Award for being the "most polite and considerate boy in our cadet corps." He attended Lehigh University in Bethlehem, Pennsylvania, in the fall of 1942 before enlisting.

He died on May 19th of 1945. The cause was unknown.

In a letter his mother, Adelaide, sent to the Marine Corps after being notified of her son's death, she wrote:

"To know that God called my son, while serving with the U. S. Marine Corps, to give his life, for the ideals and standards we know to be the highest and noblest, is my greatest comfort. In the name of those who died, as he did, to those of us left behind, I might add CARRY ON."

She received his personal effects—or at least thought she did, but the wrong inventory was sent inside the envelope, causing the Marine Corps to apologize for its carelessness. His mother later discovered through a friend who saw his grave marker in Okinawa that his name had been misspelled. The marker was corrected.

The death gratuity paid to his parents was $107.15.

John Hilbert Hebrank was the seventh player from the Mosquito Bowl to die.

He was buried on Okinawa in 6th Marine Division Cemetery No. 1, Grave 526, Row 22, Plot A.

He was twenty-one years old.

The taking of Sugar Loaf Hill was hardly the end of the campaign. For McLaughry and Schreiner and the rest of the 4th Regiment, it had just begun after they relieved the 29th in the early morning of May 19th of 1945. As the 29th withdrew and the 4th took its place, casualties piled up in what was known as the Valley of Death. Calls for corpsmen became constant: attending to the wounded, they had to chase away buddies who wanted to help but were only in the way.

James Brennan, the kid from Flushing with the rocket arm, was in Echo Company in the 2nd Battalion of the 4th Regiment. He was one of seven from the company who died on May 19th during the relief of the 29th Regiment. The cause was multiple wounds.

He had enlisted in the Marine Corps on March 18th of

1943. He had gone through basic training at Parris Island and had then been sent to Quantico, where he had fallen asleep on watch and been confined to ten days in the brig. It was a minor blemish.

James John Brennan was the eighth player from the Mosquito Bowl to die.

He was buried on Okinawa in 6th Marine Division Cemetery No. 1, Grave 546, Row 22, Plot A.

He was twenty years old.

Early the next morning of May 20th of 1945, Schreiner and McLaughry and the 4th set out to neutralize Horseshoe hill. Schreiner's platoon was close to its full strength of roughly forty-five but many were replacements, making his job only harder, trying to lead men whose names he did not know and in some instances would never know because they died so quickly. McLaughry at this point was reluctant to make any effort to befriend new men coming onto the line. He saw little point when they were going to get killed.

His heavy weapons unit lent invaluable support to the infantry. The Japanese still had the upper hand because of their vantage point but the laying down of artillery by the Americans and the resulting smoke made it difficult for the Japanese command to effectively observe. It hardly stopped them.

Schreiner frantically dug foxholes and lay flat on the ground as the enemy poured in fire. By virtue of an enveloping action that afternoon, the 4th Regiment gained the high ground on the eastern half of Horseshoe, enabling it to look down on Japanese mortar positions that had wreaked such havoc. It gained about two hundred yards before being forced to halt because of continuous fire.

That night the Japanese laid down a barrage of mortar fire in a skillfully executed counterattack. The 4th and the enemy virtually blended into one, almost impossible in the darkness to tell who was on what side. Marines were forced to toss grenades into adjacent foxholes already filled with the dead because of fear that the Japanese had infiltrated. Illumination shells from 60 mm mortars lit up the sky. There was hand-to-hand fighting. Rain came down, turning the ground into soupy mud. Ammunition had to be carried in by hand. Six battalions of marine artillery came down on the Japanese. The enemy continued to come, but no ground was lost and five hundred Japanese soldiers were killed.

Fifty-two from the 6th Division were pronounced dead that day:

Ahlgrim, Bock, Brown, Brusman, Burleigh, Callahan, Carlson, Conron, Crosby, Doyle, Eder, Fennell, Fleck, Fodi, Fornof, Fowler, Freer, Hart, Harwick, Hendricks, Hill, Holman, Jones, Jones, Keegan, Keeler, Mansfield, Martino, McCaskill, McClure, McConnell, McCormick, McLaughlin, Morris, Nation, Olson, Peavy, Player, Probst, Reiff, Robertson, Sanders, Sealy, Selig, Sims, Smith, Stoskopf, Thomas, VanCamp, Wagner, Wallace, Whitman.

Don Jones was a private from Echo Company in the 2nd Battalion of the 4th Regiment, the same company as Brennan. He had enlisted on October 9th of 1943 and was married.

He died on May 20th of 1945 of multiple wounds in the advance on Horseshoe.

Until 1947, his family held out a slim hope that he might still be alive after they had not heard from him on Okinawa. The marines finally confirmed that he had died in action.

Don Lee Jones was the ninth player from the Mosquito Bowl to die.

He was buried on Okinawa in 6th Marine Division Cemetery No. 1, Grave 412, Row 17, Plot B.

He was twenty-one years old.

III

To further its gains over the next several days, the 4th Regiment advanced to the outskirts of the capital of Naha; Schreiner's platoon and others were slowed down by stepping around the bodies of dead Japanese soldiers. Naha, a pile of rubble from previous bombardment, was taken.

Elements of the 6th Division had been in continuous combat for almost two weeks with no hot food or coffee or opportunity to bathe. A hard rain was beginning to fall. The army divisions were almost always given relief for rest and movies and hot showers. For McLaughry and Schreiner, this caused inevitable morale problems for the marines they led, further fueling the conviction that the army got everything and the marines got nothing except shit and more shit.

On May 21st of 1945, fifty-four were pronounced dead from the 6th Marine Division, fifty-one from the 4th Regiment:

Ablett, Arnold, Bowers, Bradford, Bunch, Carr, Clossen, Conroy, Crilley, Crouse, Decker, Dellagnena, Ella, Feickert, Fields, Ford, Fortier, Frank, Gibson, Higgins, Jablonicky, Jennings, Johannes, Karrio, King, Lord, Lucas, Luther, Marley, McBurney, McGee, McKenzie, Miller, Mioduski, Morgan, Munsey, Nickel, Okunevich, Owens, Paca, Phillips, Pisciotta, Richards, Roden, Schellenberg, Schildt, Sekula, Stovall, White, Wood, Zeolite.

Among those wounded that day was Hubbard Hinde, Jr., a first lieutenant in Alpha Company of the 4th Regiment. When he was a teenager in San Angelo, Texas, both his parents had been killed in a car crash. He had gone to live with his aunt Edna in Dallas in 1938 and had graduated from Southern Methodist University with a major in biology on June 8th of 1942. He appeared to be following in the footsteps of his father who had been a prominent doctor. But his career would have to wait. Nine days later, he applied to be an officer candidate in the Marine Corps.

Hinde served in the 2nd Marine Raider Battalion along with McLaughry and received a Purple Heart for a shrapnel wound received at Guam. He became a platoon leader. His last fitness report before Okinawa, based on nineteen different categories, showed fifteen "excellent" ratings and four "outstanding" ones. His commanding officer recommended that every effort be made to keep him in the Marine Corps after the war.

He received a gunshot wound in the shoulder as the 4th Regiment took control of Horseshoe on May 21st of 1945 and made its way to Naha. His prognosis was initially considered favorable, but it wasn't until an X-ray was taken that it was determined that the bullet had lodged in his left chest posterior. By the time he was evacuated to US Fleet Hospital 111 on Guam, his lower extremities were completely paralyzed. His pupils were contracted, and there were no reflexes. He passed away on May 25th of 1945.

In a letter of recommendation for Hinde in 1942 when he had applied to become an officer candidate, a Southern Methodist professor had written that after so many severe tests in his life because of the simultaneous death of his parents, he had the kind of character to withstand anything.

Hubbard Kavanaugh Hinde, Jr., was the tenth player from the Mosquito Bowl to die.

He was buried on Guam in Military Cemetery No. 2, Grave 6, Row 31, Plot C.

He was twenty-five years old.

35
Last Stand

The marines thought their days and nights of relentless combat might be over for good at the end of May. The triangle of Sugar Loaf, Crescent, and Horseshoe had been neutralized. When US troops overcame the small Japanese rear guard and climbed the high ground that had been the heart of the Shuri Line, all that was left were the skeletal carcasses of once recognizable humans.

The combat had been relentless for McLaughry, like nothing he had ever seen before, but he also knew he was lucky. His heavy-weapons platoon was utilized only during the day, allowing his men and him to retire to the rear area each night to get some rest. Other weapons platoons were not so fortunate. Howarth had been roly-poly and weighed about 170 pounds when he and McLaughry had been tentmates on Guadalcanal. When McLaughry saw him around the end of May, he weighed about 140 and figured he had slept maybe twelve hours a week during the campaign.

Rain had pounded down for ten straight days at the end of May, misery added to misery. Terrain turned to mud. Foxholes became pots of viscous stew. Vehicles came to a standstill. Even the vaunted amtracs, designed to overcome such conditions, had trouble getting through.

It rained seven inches in four days. Buckner found the weather an inconvenient delay on the way to a victory he felt was so close: "I had caught (the Japanese) napping and shoved a division past their right flank," he wrote to his wife. Once again Buckner was a victim of his own hubris and shocking underestimation of the Japanese. In another daring gamble, with cloud and rain blocking virtually all US air reconnaissance, Ushijima was in the process of withdrawing roughly forty-five thousand soldiers to another line of fortified escarpments, eleven miles farther south.

As far as some senior commanders were concerned, it wasn't simply that Buckner did not listen but the way he did not listen with his grandiose grandiloquence—witty in a mint julep recipe, perhaps, but not so much when so many soldiers, marines, and seamen were dying because of his tortoise-slow deliberateness. "Buckner is tiresome," Joseph W. "Vinegar Joe" Stilwell, a four-star general and commander of the army ground forces, wrote in his diary after he left Washington to make an inspection trip of the Pacific Theater. "I tried to tell him what I had seen, but he knew it all. Keeps repeating his wise-cracks. 'The Lord said let there be mud,' etc. etc. . . . There is NO tactical thinking or push. No plan was ever discussed at the meetings to hasten the fight or help the divisions."

The senior officers and staff of the Japanese Thirty-second Army gathered in a room next to Ushijima's office in the underground headquarters bunker around a table of canned pineapples, canned clams, and sake. Some felt that the last stand should be made at the Shuri Castle, given that there were roughly a thousand wounded who could not be moved. Yahara believed that withdrawal was the only way to continue the battle of attrition and force the Americans to keep fighting and dying. In other words, the wounded should be left behind in an underground cave that because of the rains was now flooded knee-high with water. Before Yahara left, he arranged the furniture neatly to leave a "good impression," as he put it in his memoir. Ushijima took along a folding fan. Two members of his staff guzzled beer, saying it was their last duty before they died. The seriously wounded who could not be transported south knew how to kill themselves: with cyanide, a hand grenade, or a satchel charge. By the time the Japanese retreated to the Kiyan Peninsula at the very southern tip of Okinawa, there were about thirty thousand troops remaining out of roughly a hundred thousand.

They would make their last stand.

36

Regret to Inform

The one thing in the world that Schreiner hated the most, the invasion of his privacy, happened again.

He had suffered a sprained ankle on Okinawa while playing volleyball and made for a two-line squib in papers back home. A sportswriter apparently sent it to Schreiner, thinking he would like it.[*]

Schreiner was humiliated by the image of his punching a volleyball while the bloodiest battle in the history of the Pacific war raged. He had played during breaks in combat, as there had been many breaks in

---

[*] One of the unsung miracles of Okinawa was the handling of mail. A total of 2,413,921 incoming letters and packages was handled by the military postal services. The time in transit for incoming mail averaged nine days, and mail was even delivered to men on the line during brief lulls in combat. A total of 2,030,315 pieces of outgoing mail and packages was handled. The average time of delivery was seven days.

combat, in particular during the first ten days of April, when his battalion had experienced virtually no opposition. Since his parents had given out information on him before, he may have suspected them as the source again. But he let it go.

He filled his letters with his usual abundance of love and consideration for his mother and father. He never let them know what he had seen and heard or even felt, no matter how obliquely. Servicemen were restricted in what they could say because of censorship, but some did allude to the horrors.

He sounded confident without contrivance. Like McLaughry, he had the sense that the days of combat for his battalion, the 4th Regiment, and the 6th Marine Division really were over. He could not wait to see his grandmother in Stoughton, Wisconsin, as soon as he got home. He rejoiced over the news that Hadley Hoskins, who had survived his plane being shot down, had been released from a German prisoner-of-war camp after V-E Day and was on his way back home to Lancaster. Schreiner's sister, Betty, was pregnant, and he hoped, as did Betty and her husband, that it would be a boy after their first child, a girl. He told them not to worry.

"You can count on several boys from me and Odette!"

He meant it. He could see it.

He continued to make Okinawa sound like the canoe trip he had once taken as a camp counselor in Minnesota, his only concession to war that he had gone through some "interesting experiences." He might have been one of the few marines in history to effusively praise the ration smorgasbord of canned ham and eggs, chicken and vegetables, frankfurters and beans, spaghetti and meatballs. He did eat fresh fish one night, caught by throwing grenades into the deep holes of a stream and then diving for them. He ate vegetables from an Okinawan garden. He found a cold and bracing flow of water coming down from the hills and stood under it every morning as if to liberate himself from all he had become in war. Best of all, he was reunited with Bob Bauman.

Bob's brother, Frank, had had it wrong; despite his injuries, he had not been sent home. He had decided to return to combat at the beginning of June of 1945, leaving the hospital and getting a lift back to Okinawa by plane from Guam.*

---

* His marine pilot was Tyrone Power, a matinee idol of the 1930s famous for having played the role of Zorro in *The Mark of Zorro*. In 1939, he was named the second most popular actor in the United States next to Mickey Rooney. Power had enlisted in the Marine Corps, become a cargo pilot, and had also helped ferry the wounded at both Iwo Jima and Okinawa.

The hope for the end of combat disappeared. After roughly a day of rest in early June, the 4th and 29th Regiments were ordered south to attack the Japanese on the Oroku Peninsula after they had withdrawn from Shuri. After the Motobu Peninsula and Mount Yaetake in the north, after the bloodbath of Sugar Loaf and Horseshoe in the south, how much more could a man in the 6th Division take? Luck was a finite commodity—nobody had it forever—and it was getting tired.

James Quinn was a first lieutenant and platoon leader in George Company of the 4th Regiment. He had been raised in Erie, Pennsylvania, one of seven children born to Francis Bernard and Mary Quinn. He had graduated from the College of the Holy Cross in Massachusetts, where he had been good football material as a freshman until permanently sidelined by injury. He had played excellent tennis and golf, had been at the top of the dean's list academically, had enjoyed a good book and pipe, and had given spirited discourses on the quality of various dance orchestras. He had hoped to follow in the footsteps of his father and become an attorney. In June of 1942, he had entered the marines within days of graduation as an officer candidate.

He died on June 4th of 1945 on the Oroku Peninsula.

James Matthew Quinn was the eleventh player from the Mosquito Bowl to die.

He was buried in Honolulu, Hawaii, in the National Memorial Cemetery of the Pacific, Grave 270, Row 0, Plot N.

He was twenty-four years old.

II

The same week as Quinn was killed, Bob Bauman wrote a letter to his brother. Always watching out for Frank, who was now in officer training at Quantico, Bob told him to look up an old friend there who might help make things a little easier for him.

The letter was short. Most of his letters were short when there was no beer involved. Even then they were short: "I'll write later Frank and keep in touch with you. Until next time take things easy."

He signed "Your Bro" in a fine flourish of script, then added "Semper Fi" at the bottom with a little parenthetical: ("B.S.") He did not mention that he had left the hospital.

He was going into a battle unrecognizable from the one he had left roughly a month earlier: more brutal, more unforgiving, more desperate than ever for the Japanese, pinned to the southern end of the island.

Bauman had missed the entire campaign of Sugar Loaf and the aftermath of trying to neutralize the other two hills. No regiment in the 6th Marine Division, no battalion, no company, no platoon was still the same; there had been too much loss, too much horror, too much sadness bottlenecked, too many sights and sounds that had crawled in and rang like an endless bell, too much exhaustion and fucked-up nerves. Officers had been killed, replaced by other officers, who had promptly been killed.

The Oroku Peninsula on the southern end of Okinawa was a series of escarpments facing the sea, marked by low, steep cliffs. The Japanese installations at the base of the escarpments were hidden from aerial photography. Caves had been built into the sides from which to mount a typically ruthless Japanese defense aided by excellent fields of vision from which to observe the movements as the 4th attacked from flat terrain. An estimated twelve hundred Japanese naval troops, well trained in infantry tactics, would defend the peninsula, armed with weaponry that included machine guns from aircraft converted to ground use and rocket fire.

The 4th Regiment made an amphibious landing on the peninsula in the early morning darkness of June 4th of 1945 on the west coast of Okinawa, in battered amphibious tractors that had become worn out after two months of service. Many of them broke down. The regiment still arrived on time, Bauman and Schreiner and McLaughry moving their platoons to gain ground, trying to motivate men who suffered from delayed psychoneurosis and hung on the thinnest edge of function. The advance continued on June 5th of 1945 against the stiff resistance. The roads leading to the high ground of the Japanese defense had been mined. Machine-gun and light-mortar fire and 20 mm guns attempted to impede the regiment's progress or at least buy time. The Japanese were being compressed into smaller and smaller areas with few escape routes. But they were still making effective use of caves for surprise attacks and protecting the seizure of hills with fire from the opposite slopes.

The weather on June 6th of 1945 was overcast with thick, dark clouds and light to moderate rain, the temperature at about 70 degrees with 90 percent humidity, another gloomy and sodden day. The advance stalled. Civilians were fleeing for cover. The commander of Company A, Captain Clint Eastment, went ahead with scouts and put Bauman in charge.

Schreiner's platoon got pinned down as it approached the top of one of the enemy-controlled hills. Regardless of how many men he now commanded, Bauman had to rescue his best friend, get him out of the fire. The fighting grew fiercer, the flanks of the regiment exposed.

McLaughry was on the radio with Bauman, separated only fifty feet away by a ridge, hoping to give fire support to him and Schreiner's platoon.

Bauman and his men were blindsided by enemy fire from an opposite slope. Schreiner and Sergeant Argus "Gus" Forbus were trying to get their own men out.

Schreiner turned to Forbus as they scrambled for their lives down a trail.

"That looks like Bob!"

Schreiner wanted to stop. He wanted to help. He wanted to go back. Forbus knew better. They were under attack. Their platoon was getting the shit kicked out of it. To do anything but get out was to die. Forbus could apparently see what maybe Schreiner could also see but refused to.

There was no way to save Bob Bauman.

His skull had been shattered by a bullet.

III

Back home in Harvey, Bertha Bauman heard over a Chicago radio station that Schreiner had hurt his ankle playing volleyball. It was wonderful news to Bertha since it meant he was still alive. "I'm so glad," she wrote in a letter to his mother, Anne, in mid-June of 1945. But she was worried about her own son Bob. His last letter had been on May 12th, and that had been over a month before. "This has been such a terribly long time to wait and wonder what has happened to them. Won't you please let me know if you have any more news?" She did not yet know.

On the evening of June 20th of 1945, Frank Bauman and his friend John McConnell flew to Chicago and then caught a bus to 154th Street and Center Avenue in Harvey. They had both been commissioned earlier that morning as second lieutenants at Quantico and were going home on ten days' leave to celebrate.

Frank had been thinking of his homecoming for weeks and that maybe Bob would already be there, sent back to the States because of his wounds. Frank started walking home. It was only a few blocks away. He crossed the street and was in front of Casey's pool hall. Someone inside saw him. He was puzzled by Frank's cheerful demeanor. He went outside.

"Frank, don't you know?"

"Know what?"

"I hate to be the one to tell you, but Bob was killed on Okinawa."

Frank's mother had received the telegram the day before at 7:45 p.m. She had waited to tell him in person.

Frank kept walking past a cluster of local taverns. He took a right on Center Avenue and walked another block to his house, the one with the double roof peaks and the wraparound porch, the place where he and his brother had grown up too quickly but also the place where Sunday dinner was a tradition, the place Bob had seen from the train whenever he and his University of Wisconsin teammates had taken a Chicago & North Western train to Madison.

Bertha Bauman would never be the same again. Neither would Frank, who almost immediately made two choices that would define the rest of his life. The first was to try to keep his mother's spirits up whatever it took, tell her over and over that it was God's plan for Bob to give up his life in the service of his men and did not want anyone to go through what he had and he was now where he should be. He would have wanted it this way, he kept telling her. Less than twenty-four hours earlier, Frank had become a full-fledged officer in the

United States Marine Corps, just like his brother. Now Bob was eight strips of type:

DEEPLY REGRET TO INFORM YOU THAT YOUR SON FIRST LIEUTEN- ANT ROBERT F BAUMAN USMCR WAS KILLED IN ACTION 6 JUNE 1945 AT OKINAWA ISLAND RYUKYU ISLANDS IN THE PERFORMANCE OF HIS DUTY AND SERVICE OF HIS COUNTRY WHEN INFORMATION IS RECEIVED REGARD- ING BURIAL YOU WILL BE NOTIFIED TO PREVENT POSSIBLE AID TO OUR EN- EMIES DO NOT DIVULGE THE NAME OF HIS SHIP OR STATION. PLEASE ACCEPT MY HEARTFELT SYMPATHY=
—A A VANDERGRIFT GENERAL USMC COMMANDANT OF THE MARINE CORPS

Frank kept the telegram. His daughter Patti was never quite sure why, although he did tend to keep everything.

He could not bear to look at it, just as he could never bear to talk about his brother. At night, though, sometimes in the living room of his home in South Holland outside of Chicago, he would pour himself a glass of scotch and put the Tony Bennett song "I Left My Heart in San Francisco" on the record player. Over and over he would play it in the dark.

Bob had left for overseas from the West Coast. But it wasn't Bob who had left his heart there.

Robert Frank Bauman was the twelfth player from the Mosquito Bowl to die.

He was buried on Okinawa in 6th Marine Division Cemetery No. 1, Grave 601, Row 25, Plot B.

He was twenty-four years old.

37
Why?

Johnny Perry was born in St. Mary's Township in Wake County, North Carolina, the son of Claude Perry. His mother's maiden name was Bettie Vinson. He was one of a family of eight children; his father died when he was less than a year old and his mother when he was twelve. He went to an orphanage in Tiffin, Ohio. He moved back to North Carolina, to Raleigh, when he was ready for high school. He lived with his older sister, who treated him as if he were one of her children. He was a three-sport athlete in football, basketball, and baseball at Needham Broughton High School in Raleigh. He went on to Wake Forest, where he was one of the most electrifying sophomore running backs in the country, five foot nine and 175 pounds, speedy and shifty. He went to Duke for half a year on the V-12 program and entered the Marine Corps as an officer candidate.

His road was a choppy one. At one point he changed his mind and requested a discharge to join the United States Merchant Marine. The request was turned down. He was one of nine in the forty-sixth officer candidate class of 191 who did not qualify, and he returned to the ranks as a private first class. In May of 1944, he married Elizabeth Davis Beaty. He was twenty-three, she was twenty.

He distinguished himself with great bravery on Okinawa. Because so many officers had been either killed or wounded in the area of the Shuri Line, Perry by default became a platoon leader in How Company of the 29th Regiment even though he was a corporal. On May 18th of 1945, during a furious assault on a defended enemy ridge, Perry acted on his own and went through a hail of grenades to the top of a ridge to locate an enemy pillbox. He returned to his platoon for a machine-gun squad and from an exposed position directed the fire that neutralized the pillbox and enabled his platoon to gain its objective. He was awarded the Navy Cross.

On June 8th of 1945, two days after Bob Bauman was killed, Perry died of a gunshot wound to the head as the 29th Regiment assaulted the Oroku Peninsula. He was one of four from How Company to die that day along with Clements, Taylor, and French.

His marriage had lasted one year and thirty-three days.

His wife became a widow at the age of twenty-one.

John Wesley Perry was the thirteenth player from the Mosquito Bowl to die.

He was buried on Okinawa in 6th Marine Division Cemetery No. 1, Grave 592, Row 22, Plot A.

He was twenty-five years old.

II

Four days later, on June 12th of 1945, as he moved from an observation post into a forward position in the zone of action, Captain Bob Fowler wore a baseball cap rather than a helmet. When the 2nd Battalion of the 29th seized a crucial strongpoint on the Oroku Peninsula, he was carrying only a shoulder-holstered .38-caliber pistol, his own personal weapon. Why would he make himself such an effortless target, easily identified as an officer by his unorthodox battlefield dress? Where was his helmet? Where was the carbine that officers carried?

He wasn't simply a good officer who had risen quickly through the ranks; he was a great officer, perhaps the most revered in the 29th. He was too wise for that kind of carelessness, going to the front and sticking out like that. But maybe he was one of those marines who would always be protected by their own magical aura.

He was born Robert Beals Haupt in 1920. After his mother died, he went to the Hartford, Connecticut, area to live with his aunt Ibelle Fowler and her husband. When he came of age at twenty-one, he legally changed his last name to Fowler. Ibelle and Lemuel Fowler gave him the best of everything. The Fowlers were well off, their comings and goings chronicled in the *Hartford Daily Courant* society pages, Lemuel a field supervisor of the Aetna Casualty and Surety Company in charge of fidelity and surety bond production. Bob went away to prep school at the prestigious Loomis School in Windsor in Connecticut. He graduated in 1938, then attended the University of Michigan for three and a half years until he was called up for active duty as an officer candidate.

He was appointed a second lieutenant in February of 1942, to first lieutenant in December of 1942, and then to captain in September of 1943. He fought in the Battle of Guadalcanal and in December of 1943 participated in the seizure and holding of the Cape Gloucester Airfield in New Britain in New Guinea. He was made the commanding officer of Fox Company in the 29th Regiment in June of 1944. During the Battle of Okinawa, he became the operations officer of the 2nd Battalion of the 29th.

Before he went overseas, on May 30th of 1942, he married Mary Haskell. She was from Wenatchee, Washington, and they had met at Michigan. They were a striking couple, their picture taken for the society pages as they dined at a round table for two in the Wedgwood Room of the Waldorf-Astoria hotel in New York, the leading supper club in the city, patronized by the famous and privileged and with entertainment by Frank Sinatra. They smiled at each other with the slightest touch of slyness, as if they both would always have amusing things to say to one another. He was dashing in marine uniform; she was beautiful and wore one of those forties-style hats like an exquisite bird's nest. They had that look of lasting forever through witticisms and winks and nods. You wished you could see them dance the night away in the Waldorf's grand ballroom.

Fowler commanded respect as an officer because he treated his men with respect. He was a natural-born leader. He believed in decorum and responsibility.

When some of the members of Fox Company found Japanese skulls on Guadalcanal and inserted candles in them to place outside their tents like night lights, he told them to cut it the fuck out. He handled problems himself without kicking his men upstairs into court-martial and a permanent black mark on their records. When McCallum, after a grueling twenty-mile training exercise on Guadalcanal, failed to come to attention before about-face, Fowler caught it and chewed him out. McCallum felt ashamed. The next day he saw Fowler and gave him his best salute. Fowler asked, "How are you doing, son?" The incident was forgotten.

At Sugar Loaf he conducted a personal reconnaissance in front of the lines to determine the exact nature of the terrain and the locations of the enemy positions. On June 12th of 1945, he maneuvered the 2nd Battalion into position on the Oroku Peninsula against fanatical enemy resistance.

That was where he was when he wore only the baseball cap and the shoulder holster as the mop-up began and he decided to move forward from the observation point.

Which was why he was so exposed and died of a gunshot wound in the chest.

Did he do it to be with the men of Fox Company that

he had once commanded? Was it their belief that he was immortal? Was it *his* belief that he was immortal?

Robert Beals Fowler was the fourteenth player from the Mosquito Bowl to die.

He was buried on Okinawa in 6th Marine Division Cemetery No. 1, Grave 720, Row 29, Plot A.

He was twenty-five years old.

38
Three Stars

After seventy days, the Japanese could no longer mount an effective resistance. They were losing about a thousand soldiers a day.

On June 10th, two days before Fowler died, General Buckner had done something bizarre and unprecedented in the Pacific war: he had written a letter to Ushijima telling him he should capitulate and stop the wanton bloodshed. It was similar to what Ulysses Grant had done with Buckner's father at the Battle of Fort Donelson in 1862 during the Civil War when he wrote the confederate general a note insisting on unconditional surrender. Only it had taken place ninety-three years earlier and it was common knowledge that the Japanese army never surrendered.

> The forces under your command have
> fought bravely and well. Your infantry
> tactics have merited the respect of your
> opponents in the battle for Okinawa. . . .
> Like myself, you are an infantry general
> long schooled and experienced in infan-
> try warfare. You must surely realize the
> pitiful plight of your defense forces. You
> know that no reinforcements can reach
> you. I believe, therefore, that you under-
> stand as clearly as I that the destruction
> of all Japanese resistance on the island
> is merely a matter of days. It will entail
> the necessity of my destroying the vast
> majority of your remaining troops.

The letter, sent by air, took seven days to find
Thirty-second Army headquarters. Ushijima smiled
when he read it. The letter, predictably, had no effect.

He wrote a response assuring Buckner that every
soldier under his command would fight until they were
no longer on Earth.

On June 18th of 1945, with victory so near, Buckner
decided to go to a forward observation post to watch

some of the troops. He liked doing that; it was the best possible evocation of his fearlessness and machismo that he so adored. He felt it was a way of being close to his men and the most effective way of directing the action regardless of his personal safety. He was warned not to go. There was no point. It was too dangerous.

There are differing accounts of the degree to which he exposed himself. One has him arriving in a jeep flying a flag with three stars on it, wearing a helmet with three stars on it. If that was true, it was the equivalent of a neon sign on his chest reading "Shoot me." No marine or soldier on the line would find such behavior brave, only cavalier.

He was there for at least an hour and appeared relaxed, in some ways relieved. It had been a difficult time, not simply the grumbling of other commanders over his plodding strategy, but also unheard-of criticism from print reporters over his tactics. Admiral Nimitz held an unprecedented press conference to defend Buckner, the clearest sign that the top command was in damage control mode and Buckner needed rehabilitation after a campaign that had gone so slowly. But the battle was now won except for the mop-up. He would go down in history as the victorious general of Okinawa, defeating an enemy that had employed perhaps the most ingenious defensive strategy of the Pacific war. Nobody could take that away from him. Nor could anyone take away from him his lifelong devotion to the military. He was a great patriot.

Staff Sergeant Martin Conn had just taken motion-picture footage of Buckner to memorialize his presence so near the front. Marine combat correspondent Robert Hilburn was there as well; the presence of photographers and reporters was common among generals, who were masters of the photo op. There was a flurry of men around Buckner. A marine battalion command post radioed a warning that Buckner was making himself a target.

Five rounds from a Japanese artillery unit were fired at 1:15 p.m. Buckner was sitting on a boulder. Or maybe standing next to it. Jagged pieces of coral and metal fragments flew out.

General Buckner has been hit!

He was lying on the ground, splattered with mud. A hole had been torn in the left side of his chest. Blood was gushing out. Some said he was conscious. Others said he was unconscious.

Shells were hammering down now. Colonel Clarence Wallace and Major William Chamberlin carried Buckner to a sheltered spot at the base of a cliff. A corpsman gave him plasma. A marine private held his hand and whispered to him: "You are going home, General. You are homeward bound."

He was the highest-ranking officer in World War II to be killed by enemy fire.

The Japanese, except for Ushijima, rejoiced at the news. Ushijima was sorrowful about the fate of his adversary, a fellow commander. It was a foreshadowing of his own fate five days later. Shortly before dawn on June 23rd of 1945, General Ushijima and second-in-command Cho bid farewell to those few remaining and left their cave into the open air for the first time in days. Ushijima sat on the ledge of a hill, looking out toward the ocean, with mist filling the valley. The moon shone on the sea. "It was as if everything on earth trembled, waiting with deep emotion," wrote Hiromichi Yahara. Ushijima took the traditional dagger used in hara-kiri and plunged it into the bared flesh of his abdomen. Captain Sakaguchi, standing behind him, took his sharpened sword and beheaded him. Cho committed ritual suicide as well.

Right before Ushijima died, he spoke the words of a poem he had written:

We spend arrows and bullets to stain heaven and earth,
Defending our homeland forever.

Buckner's personal effects filled several crates, given his thirty-seven-year career in the military. They were sent to his wife in San Francisco. He left behind a

Graflex camera, a 28 mm Zeitz lens, and a Dallon tele-photo lens. His clothing included two dry-cleaned wool ties, a bathrobe, blue-and-white pajamas, and the cover of a bedroll. He left behind books on Genghis Khan, the War of 1812, and tricks for camera owners. He left behind distinguished service ribbons, single stars, a set of lieutenant general insignia, and a strand of gold braid. He left behind three children.

Two days before he died, he wrote a letter to his son William Claiborne, then a plebe at West Point. He reminisced in his grand style about his own experiences at West Point:

Forty-one years ago today I entered the east rally-post, drew in my chin, alternately dropped and picked up my suitcase, was vociferously informed of my shortcomings in posture, urged to move with great alacrity and initiated into the lowest form of military servitude as a lowly beast.

He looked to the future after the war:

I shall then be content to return to Alaska and get caught up on shooting

> Kodiak bears and other small game that
> doesn't shoot back.

He talked about the end of the Okinawa campaign:

> I hope that by the time you get this our
> flag will wave over all of Okinawa.

It was the last letter he ever wrote.

Simon Bolivar Buckner, Jr., was buried on Okinawa in 7th Division Cemetery No. 1, special grave between rows 18 and 19, Plot 1.

He was fifty-eight years old.

39
Counting the Days

The day before General Buckner died, McLaughry heard a radio broadcast saying that Okinawa would be secured within a week. It was blessed news given that the assault on the Oroku Peninsula earlier in the month had been an ordeal of mud, rain, bad terrain, and constant firing at ridges and hills that were mere scaffolding for the caves of the Japanese and their connecting tunnels. His unit had fired their weapons from dawn until dark, then spent most of the night doing emergency maintenance. He and his radio operator covered mile after mile while reconnoitering approaches.

When McLaughry had landed on Okinawa seventy-seven days before, his pants had been so snug that he

502 · THE MOSQUITO BOWL

had left his belt aboard ship. Now he was down to 170 pounds, far below his playing weight at Brown and on the New York Giants, and four inches had come off his waist. To keep his pants from falling down, he resorted to tying the belt loops together with a handkerchief. But then he found something better: a discarded machine-gun belt.

Howarth copped a bottle of whiskey during a lull in combat, and together they took some snorts, mixing it with lemon powder and speculating about how great it would taste if only they had ice. McLaughry finished John Steinbeck's *Cannery Row* and started a new book sent to him by his wife, *Brainstorm* by Carlton Brown. It was about mental disintegration, a hot-button issue for McLaughry. The selection process by which some men suffering from psychoneurosis were returned to combat and some were not made no sense to him. In a letter to his parents he had displayed uncharacteristic anger:

> They have some good doctors out here, but there are few compared to the large number of meat-heads and numbskulls— particularly these psycho-neurosis doctors—with few exceptions I've never

seen them diagnose a case correctly. Guys that are obviously faking—and everyone knows it—they send home— nothing wrong at all—while guys whose nerves are really shot and are no good to themselves and a possible menace to the others in combat, get sent back to the line.

Jane had sent the book to him after meeting the author in New York. McLaughry actually liked it, and it perhaps gave him greater insight into the difficulties of diagnosis. Jane also provided unintentional comic relief by sending clippings about the 6th Marine Division and its exploits. The one that got the biggest laugh among the men was an account in the *New York Times* of the siege of Sugar Loaf that sounded like a radio announcer calling a football game: "For an unspecified time it was close-quarter fighting—grenades from the Japanese, grenades from our men, rifle answering rifle, and bayonet parrying bayonet—until one of the blades found a softer target."

The dispatch had been written from Guam, and there was no way of knowing how much of it was military hyperbole or reporter hyperbole. Marines seldom carried bayonets, and McLaughry could count on one hand the number that had been fixed to the end of a rifle. "If bayonets were all there were to worry about, the life of the infantryman would be easy," he wrote.

But he hoped it would be only a matter of days until dispatches about Okinawa would no longer be about bayonets but about victory.

40
Cessation of Hostilities

The Japanese knew the battle was over. Ushijima issued his final order on June 18th of 1945.

My Beloved Soldiers:

You have all fought courageously for nearly three months. You have discharged your duty. Your bravery and loyalty brighten the future. The battlefield is now in such chaos that all communications have ceased. It is impossible for me to command you. Every man in these fortifications will follow his superior officer's order to

fight to the end for the sake of the
motherland.

This is my final order.

Farewell.

Two days later in the early evening of June 20th of
1945, McLaughry's weapons platoon was assigned to
provide support for Schreiner's company as it attacked
the last enemy stronghold, a hill mass known as Ki-
yama Gusuku at the southernmost end of the island.
It was a mop-up of Japanese stragglers, hardly the
stuff of Sugar Loaf and Horseshoe. McLaughry spoke
briefly with Schreiner to assess objectives. Schreiner
could have sent out only enlisted men to do the scouting, but he refused. He was the company leader and
all leaders, at least the good ones, led by example. At
this point it was no big deal anyway.

Odette received the flowers that Schreiner had arranged to send her every month, pink roses and del-
phiniums. She put them under his picture.

The terrain was difficult and treacherous, an escarpment of boulders, sheer rocks, and caves. McLaughry
watched Schreiner and several other marines disappear.

Anne Schreiner had dedicated several Sunday sheets to her son's birthday on March 5th, reminding him of the one when he had been five and had his picture taken at Brintnall's department store in the blue jersey suit with stripes; the one when he had said he did not want to turn ten because he had had such a good time being nine; the one as a freshman in high school with friends featuring chocolate cake, ice cream, and an impromptu boxing match that had left Mark Hoskins with a swollen eye; the one when he had been fifteen and his father had given him a fistful of silver dollars toward a trip to Yellowstone; the one when he had gone to Wisconsin and his dad had given him a traveling bag to take to New York when the team played Columbia.

Several weeks before he left for Okinawa, she had typed out a poem, sweet and soapy and determined to rhyme:

> Dave found his girl, a winsome lass, Odette Marie,
> And then he streaked for Quantico, a bold Marine to be.
> He plies his trade in waters far—we now await war's end.
> When we will all foregather, a wedding to attend.

He and Odette had mapped out the details of their lives together in letters back and forth—the trip to Canada where they would canoe and swim and fish and make love, the home in Wisconsin where on Sunday mornings during the winter they would open the windows and turn off the radiator to feel the brace of the cold and read the funny papers and eat a big breakfast and have nothing to do the rest of the day except the rest of the day. He always read her letters twice. He wrote her day after day not because he had much to say but just to feel close to her. He apologized for not being able to articulate what he really felt when it was the very opposite.

"You are what I'm fighting to get back to and you mean more to me than anything possibly could on this earth."

Like Odysseus, love would carry Dave Schreiner home.

He was shot in his left chest, most likely by a sniper, although there were reports he had been wounded during a fake surrender. He was taken to a hospital and died the next day, on June 21st of 1945.

He had survived on Okinawa for eighty-one days.

He died on the eighty-second, the same day it was declared secure.

"Our two darling boys were real buddies and went through everything together and it seems they could not be separated and for that reason God took them both," wrote Bertha Bauman to Anne Schreiner after she learned that David had died.

"Are your days and nights getting any better, Mrs. Bauman," wrote Anne Schreiner in response. "I find mine are getting harder and harder." She expressed hope that once the war was over and all the servicemen returned to civilian life, a comforting routine might settle in, the world no longer mad. She knew it wasn't true.

"Each boy who comes back points up our own situation all the more," she wrote. "I feel that every hour as it passes is a crucifixion."

She kept his room exactly the same, as if one day he would return to where he had always belonged.

David Nathan Schreiner was the fifteenth player from the Mosquito Bowl to die.

He was buried on Okinawa in 6th Marine Division Cemetery No. 1, Grave 789, Row 32, Plot A.

He was twenty-four years old.

41
Silence

On the same day Dave Schreiner died, John McLaughry was in a bivouac behind the lines at about 11:00 p.m. when a trip flare went up, indicating the presence of infiltrators. Since enemy resistance had been broken, he thought it might be one or two stragglers planning to surrender, as so many Japanese soldiers had in the last week. He wasn't particularly worried.

He assembled a group of three other men to check it out, all of them volunteers. One had an M1 rifle, the platoon sergeant a carbine, another a shotgun with five shells filled with ball bearing–sized pellets for guarding prisoners. McLaughry grabbed the holster of his .45-caliber pistol.

The ground was irregular, mostly hillocks three to

four feet high. Alert for ambush, he went for his pistol only to realize it was *missing*. He had left it in a radio jeep after cleaning it; the weight of the two loaded clips in the holster had been heavy enough to make him think the pistol was there. Combat did not forgive.

They had advanced about twenty-five yards when Japanese soldiers jumped into view, not one or two but five or six. They were armed. This wasn't some sake-addled attack. The gap between the two groups was fifteen yards.

One Japanese fired a rifle aimed at McLaughry but somehow missed. Several others started throwing grenades. The PFC with the shotgun fired from the hip. A grenade exploded right between him and McLaughry. The PFC was blinded but kept on firing. The sergeant was behind one of the little hillocks when a grenade exploded right under his right knee. He started bleeding all over the place.

McLaughry still had no weapon.

Bullets. Grenades. Fragments. All in seconds near the stroke of midnight in the final gasps of the Battle of Okinawa.

Then silence.

Epilogue

There is a picture in an oval frame of Dave Schreiner that I keep propped up next to me on my desk. His hair is neatly parted with a little dip on the right-hand side, the eyes soft, his tie knotted tightly against the crisp white shirt. It is a college graduation picture, probably. He would have been in his early twenties. But all I see when I look at the picture is a boy who went off to war and, like so many boys in our violent and fractured world, never came back. I see such beauty of possibility in him, just as I feel such sorrow.

It was only while working on this book that for the first time I got to know members of the military and their families. What a marvelous group they are: embracing, funny, proud, proving that all my conceptions of them were misconceptions. My politics are very different from most of theirs. But nobody cares. When we gathered for the annual reunions of the Sixth Marine Division Association, I was there not only as a writer but as a lineal descendant of my father, who had been in the 6th Division. We shared something sacred—our heritage. My father, although gone for over twenty years, came back to me. I imagined him at Okinawa, a nineteen-year-old kid smoking cigarettes down to the nub and fear coursing through him but never showing it, and the image made my heart soar with pride and also break because of what he and so many had gone through. How did they do it? No book, no film or television show, nothing will ever truly capture it. Only the men who were there will ever know. Regardless of the thousands of questions I asked and all that I read and researched over the course of five years, I came to believe that this was a part of them that never could and never should be revealed.

All of the veterans of Okinawa I interviewed were in their nineties. What struck me was their spirit of eternal optimism. They loved the United States, but more than that, they *believed* in it. They laughed and occasionally cried, and not a single one of them thought that what he had done was any big deal. Some came home from the war with the irreversible burden of what they had lived through. But the men I spoke with did not; many had gone back to college on the GI Bill, expecting nothing but seizing on every opportunity the country gave them.

The phrase "The Greatest Generation" has become a tired bromide. Millions of men tried to get out of fighting in the war or find cushy desk jobs. Politics turned the draft into a free-for-all of special interests. The Marine Corps was totally segregated in World War II, and it was only during the Korean War that the capabilities of Blacks in combat were recognized. There still is far too much misogyny and racism and hatred of the Other in the United States for any generation to be great. But what made these marines special was how they were ordinary men who rose to extraordinary circumstances time and time again. It is the true measure of greatness that most of us never achieve.

When I think about the men of the Mosquito Bowl who died, there is one image I cannot get out of my mind: how they were alive, living and breathing, and then fell onto the jagged ground of Okinawa and were gone, just like that, dying alone no matter how many others surrounded them. I understand that wars have to be fought (actually I don't understand, and no one should understand), but I cannot comprehend how that happened. The word that keeps coming to me is *waste*, the absolute waste of those men's lives regardless of their unfathomable bravery and sacrifice that preserved our freedoms. They deserved so much more. They should have had so much more.

So maybe this book, without my knowing it at first, is an attempt to remind us that those who died were once so alive with the world ahead of them. Just as they must be honored in death, they must also be honored in life.

Which is why I keep the picture of Dave Schreiner next to me, for him, for all the men and women who lie beneath white crosses from one end of the globe to the other.

Anne and Herb Schreiner received dozens of letters from friends, former teammates, and young teenagers who had idolized their son, many of them two or three pages with virtually no mention of football. The letters spoke of him in a way that he never could and never would speak of himself.

It was highly unusual for a senior commander to write anything to grieving parents apart from the so-sorry-for-your-loss form letter. The death of Schreiner was such that personal letters came both from his regimental commander, Colonel Alan Shapley, and from major general, Lemuel Shepherd. Shapley wrote, "He was not just one of my lieutenants, he was one of my very good friends. . . . Dave was not just an All-American football player, but an All-American boy in all respects, and he died that way."

Although similar requests by family members to marine headquarters had been rejected, Shepherd personally made inquiries into Schreiner's death and reported that he had been on reconnaissance when killed by a sniper. With unusual tenderness, Shepherd wrote to the parents wanting them to know their son had found peace:

A stone chapel of Gothic design overlooks a field of white crosses bordered by native shrubs and tiny American flags, with the bright blue of the East China Sea beyond. The solemnity of the cemetery is such as to do full honor to the brave men whose mortal remains rest in peace in the ground they fought so gallantly to conquer.

Odette kept in touch regularly with the family she had grown to love. She related her comings and goings to help deflect their pain; she was busy with her cease-less naval duties in New York, where she took on more and more responsibility, meeting dignitaries, training new ensigns, working in a hospital to aid the wounded, going out to meet a troopship returning from Europe.

She was direct and straightforward in her letters. She worried about the impact on Schreiner's parents, given that she had the blessed diversion of being busy and they did not. She wrote to them mostly of her activities. But she was also profound in her own way: "I think we ask too much of life. Maybe if we didn't, it would be better. . . . [G]etting David back would have meant so much happiness—and maybe that was too much."

In 1946, Odette married Navy Lieutenant Commander John B. Davis, Jr., whom she had met in New York.

Anne Schreiner was as happy for her as she could possibly be. But it was another reminder that her son was gone. After learning that Bob Bauman's former fiancée, Arlene, was getting married, she wrote to Bertha Bauman in 1947:

> We were heartbroken when Odette told
> us she was to marry, and yet we kept
> saying we wanted her to do so and
> even kept looking around wondering
> whether this one or that one would not
> be good enough for her. Yet, when the

time came, then we realized how hard
it was to give her up because she had
been David's.

I know you loved Arlene as we did
Odette. We must just think how hard
it is for the girls—they have memories
way down deep that will not be erased,
and they are just doing what they can
to build another future for the one that
was taken from them, and it is right.
But oh, oh, doesn't it hurt to lose them?

In 1947, the University of Wisconsin held a dedication ceremony for the Schreiner and Bauman residence houses. The Schreiners also endowed a scholarship in their son's name. In 1949, Dave Schreiner's body was brought home. The military had decided to close the cemeteries on Okinawa and gave families the option of having their children's bodies either reinterred at the National Memorial Cemetery of the Pacific in Hawaii, known as the Punchbowl, or brought back home at military expense. All but two of the families of the players from the Mosquito Bowl who died elected to have them returned home. General Buckner returned to his Kentucky roots as well, buried next to his father and grandfather in a historic cemetery on a hilltop overlooking the state capital.

Herb Schreiner died in 1950 at the age of seventy. Some believed it wasn't only illness that caused his death but a broken heart that had never mended after the loss of his son. Anne Schreiner, a woman of indomitable spirit and strength, lived to the age of 105. Odette Hendrickson and her husband, who rose to the rank of rear admiral, raised two children. She died at the age of eighty-five in 2006.

Tony Butkovich lies next to his parents in St. Mary's Cemetery in Canton, Illinois. His sixteen touchdowns in a single season was a Big Ten record for twenty-four years, until 1967. The football field next to Lewistown High School stadium was partially named after him, but few at the school knew anything about his football exploits or his helping to lead Lewistown to its first and only appearance in the Illinois High School Boys Basketball Championship. It was seventy-six years later, in 2021, that Fulton County historian Bruce Weirauch felt something must be done, including asking the high school to make a plaque honoring Tony. In September of 2021, several hundred people attended a cemetery walk at St. Mary's featuring Tony. "World War Two took the best and brightest young men Lewistown had to offer," said Weirauch. "Everyone who was lost led an extraordinary life until then. We lost so much when we lost them."

George Murphy's widow, Mary Catherine, married again, to a former marine named Jack Rehl. He had become friendly with Murphy during training and offered to take care of Murphy's wife and infant if something happened. He made good on his promise. He looked them up after the war and after marriage adopted Mary Grace.

Rehl said that he always preserved Murphy's memory. But Murphy's grandson, John Steele, said that Rehl discouraged Murphy's name from being mentioned because of Murphy's stature as a Notre Dame football captain and fallen war hero. Steele said he had not known about the existence of his grandfather for the first seventeen or eighteen years of his life. He believes it was the same with his mother, Murphy's daughter. "It was family history that never should have been kept from me or my family or my mom."

The players from the Mosquito Bowl who survived Okinawa went on to varied careers. Not surprisingly,

522 • THE MOSQUITO BOWL

the most popular profession was football coaching at the high school or college level; in the aggregate, they won numerous conference and state championships. Others were educators, businessmen in construction, and career military. David Mears became an accounting manager and controller for a government contractor. Robert McNeil became the president of a food brokerage. David Long went into insurance. Lee Bennett worked for the San Diego County Probation Department after retiring from the military. Bob Herwig became a college coach and later a parole officer with the California Board of Parole. Hank Maliszewski became a template maker at PPG Industries. Hank Bauer became a New York Yankee, participated in seven World Series championships, and was the manager of the Baltimore Orioles team that won the World Series in 1966.

Frank Bauman became a football coach at Thornton High School in Harvey, Bob's and his alma mater. He led Thornton to a state championship in 1965 in what is considered one of the fifty best teams in the storied history of Chicagoland football.

At a parade in the small town of Three Lakes in northern Wisconsin one Memorial Day, where he was grand marshal, he committed to finally talking about Bob. But when the time came to speak, he could not do it. "It was almost like if we rip this open, I'll bleed out," said his daughter Patti Margaron.

In 2006, after being diagnosed with Alzheimer's disease, he moved into Arden Courts in South Holland. His wife, Dale, was fine physically and certainly capable of staying home. But she would not consider the idea of being without her husband and also moved into the facility, where they lived across the hall from each other. On the occasion of their sixty-fifth wedding anniversary, they renewed their vows at a simple and beautiful ceremony. Dale died at the age of eighty-nine, before her husband.

Frank passed away on April 26th of 2013 at the age of eighty-eight. His daughter Patti sat with him on the last night of his life in his room, the one decorated with pictures of Bob on the walls. She talked to him about Dale and his grandchildren and how well they were doing and how much they loved him. He squeezed her hand. She sang his favorite hymns, and she talked about Bob.

As the sun came up, Patti knew it was time. She stood up and started marching around the room like the cheerleader she had once been. She knew she maybe looked crazy, but she didn't care. Football had been the core of her father's life, so she imitated a game and told Frank there he was with the ball. She told him to start running, make it to the end zone. She was cheering just as though Frank were back at Illinois and Purdue and Thornton. She could hear her father's breath quicken as if he were running. She told him to keep going, *just keep going!* She continued to cheer and clap and laugh and cry, and she knew as strongly as she had ever known anything that he had gotten to the moment and place he had wished for in his life.

He was with his brother Bob now.

Then he let go.

The total losses at Okinawa are beyond all imagination. As many as 250,000 people were killed in eighty-two days, or more than 3,000 a day. The number of US military killed or missing in action was 4,900 from the navy, the highest of any battle in its history; 4,700 from the army; and 3,250 from the marines. The total number of US casualties was roughly 50,000, and that did not include those from battle fatigue and other non-battle-related incidents. Marine casualties (killed and wounded) were 20,000, 10 percent of the total number in combat, as opposed to 6.5 percent for the army ground forces. In the process of taking two-thirds of Okinawa, 1,622 men from the 6th Marine Division were killed. The number of fallen from the 29th Regiment, 551, was the highest of any marine regiment in World War II in a single operation. The total casualties of the division were 8,222, the highest of any marine or army division at Okinawa. In awarding the 6th Division the Presidential Unit Citation, the highest honor a division can receive, Secretary of the Navy James Forrestal wrote, "Their gallantry in overcoming a fanatic enemy in the face of extraordinary danger and difficulty adds new luster to Marine Corps History and to the traditions of the United States Naval Service."

The estimates of deaths among Japanese military personnel and Okinawan conscripts ranges from 60,000 to 100,000. The roughly 10,000 who surrendered was by far the most in any battle during the Pacific war and an indication that their willingness to die for the emperor was cracking.

The number of Okinawan civilians killed ranged from 100,000 to 150,000, as many as *one-third* of the entire population. Only the military could refer to those deaths as "collateral damage."

The correct term is *innocents.*

Forty-five days after the end of the Battle of Okinawa, the atom bomb was dropped on Hiroshima on
August 6th of 1945 and a second one on Nagasaki
on August 9th. In between these acts, which forever
altered the world, the Soviet Union declared war on
Japan on August 8th. A week later, on August 15th, a
recording of the Imperial Rescript of Surrender read
by the emperor was broadcast over the radio to the
Japanese people. Official surrender documents were
signed on board the USS *Missouri* in Tokyo Bay on
September 2nd of 1945.

World War II was over.

Men were coming back to the United States.

One of them was John McLaughry.

The silence near the stroke of midnight on the last
official day of the Okinawa campaign had not taken
him. Four Japanese soldiers were killed and the fifth
fled.

He had been careless enough to be dead. He was
lucky enough to be alive. He was brave enough despite the grenade fragments in his leg and jaw to apply
a tourniquet around the bleeding knee of the platoon
sergeant until help arrived.

On October 17th of 1945, at 4:18 p.m., his parents

and his wife, Jane (via her mother), were sent a telegram from San Francisco:

BACK AT LAST ALL WELL HERE SHORT
TIME THEN HOME LOVE—JOHN

He left for home on October 30th of 1945, lucky enough to get a train berth to Chicago and then sitting up all night, arriving at a nearly deserted Grand Central Station in New York. He came home different, quieter, more inward. His mother saw it in both her sons, "empty shells with empty eyes," as she expressed it in a letter from the late 1940s. In pictures taken before the war, there was a glint in John's eye. His mother noticed a certain nervousness after he returned, a tendency to keep to himself. He became subdued, a shadow of the big man on campus he had been at Brown. It wasn't all the time, and it did get better as he readjusted to a new world without war.

He and Jane divorced after he returned. He remarried in 1948, to Anne Van Dyck. They had three children together. Richard, the oldest, became a lawyer; David, an actuary; and Marguerite, an educator whose career has included mentoring aspiring teachers and writing a column on history and tutoring adult English-language learners. All of them are still living.

It was no surprise to anyone that McLaughry went into coaching. He was the head coach at Union College from 1947 to 1949. He moved to Amherst College in 1950 and was highly successful, with a record of 43–24–4 in nine seasons. It was only appropriate that in 1959 he moved to Brown, his alma mater and the place where Tuss had created the legend of the Iron Men.

His time at Brown was not a success, as the world measures it. It was a tough show with a record of 17–51–3 and only eight wins in Ivy League play over eight seasons. He stopped coaching after the 1966 season, when Brown went 1–8 and winless in the Ivy League. He became the director of Brown's summer and special projects and remained so until his retirement in 1979.

After he retired, he painted more than ever. His work included portraits, still lifes, landscapes, and realism as well as abstract. He was a member of the historic Providence Art Club and had an exhibit there, prompting Edward J. Sozanski, the art critic for the *Providence Journal-Bulletin*, to describe his works as "eclectic" and "provocative" with their themes of ruin and decay. He did commissioned work and was also an expert calligrapher, called upon to do scrolls and citations.

He discovered one day that his mother had kept virtually all the letters he had written while he was in the military. He read and preserved them. He also wrote an eighty-page account of the patrol he had gone on at Bougainville. He expressed himself with clarity and meticulous detail in all his writings. He hated any kind of embellishment. To exaggerate the horror of war was to trivialize the men left behind.

He died on November 28th of 2007.

John Jackson McLaughry was one of fifty players from the Mosquito Bowl to live through the Battle of Okinawa.

His ashes are held at Swan Point Cemetery in Providence.

He was ninety years old.

Notes on Sources

This section has been organized differently from the usual method. Instead of line-by-line attributions, each has been broken down by subject to show sources used and their context. The intent is to make it easier for readers to find information on a topic. The section also serves as a quasi-index in place of a formal one. To paraphrase the brilliant nonfiction writer Richard Ben Cramer, you are going to have to read the book if you want to know what is inside it. Books are meant to be read in their totality, not in snippets.

Of the hundreds of books and articles I read in researching *The Mosquito Bowl* over the course of five years, there are several that gave me special inspiration. E. B. Sledge's *With the Old Breed: At Peleliu and Okinawa*, about his experiences at the battles of Peleliu and Okinawa, is the best personal account of war that I have ever read, visceral, intense, literary, and disturbing. George Feifer's global account, *The Battle of Okinawa: The Blood and the Bomb*, is amazing in its scope, detail, and refusal to compromise on the inhuman level of blood and violence. I limited my reliance on these books as secondary sources, but their ability to delve so deeply into the heart of combat made utilizing them unavoidable at times. One other author I would like to cite is John Dower, emeritus professor of Japanese history at MIT. His book *Embracing Defeat: Japan in the Wake of World War II*, about the postwar reconstruction of Japan, is an unprecedented blend of history, research, insight, and writing. I was privileged enough to be on the jury that awarded him the 1999 National Book Award for nonfiction. It also won the Pulitzer Prize.

Chapter 1: McLaughry

The author is indebted to the family of John J. McLaughry for allowing me access to personal letters and other material dating back to McLaughry's childhood, courtesy of the estate of John J. McLaughry.

JOHN J. MCLAUGHRY, EARLY EDUCATION AND BROWN UNIVERSITY

1. "Brown's 172nd Commencement Exercises Monday; Procession Monday Leads to Diplomas," *Brown Daily Herald*, May 21, 1940.

2. "College Men Opposed to Joining Allies Now," *Brown Daily Herald*, May 13, 1940.

3. Janet M. Phillips, *Brown University: A Short History* (Providence, RI: Office of Public Affairs and University Relations, Brown University, 2000).

4. John J. McLaughry, "Introduction to the World War II Letters of John J. McLaughry," August 1990.

5. John J. McLaughry, grade reports, 1931–1935, Moses Brown School, Providence, RI.

6. Marguerite Ames, interviewed by the author.

7. "McLaughry Elected Freshman Captain," *Brown Daily Herald*, October 29, 1936.

8. "Moses Brown in Front," *New York Times*, January 31, 1936, 14.

9. *Pot Pourri* (Phillips Academy yearbook), 1936.

10. Richard McLaughry, interviewed by the author.

11. "Seniors Choose McLaughry as Class President," *Brown Daily Herald*, October 27, 1939.

12. "Students Show Aroused Spirit in Spontaneous Football Rally," *Brown Daily Herald*, October 21, 1939.

13. *"Under the Elms" Exercises, Class Day, 172nd Commencement, Class of 1940,* Brown University, 1940.

14. "Varsity Football Squad Shows Great Promise in Drills," *Brown Daily Herald,* September 17, 1936.

AMERICANS, PREWAR ATTITUDES

1. Daniel Greene and Frank Newport, "American Public Opinion and the Holocaust," Gallup, April 13, 2018.

2. Mary Gertina Feffer, "American Attitude Toward World War II During the Period from September 1939, to December, 1941," Master's thesis, Loyola University Chicago, 1951.

TUSS MCLAUGHRY

1. "Coach at Amherst Secured by Brown," *North Adams Transcript* (North Adams, MA), January 25, 1926.

2. Davis J. Walsh, "East Astounded at Brown's Wins," *Clarion-Ledger* (Jackson, MI), November 11, 1926.

3. DeOrmond McLaughry, US Census record, 1940.

4. "'They're Not Iron Men' Says M'Laughry of Brown: 'Just Eleven Boys Having Good Time,' Is Coach's Idea of Great Eleven," *Reading Times* (Reading, PA), November 19, 1926.

TUSS MCLAUGHRY, COACHING STYLE

1. "All in the Game," *Atlanta Constitution,* November 21, 1941.

2. Frank G. Henke, "Drink Milk and Practice Little, but

Brown's 'Iron Men' Attract Attention of Entire Universe," *Birmingham News*, November 28, 1926.

3. "Quick Kick and Lateral Pass Will Feature 1933 Football," *Morning Call* (Paterson, NJ), January 9, 1933.

4. "Tuss McLaughry Has Brown Players Drink Milk and Rest After Practice," *Hartford Courant* (Hartford, CT), October 27, 1926.

5. Will Murphy, "Most of Miniature Machine Only Subs Last Year," *Daily News* (New York), November 10, 1926.

IRON MEN OF BROWN, 1926 SEASON

1. "Brown Eleven Starts with 22 Men on Squad," *New York Times*, September 7, 1926.

2. John Hanlon, "How Eleven Men of Iron Flattened Harvard, Yale and Dartmouth," *Sports Illustrated*, October 7, 1968.

3. "Linemen and Backs Selected at Brown: McLaughry Has Made Tentative Choices—Huddle System Will Be Used," *New York Times*, September 12, 1926, 148.

4. Program for the 50th Anniversary Reunion of the Brown Iron Men, November 5, 1976.

5. Richards Vidmer, "Brown Again Held to Tie by Colgate," *New York Times*, November 26, 1926.

6. Tuss McLaughry to John Hanlon, April 23, 1968.

Chapter 2: Everybody's Watching

JOHN J. MCLAUGHRY, EARLY LIFE

1. "Brown Eleven Is on Upgrade; Lack of Reserves Hurts Team This Season; Son John to Help McLaughry Revive Triple Wingback," *Boston Globe*, September 17, 1937.

2. John J. McLaughry, "A Short Autobiography," courtesy of the estate of John J. McLaughry.

3. John M. Flynn, "The Referee's Sporting Chat: Young McLaughry Promising," *Berkshire Eagle* (Berkshire, MA), June 19, 1934.

4. "School Sidelights," *Boston Globe*, September 30, 1935.

JOHN J. MCLAUGHRY, ANDOVER

1. "Andover Pays Exeter Visit," *Boston Globe*, November 15, 1935.

2. "Dr. Claude M. Fuess to Be Headmaster; Succeeds Dr. Stearns at Phillips Academy," *Boston Globe*, May 29, 1933, 17.

3. Frederick S. Allis, Jr., "Admissions, Scholarships, and College Admissions," Chapter 18 in *Youth from Every Quarter* (Andover, MA: Phillips Academy, 1979).

4. John J. McLaughry, report for term ending December 19, 1935, Phillips Academy, Andover, MA, courtesy of the estate of John J. McLaughry.

5. John J. McLaughry to Florence McLaughry, assorted, December 1935 and January 1936, courtesy of the estate of John J. McLaughry.

JOHN J. AND TUSS MCLAUGHRY, BROWN

1. "Brown Football Coach Defended," *Providence Journal*, December 1, 1937, 11.
2. Jerry Nason, "Tuss' Son Sure Standout," *Boston Globe*, September 17, 1937, 24.
3. John M. Flynn, "The Referee's Sporting Chat," *Berkshire County Eagle* (Pittsfield, MA), April 3, 1940, 13.
4. "Rumor Says Former N.W. Coach May Go to Brown," *Journal Gazette* (Mattoon, IL), November 27, 1935.
5. "'Tuss' McLaughry Believes Team in 'Pretty Fair Shape,'" *Brown Daily Herald*, May 25, 1939, 3.
6. "Tuss McLaughry to Leave Brown for Dartmouth Job," *Morning News* (Wilmington, DE), January 15, 1941.

ALL-STAR GAME, 1940

1. "All-stars' Victory over Football Giants Is Hailed as a Triumph for Coach McLaughry," *New York Sun*, September 5, 1940, 31.
2. Copy of John J. McLaughry's Contract with the New York Giants, courtesy of the estate of John J. McLaughry.
3. Dave Camerer, "Giant Conquerors Rated All-Time All-Star Tops," *World-Telegram* (New York), September 5, 1940.

4. Jesse Abramson, "All-Stars' Victory over Giants Analyzed as Triumph for Coach's Ideal—the Team Player," *New York Herald Tribune*, September 6, 1940.

5. Joseph M. Sheehan, "Fans Sing Praises of All-Star Squad," *New York Times*, September 6, 1940.

McLaughry, Post-Graduation

1. "Down to Flying Weight," *Boston Post*, December 28, 1941, 21.

2. "Hanover News and Personals: McLaughry-Pitts," *Landmark* (White River Junction, VT), January 15, 1942, 7.

Reaction to Pearl Harbor Attack

1. John J. McLaughry to Florence McLaughry, January 30, 1942, courtesy of the estate of John J. McLaughry.

2. John J. McLaughry, unpublished personal account, courtesy of the estate of John J. McLaughry.

3. "The Day War Came to the Polo Grounds," *Sports Illustrated*, October 24, 1966.

Chapter 3: Schreiner

Letters and other materials dating back to childhood were donated by the family of David Schreiner to the Wisconsin Historical Society. The author is indebted to his niece, Judy Corfield, for providing additional material.

DAVID SCHREINER, PERSONAL

1. David Schreiner to himself, December 27, 1941, David N. Schreiner Letters, 1938–1947, M92–233, Box 1, 3/33/I5, Wisconsin Historical Society.

SCHREINER FAMILY

1. "City of Lancaster Honors Emma Schreiner for Years of Service to Free Library," *Wisconsin State Journal* (Madison, WI), December 10, 1942.

2. "Grant County Tire Inspectors Are Appointed; H. E. Schreiner, Chairman, Selects Aides in Various Committees," *Capital Times* (Madison, WI), January 19, 1942.

3. "Grant County Will Preserve Early History," *Wisconsin State Journal* (Madison, WI), March 20, 1935.

4. "H. E. Schreiner Elected Mayor of Lancaster," *Grant County Herald*, April 14, 1926.

5. Johannes Scheniner [sic], Lutheran Baptisms, Marriages, and Burials, Hesse, Germany, 1730–1875.

6. John Schrener [sic], US Census record, 1900.

7. Nathan, Schreiner & Co. advertisement, *Grant County Herald* (Lancaster, WI), April 13, 1876.

8. "A Park Presented to Lancaster," *Iowa County Democrat*, August 11, 1904.

9. Paul W. Schmidt, "Notes on the Schreiner Relatives, Made by Paul W. Schmidt, While Visiting Anna Virum

Schreiner, May 30, 1972," Grant County Historical Society, 1972.

10. "Schreiner's Sold; Old Lancaster Firm Changes Hands After 56 Years in Family—La Farge Man Buys," *Grant County Herald* (Lancaster, WI), February 18, 1920.

11. Sophia Nathan, Compiled Marriages for Select Counties, State of Wisconsin, 1835–1900.

GRANT COUNTY, WISCONSIN

1. "60,000 Watch Corn Shuckers," *Telegraph-Herald* (Dubuque, IA), November 13, 1931.

2. Amanda A. Tagore, "Irish and German Immigrants of the Nineteenth Century: Hardships, Improvements, and Success," Honors College Theses, Pace University, 2014, Paper 136.

3. "The Early Foundation of Lancaster," *Grant County Herald Independent*, October 14, 1987.

4. Grant County Historical Society, assorted clippings and memorabilia.

5. J. B. Keenan, *The 1931 County Agent's Report on the Progress of Grant County's Agricultural Program, Nov. 1, 1930 to Nov. 1, 1931*, The State of Wisconsin Collection.

6. Kate Everest Levi, "Geographical Origin of German Immigration to Wisconsin," *Wisconsin Historical Collections* 14 (1898): 341–93.

7. US Department of Commerce, *United States Census of Agriculture: 1935; Reports for States with Statistics for Counties and a Summary for the United States*, vol. 1 (Washington, DC: U.S. Government Printing Office, 1936).

DAVID SCHREINER, UNIVERSITY OF WISCONSIN

1. "Badgers' Play Vindicates Hank's Hunch," *Wisconsin State Journal* (Madison, WI), September 27, 1942.

2. "Badgers Tie Irish, 7 to 7," *Capital Times* (Madison, WI), November 27, 1942.

3. David Schreiner to Herbert and Anna Schreiner, April 28, 1943, David N. Schreiner Letters, 1938–1947, M92–233, Box 1, 3/33/I5, Wisconsin Historical Society.

4. Gene Ward, "Columbia Rally Nips Badgers, 7–6," *Daily News* (New York), November 10, 1940.

5. Henry J. McCormick, "Badger Lineplay Cracks," *Wisconsin State Journal* (Madison, WI), November 10, 1940.

6. Joseph C. Nichols, "Columbia Checks Wisconsin by 7–6," *New York Times*, November 10, 1940.

7. "Iowa Stops Wisconsin, 6–0; Minnesota Loses; Illinois Defeats N. U., 14–7; Notre Dame Whips Army, 13–0," *Chicago Tribune*, November 8, 1942.

8. Judy Corfield, interviewed by the author.

9. Terry Frei, *Third Down and a War to Go* (Madison: Wisconsin Historical Society Press, 2007).

DAVID SCHREINER, ALL-AMERICAN, 1941

1. "Schreiner Makes AP All-American!," *Capital Times* (Madison, WI), December 12, 1941, 17–18.

DAVID SCHREINER, ALL-AMERICAN, 1942

1. Hank Casserly, "Hank Casserly Says," *Capital Times* (Madison, WI), December 6, 1942, 23.
2. "Schreiner Is All-America Choice in the Marines," *Capital Times* (Madison, WI), December 16, 1942, 17.

Chapter 4: Butkovich

The Harvard Library digital collection Immigration to the United States, 1789–1930, is a treasure trove. It contains more than 400,000 pages from more than 2,200 books. Of all the fine works on the subject, the one that stands out the most to me is Harvard University history professor emeritus Oscar Handlin's Pulitzer Prize–winning book, *The Uprooted: The Epic Story of the Great Migrations That Made the American People*, on the great migrations to America. It is both superb history and superbly written. Fulton County historian Bruce Weirauch was instrumental in helping to draw a portrait of the Butkovich family and the community.

TONY BUTKOVICH, EARLY COLLEGE ATHLETICS

1. Nelson Campbell, "Four All-Staters on Freshman Cage Squad," *Daily Illini*, November 12, 1940.

2. "Zuppke Looks Over Four Sophomore Backs," *Daily Illinois State Journal*, September 17, 1941, 17.

3. Fritz Jauch, "Pete Adams Has Off Day as Eager Sideliners Seep Through Gate," *Daily Illini*, October 9, 1941.

TONY BUTKOVICH, ILLINOIS 1942 SEASON

1. Fritz Jauch, "The Morning After," *Daily Illini*, October 11, 1942.

2. Jack Adams, "Illini Grimly Prepare for Irish with 90-Minute Scrimmage," *Daily Illini*, October 21, 1942.

3. Wilfrid Smith, "New Coach and Three of His Fighting Illini: Sophomore Tackles Will Be Measure of Illinois' Success," *Chicago Daily Tribune*, September 9, 1942, 25.

4. "Wolverines Open Intensive Drill for Illini," *Chicago Tribune*, October 28, 1942, 26.

THE BUTKOVICH BROTHERS, ATHLETICS

1. "All-State Prep Team Picked," *Decatur Daily Review*, December 12, 1938, 5.

2. "Bill Butkovich Sparks Illinois," *Daily Independent* (Kannapolis, NC), September 23, 1945, 7.

3. "Blackhawks Beat Eau Claire," *La Crosse Tribune* (La Crosse, WI), April 29, 1940, 9.

4. Bruce Weirauch, interviewed by the author.

5. "Butkovich's 2 Touchdowns Paces Victory," *South Bend Tribune*, September 23, 1945, 29.

6. "Canton Boy Leads State Loop Batters," *Pantagraph* (Bloomington, IL), July 9, 1940.

7. *The Cantonian* (Canton High School yearbook), 1938, 1939, and 1940.

8. "Eighth Annual All-State Team," *Times* (Streator, IL), March 20, 1940.

9. "Ex-Collegians Dot Pro Squad," *Statesman Journal* (Salem, OR), October 4, 1942, 12.

10. "Harmon Chooses All-State Grid Teams for 1938," *Freeport Journal-Standard* (Freeport, IL), November 29, 1938, 9.

11. "Indians Nose Farmington Out in One Point Victory," *Fulton Democrat*, October 25, 1939.

12. Jim Starcevic, interviewed by the author.

13. Jimmie Murphy, "Press Passing," November 13, 1939.

14. Larry J. Krulac, interviewed by the author.

15. "Put and Take, Quips with a Punch," *Daily Sentinel* (Woodstock, IL), March 15, 1940, 4.

16. Roger and Mary Parmenter, interviewed by the author.

17. Tracy Shryock, "Anthony 'Blondie' Butkovich; 'Touchdown Tony,'" *Fulton Democrat*, January 20, 1981.

18. University of Oregon football roster, Oregon v. UCLA game program, Hayward Field, University of Oregon, Eugene, OR, November 9, 1940.

19. "Varsity Hoopsters Look O. K. in Pre-season Tilt," *Fulton Democrat*, November 14, 1938.

20. "Veteran Illini Eleven Defeats Pittsburgh, 23–6," *Chicago Tribune*, September 23, 1945, 25.

TONY BUTKOVICH, HIGH SCHOOL ATHLETICS

1. "Butkovich Stars as Ducks Lose to Indians," *Fulton Democrat*.
2. "Canton to Meet Lewistown Team at 7:30 Tonight," *Fulton Democrat*.
3. "Dundee Beaten by Granite City in State Meet," *Chicago Tribune*, March 18, 1940.
4. "Indians Nose Farmington Out in One Point Victory," *Fulton Democrat*, October 25, 1939.
5. "LCHS Salutes the 1940 State Tournament Team," *Fulton Democrat*.

CROATIAN IMMIGRANTS

1. Carl D. Oblinger, *Divided Kingdom: Work, Community, and the Mining Wars in the Central Illinois Coal Fields During the Great Depression* (Springfield: Illinois State Historical Society, 1991).
2. David R. Roediger, *Working Toward Whiteness: How America's Immigrants Became White—The Strange Journey from Ellis Island to the Suburbs* (New York: Basic Books, 2018).
3. Dubravka Mlinarić, Mario Bara Snježana Gregurović, Drago Župarić-Iljić, and Simona Kuti, "Croatian Migra-

tion History and the Challenges of Migrations Today," Institute for Migration and Ethnic Studies, Zagreb, January 8, 2015.

4. Francis H. Eterovich and Christopher Spalatin, *Croatia: Land, People, Culture*, vol. 2 (Toronto: University of Toronto Press, 1970).

5. George J. Prpic, *The Croatian Immigrants in America* (New York: Philosophical Library, 1971).

6. Jacob Riis, *How the Other Half Lives: Studies Among the Tenements of New York* (New York: Scribner's, 1890).

7. "Keweenaw Ethnic Groups: The Croatians," Michigan Technical University Archives.

8. "The Mine Wars," Lithuanians in Springfield, Illinois, https://lithspringfield.com/an-indelible-role-in-our-history/lithuanian-local-history-2/the-mining-life/the-mine-wars/.

9. Pat Taylor, Dave Bishop, Brooks Carver, and Sue Rusch, eds., *Spoon River Country: The Immigrant Story* (Canton, IL: Prairie Sky Press).

BLAŽ BUTKOVICH, IMMIGRATION

1. Ana Butković, New York passenger arrival list (Ellis Island), January 15, 1906.

2. Blaž Butković, New York passenger arrival list (Ellis Island), January 15, 1906.

3. Lidija Smbunjak, "Research Report: Butković–Grubišić Case, Mrkopalj Parish, Croatia," Mrkopalj parish records, Zagreb State Archive.

4. Raymond L. Cohn, "The Transition from Sail to Steam in Immigration to the United States," *Journal of Economic History* 65, no. 2 (June 2005): 469–95.

ELLIS ISLAND

1. Anne-Emanuelle Birn, "Six Seconds Per Eyelid: The Medical Inspection of Immigrants at Ellis Island, 1892–1914," *Dynamis* 17 (1997): 281–316.

2. *Annual Report of the Commissioner of Immigration for the Port of New York with Reference to Ellis Island Affairs for the Year Ended June 30, 1911*, US Senate, 62nd Cong., 2nd sess., December 5, 1911.

3. Broughton Brandenburg, *Imported Americans: The Story of the Experiences of a Disguised American and His Wife Studying the Immigration Question* (New York: Stokes, 1904).

4. Dave and Patricia Kustra, "Their Journey to America," Allegheny-Kiski Valley Heritage Museum.

5. "Dictionary of Races or Peoples," in US Senate, *Reports of the Immigration Commission. Abstracts of Reports of the Immigration Commission with Conclusions and Recommendations and Views of the Minority* 1, 61st Cong., 3rd sess., December 5, 1910.

6. Edith Abbott, "Historical Aspects of the Immigration Problem; Select Documents," *Immigration to the United States, 1789–1930*, Harvard Library.

7. Elizabeth C. Barney Buel, *Manual of the United States for the Information of Immigrants and Foreigners* (Washington, DC: The National Society, Daughters of the American Revolution, 1926), *Immigration to the United States, 1789–1930*, Harvard Library.

8. Henry P. Guzda, "Ellis Island a Welcome Site? Only After Years of Reform," *Monthly Labor Review* 109, no. 7 (1986).

9. "Immigrants in Industries. Part 1: Bituminous Coal Mining" in US Senate, *Reports of the Immigration Commission*, 61st Cong., 2nd sess., June 15, 1911, doc. 633.

10. "Occupations of the First and Second Generations of Immigrants in the United States," in *Reports of the Immigration Commission. Abstracts of Reports of the Immigration Commission with Conclusions and Recommendations and Views of the Minority* 1, 61st Cong., 3rd sess., December 5, 1910.

11. Peter Morton Coan, *Ellis Island Interviews* (New York: Barnes & Noble, 1997).

12. State Department of Labor, New York, *Thirteenth Annual Report of the Commissioner of Labor for the*

Twelve Months Ended September 30, 1913 (Albany, NY: State Department of Labor, 1914).

13. "Statistical Review of Immigration to the United States, 1820 to 1910," in *Reports of the Immigration Commission. Abstracts of Reports of the Immigration Commission with Conclusions and Recommendations and Views of the Minority,* 61st Cong., 3rd sess., December 5, 1910.

14. "Steerage Conditions; Importation and Harboring of Women for Immoral Purposes; Immigrant Homes and Aid Societies; Immigrant Banks," in US Senate, *Reports of the Immigration Commission,* 61st Cong., 3rd sess., December 5, 1910, doc. 753.

Chapter 5: Land of the Free

IMMIGRATION

1. Franz Boas, "Changes in the Bodily Form of Descendants of Immigrants," *American Anthropologist* 14, no. 3 (July–September 1912): 530–62.

2. Howard B. Grose, *Aliens or Americans?* (New York: Eaton & Mains, 1906).

3. John R. Commons, *Races and Immigrants in America* (New York: Macmillan, 1907).

4. Oscar Handlin, *The Uprooted: The Epic Story of the*

Great Migrations That Made the American People (Boston: Little, Brown, 1951).

5. Rita J. Simon and Susan H. Alexander, *The Ambivalent Welcome: Print Media, Public Opinion, and Immigration* (Westport, CT: Praeger, 1993).

6. "Various Facts and Opinions Concerning the Necessity of Restricting Immigration," *Publications of the Immigration Restriction League*, no. 3 (Immigration Restriction League, 1894), Immigration to the United States, 1789–1930, Harvard Library.

EUGENICS

1. Daniel Okrent, *The Guarded Gate: Bigotry, Eugenics, and the Law That Kept Two Generations of Jews, Italians, and Other European Immigrants Out of America* (New York: Scribner, 2019).

2. Lothrop Stoddard, *The Revolt Against Civilization: The Menace of the Under Man* (New York: Charles Scribner's Sons, 1922).

3. Lothrop Stoddard, *The Rising Tide of Color: Against White World-Supremacy* (New York: Charles Scribner's Sons, 1922).

4. Madison Grant, *The Passing of the Great Race*, The American Immigration Collection Series, vol. 2 (New York: Arno Press, 1970).

5. Thomas C. Leonard, "Retrospectives: Eugenics and

Economics in the Progressive Era," *Journal of Economic Perspectives* 19, no. 4 (Fall 2005): 207–24.

BLAŽ AND ANA BUTKOVICH, ST. DAVID, ILLINOIS

1. Blaž Butkovich, New York passenger arrival list (Ellis Island), May 25, 1904.

2. "Blaž Butkovich," *Galesburg Register-Mail* (Galesburg, IL), October 13, 1959.

3. Blaž Butkovich, petition for naturalization.

4. Blaž Butkovich, US Census records, 1920 and 1930.

5. Butković, Blaž; Grubisic, Ana, Croatia, Church Books, 1516–1994, Roman Catholic, Mrkopalj, Marriages (Vjencani), 1890–1916.

CHERRY MINE DISASTER

1. Miss Cellania, "The 1909 Cherry Mine Disaster," Mental Floss, May 30, 2016.

ST. DAVID; FULTON COUNTY

1. C. Chenoweth and Alan R. Myers, *Directory of Coal Mines in Illinois, 7.5-Minute Quadrangle Series: St. David Quadrangle, Fulton & Mason Counties* (Champaign: Prairie Research Institute, Illinois State Geological Survey, 2015).

2. Fulton County Historical and Genealogical Society, *Fulton County Heritage* (Dallas: Curtis Media, 1988).

3. Helen Hollandsworth Clark, ed., *A History of Fulton County, Illinois, in Spoon River Country, 1818–1968* (Fulton County, IL: Fulton County Board of Supervisors, 1969).

4. *History of Fulton County* (Peoria, IL: Chapman, 1879).

5. John Drury, *This Is Fulton County, Illinois*, American Aerial County History Series, no. 2 (Chicago: Loree, 1954).

6. Ken Huggins and Lori McLouth, *The Illustrated Book of Fulton County Illinois* (Canton: West Central Publications of Illinois, 2014).

7. United States Bureau of the Census, *Thirteenth Census of the United States Taken in the Year of 1910: Statistics for Illinois* (Washington, DC: U.S. Government Printing Office, 1913).

LABOR CONDITIONS

1. Grace Abbott, *Bulletin of the Immigrants Commission No. 2: The Immigrant and Coal Mining Communities of Illinois* (Springfield: State of Illinois Department of Registration and Education, 1920).

2. W. Jett Lauck and Edgar Sydenstricker, *Conditions of Labor in American Industries: A Summarization of the Results of Recent Investigations* (New York: Funk & Wagnalls, 1917), 30–38, 85, 120–35, 194, 202–6, 231, 248–56, 272, 288–94, 308, 318–19, 327–41, 352, 360–76.

3. Floyd Mansberger and Christopher Stratton, *"Pick, Shovel, Wedge, and Sledge": A Historical Context for Evaluating Coal Mining Resources in Illinois* (Springfield, IL: Fever River Research, 2005).

4. Illinois Bureau of Labor Statistics, *Twenty-Eighth Annual Coal Report of the Illinois Bureau of Labor Statistics, 1909* (Springfield, IL: Illinois State Journal Co., State Printers, 1909).

5. Illinois Bureau of Labor Statistics, *Twenty-Fourth Annual Coal Report of Illinois for the Year Ended September 30, 1905* (Springfield, IL: Illinois Bureau of Labor Statistics, 1906).

6. United States Bureau of Mines, *Coal-Mine Fatalities in the United States 1870–1914*, compiled by Albert H. Fay (Washington, DC: U.S. Government Printing Office, 1916).

LEWISTOWN V. HEBRON, BASKETBALL

1. "Hebron Battles Lewiston in State Tourney Tonight," *Freeport Journal-Standard*, March 14, 1940, 21.

2. "Lewistown in Big Rally to Win Contest," *Woodstock Daily Sentinel* (Woodstock, IL), March 15, 1940, 1, 4.

3. "Lewistown Is Opponent in Game Tonight; County Fans Back Hebron," *Woodstock Daily Sentinel* (Woodstock, IL), March 14, 1940, 1.

4. "Little Hebron Falls in Close 31–30 Battle," *Pantagraph* (Bloomington, IL), March 15, 1940, 16.

5. Tom Siler, "46,256 Fans See State Cage Meet; Phillip Is Star," *Times* (Streator, IL), March 18, 1940, 5.

TONY BUTKOVICH, EARLY UNIVERSITY OF ILLINOIS CAREER

1. Joe Arndt, "The Brawn Patrol," *Daily Illini*, September 27, 1940.

2. Joe Arndt, "Milosevich, Bernhardt, Rettinger Batter Frosh Line; Varsity Tallies 27–6 Triumph over Plebes; Butkovich Counts Lone Score for Freshmen; Riggs, Phillips, Engel Star," *Daily Illini*, September 27, 1940.

3. Fritz Jauch, "Pete Adams Has Off Day as Eager Sideliners Seep Through Gate," *Daily Illini*, October 9, 1941.

4. "Zuppke Looks Over Four Sophomore Backs," *Daily Illinois State Journal*, September 17, 1941, 17.

Chapter 6: The Army Way

JOHN J. MCLAUGHRY, ARMY AIR CORPS

1. John J. McLaughry to Tuss and Florence McLaughry, assorted, January through August 1942.

2. United States Army, *Field Service Regulations— Operations May 22, 1941*, FM 100–5 (Washington, DC: United States Army, 1941).

U.S. ARMY, 1940–42

1. James A. Huston, "Selective Service in World War II," *Current History* 54, no. 322 (June 1968): 345–50, 368, 384.
2. "This Is What the Soldiers Complain About," *Life*, August 18, 1941, 16–21.

JAPANESE IMMIGRATION

1. Chester H. Rowell, "Chinese and Japanese Immigrants—A Comparison," *Annals of the American Academy of Political and Social Science* 34, no. 2 (1909): 3–10.
2. Doug Blair, "The 1920 Anti-Japanese Crusade and Congressional Hearings," Seattle Civil Rights & Labor History Project, 2006,
3. Isami Arifuku Waugh, Alex Yamato, and Raymond Y. Okamura, "A History of Japanese Americans in California: Immigration," Five Views: An Ethnic Historic Site Survey for California, National Park Service, 2004.
4. Jeremiah W. Jenks and W. Jett Lauck, *The Immigration Problem: A Study of American Immigration Conditions and Needs* (Boston: World Peace Foundation, 1924), 237–60, 292, 608, Immigration to the United States, 1789–1930, Harvard Library.
5. Raymond Leslie Buell, "Japanese Immigration," *World Peace Foundation Pamphlets* 7, nos. 5–6 (1924):

287–305, 314–18, Immigration to the United States, 1789–1930, Harvard Library.

6. "The Senate's Declaration of War," *Japan Times and Mail*, April 19, 1924, 4.

7. Sidney Lewis Gulick, *The American Japanese Problem: A Study of the Racial Relations of the East and the West* (New York: Charles Scribner's Sons, 1914), 3–35, Immigration to the United States, 1789–1930, Harvard Library.

8. Tasuku Harada, ed., *The Japanese Problem in California: Answers (by Representative Americans) to Questionnaire* (San Francisco: Printed for private circulation, 1922).

JAPANESE AMERICANS, RESPONSE TO EXCLUSION ACT

1. "Japanese Kills Himself Near Tokio Embassy," *New York Times*, June 1, 1924, 1.

2. "Bill Barring Japs Signed by Coolidge," *Omaha Morning News*, May 27, 1924.

3. Committee on Immigration, *Hearings Before the Committee on Immigration on S. 2576, a Bill to Limit the Immigration of Aliens into the United States, and for Other Purposes, March 11, 12, 13, and 15, 1924*, US Senate, 68th Cong., 1st sess. (Washington, DC: U.S. Government Printing Office, 1924).

4. Committee on Immigration and Naturalization and Albert Johnson, *Restriction of Immigration: Hearings*

Before the Committee on Immigration and Naturalization, House of Representatives, Sixty-eighth Congress, First Session, on H.R.5, H.R.101, H.R.561 [H.R.6540], US House of Representatives, 68th Cong., 1st sess. (Washington, DC: U.S. Government Printing Office, 1924).

5. "Exclusion Law Is Scored: President Calls That Part of Act 'Unnecessary and Deplorable,'" *New York Times*, May 27, 1924, 1–2.

6. "The Immigration Act of 1924," History, Art & Archives, United States House of Representatives.

7. Izumi Hirobe, *Japanese Pride, American Prejudice: Modifying the Exclusion Clause of the 1924 Immigration Act* (Stanford, CA: Stanford University Press, 2001), 21–53.

8. "Japanese Protest Says Exclusion Violates Treaty," *New York Times*, June 1, 1924, 1, 13.

9. Nancy Stalker, "Suicide, Boycotts and Embracing Tagore: The Japanese Popular Response to the 1924 US Immigration Exclusion Act," *Japanese Studies* 26, no. 2 (2006): 153–70.

EFFECT ON JAPANESE AMERICAN RELATIONS

1. Department of State, *Peace and War: United States Foreign Policy, 1931–1941* (Washington, DC: U.S. Government Printing Office, 1943), 87–97.

2. International Treaty for the Limitation and Reduction of Naval Armament, April 22, 1930.

3. Irvine H. Anderson, Jr., "The 1941 de Facto Embargo on Oil to Japan: A Bureaucratic Reflex," *Pacific Historical Review* 44, no. 2 (May 1975): 201–31.

4. John J. McLaughry, recollections from "The World War II Letters of John J. McLaughry," 1990, courtesy of the estate of John J. McLaughry.

5. Joseph C. Grew, *Ten Years in Japan: A Contemporary Record Drawn from the Diaries and Private and Official Papers of Joseph G. Grew, United States Ambassador to Japan, 1932–1942* (New York: Simon and Schuster, 1944).

6. Kallie Szczepanski, "What Motivated Japanese Aggression in World War II?," ThoughtCo., July 27, 2019.

7. "London Naval Conference," Modern Japan in Archives: Political History from the Opening of the Country to Post-War, National Diet Library, 2010.

8. Shiho Imai, "Gentlemen's Agreement," Densho Encyclopedia.

9. Stewart Brown, "Japan Stuns World, Withdraws from League," United Press, February 24, 1933.

10. "United States Freezes Japanese Assets," History, November 19, 2009.

Chapter 7: The Letter

Iowa State University history professor Amy J. Rutenberg's book *Rough Draft: Cold War Military Manpower Policy and the Origins of Vietnam-Era Draft Resistance* is particularly useful in offering a measured argument on our perceptions of "the Greatest Generation" and the idea that its wholehearted support of the war was to some degree patriotic propaganda. George Q. Flynn's book *The Draft, 1940–1973* is a thorough and comprehensive account of the draft during the war.

DAVID SCHREINER, BEFORE ENLISTING

1. David Schreiner to Herbert and Anna Schreiner, September 13, 1942, Wisconsin Historical Society.
2. David Schreiner to Mr. Oz Callan, local draft board, September 21, 1942, David N. Schreiner Letters, 1938–1947, M92–233, Box 1, 3/33/I5, Wisconsin Historical Society.

THE DRAFT

1. "23 Churches Score New Draft Ruling," *New York Times*, May 8, 1944, 1, 25.
2. Albert A. Blum, "The Army and Student Deferments During the Second World War," *Journal of Higher Education* 31, no. 1 (January 1960): 41–45.
3. Amy J. Rutenberg, *Rough Draft: Cold War Military Manpower Policy and the Origins of Vietnam-Era*

Draft Resistance (Ithaca, NY: Cornell University Press, 2019), 24, 28–31.

4. David Schreiner to Herbert and Anna Schreiner, assorted, September 1942, Wisconsin Historical Society.

5. "Draft Age to Stay at 18," *New York Times*, April 16, 1943, 11.

6. George Q. Flynn, *The Draft, 1940–1973* (Lawrence: University Press of Kansas, 1993), 55, 60–62, 69.

7. John H. McMinn and Max Levin, "Procurement, 1941–45: Medical, Dental and Veterinary Corps," in *Personnel in World War II* (Washington, DC: Office of the Surgeon General, 1963), 167–210.

8. "Movies Are Put in Essential Class by Draft Ruling," *New York Times*, February 9, 1942, 1.

9. "New Draft Order Exempts 135,000," *New York Times*, April 13, 1944, 16.

10. "Occupational Deferments," *Indiana Law Journal* 17, no. 4 (April 1942): 316.

11. "Predicts Deferment for 95% over 26," *New York Times*, April 14, 1944, 11.

12. "Research Starters: US Military by the Numbers," The National WWII Museum.

13. Sally C. Curtin and Paul D. Sutton, "Marriage Rates in the United States, 1900–2018," National Center for Health Statistics, 2020.

14. *Selective Service Bulletin* 1, no. 11 (January 1, 1945).

15. *Selective Service Bulletin* 5, no. 3 (March 1, 1945).
16. Selective Service System, *Problems of Selective Service, Special Monograph* 1, no. 16 (1952).

Chapter 8: Murphy

Murray Sperber, professor emeritus of English and American Studies at Indiana University, has been the nation's preeminent author for three decades on the often pernicious impact of sports on American colleges. *Shake Down the Thunder: The Creation of Notre Dame Football* is an eye-opening look into Notre Dame football, written with Sperber's typical combination of exhaustive research and engaging style. Robert E. Burns's *Being Catholic, Being American: The Notre Dame Story* is a candid and comprehensive history of the school and its unique place in academia. For anyone who wants to know more about the impact of the war on a college football team, Terry Frei's *Third Down and a War to Go: The All-American 1942 Wisconsin Badgers* is an excellent and highly readable account of the legendary 1942 Wisconsin team. Among its characters are Dave Schreiner and Robert Bauman, who both played in the Mosquito Bowl.

NOTRE DAME FOOTBALL

1. "It's a Murphy Leading the Irish in 1942," *Notre Dame Scholastic* 75, no. 12 (January 16, 1942).

2. Murray A. Sperber, *Shake Down the Thunder: The Creation of Notre Dame Football* (Bloomington: Indiana University Press, 2002), 496.

3. "Sport Shorts," *Yank: The Army Weekly*, December 9, 1942, 23.

4. Steve Delsohn, *Talking Irish: The Oral History of Notre Dame Football* (New York: Avon, 1998).

FRANK LEAHY

1. Al Lamb, "Spinning the Sports Top," *Press and Sun-Bulletin* (Binghamton, NY), October 14, 1942, 24.

2. Arch Ward, "Fate Brings a Date with Destiny," in *Frank Leahy and the Fighting Irish: The Story of Notre Dame Football* (New York: G. P. Putnam's Sons, 1944).

3. Arthur Daley, "The Football Master of His Day; Hall Honor Reward for Leahy," *Indianapolis Star*, February 10, 1970, 22.

4. Arthur Daley, "Sports of the Times: No More Self-Torture," *New York Times*, February 2, 1954, 22.

5. Arthur Daley, "Sports of the Times: The Fighting Irish; the Accusation; the Freeze-Out; Too Little, Too Late," *New York Times*, December 7, 1956, 46.

6. "Autumn of '42: Leahy Ditched Rockne's System and Still Won," *Los Angeles Times*, November 27, 1992.

7. Bernard J. Williams, *The Frank Leahy Legend* (Torrance, CA: JCL Services, 1974), 150–15, 331.

8. Bill Dwyre, "Leahy Had Irish Stand Tall—or Else," *Los Angeles Times*, October 20, 2012, 23.

9. "Coach Frank Leahy's Final Hours," *San Francisco Examiner*, June 22, 1973, 61.

10. Commencement Exercises, University of Notre Dame, Notre Dame, IN, December 20, 1942.

11. Ed Hayes, "The Coach Fired by Notre Dame," *Orlando Sentinel*, June 24, 1943, 3-D.

12. Edward Prell, "Leahy Follows Rockne Path to Success; a Quarter Century in the Life of Frank Leahy, Notre Dame '31; Belonged Under Golden Dome as Freshman to Gridiron Coach," *Chicago Tribune*, February 1, 1954, 49.

13. "Football Giant Leahy, 65, Dies," *Boston Globe*, June 22, 1973, 47.

14. Frank Dolson, "How Many Sleepless Nights," *Philadelphia Inquirer*, December 20, 1979, 72.

15. "Frank Leahy Always Had Notre Dame Standing Tall and Up Straight," *Los Angeles Times*, October 19, 2012.

16. "Frank Leahy at Notre Dame," *New York Times*, September 28, 1941.

17. "Frank Leahy Buried in Somber Ceremony," *Los Angeles Times*, June 24, 1973, B5.

18. "Frank Leahy, Notre Dame Coach, Dead," *New York Times*, June 22, 1973, 38.

19. "Frank Leahy, Notre Dame Coach, Dies," *Washington Post*, June 22, 1973.

20. Gerald Holland, "The Coach," *Sports Illustrated*, October 13, 1958.

21. Gerald Holland, "Subject: Frank Leahy," *Sports Illustrated*, October 31, 1955.

22. "Hall Honor Reward for Leahy," *Indianapolis Star*, February 10, 1970, 22.

23. "'I'm Not Ashamed': Injury Feint Defended by Frank Leahy," *Washington Post*, January 15, 1954, 29.

24. Jim Murray, "Frank Leahy's Life a Greek Tragedy," *Indianapolis Star*, December 8, 1974, 54.

25. "Leahy in Clinic, McKeever Pilot," *Daily News* (New York), October 10, 1942, 29.

26. "Leahy in Hospital to Miss N. D. Game," *Brooklyn Daily Eagle*, October 10, 1942, 9.

27. "Leahy Leaves Mayo," *St. Louis Globe-Democrat*, December 21, 1942, 12.

28. "Leahy Quits Notre Dame Because of Ill Health," *Washington Post*, February 1, 1954.

29. "Leahy to Junk 'Rockne Shift' as Irish Style," *Journal and Courier*, February 27, 1942, 15.

30. Notre Dame Department of Sports Publicity, "Football—1940–49."

31. "Notre Dame's Leahy Drops Rockne, Turn to 'T,'" *Daily News* (New York), April 19, 1942, 1.

32. "A Time for Greatness," in *Many Autumns Ago: The Frank Leahy Era at Boston College and Notre Dame,*

edited by Mike Bynum (Birmingham, AL: October Football Corp., 1988).

33. Wells Twombly, "Coach Frank Leahy's Final Hours," *San Francisco Examiner*, June 22, 1973, 61.

CATHOLICISM AT NOTRE DAME

1. Andrew M. Greeley, *From Backwater to Mainstream: A Profile of Catholic Higher Education* (New York: McGraw-Hill, 1969).

2. "The Devil Writes a Letter Home," *University of Notre Dame Religious Bulletin*, September 23, 1942.

3. "A Father Writes to His Son," *University of Notre Dame Religious Bulletin*, September 19, 1942.

4. "Get Up Saturday for the Team," *University of Notre Dame Religious Bulletin*, September 24, 1942.

5. "It's God's Wish—Be on Time," *University of Notre Dame Religious Bulletin*, October 19, 1942.

6. Kevin Schmiesing, "Sports, Catholicism, and Culture: The History of Notre Dame Football," Catholic Exchange, November 3, 2006.

7. "A Maid and Chastity," *University of Notre Dame Religious Bulletin*, December 1, 1942.

8. "Mass and Communion for the Team Tomorrow," *University of Notre Dame Religious Bulletin*, October 2, 1942.

9. "The Only Divorce Permitted in the Catholic Church,"

University of Notre Dame Religious Bulletin, December 12, 1942.

10. Patrick F. Scanlan, "Notre Dame and Over Emphasis," *Tablet* (Brooklyn, NY), December 13, 1930, 11.

11. Philip Gleason, *Contending with Modernity: Catholic Higher Education in the Twentieth Century* (Oxford, UK: Oxford University Press, 1995).

12. Robert E. Burns, *Being Catholic, Being American: The Notre Dame Story* (Notre Dame, IN: University of Notre Dame Press, 1999).

13. "Survey of Fifteen Religious Surveys, 1921–1936," *Bulletin of the University of Notre Dame* 34, no. 1 (1939).

14. "These Won't Think," *University of Notre Dame Religious Bulletin*, October 21, 1942.

15. "Your Lack of Support—Plenty," *University of Notre Dame Religious Bulletin*, November 23, 1942.

FREE SPEECH AT NOTRE DAME

1. "Professor Out in Notre Dame Speech Dispute," *Chicago Tribune*, November 9, 1943, 7.

2. "Statements on Ouster of Notre Dame Professor," *Boston Globe*, November 9, 1943, 9.

NOTRE DAME STUDENTS; THE WAR

1. "Twenty-Fourth N.D. Man Makes Supreme Sacrifice,"

University of Notre Dame Religious Bulletin, November 21, 1942.

NOTRE DAME FOOTBALL, 1942

1. *The Dome* (Notre Dame University yearbook), 1942.
2. Frank Leahy to George Murphy, October 18, 1942, courtesy of the Steele family.
3. "Georgia Boys Score in Last Two Quarters," *South Bend Tribune*, October 4, 1942.
4. "Hopes for Undefeated Irish Squad Grounded by Georgia Engineers," *Notre Dame Scholastic* 77, no. 3 (October 9, 1942): 28.
5. Jim Costin, "Irish at All-Time Tops on Saturday; Never Better for One Game at Any Time," *South Bend Tribune*, October 19, 1942, 12.

WISCONSIN V. OHIO STATE, 1942

1. "Capacity Throng Expected for Big Ten Classic at Madison Tomorrow," *Daily Dispatch* (Moline, IL), October 30, 1942, 23.
2. "Badgers Humble Buckeyes, 17–7, Giving Ohio State Its First Defeat," *Wisconsin State Journal* (Madison, WI), November 1, 1942, 1.
3. James S. Kearns, "Hirsch Cracked Ohio State," *Wisconsin State Journal* (Madison, WI), November 3, 1942, 11.

4. "Schreiner Heaps," *Wisconsin State Journal* (Madison, WI), November 1, 1942, 22.

5. Terry Frei, *Third Down and a War to Go: The All-American 1942 Wisconsin Badgers* (Madison: Wisconsin Historical Society Press, 2007), 99, 132.

6. "Wisconsin Underdog Against Ohio State; Schreiner Leads Badgers in Nation's No. 1 College Game," *Wisconsin State Journal* (Madison, WI), October 31, 1942, 1–2.

UNIVERSITY OF WISCONSIN FOOTBALL, 1942

1. "Iowa Ends Badger Dreams, 6–0," *Des Moines Register*, November 8, 1942.

2. Terry Frei, *Third Down and a War to Go: The All-American 1942 Wisconsin Badgers* (Madison: Wisconsin Historical Society Press, 2007).

3. "Wisconsin Beats Minnesota, 20 to 6," *New York Times*, November 22, 1942.

DAVID SCHREINER AND GEORGE MURPHY, POSTSEASON AND ENLISTMENT

1. "21 Lettermen Finish at N.D.," *South Bend Tribune*, December 21, 1942, 16.

2. David Schreiner to Herbert and Anna Schreiner, assorted, February through May, 1943, David N. Sch-

reiner Letters, 1938–1947, M92–233, Box 1, 3/33/I5, Wisconsin Historical Society.

3. David Schreiner, official military personnel file.

4. David Schreiner, Application for Appointment to Candidates' Class for Commission, U.S.M.C. Reserve, December 5, 1942, Wisconsin Historical Society.

5. "Face Immediate Induction After Mid-year Exams," *Wisconsin State Journal* (Madison, WI), January 26, 1943, 13.

6. George Murphy, official military personnel file.

7. "East Strikes Through Air to Win," *San Francisco Examiner*, January 2, 1943, 19.

8. "Governali and Filipowicz Star as East Turns Back West, 13–12; Schreiner Scores on Columbia Ace's Pass and Fordham Back Plunges to Winning Touchdown—58,000 See Charity Game," *New York Times*, January 2, 1943, 17.

9. "Governali Paces Late Comeback: 58,000 See Annual Battle with West All-Stars; Passes Prove Decisive," *Washington Post*, January 2, 1943.

10. "Pro Clubs Draw for 'Players;' Wildung No. 1 Packer Choice; Detroit Lions Get Frankie Sinkwich and Dave Schreiner," *Post-Crescent* (Appleton, WI), April 9, 1943.

11. "Sinkwich, Schreiner Most Popular Gridmen," *Des Moines Register*, December 12, 1942, 17.

Chapter 9: Odette

The author is indebted to the family of Odette Hendrickson Davis for allowing access to letters and other material, courtesy of the family of Odette Hendrickson Davis.

1. Ann Norman and Charlotte Rudowicz, interviewed by the author, December 31, 2021.
2. "Delta Gamma Initiation," *Capital Times*, April 1, 1940, 7.
3. "Guest List Told for Epsilon Eta Dance Saturday," *Capital Times*, March 24, 1939, 15.
4. "Johnson Dance Pupils, Symphony Give Recital," *Wisconsin State Journal* (Madison, WI), May 19, 1935, 16.
5. "State Revenues Soar; Income Tax Up 48 Pct.," *Wisconsin State Journal* (Madison, WI), April 12, 1937, 2.
6. David Schreiner to Lula Hendrickson, May 29, 1943, courtesy of the family of Odette Hendrickson Davis.

Chapter 10: Football Is War

Karen Marie Wood's *Gridiron Courage: The Navy, Purdue, and World War II* is an excellent account of the 1943 Purdue season that starred Tony Butkovich. Wilbur D. Jones, *"Football! Navy! War!": How Military "Lend-Lease" Players Saved the College Game and Helped Win World War II* was extremely helpful in depicting the era of V-12 college football during the war. Jack Cavanaugh's *Mr.*

Inside and Mr. Outside: World War II, Army's Undefeated Teams, and College Football's Greatest Backfield Duo was of great help in showing how football players at Army were insulated from the draft.

ST. DAVID; WAR

1. *The Cantonian* (Canton High School Yearbook), 1938.
2. Lawrence Grubisich, US Census record, 1940.
3. Lawrence Grubisich, draft card.
4. *The Legend* (Lewistown Community High School yearbook), 1946.
5. "Men from St. David Serve Near and Far in Armed Forces," *Peoria Star*, August 22, 1943.
6. *Service Record Book of Men and Women of St. David, Illinois and Community* (St. David, IL: St. David Bible Class and St. David Community Business Men, 2013).

TONY BUTKOVICH, UNIVERSITY OF ILLINOIS

1. Fred Young, "Football Pendulum at Illinois Is on Upswing This Autumn," *Pantagraph* (Bloomington, IL), September 25, 1940, 10.
2. Fritz Jauch, "The Morning After: Tony," *Daily Illini*, April 18, 1946.
3. Fritz Jauch, "Pete Adams Has Off Day as Eager Sideliners Seep Through Gate," *Daily Illini*, October 9, 1941.

ILLINOIS V. MINNESOTA, 1942

1. Dick Walker, "Assyrian Star Wins Praise of Eliot; Tony Butkovich Scorns 'Nat'l Champ' Title of Golden Gopher Eleven," *Daily Illini*, October 11, 1942.

2. Fred Young, "Alert Illinois Eleven Scores 20–13 Triumph over Minnesota," *Pantagraph* (Bloomington, IL), October 11, 1942, 8.

3. Fritz Jauch, "Inspired Illini Win! Alert, Charging Team Outplays Nat'l Champs at Homecoming, 20–13," *Daily Illini*, October 11, 1942.

FOOTBALL AND THE NAVY; V-12 PROGRAM

1. Carolyn Alison, "V-12: The Navy College Training Program," WWII Committee.

2. "Draft Board Seeks Inquiry on Status of Buck Gridders," *Cincinnati Enquirer*, October 25, 1941, 13.

3. "Future of Sports Is Doubtful," *Cincinnati Enquirer*, December 24, 1941, 25.

4. Henry C. Herge, *Navy V-12* (Paducah, KY: Turner Publishing, 1996).

5. James G. Schneider, *The Navy V-12 Program: Leadership for a Lifetime* (Champaign, IL: Marlow Books, 1987).

6. Sara W. Bock, "V-12 Marines in World War II: The Corps Needed Officers and the Nation's Universities Answered the Call," *Leatherneck* 100, no. 12 (December 2017).

7. Wilbur D. Jones, *"Football! Navy! War!": How Military "Lend-Lease" Players Saved the College Game and Helped Win World War II* (Jefferson, NC: McFarland, 2009).

ARMY; SPORTS

1. Allison Danzig, "Army Football Reserves Hit by Loss of Players to Advanced Flying Course," *New York Times*, October 9, 1942, 27.
2. Allison Danzig, "Army-Navy Ruling Will Decide Fate of College Sports," *New York Times*, January 3, 1943, 185–86.
3. Allison Danzig, "N.C.A.A. to Carry On in 1943 with Sports Based on Nation's Wartime Needs," *New York Times*, December 31, 1942, 10.
4. Allison Danzig, "Sports Carry On, but The Picture Changes," *New York Times*, May 23, 1943, 166, 186.
5. "Annapolis Gets Army-Navy Game; Outsiders Barred to Reduce Travel," *New York Times*, October 23, 1942, 1, 12.
6. "Army Edict Seen Blow to Sports," *Philadelphia Inquirer*, February 13, 1943, 20.
7. "Army Students in Colleges Barred from Sports," *St. Louis Star and Times*, February 12, 1943, 20.
8. Associated Press, "Order Cancels Football Program at Army Air Technician Schools; but Great Lakes Naval

Training Station Arranges Schedule of 12 Games with Strong Teams—Notre Dame Booked," *New York Times*, August 21, 1942, 23.

9. Bus Ham, "Secretary of War Stimson Hits College Sports Hard," *Morning Call* (Paterson, NJ), August 16, 1943, 14.

10. Bus Ham, "Stimson Regrets That Soldiers Can't Play," *Knoxville Journal*, August 16, 1943, 9.

11. Jim McCulley, "Fordham Drops Football, 'Shortage of Grid-Power,'" *Daily News* (New York), July 15, 1943, 324.

12. Louis E. Keefer, "Birth and Death of the Army Specialized Training Program," *Army History* no. 33 (Winter 1995): 1–7, http://jstor.com/stable/26304217.

13. "Most Major Colleges Intend to Carry On in Football; 17-Year-Olds Are to Form Nucleus," *Cincinnati Enquirer*, February 14, 1943, 30.

14. "Navy Football Program Planned Despite Army," *Christian Science Monitor*, August 11, 1943, 16.

FOOTBALL, IMPORTANCE OF

1. Harry Keck, "Late Sec. Knox Responsible for Athletics in the Navy," *Pittsburgh Sun-Telegraph*, May 4, 1944, 18.

2. Jon Johnston, "Football History: Clark Shaughnessy and the T Formation," Corn Nation, April 12, 2007.

3. "Navy Head Favors Continuation of Wartime Sports," *Marine Corps Chevron*, January 15, 1944, 14.

4. "Navy Secretary Frank Knox and Lieut. Gen. A. A. Vandegrift, Marine Commandant, Dwell on Importance of Previous Training for War Duties—Effect of National Service Legislation," *Times-Tribune* (Scranton, PA), January 12, 1944, 17.

5. "Stay in Shape," *Rocky Mount Telegram* (Rocky Mount, NC), January 13, 1944, 4.

6. Wilbur D. Jones, Jr., *"Football! Navy! War!": How Military "Lend-Lease" Players Saved the College Game and Helped Win World War II* (Jefferson, NC: McFarland, 2009).

PURDUE; THE WAR

1. Karen Marie Wood, "Gridiron Courage: The Navy, Purdue, and World War II," Master's thesis, Indiana University, 2011.

2. Ray Schmidt, "The Purdue Marines," *College Football Historical Society Newsletter*, August 1988.

3. Thomas R. Johnston, "Purdue University in the War," *Purdue Alumnus*, 1943.

GENE TUNNEY

1. Guy Butler, "Topics of the Tropics: Sports Important, but Chiefly as Recreational Factor, Tunney Says; Skilled

Athletes No Better Fighters," *Miami News*, July 13, 1942, 11.

2. "Tunney Favors Compulsory Fitness," *Poughkeepsie Journal*, October 19, 1944, 16.

3. "Tunney Fears Military Athletics Detract from Warrior Psychology," *New York Times*, August 20, 1942, 27.

4. "Tunney Says Football Should Be Abandoned," *Sacramento Bee*, December 2, 1943, 29.

ELMER BURNHAM

1. George A. Barton, "Sport-Graphs," *Star Tribune* (Minneapolis, MN), September 16, 1943.

2. Glen Perkins, "Burnham's Boys Play for Fun," *Purdue Alumnus* 30, no. 8 (August 1943): 5.

3. "Survey Reveals Many Outstanding Prospects," *Purdue Exponent*, August 14, 1943.

ATHLETIC PREFERENCE

1. Arthur R. H. Morrow, "In Order to Carry On," *Philadelphia Inquirer*, March 26, 1944, 117.

2. Bill Davidson, "Sports During the War?," *Yank: The Army Weekly* 3, April 27, 1945, 23.

3. George C. Marshall, "5–005 Memorandum for General Handy, January 3, 1945," in *The Papers of George Catlett Marshall*, vol. 5, *"The Finest Soldier," January 1, 1945–January 7, 1947*, edited by Larry I. Bland and

Sharon Ritenour Stevens (Baltimore: Johns Hopkins University Press, 1991), 6–7.

4. Jim O'Brien, "Sidelines," *Journal Times* (Racine, WI), December 27, 1944, 10.

5. Joe Williams, "Re-examination, Induction of 4-F Athletes Would Be Unwise, Declares Army Examiner," *El Paso Herald Post*, December 27, 1943, 8.

6. "Sport: Frnka's 4-Fs," *Time*, December 13, 1943.

US MILITARY ACADEMY FOOTBALL

1. *Army vs. Notre Dame*, November 11, 1944, Yankee Stadium (New York: Blanchard Press; Harry M. Stevens, Inc., 1944).

2. Bob Curran, "In War, Jocks Were Home Free," *Buffalo News*, June 14, 1994.

3. Charles Einstein, "When Football Went to War," *Sports Illustrated*, December 6, 1971, https://www.si.com/vault/1971/12/06/615072/when-football-went-to-war/.

4. Jack Cavanaugh, *Mr. Inside and Mr. Outside: World War II, Army's Undefeated Teams, and College Football's Greatest Backfield Duo* (Chicago: Triumph, 2014), xvii–12, 21, 36, 38, 40, 45, 50, 55, 58–61, 121, 206, 213, 223.

5. Joseph Paul Vasquez III, "America and the Garrison Stadium: How the US Armed Forces Shaped College Football," *Armed Forces & Society* 38, no. 3 (July 2012): 353–72.

6. Randy Roberts, "College Football: The Army-Navy Game Nobody Missed," *Wall Street Journal*, December 9, 2011.

7. "Says Grid Stars Who Quit Service Schools Look like Draft Dodgers," *Boston Globe*, September 17, 1946, 35.

8. Wilbur D. Jones, Jr., *"Football! Navy! War!": How Military "Lend-Lease" Players Saved the College Game and Helped Win World War II* (Jefferson, NC: McFarland, 2009), 9.

9. ZappaOMatic, "[OC] History of Service Teams and the Service Academies During World War II," Reddit, April 17, 2017.

GEORGE BARNEY POOLE

1. Associated Press, "Poole Spent 7 Seasons at Ole Miss, UNC, Army," ESPN, April 12, 2005.

2. "Barney Poole Is Flunked from Point," *Californian* (Salinas, CA), May 31, 1947, 14.

3. "Barney Poole—No Longer a 'Simon Pure,'" *Times and Democrat* (Orangeburg, SC), May 28, 1949, 6.

4. William Tucker, "Ole Mis' Barney Poole Out to Break Endurance Record for Going to College," *Tennessean* (Nashville, TN), June 16, 1947, 10.

DEWITT "TEX" COULTER

1. Oscar Fraley, "Break for Tex," *Star-Gazette* (Elmira, NY), October 15, 1947, 14.

2. Sam Blair, "In Memory of DeWitt 'Tex' Coulter—All-Time Area Player: Tex Coulter of Masonic Home Was Greatest Among Greats," *Dallas Morning News*, December 16, 1984.

Chapter 11: Separate and Unequal

Ulysses Lee's *The Employment of Negro Troops* is an exhaustive account of Black troops in World War II and the shocking degree of segregation and racism against them. The *Pittsburgh Courier*, a weekly for the African American community, did landmark reporting on racism in the military while the rest of the print media remained largely silent.

JOHN J. MCLAUGHRY, OFFICER TRAINING

1. John J. McLaughry to Tuss and Florence McLaughry, assorted, January through April 1943, courtesy of the estate of John J. McLaughry.

JOHN J. MCLAUGHRY, MONTFORD POINT

1. John J. McLaughry to Tuss and Florence McLaughry, assorted, May through July 1943, courtesy of the estate of John J. McLaughry.
2. Melton A. McLaurin, *The Marines of Montford Point: America's First Black Marines* (Chapel Hill: University of North Carolina Press, 2007).

THE KILLING OF ROBERT STAFFORD

1. Branch Office of the Judge Advocate General with the European Theater of Operations, *United States v. Private William C. Forester (34686405) and Private Tracey Bryant (34686280)*, both of *425th Military Police Escort Guard Company* (Washington, DC: War Department, 1944).

BLACK TROOPS, DISCRIMINATION AGAINST IN COURTS-MARTIAL AND SENTENCING

1. J. Robert Lilly, "Death Penalty Cases in WWII Military Courts: Lessons Learned from North Africa and Italy," paper presented at the 41st Annual Meeting of the Academy of Criminal Justice Sciences, Las Vegas, NV, March 10–13, 2004.

2. United States, War Department, General Courts Martial, "Offenses by Type; Monthly Average 1943, Jan and Feb 1944," Administrative History Collection, Folder Title: Negro Troops, ADM NR. 218 (Washington, DC: War Department, 1943).

3. United States War Department, General Courts Martial, "Persons Involved—Convicted and Acquitted Monthly Average 1943 and Jan 1944," Administrative History Collection, Folder Title: Negro Troops, ADM NR. 218 (Washington, DC: War Department, 1943).

4. United States War Department, General Courts Martial, "Sentences: Monthly Average 1943, Jan and Feb

1944," Administrative History Collection, Folder Title: Negro Troops, ADM NR. 218 (Washington, DC: War Department, 1944).

5. "Walter White Defends Seamen: Navy Court Sentenced 45 Sailors for Guam Rioting," *Pittsburgh Courier*, July 21, 1945.

BLACK TROOPS, RACISM AGAINST, GENERAL

1. Alan Rice, "Black Troops Were Welcome in Britain, but Jim Crow Wasn't: The Race Riot of One Night in June 1943," The Conversation, June 22, 2018.

2. Alexis Clark, "When Jim Crow Reigned amid the Rubble of Nazi Germany," *New York Times Magazine*, February 19, 2020.

3. "Background on Detroit's Race Rioting," *Pittsburgh Press*, June 22, 1943.

4. Bernard C. Nalty, *The Right to Fight: African-American Marines in World War II*, Marines in World War II Commemorative Series (Washington, DC: U.S. Government Printing Office, 1995).

5. Chris Dixon, *African Americans and the Pacific War, 1941–1945: Race, Nationality, and the Fight for Freedom* (Cambridge, UK: Cambridge University Press, 2018).

6. Christopher Paul Moore, *Fighting for America: Black Soldiers, The Unsung Heroes of World War II* (New York: One World, 2005).

7. David Schindler and Mark Westcott, "Shocking Racial Attitudes: Black G.I.s in Europe," *Review of Economic Studies* 88, no. 1 (January 2021): 489–520.

8. Douglas A. Blackmon, *Slavery by Another Name: The Re-Enslavement of Black People in America from the Civil War to World War II* (New York: Doubleday, 2008).

9. "Harlem Is Orderly with Heavy Guard Ready for Trouble," *New York Times*, August 3, 1943, 1.

10. Henry I. Shaw, Jr., and Ralph W. Donnelly, *Blacks in the Marine Corps* (Washington, DC: U.S. Marine Corps History and Museums Division, 2002).

11. James Baldwin, "Letter from a Region in My Mind," *New Yorker*, November 17, 1962.

12. Linda Hervieux, *Forgotten: The Untold Story of D-Day's Black Heroes, at Home and at War* (New York: Harper, 2015).

13. Phillip McGuire, "Desegregation of the Armed Forces: Black Leadership, Protest and World War II," *Journal of Negro History* 68, no. 2 (Spring 1983): 147–58.

14. "Racial Killings of Black Soldiers, 1941–1942: The War at Home," Civil Rights & Restorative Justice Project, Northeastern University.

15. Roger Didier, "The Hastie Report!," *Pittsburgh Courier*, February 6, 1943.

16. "Soldier Is Killed in Negro Troop Riot," *New York Times*, June 11, 1943, 12.

17. Ulysses Lee, *The Employment of Negro Troops* (Washington, DC: U.S. Army Center of Military History, 2001).

18. United States War Department, Army War College, Office of the Commandant, Memorandum for the Chief of Staff: Subject: Employment of Negro Man Power in War (Washington, DC: War Department, 1925).

19. United States War Department, *Command of Negro Troops*, Pamphlet no. 20–4 (Washington, DC: War Department, 1944).

20. United States War Department, *History of the VIII Air Force Service Command*, chap. 1, "Mission" (Washington, DC: War Department, 1943).

21. United States War Department, Special Staff, Historical Division, *The Training of Negro Troops*, Study No. 36 (Washington, DC: War Department, 1946).

22. U.S. Army, Administrative History Collection, Folder Title: Anglo-American Relations, File No. 23 (Washington, DC: U.S. Army, 1944).

23. U.S. Army, Administrative History Collection, "Policy on Negroes," Folder Title: Negro Troops, File No. 218 (Washington, DC: U.S. Army, 1942).

24. U.S. Army, Administrative History Collection, Folder Title: American Red Cross, File No. 20B (Washington, DC: U.S. Army, 1945): 17.

25. U.S. Army, "Censorship Report on Inter-Racial Relations for Period 16–30 April 1945," Administrative History Collection, Folder Title: Censorship, File No. 58 (Washington, DC: U.S. Army, 1945).

26. U.S. Army, "Extracts on Negro Morals," Administrative History Collection, Folder Title: Morals and Conduct, File No. 213 (Washington, DC: U.S. Army, 1944).

27. U.S. Army, Headquarters European Theater of Operations, Historical Section, "American Red Cross in Great Britain, 1942–1944" (Washington, DC: U.S. Army, 1944).

28. U.S. Army, Headquarters European Theater of Operations, Historical Section, "First Eisenhower Period, ETO Monograph, 1941–43" (Washington, DC: U.S. Army, 1944).

29. U.S. Army, "History Branch Office of the Judge Advocate General with the United States Forces European Theatre 18 July–1 November 1945, vol. 1," Administrative History Collection, Folder Title: Judge Advocate History of the Branch Office, ETO, ADM NR. 559A (Washington, DC: U.S. Army, 1944).

30. William Doyle, *Inside the Oval Office: The White House Tapes from FDR to Clinton* (New York: Kodansha, 1999).

Chapter 12: Remember the McKean

JOHN J. MCLAUGHRY, OVERSEAS

1. John J. McLaughry to Tuss and Florence McLaughry, assorted, August through November 1943, courtesy of the estate of John J. McLaughry.

USS *MCKEAN*

1. U.S. Fleet, South Pacific Force, USS *McKean*, *Action Report Involving the Loss of the USS* McKean *as a Result of Enemy Action on November 17, 1943—Forwarding of*, November 23, 1945.

Chapter 13: Sunday Sheet

DAVID SCHREINER

1. Anna Schreiner, "Schreiner Sunday Sheet," assorted, May 1943 through March 1945, David N. Schreiner Letters, 1938–1947, M92–233, Box 1, 3/33/I5, Wisconsin Historical Society.

Chapter 14: Bauman

The author is indebted to Patti and Brett Margaron for allowing access to letters and other material relating to Robert and Frank Bauman, courtesy of the Bauman Family Legacy.

ROBERT AND FRANK BAUMAN, GROWING UP

1. Bertha Bauman, US Census record, 1920.

2. Cook County, Illinois, birth certificates, 1878–1922, Illinois Department of Public Health, Division of Vital Records, Springfield, IL.

3. "Frank Bauman, Harvey Police Marksman, Dies," *Chicago Tribune*, September 21, 1934.

4. Frank L. Bauman [*sic*], US Census record, 1930.

5. Patti, Brett, Frank, and Matt Margaron, interviewed by the author.

6. R. B. McCandless, Supervising Receiver, Division of Insolvent National Banks, to Mrs. F. Bauman, Mary 4, 1938, Bauman Family Legacy.

7. Robert Bauman, grade report, school year 1934–1935, Harvey Public Schools, District 152, Cook County, IL, Bauman Family Legacy.

ROBERT AND FRANK BAUMAN, FOOTBALL

1. Bob Bauman to Emma Bauman, assorted January 1941 through April 1942, Bauman Family Legacy.

2. Bob Bauman to Bertha Bauman, assorted, March 1942 through July 1945, Bauman Family Legacy.

3. Bob Bauman to Frank Bauman, April 23, 1942, Bauman Family Legacy.

4. Burlington Route, *Chicago Railroad Fair*, 1948.

5. "Grid Aces Move to Purdue; Purdue Gets Illinois'

Best," *Baltimore American Sports*, September 26, 1943.

6. Illinois Central Railroad, timetables, No. 118; September 29, 30, October, November, December 1946.

HARVEY, ILLINOIS

1. Cheryl Corley, "Once a Blue-Collar Powerhouse, a Chicago Suburb Now Faces a Dim Future," NPR, September 6, 2017.
2. "Harvey, IL," Encyclopedia of Chicago, Chicago Historical Society, 2005.

Chapter 15: Forget Me Not

DAVID SCHREINER, ENGAGEMENT

1. David Schreiner to Betty Johnson, assorted, July through December 1943, David N. Schreiner Letters, 1938–1947, M92–233, Box 1, 3/33/I5, Wisconsin Historical Society.
2. David Schreiner to Betty, Hal, and Judy Johnson, assorted, June and July 1943, Wisconsin Historical Society.
3. David Schreiner to Herbert and Anna Schreiner, assorted, June through November, 1943, Wisconsin Historical Society.
4. David Schreiner to Herbert and Anna Schreiner, telegram, November 16, 1943, Wisconsin Historical Society.

5. "Miss Odette M. Hendrickson Engaged to David Schreiner, Famous U. W. Football Star," *Wisconsin State Journal* (Madison, WI), June 6, 1943.

Chapter 16: Committed to the Deep

Much of this chapter was based on well over a thousand pages of action reports submitted by the military after the battle. *Time* war correspondent Robert Sherrod's book *Tarawa: The Incredible Story of One of World War II's Bloodiest Battles* is a gripping and brave eyewitness account of the battle. Sherrod, who also covered Okinawa, was Ernie Pyle without the hokum. He was the best correspondent of the war.

THE BATTLE OF TARAWA

1. Brig. Gen. J. L. Underhill, USMC, Fifth Amphibious Corps, Marine Corps, "Observations on the 2d Marine Division Operations, TARAWA," in Report on Galvanic, January 11, 1944.

2. Captain J. B. O'Neill (MC), USN, Fifth Amphibious Corps, Marine Corps, "TARAWA Atoll; Report of Sanitary Inspection of, and Corrective Measures Taken," in Report on Galvanic, January 11, 1944.

3. Captain R. F. Whitehead, Fifth Amphibious Corps, Marine Corps, "Report of Capt. R. F. Whitehead, USN," in Report on Galvanic, January 11, 1944.

4. Commander Group Two, Commander Task Force Fifty-three, Fifth Amphibious Corps, Marine Corps (Rear Admiral H. W. Hill), Japanese Defenses on Bititu Island, December 13, 1943.

5. Commander Group Two, Commander Task Force Fifty-three, Fifth Amphibious Corps, Marine Corps (Rear Admiral H. W. Hill), Report of TARAWA Operations, December 13, 1943.

6. Commander in Chief C. W. Nimitz, U.S. Pacific Fleet and Pacific Ocean Areas, Operations in Pacific Ocean Areas, November 1943.

7. Commander, Transports Division Four, Pacific Fleet, Action Report—Tarawa Atoll, Gilbert Islands, December 30, 1943.

8. Commanding Officer, USS *Harry Lee*, "Comments of Lieut. Comdr. T. D. Slagle (MC) USNR, Senior Medical Officer, USS *Harry Lee*," in Report of Operations at Tarawa (GALVANIC), January 9, 1944.

9. Commanding Officer, USS *Harry Lee*, "Comments of Lieut. (jg) A. D. Callow, (MC) USNR, Beach Party Medical Officer," in Report of Operations at Tarawa (GALVANIC), January 9, 1944.

10. Commanding Officer, USS *Pursuit* (AM 108), Suggestions and Recommendations on Operations Against Tarawa Atoll, Gilbert Islands, November 20–28, 1943.

11. Edward Theriot, *Dodging Tides: The Battle of Tarawa* (Kindle, 2014).

12. Fifth Amphibious Corps, Marine Corps, "Analysis of Communication Reports," in Report on Galvanic, January 11, 1944.

13. Fifth Amphibious Corps, Marine Corps, "Engineer Report on Action Galvanic, 5 January 1944," in Report on Galvanic, January 11, 1944.

14. Fifth Amphibious Corps, Marine Corps, Epidemiology Unit no. 45, "Summary of Sanitary Survey of Betio Island of the Tarawa Atoll made on 12–3–43," in Report on Galvanic, January 11, 1944.

15. Fifth Amphibious Corps, Marine Corps, "G-1 Report," in Report on Galvanic, January 11, 1944.

16. Fifth Amphibious Corps, Marine Corps, "G-2 Report, 8 December 1943," in Report on Galvanic, January 11, 1944.

17. Fifth Amphibious Corps, Marine Corps, "G-4 Activities, 4 January 1944," in Report on Galvanic, January 11, 1944.

18. Fifth Amphibious Corps, Marine Corps, "Kourbash Air Situation—21 November 1943," in Report on Galvanic, January 11, 1944.

19. Fifth Amphibious Corps, Marine Corps, "LONGSUIT Operation, Observations of," in Report on Galvanic, January 11, 1944.

20. Fifth Amphibious Corps, Marine Corps, Medical Observer, Forward Echelon, Galvanic, "Medical Situation, Galvanic," in Report on Galvanic, January 11, 1944.

21. Fifth Amphibious Corps, Marine Corps, "Memorandum for the Chief of Staff, Fifth Amphibious Corps: Ordnance Material and Ammunition, Salvage of—2 January 1944," in Report on Galvanic, January 11, 1944.

22. Fifth Amphibious Corps, Marine Corps, "Report of Galvanic Operation LONGSUIT, 2 December 1943," in Report on Galvanic, January 11, 1944.

23. Fifth Amphibious Corps, Marine Corps, "Report of Observations on GALVANIC Operation," in Report on Galvanic, January 11, 1944.

24. Fifth Amphibious Corps, Marine Corps, "Report on Naval Gunfire During Galvanic," in Report on Galvanic, January 11, 1944.

25. Peter Neushul and James D. Neushul, "With the Marines at Tarawa," *U.S. Naval Institute Proceedings* 125, no. 4 (April 1999): 1154.

26. Robert Citino, "Photo Finish: The Battle of Tarawa," The National WWII Museum, August 16, 2018.

27. Sam Roberts, "Norman T. Hatch, Who Filmed Grisly World War II Combat, Dies at 96," *New York Times*, April 28, 2017.

28. USS *Arthur Middleton*, Report of Boat Operations on "Helen Island," December 1, 1943.

29. USS *Doyen* (APA-1), Report of Galvanic Operation, December 3, 1943.

30. USS *La Salle*, Report on Landing Phase of Operations at Tarawa, November 28, 1943.

THE BATTLE OF TARAWA, UNKNOWNS

1. Commanding Officer, USS *Harry Lee*, Report of Operations at Tarawa (GALVANIC), January 9, 1944.

2. Joseph H. Alexander, *Across the Reef: The Marine Assault on Tarawa*, Marines in World War II Commemorative Series (Washington, DC: U.S. Marine Corps), 2–4.

3. Rick Stone, *The Tarawa Unknowns*, Report Prepared for the 2nd Marine Division Association, 2013.

4. W. Wyeth Willard, navy chaplain, private journal.

TENSIONS BETWEEN THE ARMY AND THE MARINES

1. David John Ulbrich, "The Importance of the Battle of Belleau Wood," *War on the Rocks*, June 4, 2018.

2. James A. Warren, "Gallipoli: WWI's Most Disastrous Battle," Daily Beast, August 27, 2019.

3. "The Myths of the Battle of Gallipoli," History Extra, April 25, 2018.

AMPHIBIOUS ASSAULT STRATEGY

1. Dirk Anthony Ballendorf and Merrill Lewis Bartlett,

Pete Ellis: An Amphibious Warfare Prophet, 1880–1923 (Annapolis, MD: Naval Institute Press, 2010).

2. Earl H. Ellis, "Advanced Base Operations in Micronesia," July 23, 1921.

3. F. H. Schofield and E. H. Ellis, *Report of Naval War College Committee on Defense of Guam* (Newport, RI: U.S. Naval War College, 1913).

4. Philip A. Crowl and Jeter A. Isely, *The U.S. Marines and Amphibious Warfare* (Princeton, NJ: Princeton University Press, 1951).

HOLLAND M. SMITH

1. Anne Cipriano Venzon, *From Whaleboats to Amphibious Warfare: Lt. Gen. "Howling Mad" Smith and the U.S. Marine Corps* (Westport, CT: Praeger, 2003).

2. Harry A. Gailey, *Howlin' Mad vs. the Army: Conflict in Command, Saipan, 1944* (Novato, CA: Presidio, 1986).

3. Holland M. Smith and Percy Finch, *Coral and Brass* (New York: Charles Scribner's Sons, 1949).

4. James R. Stockman, *The Battle for Tarawa* (Washington, DC: U.S. Marine Corps, Division of Public Information, Historical Section, 1947).

5. Norman V. Cooper, *A Fighting General: The Biography of Gen. Holland M. "Howlin' Mad" Smith* (Quantico, VA: Marine Corps Association, 1987).

BETIO

1. Col. Joseph H. Alexander, USMC, "A Bloody Proving Ground," *Naval History Magazine* 22, no. 6 (December 2008).

2. James R. Stockman, *The Battle for Tarawa* (Washington, DC: U. S. Marine Corps, Division of Public Information, Historical Section, 1947), 7, 13–15, 19–28.

3. Robert Sherrod, "Report on Tarawa: Marines' Show," *Time*, December 6, 1943.

4. Robert Sherrod, *Tarawa: The Incredible Story of One of World War II's Bloodiest Battles* (New York: Skyhorse, 2013; originally published 1944), 51.

TARAWA, TIDES

1. Fifth Amphibious Corps, Marine Corps, "Report of Observations on GALVANIC Operation," in Report on Galvanic, January 11, 1944.

2. George C. Dyer, *The Amphibians Came to Conquer: The Story of Richmond Kelly Turner* (Verdun Press, 2015), 715, 719, 727.

3. Hanson W. Baldwin, "The Bloody Epic That Was Tarawa," *New York Times*, November 16, 1958, 19.

4. "How Marines Beat Unbeatable in Bloody Victory at Tarawa," *Daily News* (New York), December 4, 1943, 22.

5. Josh Hudak, "Through Crimson Tides: Tarawa's Effect on Military Tactics and Public Perception of War," Clemson University, 2014.

6. Patrick L. McKiernan, "Tarawa: The Tide That Failed," *U.S. Naval Institute Proceedings*, February 1962, 50–57.

7. Robert Sherrod, *Tarawa: The Incredible Story of One of World War II's Bloodiest Battles* (New York: Skyhorse, 2013; originally published 1944), 66.

HIGGINS BOATS

1. Charles M. Madigan, "Stories in the Stars," *Chicago Tribune*, November 20, 1998.

2. Daniel Strohl, "The Man Behind the Higgins Boats That Made D-Day Possible Also Proposed Rolling onto Beaches in Monster Swamp Buggies," Hemmings, June 6, 2019.

3. Jerry E. Strahan, *Andrew Jackson Higgins and the Boats That Won World War II* (Baton Rouge: Louisiana State University Press, 1998).

DONALD ROEBLING, PERSONAL

1. Al Burgert, "Roebling's 'Alligator' for Florida Rescues," *Life*, October 4, 1937, 94.

2. "Alligators by Roebling," *Time*, January 11, 1943.

3. Lemuel Parton, "Sea-Going Truck Used in Invasion," *Ventura County Star-Free Press*, September 1, 1942, 12.

4. "Navy Orders Seagoing Tank," *Times* (San Mateo, CA), February 19, 1941, 16.

5. Ralph Reed, "Mud-Spattered Senator Declares Tank Ride Is 'Thrilling, Satisfying,'" *Tampa Bay Times*, September 4, 1941.

6. "Tank That Swims Built to Reach Disaster Areas," *Chicago Tribune*, October 16, 1935, 9.

7. "'Vehicle of Mercy' Built by Clearwater Sportsman," *Tampa Tribune*, October 16, 1935, 1.

JOHN A. ROEBLING

1. Hamilton Schuyler, *The Roeblings: A Century of Engineers, Bridge Builders and Industrialists* (Princeton, NJ: Princeton University Press, 1931).

2. "John A. Roebling, Engineer, 84, Dies," *New York Times*, February 3, 1952, 85.

3. John A. Roebling, *Washington Roebling's Father: A Memoir of John A. Roebling*, edited by Donald Sayenga (Reston, VA: American Society of Civil Engineers Press, 2009).

DONALD ROEBLING; LVTS IN COMBAT

1. "Alligators by Roebling," *Time*, January 11, 1943.

2. Gen. Julian C. Smith, Marine Corps, Second Marine Division War Diary, January 12, 1944.

3. J. David Rogers, "Donald Roebling and the Origins of the Amphibious Tractor," paper presented at American Society of Civil Engineers World Environmental and Water Resources Congress, 2016.

4. *Operations in Pacific Ocean Areas—November 1943* (secret report from U.S. Pacific Fleet Commander in Chief [Admiral Chester Nimitz] to his superior, U.S. Fleet Commander in Chief [Admiral Ernest King]), February 28, 1944, Annex E: Occupation of the Gilbert Islands.

5. Richard W. Roan, *Roebling's Amphibian: The Origin of the Assault Amphibian* (Quantico, VA: Marine Corps Development and Education Command, 1987).

6. Robert E. Schrader IV, "From Belleau Wood to Pacific Beaches: Major Developments in the U.S. Marine Corps," The Strategy Bridge, May 24, 2018.

BATTLE OF TARAWA, CASUALTIES

1. Fifth Amphibious Corps, Marine Corps, "G-1 Report," in Report on Galvanic, January 11, 1944.

2. Gen. Julian C. Smith, Marine Corps, Second Marine Division War Diary, January 12, 1944.

3. Gordon L. Rottman, *U.S. Marine Corps World War II*

Order of Battle: Ground and Air Units in the Pacific War, 1939–1945 (Westport, CT: Greenwood, 2002).

4. James R. Stockman, *The Battle for Tarawa* (Washington, DC: Historical Section, Division of Public Information, U.S. Marine Corps, 1947).

5. Logbook of the USS *Harry Lee*, November 21, 1943.

6. Robert Trumbull, "Reborn Tarawa Still Bears Evidence of the Historic Pacific Battle 25 Years Ago," *New York Times*, November 23, 1968.

7. Secret After Action Report from Medical Observer, Forward Echelon, Galvanic, Fifth Amphibious Corps, Marine Corps, to Maj. Gen. H. M. Smith's Chief of Staff at Headquarters of the Fifth Amphibious Corps, December 1, 1943.

LANDING ON TARAWA, COMMUNICATION BREAKDOWN

1. Brig. Gen. J. L. Underhill, Observations on the 2d Marine Division Operations, Tarawa, January 11, 1944.

2. Commander, Task Force 53, [Rear Admiral Harry Hill] Tarawa Operations Report to Commander in Chief, U.S. Pacific Fleet, December 13, 1943.

3. Commander, Transport Group for Task Force 53, After Action Report to Rear Admiral Hill, December 1, 1943.

4. Engineer Report on Action Galvanic, Part II: Engineer Report Subsequent to Operation, January 5, 1944.

5. Fifth Amphibious Corps, Marine Corps, "Enclosure 'F'

to Fifth Amphibious Corps Report on Galvanic: Transport Quartermaster Report on Galvanic," December 30, 1943.

6. Fifth Amphibious Corps, Marine Corps, "Kourbash—Galvanic Operating Report of Communications," in Report on Galvanic, December 2, 1944.

7. George C. Dyer, *The Amphibians Came to Conquer: The Story of Richmond Kelly Turner* (Verdun Press, 2015), 8, 52, 710.

8. George F. Horne, "Tarawa's Captor Reviews Victory," *New York Times*, November 30, 1943, 3.

9. Gordon L. Rottman, *U.S. Special Warfare Units in the Pacific Theater, 1941–45* (Oxford, UK: Osprey Publishing, 2019), 21.

10. Hanson W. Baldwin, "The Bloody Epic That Was Tarawa," *New York Times*, November 16, 1958.

11. Henry L. Shaw, Jr., Bernard C. Nalty, and Edwin T. Turnbladh, *Central Pacific Drive: History of U.S. Marine Corps Operations in World War II* (Washington, DC: Historical Branch, G-3 Division, Headquarters, U.S. Marine Corps, 1966).

12. Lt. Gen. Julian Smith, USMC, "Tarawa," *U.S. Naval Institute Proceedings*, November 1953.

13. Maj. Gen. Holland M. Smith, Fifth Amphibious Corps, USMC, Report of GALVANIC Operation (Gilbert Islands), 1943.

14. *Operations in Pacific Ocean Areas—November 1943* (secret report from U.S. Pacific Fleet Commander in Chief [Admiral Chester Nimitz] to his superior, U.S. Fleet Commander in Chief [Admiral Ernest King]), February 28, 1944, Annex F.

15. "Shoup Defends Tarawa Tactics 20 Years After Marines' Battle," *New York Times*, November 21, 1963, 29.

COMMAND STRUCTURE, RESPONSIBILITY FOR CASUALTIES

1. Commander in Chief, US Pacific Fleet, *United States Naval Administration in World War II: Marshall—Gilbert Area*, 1946.

2. Craig L. Symonds, *World War II at Sea: A Global History* (Oxford, UK: Oxford University Press, 2018), 606.

3. Forrest C. Pogue, *George C. Marshall: Organizer of Victory, 1943–1945* (New York: Viking, 1963), 440.

4. George F. Horne, "1,026 Marines Lost in Tarawa Capture," *New York Times*, December 2, 1943, 19.

5. Hanson W. Baldwin, "The Bloody Epic That Was Tarawa," *New York Times*, November 16, 1958.

6. Hanson W. Baldwin, "Pacific Technique Gains: A Realistic Study of Tarawa Lessons Helped Prepare Marshall Invasion," *New York Times*, February 25, 1944, 4.

7. Joseph H. Alexander, "Significance of Tarawa," in *Across the Reef: The Marine Assault on Tarawa*, Ma-

rines in WWII Commemorative Series (Washington, DC: U.S. Marine Corps, 1993).

8. "Knox Upholds Plan of Tarawa Action; Attack So Costly to Marines in Part Because Wind's Shift Stranded Landing Craft," *New York Times*, December 1, 1943, 4.

9. "Navy Reports Cut in Tarawa Losses," *New York Times*, January 6, 1944, 4.

10. "Nimitz Visits Tarawa; Vows New Blow at Japs," *Los Angeles Times*, December 1, 1943.

11. Robert Sherrod, *Tarawa: The Incredible Story of One of World War II's Bloodiest Battles* (New York: Skyhorse, 2013; originally published 1944), 147–51.

12. "Smith Decries Tarawa Battle as 'Mistake,'" *Times Dispatch* (Richmond, VA), November 3, 1948, 9.

13. "Vandegrift Backs Method at Tarawa; Calls Attack Well Planned but Warns That Low-Cost Victories Are Over," *New York Times*, December 18, 1943, 2.

14. William F. Tyree, "U.S. Casualties 3,772 in Gilbert Isle Attack," *Daily News* (New York), December 2, 1943.

Chapter 17: The Patrol

This chapter is almost entirely based on an eighty-page account of a three-day patrol in Bougainville, written by John McLaughry in 1974 and revised after meeting with one of the other participants. The details have been cross-checked to the degree possible, and the accuracy is impeccable except for a very few minor details.

PATROL, BOUGAINVILLE

1. John J. McLaughry, "The World War II Letters of John J. McLaughry," 1990, courtesy of the estate of John J. McLaughry.

BOUGAINVILLE, GENERAL

1. David D. Duncan, "Fiji Patrol on Bougainville," *National Geographic*, January 1945, 87–93.
2. First Amphibious Corps, Marine Corps, Report on Bougainville Operation, 3 November 1943 to 15 December 1943, Bougainville Beachhead: Phase II.
3. Harry A. Gailey, *Bougainville, 1943–1945: The Forgotten Campaign* (Lexington: University Press of Kentucky, 1991).
4. John N. Rentz, *Bougainville and the Northern Solomons*, Marine Corps Monographs Series (Nashville, TN: Battery Press, 1989; originally published by Historical Section, U.S. Marine Corps, 1948).

MALARIA

1. Fiammetta Rocco, *The Miraculous Fever Tree: Malaria and the Quest for a Cure That Changed the World* (New York: HarperCollins, 2003).

2. Karen Masterson, *The Malaria Project: The U.S. Government's Secret Mission to Find a Miracle Cure* (New York: New American Library, 2014).

3. Randall M. Packard, *The Making of a Tropical Disease: A Short History of Malaria*, 2nd ed., Johns Hopkins Biographies of Disease (Baltimore: Johns Hopkins University Press, 2021).

4. Timothy C. Winegard, *The Mosquito: A Human History of Our Deadliest Predator* (New York: Dutton, 2019).

Chapter 18: Pen Pal

TONY BUTKOVICH, PURDUE FOOTBALL

1. "Boilermaker Squad Hit Hard by Loss of V-12 Seniors," *Purdue Exponent*, November 3, 1943, 3.

2. "Butkovich Sets Big 9 Mark as Purdue Whips Badgers," *Chicago Tribune*, October 31, 1943.

3. *Debris* (Purdue University yearbook), 1943 and 1944.

4. Harold Harrison, "Purdue Foes Await News from Marines on Butkovich Status," *Register-Republic* (Rockford, IL), October 26, 1943.

5. Irving Vaughn, "Boilermakers Set to Crush Badgers Today; Butkovich Will Play Final Contest," *Chicago Tribune*, October 30, 1943.

6. Irving Vaughn, "Butkovich, Boilermaker Pals Do a 32

to 0 Job on Wisconsin," *Chicago Tribune*, October 31, 1943.

7. Ken Thompson, "1943 Win over Badgers Bittersweet," *Journal and Courier* (Lafayette, IN), November 6, 1999.

8. "Nine Marine Trainees to Be Lost to Purdue; Butkovich Among Football Men Facing Transfer Next Week," *New York Times*, October 27, 1943.

9. "Photographic Proof That 'Touchdown Tony' Butkovich Can Be Stopped; Badgers Hold on 1-Yard Line," *Wisconsin State Journal* (Madison, WI), October 31, 1943.

10. "Purdue Trims Game Badger Team, 32–0; Butkovich Sets New Big 10 Scoring Record of 78 Points," *Wisconsin State Journal* (Madison, WI), October 31, 1943.

11. "Tony Butkovich Is Cleveland Choice," *Journal and Courier* (Lafayette, IN), April 20, 1944.

TONY BUTKOVICH, PARRIS ISLAND

1. "Grid Greats on Uncle Sam's Team," *Globe-Gazette* (Mason City, IA), January 6, 1944.

US ECONOMY DURING WORLD WAR II

1. Christopher J. Tassava, "The American Economy During World War II," Economic History Association.

2. Paul Fussell, *Wartime: Understanding and Behavior in*

the Second World War (Oxford, UK: Oxford University Press, 1989).

TOM MILLIGAN

1. "Brings 'Special Delivery' from Boy's Hero in Pacific," *Palladium-Item* (Richmond, IN), December 17, 1944.

2. "Camp Clements to Be Used by 4-H Boys, Girls Aug. 19–25," *Palladium-Item* (Richmond, IN), August 14, 1945.

3. Carolyn Maund, "All in a Day's Work . . . Mother's Duties Keep Her Busy and Happy," *Palladium-Item* (Richmond, IN), June 3, 1945.

4. "Children Inspect Milkweed Pod Collection," *Palladium-Item* (Richmond, IN), September 18, 1944.

5. "Four-H News," *Palladium-Item* (Richmond, IN), March 10, 1945.

6. "Keesling Brought Letter to Local Boy from Butkovich," *Palladium-Item* (Richmond, IN), May 9, 1945.

7. Mike Emery, "Retro Richmond: Once Known as the Lawn Mower Capital of the World," *Palladium-Item* (Richmond, IN), September 28, 2018.

8. Tom Milligan, interviewed by the author.

9. "Wayne County 4-H Fair Awards," *Palladium-Item* (Richmond, IN), August 9, 1945.

Chapter 19: Not a Damn Thing

KING NEPTUNE CEREMONY

1. Virgil A. Cowart, "Crossing the Line: A Story of the Ceremonies Attending the Crossing of the Equator: The United States Ship *Mississippi* en Route American Polynesia, July 19–29, 1940" (Washington, DC: U.S. Navy, 1940).

DAVID SCHREINER, GUADALCANAL

1. David Schreiner to Betty and Hal Johnson, March 20, 1944, David N. Schreiner Letters, 1938–1947, M92–233, Box 1, 3/33/I5, Wisconsin Historical Society.
2. David Schreiner to Herbert and Anna Schreiner, assorted, February 1944 through May 1945, Wisconsin Historical Society.

Chapter 20: Temptation

JOHN J. MCLAUGHRY, BOUGAINVILLE COMBAT

1. John J. McLaughry, "January 1–15, 1944" insert in "The World War II Letters of John J. McLaughry," 1990, courtesy of the estate of John J. McLaughry.
2. John J. McLaughry to Florence and Tuss McLaughry, assorted, November through December 1943, courtesy of the estate of John J. McLaughry.

JOHN J. MCLAUGHRY, GUAM TRAINING

1. John J. McLaughry to Tuss and Florence McLaughry, assorted, January through May 1944, courtesy of the estate of John J. McLaughry.

ODETTE HENDRICKSON

1. David Schreiner to Betty Johnson, September 4, 1944, David N. Schreiner Letters, 1938–1947, M92–233, Box 1, 3/33/I5, Wisconsin Historical Society.

2. David Schreiner to Herbert and Anna Schreiner, October 31, 1944, Wisconsin Historical Society.

3. David Schreiner to Odette Hendrickson, June and December 1944, courtesy of the family of Odette Hendrickson Davis.

4. "Graduation Exercises," Naval Reserve Midshipmen's School (WR), Northampton, MA, February 8, 1944.

5. "Hendrickson Returns from War to Find Sister in Service, Too," *Wisconsin State Journal* (Madison, WI), November 26, 1943, 1.

6. Odette Hendrickson to Lula Hendrickson, December 1943 and January 1944, courtesy of the family of Odette Hendrickson Davis.

FRANK KNOX, RACISM TOWARD WAVES

1. Morris J. MacGregor, Jr., *Integration of the Armed*

Forces, 1940–1965, Defense Studies Series (Washington, DC: U.S. Army Center of Military History, 2001).

Chapter 21: Millimeter

JOHN J. MCLAUGHRY, COMBAT ON GUAM

1. "John J. McLaughry's account of Mid May through August, 1944," courtesy of the estate of John J. McLaughry.
2. John J. McLaughry to Tuss and Florence McLaughry, assorted, August 1944, courtesy of the estate of John J. McLaughry.

DAVID SCHREINER, COMBAT ON GUAM

1. David Schreiner to Betty and Hal Johnson, July 4, 1944, David N. Schreiner Letters, 1938–1947, M92–233, Box 1, 3/33/I5, Wisconsin Historical Society.
2. David Schreiner to Herbert and Anna Schreiner, assorted, August 1944, Wisconsin Historical Society.

SAIPAN

1. 27th Infantry Division, *Report of Intelligence Activities 27th Infantry Division, Saipan Operation,* April 1–August 6, 1944.

2. Harold J. Goldberg, *D-Day in the Pacific: The Battle of Saipan*, Twentieth-Century Battles (Bloomington: Indiana University Press, 2007).

3. Harry A. Gailey, *Howlin' Mad vs. the Army: Conflict in Command, Saipan, 1944* (Novato, CA: Presidio, 1986).

4. Holland M. Smith and Percy Finch, *Coral and Brass* (New York: Charles Scribner's Sons, 1949).

5. James H. Hallas, *Saipan: The Battle That Doomed Japan in World War II* (Guilford, CT: Stackpole Books, 2019).

6. John C. Chapin, *Breaching the Marianas: The Battle for Saipan*, Marines in World War II Commemorative Series (Washington, DC: History and Museums Division, U.S. Marine Corps, 1994).

7. United States Strategic Bombing Survey, Over-all Economic Effects Division, *The Effects of Strategic Bombing on Japan's War Economy* (Washington, DC: U.S. Government Printing Office, 1946), 28, 29, 32, 57.

MARPI POINT

1. Robert Lee Sherrod, "Civilians Committed Mass Suicide," *Life*, August 28, 1944, 80–81.

2. Robert Lee Sherrod, "War's Terror Struck at the Innocent," *Life*, August 28, 1944.

GUAM, RECAPTURE OF

1. Cyril J. O'Brien, "Guam in World War II," in *LIBER-ATION: Marines in the Recapture of Guam*, Marines in World War II Commemorative Series (Washington, DC: National Park Service, 1994).
2. O. R. Lodge, *The Recapture of Guam 1954* (Washington, DC: Historical Branch, G-3 Division, Headquarters, U.S. Marine Corps, 1954).

BABE RUTH

1. Winston Groom, *1942: The Year That Tired Men's Souls* (New York: Atlantic Monthly Press, 2005).

Chapter 22: March of the Crabs

BOB BAUMAN, GUADALCANAL

1. Bob Bauman to Dale Spilsbury, February and November 1944, Bauman Family Legacy.
2. Bob Bauman to Dorothy Spindler, February 1944, Bauman Family Legacy.
3. Bob Bauman to Emma Bauman, October 22, 1944, Bauman Family Legacy.
4. Bob Bauman to Frank Bauman, undated 1943 and December 1944, Bauman Family Legacy.
5. Bob Bauman, "To the Tune of Halls of Montezuma," Bauman Family Legacy.

6. U.S. Marine Corps to Bertha L. Bauman, Notice of receipt of allotment, November 30, 1944, Bauman Family Legacy.

FRANK BAUMAN, PURDUE

1. "2 of Hoosier Big 3 Face Toughest Tests," *Indianapolis News*, October 27, 1944.
2. "Sporting News All-Americans Announced," *Morning Call* (Allentown, PA), December 6, 1944.
3. "Writers Pick All-American Football Team," *Chico Record* (Chico, CA), December 10, 1944.

GUADALCANAL, PHYSICAL DESCRIPTION

1. 25th Naval Construction Battalion, *War Diary* (Washington, DC: War Department, 1945).
2. Bill Pierce (Weapons Co., 29th Marine Regiment), "Discipline and Duty—Marine Corps Life," in *Okinawa 1945: Personal Recollections of the Battle of Okinawa by Marines of the Sixth Marine Division*, vol. 3, edited by Kenneth J. Long (Sixth Marine Division Association), 45–46.
3. C. Edward Gideon, *History of the Fifty-eighth United States Naval Construction Battalion, 1942–1945* (Brooklyn, NY: Foxcroft Commercial Press, 1945).
4. Gordon L. Rottman, *World War II Pacific Island Guide: A Geo-Military Study* (Westport, CT: Greenwood Press, 2002), 97–98, 105–6, 116.

5. H. B. Guppy, *The Solomon Islands and Their Natives* (London: S. Sonnenschein, Lowrey & Co., 1887).

6. Kenneth J. Long, "Preface," in *Okinawa 1945: Personal Recollections of the Battle of Okinawa by Marines of the Sixth Marine Division*, vol. 4, edited by Kenneth J. Long (Sixth Marine Division Association), 4.

7. Neal McCallum, interviewed by the author.

8. *The Odyssey: Eighteenth U.S. Naval Construction Battalion* (San Francisco: Schwabacher-Frey, 1946).

9. Office of the Chief of Naval Operations, Navy Department, *Amphibious Operations: Capture of Okinawa (Ryukyus Operation), 27 March to 21 June 1945* (Washington, DC: Navy Department, 1946).

10. Osa Johnson, *Bride in the Solomons* (Boston: Houghton Mifflin, 1944).

11. Paul S. Higginbotham, *The Anxiety of the 46th U.S. Naval Construction Battalion 18 November 1942–1 May 1945* (n.p., n.d.).

12. Pedro A. Del Valle, *Semper Fidelis: An Autobiography* (Hawthorne, CA: Christian Book Club of America, 1976), 186.

13. S. E. Smith, *The United States Marine Corps in World War II: The One-Volume History, from Wake to Tsingtao, by the Men Who Fought in the Pacific and by Distinguished Marine Experts, Authors, and Newspapermen* (New York: Random House, 1969), 628–29.

14. Sixth Marine Division, Fourth Marine Regiment, First Battalion, Marine Corps, "Special Action Report: First Battalion, Fourth Marine Regiment, Phase I Okinawa," in *Special Action Report, Phases I and II, Okinawa Operation, May 1, 1945.*

15. Sixty-first U.S. Naval Construction Battalion, *Sixty-first Seafoam: A Logbook* (Baton Rouge, LA: Army & Navy Pictorial Publishers, 1945).

16. Sixty-third U.S. Naval Construction Battalion, *Can Do!* (Washington, DC: War Department, 1945).

17. Third Amphibious Corps, Marine Corps, *Action Report: Ryukyus Operation, Phases I & II (Okinawa),* July 1, 1945.

18. Third Amphibious Corps, Marine Corps, *Action Report: Ryukyus Operation, Appendices, Corps Operation Orders and G-3 Periodic Reports,* July 1, 1945.

19. U.S. Navy, *Pacific Diary of the Twenty-Fifth U.S. Naval Construction Battalion* (Washington, DC: U.S. Navy Seabee Museum).

20. William Bradford Huie, *Can Do! The Story of the Seabees* (New York: Dutton, 1944).

21. William Bruce Johnson, *The Pacific Campaign in World War II: From Pearl Harbor to Guadalcanal,* Cass Series—Naval Policy and History, vol. 35 (London: Routledge, 2006), 201–3, 209–10, 288, 292.

22. William T. Atu, "Fishing for Drummerfish (Kyphosidae)

with Termites and Spider Webs on the Weather Coast of Guadalcanal, Solomon Islands," *SPC Traditional Marine Resource Management and Knowledge Information Bulletin* 18 (2005): 3–8.

23. Mack Morriss, *South Pacific Diary, 1942–43* (Lexington: University of Kentucky Press, 1996).

24. Judith A. Bennett, *Natives and Exotics: World War II and Environment in the Southern Pacific* (Honolulu: University of Hawaii Press, 2009).

Chapter 23: The Mosquito Bowl

The printed program for the Mosquito Bowl, available online, contains the rosters for the 29th and 4th Regiments. All the names were cross-checked against Marine Corps muster rolls, available biographical information, and more than eighty newspaper databases to confirm their identities and football and professional careers. There were several I was unable to confirm. I found several sources to be of particular help. John Gunn wrote two comprehensive books on the history of marine football in which he dedicated a short section to the Mosquito Bowl. Terry Frei wrote about the game as well in *Third Down and a War to Go: The All-American 1942 Wisconsin Badgers.*

THE MOSQUITO BOWL, THE PLAYERS

1. Fred Abbott to Helen Abbott, December 25, 1944.

2. John Gunn, *The Old Core: Parris Island, San Diego, the All-Marines, the Great Goettge, President's Cup Series, Mare Island, the Rose Bowl Games, Swede Larson, John Beckett, and More* (Costa Mesa, CA: J&J Publishing, 1992).

3. John Gunn, *(Quite) A Few Good Men* (Costa Mesa, CA: J&J Publishing, 1992).

4. Kenneth J. Long, ed., *Okinawa 1945: Personal Recollections of the Battle of Okinawa by Marines of the Sixth Marine Division*, vol. 2 (Sixth Marine Division Association).

5. Melvin D. Heckt to Mr. and Mrs. Wesley G. Heckt, December 25, 1944.

6. Neal McCallum, interviewed by the author.

7. Terry Frei, *Third Down and a War to Go: The All-American 1942 Wisconsin Badgers* (Madison: Wisconsin Historical Society Press, 2007).

THE MOSQUITO NETWORK

1. Mark Durenberger, "Meet the Mosquito Network," RadioWorld, July 5, 2020.

2. Martin Hadlow, "The Mosquito Network: American Military Broadcasting in the South West Pacific During World War Two," *Journal of Radio Studies* 11, no. 4 (2004): 73–86.

3. "Radio: Mosquito Network," *Time*, July 17, 1944.

JOHN J. MCLAUGHRY, THE MOSQUITO BOWL

1. John J. McLaughry to Tuss and Florence McLaughry, assorted, December 1944, courtesy of the estate of John J. McLaughry.

Chapter 24: Bound for Hell

OKINAWA, HEADING FOR

1. Roy Edgar Appleman, James M. Burns, Russell A. Gugeler, and John Stevens, *Okinawa: The Last Battle* (Washington, DC: Historical Division, Department of the Army, 1948), 1, 7, 9, 26.
2. Sixth Marine Division, U.S. Marines, *Special Action Report: Phases I & II Okinawa Operation*, Annex A: "4th Marines," May 1, 1945.

ULITHI

1. Capt. James R. Stockman, "The Landing," in *Okinawa 1945: Personal Recollections of the Battle of Okinawa by Marines of the Sixth Marine Division*, vol. 4, edited by Kenneth J. Long (Sixth Marine Division Association), 15–16.
2. David Schreiner to Herbert and Anna Schreiner, assorted, March 1945, David N. Schreiner Letters, 1938–1947, M92–233, Box 1, 3/33/I5, Wisconsin Historical Society.

Chapter 25: Buckner

SIMON BOLIVAR BUCKNER

1. Arndt Mathis Stickles, *Simon Bolivar Buckner: Borderland Knight* (Chapel Hill: University of North Carolina Press, 1940).

2. "Buckner and Son," *Washington Post*, April 19, 1910, 6.

3. "Gen. Buckner Indicted for Treason," *Chicago Tribune*, February 22, 1862.

4. "Gen. Buckner Is Happy. He Has His Cabin, His Mintbed, His Toddy and His Dog," *New York Times*, December 3, 1910.

5. "Gen. Buckner's Burial Today: Special Train Will Carry Family to Frankfort for Interment," *Washington Post*, January 10, 1914, 4.

6. "Happiest Man Living: Gen. Buckner Wouldn't Trade His Mint Bed for Rockefeller's Riches," *Washington Post*, December 3, 1910, 6.

7. John E. Bierck, "Buckner's Father First to Face Unconditional Surrender Terms," *Washington Post*, June 24, 1945, B1.

8. "War Worn Veterans Who Fought for Dixie Once More in Reunion," *Atlanta Constitution*, June 15, 1905.

SIMON BOLIVAR BUCKNER, JR., U.S. MILITARY ACADEMY

1. "Buckner's Son Is Chosen: Selected by President to Go to West Point," *Atlanta Constitution*, June 19, 1903.

2. *Bugle Notes* (handbook of the United States Corps of Cadets) (West Point, NY: United States Military Academy, 1908).

3. *The Howitzer* (United States Military Academy yearbook), 1910.

SIMON BOLIVAR BUCKNER, JR., EARLY MILITARY CAREER

1. "New Cadet Commandant: Lieut. Col. Buckner Succeeds Lieut. Col. Richardson at West Point," *New York Times*, March 17, 1933.

SIMON BOLIVAR BUCKNER, JR., MINT JULEP RECIPE

1. Robert L. Wolke, "One Mint Julep," *Washington Post*, April 30, 2003, FB1.

2. Simon Bolivar Buckner, Jr., and W. D. Connor, "The Buckner Mint Julep Ceremony," The Buckner Home, 1937.

3. William C. Buckner, "The Great Mint Julep Recipe," *Assembly* 56, nos. 4–6 (1998).

SIMON BOLIVAR BUCKNER, JR., FAMILY LIFE

1. Mary Buckner Brubaker, personal account of her early life.

2. "Obituaries: Mary Buckner Brubaker," *Mail Tribune* (Medford, OR), January 5, 2014.

SIMON BOLIVAR BUCKNER, JR., SOCIAL LIFE

1. "First Army Winter Dance Is Brilliant: Hurleys Head the Line Receiving Guests; Many Dinners," *Washington Post*, November 22, 1930, 9.

2. "Japan Envoy Honored at Costume Ball: Kentucky Society Gives Brilliant Dance at Mayflower," *Washington Post*, March 2, 1930, S7.

3. "Kentucky Society Plans Costume Ball," *Washington Post*, November 16, 1930, S6.

4. Marriage announcement, *Hopkinsville Kentuckian*, December 28, 1916.

5. "Mrs. Maurice H. Thatcher Entertains at Luncheon," *Washington Post*, May 25, 1929, 7.

6. "Party Given to Mrs. Gann by Mrs. Henry: Many Social Leaders Attend Function at Willard Hotel," *Washington Post*, December 3, 1930.

SIMON BOLIVAR BUCKNER, JR., ALEUTIAN ISLANDS CAMPAIGN

1. "Alaskan Defense Head's Cut in Liquor Hours Poorly Heeded," *Christian Science Monitor*, February 5, 1943.

2. Don Eddy, "A Tough Guy Holds Alaska," *Los Angeles Times*, January 31, 1943, G4.

3. "Honored for Alaskan Defense," *New York Times*, October 2, 1943, 9.

4. "Southern Gentleman, Commanding Alaska Defenses, Anxious for Crack at Japanese," *Atlanta Constitution*, March 17, 1942, 1.

5. "Troops Occupy Kiska and Find All Japs Gone," *Chicago Tribune*, August 22, 1943, 5.

6. William Gilman, "Keen for Action: Army Head Represents Fist of Defense Arm; Looks at Asia," *Arizona Daily Star*, March 17, 1942.

7. Joseph Driscoll, "Buckner Ideal Alaska Chief," *Oakland Tribune*, October 8, 1942.

8. "Buckner Son of General: 'Big Bear of a Man' Was as Tough as He Looked," *Sun* (Baltimore, MD), June 19, 1945.

SIMON BOLIVAR BUCKNER, JR., APPOINTMENT AS GENERAL

1. "Buckner, Invader of Ryukyus, Son of Confederate General," *Sun* (Baltimore, MD), April 2, 1945, 4.

2. "Japs Will Find 'Bull' Buckner Tough Opponent," *Chicago Daily Tribune*, April 2, 1945, 4.

SIMON BOLIVAR BUCKNER, JR., MEETING WITH ROOSEVELT

1. "Gen. Buckner Sees President," *New York Times*, September 25, 1943, 25.

CONFLICTS OVER COMMAND STRUCTURE

1. Alan Rems, "At War with the Army," *Naval History Magazine*, February 2012.

RACISM

1. Brian Garfield, *The Thousand-Mile War: World War II in Alaska and the Aleutians* (Fairbanks: University of Alaska Press, 1995).
2. Ernest Gruening, "Introduction: The Alaskan Eskimos in World War II," in Muktuk Marston, *Men of the Tundra: Alaska Eskimos at War* (New York: October House, 1972).

REPLACING BUCKNER IN ALASKA

1. George C. Marshall, 3–148 Memorandum for General McNair, March 27, 1942, in *The Papers of George Catlett Marshall*, vol. 3, *"The Right Man for the Job": December 7, 1941–May 31, 1943*, edited by Larry I. Bland and Sharon Ritenour Stevens (Baltimore: Johns Hopkins University Press, 1991).
2. George C. Marshall, 3–311 to Lieutenant General John L. De Witt, September 3, 1942, in *The Papers of George Catlett Marshall*, vol. 3, *"The Right Man for the Job": December 7, 1941–May 31, 1943*, edited by Larry I. Bland and Sharon Ritenour Stevens (Baltimore: Johns Hopkins University Press, 1991).

3. George C. Marshall, 3–351 to Lieutenant General John L. De Witt, October 2, 1942, in *The Papers of George Catlett Marshall*, vol. 3, *"The Right Man for the Job": December 7, 1941–May 31, 1943*, edited by Larry I. Bland and Sharon Ritenour Stevens (Baltimore: Johns Hopkins University Press, 1991).

ALEUTIANS CAMPAIGN

1. Center of Military History, Department of the Army, *Aleutian Islands*, The Campaigns of World War II, no. 72–7 (Washington, DC: Center of Military History, 2003).

2. Charles River Editors, *The Aleutian Islands Campaign: The History of Japan's Invasion of Alaska During World War II* (Charles River Editors, 2016).

3. Claus-M. Naske, "The Battle of Alaska Has Ended and . . . the Japs Won It," *Military Affairs* 49, no. 3 (1985): 144–51.

4. Foster Hailey, "Cold, Fog, Mud—Life in the Aleutians," *New York Times*, August 22, 1943, SM4.

5. "General Gets $1 Hunting License," *Klamath News* (Klamath Falls, OR), September 19, 1941.

6. John Farley, "The Aleutian Islands Campaign: An Operational Art Perspective," Naval War College, Newport, RI, 1997.

7. Joseph Driscoll, *War Discovers Alaska* (Philadelphia: Lippincott, 1943).

8. Muktuk Marston, *Men of the Tundra: Alaska Eskimos at War* (New York: October House, 1969).

9. Samuel Eliot Morison, *Victory in the Pacific, 1945,* History of United States Naval Operations in World War II, vol. 14 (Boston: Little, Brown, 1960).

10. Stephen Dennis, "A War of Words: The U.S. Army vs. the Alaska Game Commission," *Fairbanks News-Miner,* January 18, 2009.

AFRICAN AMERICAN TROOPS, TREATMENT OF

1. Bill Gifford, "Great Black North," *Washington City Paper,* October 8, 1993.

2. John Virtue, *The Black Soldiers Who Built the Alaska Highway: A History of Four Army Regiments in the North, 1942–1943* (Jefferson, NC: McFarland, 2013).

THE PELELIU CAMPAIGN

1. Jack R. Ainsworth, *Among Heroes: A Marine Corps Rifle Company on Peleliu,* edited by Laurence Pope (Quantico, VA: Marine Corps University Press, 2012).

2. James H. Hallas, *The Devil's Anvil: The Assault on Peleliu* (Westport, CT: Praeger, 1994).

3. Peter Margaritis, *Landing in Hell: The Pyrrhic Victory of the First Marine Division on Peleliu, 1944* (Philadelphia: Casemate, 2018).

THE SAIPAN CAMPAIGN

1. 27th Infantry Division, *Report of Intelligence Activities 27th Infantry Division, Saipan Operation,* April 1–August 6, 1944.

2. Harold J. Goldberg, *D-Day in the Pacific: The Battle of Saipan,* Twentieth-Century Battles (Bloomington: Indiana University Press, 2007).

3. Harry A. Gailey, *Howlin' Mad vs. the Army: Conflict in Command, Saipan, 1944* (Novato, CA: Presidio, 1986).

4. Holland M. Smith and Percy Finch, *Coral and Brass* (New York: Charles Scribner's Sons, 1949).

5. James H. Hallas, *Saipan: The Battle That Doomed Japan in World War II* (Guilford, CT: Stackpole Books, 2019).

Chapter 26: April Fool

The names of marines from the 6th Marine Division killed in this and succeeding chapters were extrapolated from a database of all marine deaths from 1941 to 1945, compiled by Gordon Smith of the Naval-History.Net archive at the Library of Congress. The sources he used were USMC casualty cards, the American Battle Monuments Commission, the Defense POW/MIA Accounting Agency, and a listing of all casualties state by state. Julia Bell, a researcher for the book, entered the names of men from the 6th Division at Okinawa who died into a database. It was then possible to break the data down in a variety of ways, including date of death, regiment, battalion, and company. The author is aware that there may be some omissions. There may also be some discrepancies in the actual date of death because of when the bodies of the fallen were recovered.

In addition to the E. B. Sledge and George Feifer books, two personal accounts were extremely helpful in depicting the battle. For the perspective of the Battle of Okinawa from the Japanese viewpoint, Hiromichi Yahara's *The Battle for Okinawa: A Japanese Officer's Eyewitness Account of the Last Great Campaign of World War II* is written with both candor and poignance in depicting the fatal hopelessness of the Japanese soldier and officer. Philips D. Carleton's *The Conquest of Okinawa: An Account of the Sixth Marine Division* was written for the U.S. Marine Corps Historical Division and based on personal observances. Max Hastings's book *Retribution: The Battle for Japan, 1944–45* is excellent for an extended account of the final years of the Pacific war.

THE LANDING AT OKINAWA

1. Bevan G. Cass, ed., *History of the Sixth Marine Division* (Washington, DC: Infantry Journal Press, 1948), 45–47, 231.

2. Bill Sloan, *The Ultimate Battle: Okinawa 1945—the*

Last Epic Struggle of World War II (New York: Simon & Schuster, 2008), 16–17.

3. Frank Kukuchka (Co. I, 3rd Bn., 29th Marine Regiment), "My Days on Okinawa—1945," in *Okinawa 1945: Personal Recollections of the Battle of Okinawa by Marines of the Sixth Marine Division*, vol. 3, edited by Kenneth J. Long (Sixth Marine Division Association), 91, 104–7.

4. George Feifer, *The Battle of Okinawa: The Blood and the Bomb* (Guilford, CT: Lyons Press, 2001), 101, 105.

5. Gil Kanter, "Recollection of PFC Gil Kanter, USMC (K Co., 3rd Bn, 22nd Marines)," in *Okinawa 1945: Personal Recollections of the Battle of Okinawa by Marines of the Sixth Marine Division*, vol. 3, edited by Kenneth J. Long (Sixth Marine Division Association), 88.

6. James S. White, *On the Point of the Spear: Some Experiences of a Marine Rifleman During the Battle for the Island of Okinawa in April, May and June of 1945* (1995), 52–53.

7. John J. McLaughry, commentary insert no. 8, Mid March to April 1945, in "The World War II Letters of John J. McLaughry," 1990, courtesy of the estate of John J. McLaughry.

8. Joint War Plans Committee, *Plan for Seizure of the Ryukyus—6 November 1944*, 116/4 (Washington, DC: Joint War Plans Committee, 1944).

9. Joseph H. Alexander, *The Final Campaign: Marines in the Victory on Okinawa*, Marines in World War II Commemorative Series (Washington, DC: Marine Corps Historical Center, 1996).

10. Keil R. Gentry, "Land the Landing Force," *Marine Corps Gazette*, August 2019.

11. Mark Ealey, Tatsuro Higa, Alastair McLauchlan, and Masahide Ota, *Descent into Hell: Civilian Memories of the Battle of Okinawa* (Portland, ME: MerwinAsia, 2014).

12. Patrick O'Donnell, *Into the Rising Sun: World War II's Pacific Veterans Reveal the Heart of Combat* (New York: Free Press, 2010), 262.

13. Philips D. Carleton, *The Conquest of Okinawa: An Account of the Sixth Marine Division* (Washington, DC: U.S. Marine Corps, Historical Division, 1946), 26.

14. Robert Lee Sherrod, *History of Marine Corps Aviation in World War II* (Washington, DC: Combat Forces Press, 1948), 53–54.

15. Roy Edgar Appleman, James M. Burns, Russell A. Gugeler, and John Stevens, *Okinawa: The Last Battle* (Washington, DC: Historical Division, Department of the Army, 1948), 15, 89–91.

16. Simon Bolivar Buckner, Jr., and Joseph Warren Stilwell, *Seven Stars: The Okinawa Battle Diaries of Simon Bolivar Buckner, Jr., and Joseph Stilwell*, edited by Nicholas

Evan Sarantakes, Texas A&M Military History Series, vol. 93 (College Station: Texas A&M University Press, 2004), 29.

17. Sixth Marine Division, Marine Corps, *Special Action Report, Phases I and II, Okinawa Operation*, April 30, 1945.

18. "Typhoon of Steel: Fear of Capture Linked to Group Suicides in Battle of Okinawa (Pt. 7)," *Mainichi*, July 1, 2021.

19. Walter "Walt" G. Rutkowski, "The Battle of Okinawa . . . I Was There," in *Okinawa 1945: Personal Recollections of the Battle of Okinawa by Marines of the Sixth Marine Division*, vol. 3, edited by Kenneth J. Long (Sixth Marine Division Association, Inc.), 122.

BOMBARDMENT

1. Allan Reed Millett, *Semper Fidelis: The History of the United States Marine Corps* (Toronto: Free Press, 1991).

2. Simon Bolivar Buckner, Jr., and Joseph Warren Stilwell, *Seven Stars: The Okinawa Battle Diaries of Simon Bolivar Buckner, Jr., and Joseph Stilwell*, edited by Nicholas Evan Sarantakes, Texas A&M Military History Series, vol. 93 (College Station: Texas A&M University Press, 2004).

SUBSEQUENT TO LANDING

1. Hiromichi Yahara, *The Battle for Okinawa: A Japanese Officer's Eyewitness Account of the Last Great Campaign of World War II* (New York: Wiley, 1995).

2. Jon Diamond, *The Battle of Okinawa 1945: The Pacific War's Last Invasion*, Images of War (South Yorkshire, UK: Pen & Sword Military, 2019).

3. Richard Wheeler, *A Special Valor: The U.S. Marines and the Pacific War* (Annapolis, MD: Naval Institute Press, 2006), 413.

THE INVASION OF IE SHIMA

1. "Okinawa Campaign: Invasion of Ie Shima, April 16, 1945," National Museum of the U.S. Navy.

NAPALM AND FLAMETHROWERS

1. 713th Tank Battalion, After Action Report: 713th Tank Battalion. Armored Flame Thrower Provisional, November 10, 1944–June 30, 1945.

2. Chris McNab, *The Flamethrower* (Oxford, UK: Osprey Publishing, 2015).

3. David W. Van Wyck, "Beyond the Burn: Studies on the Physiological Effects of Flamethrowers During World War II," *Military Medical Research* 7, no. 8 (2020).

4. George Feifer, *The Battle of Okinawa: The Blood and the Bomb* (Guilford, CT: Lyons Press, 2001).

5. Louis F. Fieser, *The Scientific Method: A Personal Account of Unusual Projects in War and in Peace* (New York: Reinhold, 1964).

6. Louis F. Fieser et al., "Napalm," *Industrial & Engineering Chemistry* 38, no. 8 (1946): 768–73.

7. Marine Guillaume, "Napalm in US Bombing Doctrine and Practice, 1942–1975," *Asia-Pacific Journal* 14, no. 23 (2016): article 5.

8. Yasuo Kuwahara and Gordon T. Allred, *Kamikaze* (New York: Ballantine, 1957), 33–34.

BUCKNER, STRATEGY

1. Nicholas Evan Sarantakes, "Warriors of Word and Sword: The Battle of Okinawa, Media Coverage, and Truman's Reevaluation of Strategy in the Pacific," *Journal of American–East Asian Relations* 23, no. 4 (2016): 334–67.

2. Owen T. Stebbins, "A Maneuver That Might Have . . . ?," *Marine Corps Gazette* (June 1995): 69.

3. Paul E. Cunningham II, "Command and Control of the U.S. Tenth Army During the Battle of Okinawa," Master of Military Art and Science thesis, Military History, U.S. Army Command and General Staff College, 2009.

INTELLIGENCE FAILURES

1. Arnold G. Fisch, Jr., *Ryukyus*, U.S. Army Campaigns

of World War II (Washington, DC: Center for Military History, 1995), 24–25.

2. Colwell, Robert N. Colwell, "Intelligence and the Okinawa Battle," *Naval War College Review* 38, no. 2 (1985): article 9.

3. E. B. Sledge, *With the Old Breed at Peleliu and Okinawa* (New York: Presidio, 2010), 370.

4. Jeter Allen Isely and Philip A. Crowl, *The U.S. Marines and Amphibious War: Its Theory, and Its Practice in the Pacific* (Princeton, NJ: Princeton University Press, 1951), 552–53.

5. Roy Edgar Appleman, James M. Burns, Russell A. Gugeler, and John Stevens, "Tactics and Tactical Decisions," in *Okinawa: The Last Battle* (Washington, DC: Department of the Army, Historical Division, 1948), 249–64.

Chapter 27: Abandon Ship

The reconstruction in this chapter was based on extremely detailed action reports written for the USS *Bush* and USS *Colhoun*. The author gratefully acknowledges the use of the excellent website www.ussbush.com for its personal accounts. Robin L. Reilly's *Kamikaze Attacks of World War II: A Complete History of Japanese Suicide Strikes on American Ships, by Aircraft and Other Means* is a comprehensive account of the Japanese use of suicide planes.

WILLARD C. HOFER, DICK BAUMHARDT, AND ROBERT PETH-
ICK, SIXTH MARINE DIVISION

1. Bill Pierce (Weapons Co., 29th Marine Regiment),
"Discipline and Duty—Marine Corps Life," in *Okinawa 1945: Personal Recollections of the Battle of Okinawa by Marines of the Sixth Marine Division*, vol. 3,
edited by Kenneth J. Long (Sixth Marine Division Association), 61.

2. Robert G. Thobaben, *For Comrade and Country: Oral
Histories of World War II Veterans* (Jefferson, NC:
MacFarland, 2003).

3. Willard Clair Hofer, assorted military records.

SIMON BOLIVAR BUCKNER, JR., STRATEGY

1. Nicholas Evan Sarantakes, "Warriors of Word and
Sword: The Battle of Okinawa, Media Coverage, and
Truman's Reevaluation of Strategy in the Pacific," *Journal of American–East Asian Relations* 23, no. 4 (2016):
334–67.

2. Simon Bolivar Buckner, Jr., "Lt. Gen. Simon Boli-
var Buckner: Private Letters Relating to the Battle of
Okinawa," edited by A. P. Jenkins, *Ryudai Review of
Euro-American Studies* 42 (1997).

3. Simon Bolivar Buckner, Jr., and Joseph Warren Stilwell,
*Seven Stars: The Okinawa Battle Diaries of Simon Boli-
var Buckner, Jr., and Joseph Stilwell*, edited by Nicholas

Evan Sarantakes, Texas A&M Military History Series 93 (College Station: Texas A&M University Press, 2004).

KAMIKAZE

1. Albert Axell and Hideaki Kaze, *Kamikaze: Japan's Suicide Gods* (Harlow, UK: Pearson Education, 2002).

2. Emiko Ohnuki-Tierney, *Kamikaze, Cherry Blossoms, and Nationalisms: The Militarization of Aesthetics in Japanese History* (Chicago: University of Chicago Press, 2002).

3. Emiko Ohnuki-Tierney, *Kamikaze Diaries: Reflections of Japanese Student Soldiers* (Chicago: University of Chicago Press, 2006).

4. Mordecai G. Sheftall, *Blossoms in the Wind: The Human Legacy of the Kamikaze* (New York: NAL Caliber, 2005).

5. Peter C. Smith, *Kamikaze: To Die for the Emperor* (Barnsley, South Yorkshire, UK: Pen & Sword Aviation, 2014).

6. Robin L. Rielly, *Kamikaze Attacks of World War II: A Complete History of Japanese Suicide Strikes on American Ships, by Aircraft and Other Means* (Jefferson, NC: McFarland, 2010).

7. Ryūji Nagatsuka, *I Was a Kamikaze*, Eyewitness Accounts (Stroud, Gloucestershire, UK: Amberley, 2014).

8. Yasuo Kuwahara and Gordon T. Allred, *Kamikaze* (New York: Ballantine, 1957).

USS *BUSH*

1. USS *Bush*, Action Report—Okinawa Operation, March 15–April 6, 1945.

2. "USS *BUSH* (DD 529): Fourth Set of Memories, Rescue at Okinawa," http://www.ussbush.com/memory4.htm.

3. "USS *BUSH* (DD 529): Glossary of Terms."

4. "USS *BUSH* (DD 529): Third Set of Memories, Lost at Okinawa."

5. "USS *BUSH* (DD 529): 'Sailors Lost. '"

USS *COLHOUN*

1. USS *Colhoun* (DD801), Action Report, Invasion and Occupation of Okinawa, Nansei Shoto, April 1–April 6, 1945, and loss of the USS *Colhoun* (DD801), April 27, 1945.

Chapter 28: The Tortoise

NIMITZ VISIT

1. Benis M. Frank and Henry I. Shaw, Jr., *History of the U.S. Marine Corps Operations in World War II: Victory and Occupation*, vol. 5 (Washington, DC: U.S. Marine Corps, Historical Branch, 1968).

2. E. B. Potter, *Nimitz* (Annapolis, MD: Naval Institute Press, 2008).

3. Frank H. Haigler (22nd Marines), "Okinawa Diary," in *Okinawa 1945: Personal Recollections of the Battle of*

Okinawa by Marines of the Sixth Marine Division, vol. 3, edited by Kenneth J. Long (Sixth Marine Division Association), 185.

4. Neal McCallum, interviewed by the author.

5. Simon Bolivar Buckner, Jr., and Joseph Warren Stilwell, *Seven Stars: The Okinawa Battle Diaries of Simon Bolivar Buckner, Jr., and Joseph Stilwell*, edited by Nicholas Evan Sarantakes, Texas A&M Military History Series 93 (College Station: Texas A&M University Press, 2004).

MOTOBU PENINSULA/MOUNT YAETAKE

1. John J. McLaughry to Tuss and Florence McLaughry, assorted, April 1945, courtesy of the estate of John J. McLaughry.

2. Kenneth J. Long, "Edwin H. Denty," in *Okinawa 1945: Personal Recollections of the Battle of Okinawa by Marines of the Sixth Marine Division*, vol. 3, edited by Kenneth J. Long (Sixth Marine Division Association), 128–29.

3. Philips D. Carleton, *The Conquest of Okinawa: An Account of the Sixth Marine Division* (Washington, DC: Marine Corps Historical Division, 1946).

Chapter 29: The Little Girl

Haruko Taya Cook and Theodore Failor Cook's *Japan at War: An Oral History* is a terrifying depiction of what citizens of Japan and the neighboring countries suffered during the war. Raymond Gillespie's personal oral history is admirably candid and vivid.

BOB BAUMAN, BRONZE STAR

1. Bob Bauman to Emma Bauman, April 1945, Bauman Family Legacy.

JAPANESE DEFENSE

1. Roy Edgar Appleman, James M. Burns, Russell A. Gugeler, and John Stevens, *Okinawa: The Last Battle* (Washington, DC: Historical Division, Department of the Army, 1948).

CIVILIANS

1. David M. Brownstone, Irene M. Franck, and Douglass L. Brownstone, *Island of Hope, Island of Tears* (New York: Penguin, 1986).

2. Donald Smith, "Dark Caverns Entomb Bitter Memories, Bodies of Okinawan 'Lily Girls': Pacific Theater: Women Were Forced into Service as Nurses by the Japanese During World War II," *National Geographic*, June 4, 1995.

3. Fletcher Pratt, *The Marines' War: An Account of the Struggle for the Pacific from Both American and Japanese Sources* (New York: Sloane, 1948), 376, 369.

4. Fred Addison (Co. A, 1st Armored Amphib. Bn.), "Okinawa," in *Okinawa 1945: Personal Recollections of the
Battle of Okinawa by Marines of the Sixth Marine Division*, vol. 2, edited by Kenneth J. Long (Sixth Marine
Division Association), 100–101.

5. George Feifer, *The Battle of Okinawa: The Blood and the
Bomb* (Guilford, CT: Lyons Press, 2001), 188, 251, 371.

6. Gerald Astor, *Operation Iceberg: The Invasion and Conquest of Okinawa in World War II* (New York: Fine,
1995), 309.

7. Haruko Taya Cook and Theodore Failor Cook, *Japan
at War: An Oral History* (New York: New Press, 1992),
341–42.

8. Mark Ealey, Tatsuro Higa, and Alastair McLauchlan,
*Descent into Hell: Civilian Memories of the Battle of
Okinawa* (Portland, ME: MerwinAsia, 2014), 422.

9. Marvin Skeath, interviewed by the author.

10. Patrick O'Donnell, *Into the Rising Sun: World War
II's Pacific Veterans Reveal the Heart of Combat* (New
York: Free Press, 2010), 264.

11. PFC Charles W. Pugh (K Company, 22nd Marine Regiment), "One Marine's Story," in *Okinawa 1945: Personal Recollections of Okinawa by Marines of the Sixth
Marine Division*, vol. 3, edited by Kenneth J. Long
(Sixth Marine Division Association), 221–23.

12. Prabhu Silvam, "'Worse than Death': The Children

Who Survived the Battle for Okinawa," *South China Morning Post*, May 6, 2018.

13. Raymond P. Gillespie, "Sixth Marine Division," in *Okinawa 1945: Personal Recollections of the Battle of Okinawa by Marines of the Sixth Marine Division*, vol. 2, edited by Kenneth J. Long (Sixth Marine Division Association), 124–26, 128, 130–31, 134.

JAPANESE ATROCITIES

1. Arnaud Doglia, "Japanese Mass Violence and Its Victims in the Fifteen Years War (1931–45)," Mass Violence and Resistance—Research Network, SciencesPo, October 7, 2011.

2. "Bronx Marine Tells How Japanese Hanged Lieutenant in Form of Cross," *New York Times*, May 10, 1945.

3. Edward Drea et al., *Researching Japanese War Crimes Records* (Washington, DC: National Archives and Records Administration Nazi War Crimes and Japanese Imperial Government Records Interagency Working Group, 2006).

4. James J. Orr, *The Victim as Hero: Ideologies of Peace and National Identity in Postwar Japan* (Honolulu: University of Hawaii Press, 2001).

5. Nikola Budanovic, "'Just' 10 Japanese Atrocities from World War II," War History Online, January 24, 2018.

6. R. J. Rummel, "Statistics of Japanese Democide: Es-

timates, Calculations, and Sources," in *Statistics of Democide: Genocide and Mass Murder Since 1900* (Charlottesville: University of Virginia, Center for National Security Law, Transaction Publishers, and Rutgers University, 1997).

7. Timothy Lang Francis, "'To Dispose of the Prisoners': The Japanese Executions of American Aircrew at Fukuoka, Japan, During 1945," *Pacific Historical Review* 66, no. 4 (November 1997): 469–501.

8. United States Department of the Army, Historical Division, Military Intelligence Section, General Headquarters, Far East Command, *Statements of Japanese Officials on World War II* (English translations) (Washington, DC: Department of the Army, 1950).

9. United States Strategic Bombing Survey, Over-All Economic Effects Division, *The Effects of Strategic Bombing on Japan's War Economy* (Washington, DC: U.S. Government Printing Office, 1946).

HUMAN EXPERIMENTATION, BIOLOGICAL WARFARE

1. "1980s: Evidence of Atrocities Begins to Emerge from the Shadows," Alliance for Human Research Protection, December 10, 2011.

2. Gregory Dean Byrd, "General Ishii Shiro: His Legacy Is That of Genius and Madman," Master's thesis, East Tennessee State University, 2005.

3. Justin McCurry, "Japanese Veteran Admits Vivisection Tests on POWs," *Guardian*, November 27, 2006.

4. Michael Daly, "Japan Dissected My Granddad Alive in World War II," Daily Beast, May 22, 2020.

5. Nicholas D. Kristof, "Unmasking Horror—A Special Report; Japan Confronting Gruesome War Atrocity," *New York Times*, March 17, 1995.

6. Otozō Yamada, *Materials on the Trial of Former Servicemen of the Japanese Army Charged with Manufacturing and Employing Bacteriological Weapons* (Moscow: Foreign Languages Publishing House, 1950).

7. Richard James Havis, "Japanese Soldiers Finally Tell Their Story/Hell in the Pacific—From Vivisection to Cannibalism," SF Gate, March 17, 2002.

8. Sheldon H. Harris, "Japanese Biomedical Experimentation During the World-War-II Era," *Military Medical Ethics* 2 (2003): 463–81.

9. Toshiyuki Tanaka, *Hidden Horrors: Japanese War Crimes in World War II* (Boulder, CO: Westview Press, 1996).

NAVY WAR CRIMES TRIALS, JAG CASE FILES

1. Department of the Navy, Memorandum in the Military Commission Case of Kobayashi, Masashi, Former Vice Admiral, Imperial Japanese Navy, 1948.

2. Headquarters Army Garrison Force, *Investigation of Atrocities*, August 1, 1944.

3. Judge Advocate General, United States Navy, *Case Files of Pacific Area War Crimes Trials, 1945–1949: Yoshio Tachibana et al., c. 1946* (Washington, DC: Office of the Navy Judge Advocate General, 1946).

4. Judge Advocate General, United States Navy, *File of Proceedings in the Case of Chuichi Hara, 1948* (Washington, DC: Office of the Navy Judge Advocate General, 1948).

5. Judge Advocate General, United States Navy, *Memorandum in the Military Commission Trial of Seisaku Wakabayashi, Former Vice Admiral, IJN* (Washington, DC: Office of the Navy Judge Advocate General, 1946).

6. Judge Advocate General, United States Navy, *Military Commission Case of Captain Masaharu Tanaka, I.J.N., Tried in Joinder with Lieutenant Commander Tomeroku Danzaki, I.J.N., and Lieutenant, Junior Grade, Yoshiharu Yoshinuma, I.J.N. on 5 November 1946* (Washington, DC: Office of the Navy Judge Advocate General, 1947).

7. Judge Advocate General, United States Navy, *Record of Proceedings of Military Commission at Guam in the Case of Kasuro Nakamura et al.* (Washington, DC: Office of the Navy Judge Advocate General, 1948).

8. Judge Advocate General, War Crimes Office, *Atrocities on Island of Saipan* (Washington, DC: War Department, 1944).

9. Judge Advocate General, War Crimes Office, *Brutal Treatment of POWs by Japanese: Ryoji, Durand, Marquis* (Washington, DC: War Department, 1946).

10. Judge Advocate General, War Crimes Office, *Interview: Pfc. Edward A. Johnston* (Washington, DC: War Department, 1945).

11. Judge Advocate General, War Crimes Office, *Killing of Unknown U.S. Marine Lieutenant on Saipan* (Washington, DC: War Department, 1945).

12. Judge Advocate General, War Crimes Office, *Military Commission Case of Captain Masaharu Tanaka, I.J.N., Tried in Joinder with Lieutenant Commander Tomeroku Danzaki, I.J.N., and Lieutenant, Junior Grade, Yoshiharu Yoshinuma, I.J.N.* (Washington, DC: War Department, 1946).

13. Judge Advocate General, War Crimes Office, *Record of Proceedings of Military Commission Convened at United States Pacific Fleet, Commander Marianas, Guam, Marianas Islands: Case of Shimpei Asano et al.* (Washington, DC: War Department, 1948).

14. Judge Advocate General, War Crimes Office, *Report from Captured Personnel and Material Branch, Military Intelligence Division, War Department* (Washington, DC: Office of the Army Judge Advocate General, 1945).

15. Sgt. Stanley Fink, *Probate: Juan Perrez* (Washington, DC: Office of the Army Judge Advocate General, 1945).

16. United States Pacific Command and United States Pacific Fleet, *Review of the Record of Trial by a Military Commission of Former Surgeon Second Lieutenant Teraki, Tadashi, IJA* (Washington, DC: Office of the Navy Judge Advocate General, 1947).

INTERNATIONAL MILITARY TRIBUNAL FOR THE FAR EAST

1. David Nelson Sutton, *Crimes Against Humanity Committed by Japanese Troops in China, 1937–1945: Brief of Atrocities, Class C Offenses*, International Military Tribunal for the Far East Digital Collection, University of Virginia Law Library.

2. Neil Boister and Robert Cryer, eds., *Documents on the Tokyo International Military Tribunal: Charter, Indictment and Judgment* (Oxford, UK: Oxford University Press, 2008).

3. "The Pacific War" and "Conventional War Crimes (Atrocities)," in International Military Tribunal for the Far East, *Judgment of the International Military Tribunal for the Far East*, November 1948, 843–1135, International Military Tribunal for the Far East Digital Collection, University of Virginia Law Library.

Chapter 30: Return to Sender

1. Tony Butkovich to Ana and Blaž Butkovich, February 10, 1945.
2. Tom Milligan to Tony Butkovich, April 6, 1945.

Chapter 31: A Thousand Ants

The author is greatly appreciative of Robert McGowan II for sharing his father's story in meticulous detail over the course of several extended interviews and supplying letters written by him.

27TH ARMY INFANTRY DIVISION

1. "27th Division Converts; State Guard Unit Shifts Today to Armored Status," *New York Times*, February 1, 1955, 23.
2. "27th Infantry Division, World War Two," New York State Military Museum and Veterans Research Center.
3. "27th Gets Ready for Battle Games," *New York Times*, May 11, 1941, 37.
4. Arnold G. Fisch, Jr., *Ryukyus*, The U.S. Army Campaigns of World War II (Washington, DC: Center for Military History, 1995), 31.
5. Charles S. Kaune, "The National Guard in War: An Historical Analysis of the 27th Infantry Division (New York National Guard) in World War II," Master's thesis,

U.S. Army Command and General Staff College, Fort Leavenworth, KS, 1990.

6. "Civil War: Remembering the 7th Regiment," New York Almanack, May 5, 2011.

7. Clifton La Bree, *The Gentle Warrior: General Oliver Prince Smith, USMC* (Kent, OH: Kent State University Press, 2001).

8. David Lippman, "Saipan 1944: Smith vs. Smith, Part Three," Avalanche Press, April 2016.

9. Edmund Love, *The 27th Infantry Division in World War II* (Washington, DC: Infantry Journal Press, 1949).

10. George Feifer, *The Battle of Okinawa: The Blood and the Bomb* (Guilford, CT: Lyons Press, 2001), 186–89.

11. Gerald Astor, *Operation Iceberg: The Invasion and Conquest of Okinawa in World War II* (New York: Fine, 1995), 288–89, 297, 300, 312, 320.

12. Holland M. Smith and Percy Finch, *Coral and Brass* (New York: Charles Scribner's Sons, 1949), 118–19, 126, 174–75.

13. James Whitaker, interviewed by the author.

14. Jeter Allen Isely and Philip A. Crowl, *The U.S. Marines and Amphibious War: Its Theory, and Its Practice in the Pacific* (Princeton, NJ: Princeton University Press, 1951), 202, 552–53.

15. Laura Homan Lacey, *Stay Off the Skyline: The Sixth*

Marine Division on Okinawa: An Oral History (Washington, DC: Potomac Books, 2005), 165.

16. Neal McCallum, interviewed by the author.
17. Norman V. Cooper, *A Fighting General: The Biography of Gen. Holland M. "Howlin' Mad" Smith* (Quantico, VA: Marine Corps Association, 1987).
18. Richard Wheeler, *A Special Valor: The U.S. Marines and the Pacific War* (Annapolis, MD: Naval Institute Press, 2006), 424–26.

ROBERT W. MCGOWAN

1. Robert McGowan II, interviewed by the author.
2. Robert W. McGowan to his father, G. R. McGowan, June 3, 1945.
3. Robert W. McGowan to his mother, Margaret McGowan, January 22, 1945.
4. Robert W. McGowan to his mother, Margaret McGowan, June 18, 1945.

SUGAR LOAF HILL, EARLY STAGES

1. James S. White (29th Mar-3-G), "On the Point of the Spear," in *Okinawa 1945: Personal Recollections of the Battle of Okinawa by Marines of the Sixth Marine Division*, vol. 2, edited by Kenneth J. Long (Sixth Marine Division Association), 198.
2. Roy Edgar Appleman, James M. Burns, Russell A.

Gugeler, and John Stevens, *Okinawa: The Last Battle* (Washington, DC: Historical Division, Department of the Army, 1948), 318.

Chapter 32: At All Costs

James Hallas's *Killing Ground on Okinawa: The Battle for Sugar Loaf Hill* was an essential resource. Laura Homan Lacey's *Stay Off the Skyline: The Sixth Marine Division on Okinawa: An Oral History* was also quite helpful.

GEORGE MURPHY AND HIS FAMILY

The author is indebted to the Steele Family for allowing access to letters and other material relating to George Murphy.

1. David Alonzo Mears, interviewed by the author.
2. George Murphy to Mary Murphy, March 29, 1945, courtesy of the Steele Family.

SUGAR LOAF, GENERAL

1. 1st Lt. Roger W. Jamieson (F Co., 2nd Bn., 22nd Marine Reg.), "Okinawa–1945," in *Okinawa 1945: Personal Recollections of the Battle of Okinawa by Marines of the Sixth Marine Division*, vol. 3, edited by Kenneth J. Long (Sixth Marine Division Association), 24–25.
2. Capt. Phillip "Phil" Morell (Cmdr. A Co., 6th Tank Bn., 6th Marine Div.), "Sugar Loaf Hill, Okinawa—1945,"

in *Okinawa 1945: Personal Recollections of Okinawa by Marines of the Sixth Marine Division*, vol. 3, edited by Kenneth J. Long (Sixth Marine Division Association), 241, 250.

3. Cmdr. Donald B. Long, "Diary of Ben Love (Australian Trooper)," in *Okinawa 1945: Personal Recollections of the Battle of Okinawa by Marines of the Sixth Marine Division*, vol. 3, edited by Kenneth J. Long (Sixth Marine Division Association), 201–3, 208–10.

4. George Thompson, *82 Days of Hell and Glory: The Okinawa Campaign with the Sixth Marine Division* (Washington, DC: War Department, 1945), 10–14.

5. James H. Hallas, *Killing Ground on Okinawa: The Battle for Sugar Loaf Hill* (Annapolis, MD: Naval Institute Press, 2007).

6. PFC Charles W. Pugh (K Co., 22nd Marine Regiment), "One Marine's Story," in *Okinawa 1945: Personal Recollections of Okinawa by Marines of the Sixth Marine Division*, vol. 3, edited by Kenneth J. Long (Sixth Marine Division Association), 226–30, 235.

7. Major Bernard W. Green, "History of the First Battalion—Fourth Marine Regiment," in *Okinawa 1945: Personal Recollections of the Battle of Okinawa by Marines of the Sixth Marine Division*, vol. 3, edited by Kenneth J. Long (Sixth Marine Division Association), 198.

8. Neal McCallum, interviewed by the author.

9. Pedro A. Del Valle, *Semper Fidelis: An Autobiography* (Hawthorne, CA: Christian Book Club of America, 1976), 281, 331, 339, 364.

10. PFC LeRoy K. Hammond (Co. K, 3rd Bn., 4th Marine Regiment), in *Okinawa 1945: Personal Recollections of the Battle of Okinawa by Marines of the Sixth Marine Division*, vol. 3, edited by Kenneth J. Long (Sixth Marine Division Association), 261–62.

11. Philips D. Carleton, *The Conquest of Okinawa: An Account of the Sixth Marine Division* (Washington, DC: Marine Corps Historical Division, 1946), 26.

12. Private Wendell K. Majors, "Account of Private Wendell K. Majors, G-2-22," in *Okinawa 1945: Personal Recollections of the Battle of Okinawa by Marines of the Sixth Marine Division*, vol. 3, edited by Kenneth J. Long (Sixth Marine Division Association), 117, 241.

13. Sixth Marine Division, Marine Corps, Second Battalion, Fourth Marine Regiment, *Special Action Report—Okinawa Operation Phase III, June 23, 1945.*

14. Sixth Marine Division, Marine Corps, Third Battalion, Fourth Marine Regiment, *Special Action Report—Okinawa Operation Phase III, June 29, 1945.*

THE JAPANESE AT SUGAR LOAF

1. George Thompson, "Japs Are Driven Out of Stiffest Defenses," *Gazette* (Cedar Rapids, IA), August 9, 1945.

2. Joseph H. Alexander, *The Final Campaign: Marines in the Victory on Okinawa,* Marines in World War II Commemorative Series (Washington, DC: Marine Corps Historical Center, 1996), 49–53.

3. Hiromichi Yahara, *The Battle for Okinawa: A Japanese Officer's Eyewitness Account of the Last Great Campaign of World War II* (New York: John Wiley & Sons, 1995).

4. Patrick O'Donnell, *Into the Rising Sun: World War II's Pacific Veterans Reveal the Heart of Combat* (New York: Free Press, 2010), 260–61.

THE SHURI LINE

1. Fletcher Pratt, *The Marines' War, an Account of the Struggle for the Pacific from Both American and Japanese Sources* (New York: W. Sloane Associates, 1948), 372–73.

2. Frank J. Kukuchka (Co. I, 3rd Bn., 29th Marine Regiment), in *Okinawa 1945: Personal Recollections of the Battle of Okinawa by Marines of the Sixth Marine Division,* vol. 3, edited by Kenneth J. Long (Sixth Marine Division Association), 117.

3. Laura Homan Lacey, *Stay Off the Skyline: The Sixth Marine Division on Okinawa: An Oral History* (Washington, DC: Potomac Books, 2005), 118–20.

4. Raymond P. Gillespie, "Sixth Marine Division," in *Okinawa 1945: Personal Recollections of the Battle of Okinawa by Marines of the Sixth Marine Division*, vol. 2, edited by Kenneth J. Long (Sixth Marine Division Association), 141.

5. Roy Edgar Appleman, James M. Burns, Russell A. Gugeler, and John Stevens, "Chapter X: Tactics and Tactical Decisions," in *Okinawa: The Last Battle* (Washington, DC: Department of the Army, Historical Division, 1948), 249–64.

6. Thomas M. Huber, *Japan's Battle of Okinawa, April–June 1945*, Leavenworth Papers, vol. 18 (Washington, DC: U.S. Government Printing Office, 1990).

7. "Major Henry Alexius Courtney Junior, 'Hero of Sugar Loaf Hill,'" compiled by Royleen Newman, Greysolon Daughters of Liberty Chapter NSDAR, Minnesota Medal of Honor Memorial.

8. Declan F. Klingenhagen (Co. D, 2nd Bn., 29th Marine Regiment), "My Campaign on Okinawa (A Darker Side)," in *Okinawa 1945: Personal Recollections of the Battle of Okinawa by Marines of the Sixth Marine Division*, vol. 3, edited by Kenneth J. Long (Sixth Marine Division Association), 12–15.

9. First Lt. Roger W. Jamieson (Co. F, 2nd Bn., 22nd Marines), in *Okinawa 1945: Personal Recollections of the*

Battle of Okinawa by Marines of the Sixth Marine Division, vol. 3, edited by Kenneth J. Long (Sixth Marine Division Association), 22–26.

10. James H. Hallas, *Killing Ground on Okinawa: The Battle for Sugar Loaf Hill* (Annapolis, MD: Naval Institute Press, 2007).

11. "Japs Fear Leatherneck-Led Landing," *Marine Corps Chevron*, June 30, 1945.

Chapter 33: Crazy for Revenge

CASUALTIES, MAY 15, 1945

1. Neal McCallum, interviewed by the author.

CHARLES BEHAN

1. James Whitaker, interviewed by the author.
2. Neal McCallum, interviewed by the author.
3. William Hulek, personal account.

CASUALTIES, MAY 16, 1945

1. Arnold G. Fisch, Jr., *Ryukyus*, U.S. Army Campaigns of World War II (Washington, DC: Center for Military History, 1995), 22–23.
2. Compilation by the author.
3. Richard Wheeler, *A Special Valor: The U.S. Marines*

and the Pacific War (Annapolis, MD: Naval Institute Press, 2006), 429–33.

Chapter 34: Carry On

SECURING SUGAR LOAF HILL

1. Declan F. Klingenhagen (Co. D, 2nd Bn., 29th Marine Regiment), "My Campaign on Okinawa (A Darker Side)," in *Okinawa 1945: Personal Recollections of the Battle of Okinawa by Marines of the Sixth Marine Division*, vol. 3, edited by Kenneth J. Long (Sixth Marine Division Association), 11–16.

2. First Lt. Roger W. Jamieson (Co. F, 2nd Bn., 22nd Marines), in *Okinawa 1945: Personal Recollections of the Battle of Okinawa by Marines of the Sixth Marine Division*, vol. 3, edited by Kenneth J. Long (Sixth Marine Division Association), 26.

3. Hiromichi Yahara, *The Battle for Okinawa: A Japanese Officer's Eyewitness Account of the Last Great Campaign of World War II* (New York: John Wiley & Sons, 1995).

4. James H. Hallas, *Killing Ground on Okinawa: The Battle for Sugar Loaf Hill* (Annapolis, MD: Naval Institute Press, 2007).

5. Patrick O'Donnell, *Into the Rising Sun: World War*

II's Pacific Veterans Reveal the Heart of Combat (New York: Free Press, 2010), 261.

6. Philips D. Carleton, *The Conquest of Okinawa: An Account of the Sixth Marine Division* (Washington, DC: Marine Corps Historical Division, 1946), 26.

HORSESHOE

1. Benis M. Frank and Henry I. Shaw, Jr., *History of the U.S. Marine Corps Operations in World War II: Victory and Occupation,* vol. 5 (Washington, DC: U.S. Marine Corps, Historical Branch, 1968), 253.

2. Bevan G. Cass, ed., *History of the Sixth Marine Division* (Washington, DC: Infantry Journal Press, 1948), 129–30.

3. Neal McCallum, private correspondence with author, February 2022.

4. Sixth Marine Division, Marine Corps, Special Action Report—Okinawa Operation Phase III, June 30, 1945, 838.

CASUALTIES, MAY 18, 1945

1. Compilation by the author.

CASUALTIES, MAY 19, 1945

1. Compilation by the author.

CASUALTIES, MAY 20, 1945

1. Compilation by the author.

CASUALTIES, MAY 21, 1945

1. Compilation by the author.

Chapter 35: Last Stand

OKINAWA, JAPANESE WITHDRAWAL

1. Hiromichi Yahara, *The Battle for Okinawa: A Japanese Officer's Eyewitness Account of the Last Great Campaign of World War II* (New York: John Wiley & Sons, 1995), 71–73.
2. John J. McLaughry to Tuss and Florence McLaughry, assorted, May and June 1945, courtesy of the estate of John J. McLaughry.

SIMON BOLIVAR BUCKNER, JR., STUBBORNNESS OF

1. Simon Bolivar Buckner, Jr., and Joseph Warren Stilwell, *Seven Stars: The Okinawa Battle Diaries of Simon Bolivar Buckner, Jr., and Joseph Stilwell*, edited by Nicholas Evan Sarantakes, Texas A&M Military History Series 93 (College Station: Texas A&M University Press, 2004), 64, 74–75.

Chapter 36: Regret to Inform

OROKU PENINSULA

1. David Schreiner to Herbert and Anna Schreiner, as-

sorted, April through June 1945, David N. Schreiner Letters, 1938–1947, M92–233, Box 1, 3/33/I5, Wisconsin Historical Society.

2. Fourth Marine Regiment, Marine Corps, *Annex A to Sixth Marine Division Special Action Report: Phase III—Okinawa Operation, June 30, 1945.*

3. Neal McCallum, interviewed by the author.

4. Sixth Marine Division, Marine Corps, *G-2 Periodic Report,* no. 67, June 7, 1945.

5. "Volleyball Game, Not Jap Bullets, 'Bench' Schreiner," *Wisconsin State Journal* (Madison, WI), June 11, 1945.

MARK HADLEY HOSKINS

1. "Charles Hoskins Killed in Action," *Wisconsin State Journal* (Madison, WI), February 23, 1945.

2. "Hoskins, Badger Grid Captain Is Liberated," *Waukesha Daily Freeman* (Waukesha, WI), June 15, 1945.

3. "Lieut. Hoskins Back in U.S.," *Wisconsin State Journal* (Madison, WI), June 14, 1945.

4. "Lt. Mark Hoskins Reported Missing in Action over Hungary; Co-Pilot," *Kenosha News* (Kenosha, WI), July 12, 1944.

5. "Mark Hoskins Freed from German Camp," *Leader-Telegram* (Eau Claire, WI), May 22, 1945.

BOB BAUMAN

1. Bob Bauman to Frank Bauman, June 2, 1945, Bauman Family Legacy.
2. Bertha Bauman to Anna Schreiner, June 14, 1945, Bauman Family Legacy.

Chapter 37: Why?

JOHN PERRY

1. "Football Forecast: Southern Conference," *Shreveport Journal* (Shreveport, LA), September 17, 1942.
2. John D. Wood, "Now Hear This," *Gastonia Gazette* (Gastonia, NC), September 19, 1947.
3. "Johnny Perry and Red Cochran Set Pace; Duke Is Outclassed," *Asheville Citizen-Times* (Asheville, NC), October 4, 1942.
4. "Mary Haskell Wed in New York to Lieut. R. B. Fowler," *Hartford Daily Courant* (Hartford, CT), June 4, 1942.
5. "Perry Is Star," *Tampa Times*, October 5, 1943.
6. "Perry Leaves Deacs to Join Air Corps," *Charlotte News* (Charlotte, NC), January 26, 1942.

ROBERT FOWLER

1. "Mary Haskell Wed in New York to Lieut. R. B. Fowler," *Hartford Daily Courant* (Hartford, CT), June 4, 1942.
2. Matthew Mills Stevenson, "War's End on Okinawa: In

Notes On Sources

Search of Captain Robert Fowler," *Journal of Military History* 67, no. 2 (April 2003): 517–28.

3. Neal McCallum, private correspondence with author, August 28, 2021.
4. *The Perigon* (Loomis Chaffee High School yearbook), 1937.
5. Robert Beals Fowler and Mary Haskell, marriage license, May 30, 1942.
6. "Robert Fowler Wins Marine Commission," *Hartford Daily Courant* (Hartford, CT), February 4, 1942.
7. Robert Haupt, Notarized Record of Legal Name Change of Robert Haupt to Robert Fowler.
8. Robert Sherer, "Fox Company, 2–29: The Battle of Okinawa," letter, undated.
9. "Society and Clubs—Captain and Mrs. Robert B. Fowler," *Hartford Daily Courant* (Hartford, CT), April 8, 1944.

Chapter 38: Three Stars

OKINAWA, END OF CAMPAIGN

1. Odette Hendrickson to Herbert and Anna Schreiner, June 20, 1945, David N. Schreiner Letters, 1938–1947, M92–233, Box 1, 3/33/I5, Wisconsin Historical Society.

MITSURU USHIJIMA

1. George Feifer, *The Battle of Okinawa: The Blood and the Bomb* (Guilford, CT: Lyons Press, 2001).

2. Hiromichi Yahara, *The Battle for Okinawa: A Japanese Officer's Eyewitness Account of the Last Great Campaign of World War II* (New York: John Wiley & Sons, 1995).

SIMON BOLIVAR BUCKNER, JR., LETTERS, DIARIES

1. Simon Bolivar Buckner, Jr., "Lt. Gen. Simon Bolivar Buckner: Private Letters Relating to the Battle of Okinawa," edited by A. P. Jenkins, *Ryudai Review of Euro-American Studies* 42 (1997): 63–113.
2. Simon Bolivar Buckner, Jr., and Joseph Warren Stilwell, *Seven Stars: The Okinawa Battle Diaries of Simon Bolivar Buckner, Jr., and Joseph Stilwell*, edited by Nicholas Evan Sarantakes (College Station: Texas A&M University Press, 2004).

BUCKNER STRATEGY, MEDIA CRITICISM OF

1. Homer Bigart, "Okinawa Tactics No 'Fiasco,' Says Homer Bigart; He Thinks Marines Could Have Been Better Used," *St. Louis Post-Dispatch*, June 18, 1945, 1, 13.
2. Joseph H. Alexander, Don Horan, and Norman Stahl, *A Fellowship of Valor: The Battle History of the United States Marines* (New York: HarperCollins, 1997), 237.
3. Nicholas Evan Sarantakes, "Warriors of Word and Sword: The Battle of Okinawa, Media Coverage, and Truman's Reevaluation of Strategy in the Pacific," *Jour-*

nal of American–East Asian Relations* 23, no. 4 (2016): 334–67.

NIMITZ, DEFENSE OF BUCKNER

1. "Backs Tactics of Buckner in Campaign," *Chicago Tribune*, June 17, 1945, 1.
2. "Nimitz Answers Critic of Okinawa Campaign," *Los Angeles Times*, June 17, 1945, 1.
3. "Nimitz Defends Okinawa Campaign," *New York Times*, June 17, 1945.

Chapter 39: Counting the Days

FINAL DAYS OF CAMPAIGN

1. John J. McLaughry, personal commentary, courtesy of the estate of John J. McLaughry.

Chapter 40: Cessation of Hostilities

OKINAWA DECLARED SECURE

1. Anna Schreiner to Bertha Bauman, assorted, June 22 through September 1945, Bauman Family Legacy.
2. Anna Schreiner, "Schreiner Spasmodic Sheet, vol. 42: Birthday Edition! Saluting Lt. David N. Schreiner, United States Marine Corps," March 5, 1945, David

N. Schreiner Letters, 1938–1947, M92–233, Box 1, 3/33/I5, Wisconsin Historical Society.

3. David Schreiner to Herbert and Anna Schreiner, June 18, 1945, Wisconsin Historical Society

4. Bertha Bauman to Anna Schreiner, July 3, 1945, Wisconsin Historical Society.

5. David Schreiner to Odette Hendrickson, assorted, February through March 1945, courtesy of the family of Odette Hendrickson Davis.

6. Emma Bauman to Anna Schreiner, June 20, 1945, Wisconsin Historical Society.

7. Hiromichi Yahara, *The Battle for Okinawa: A Japanese Officer's Eyewitness Account of the Last Great Campaign of World War II* (New York: John Wiley & Sons, 1995).

8. Odette Hendrickson to Herbert and Anna Schreiner, June 20, 1945, Wisconsin Historical Society.

9. Terry Frei, "Dave Schreiner, Badger and Marine," adapted from *Third Down and a War to Go* (Madison, WI: Wisconsin Historical Society Press, 2007).

10. Terry Frei, *Third Down and a War to Go* (Madison: Wisconsin Historical Society Press, 2007).

Chapter 41: Silence

1. John J. McLaughry, personal commentary, courtesy of the estate of John J. McLaughry.

Bibliography

XXIV Corps. *G-3 Reports*, nos. 1–50. N-9099. 1945.

25th Naval Construction Battalion. *War Diary.* 1945.

Abbott, Grace. *Bulletin of the Immigrants Commission No. 2: The Immigrant and Coal Mining Communities of Illinois.* Springfield: State of Illinois Department of Registration and Education, 1920.

"Abstracts of Reports of the Immigration Commission with Conclusions and Recommendations and Views of the Minority, Vol. 1." In US Senate, *Reports of the Immigration Commission*, 61st Cong., 3rd sess., December 5, 1910. Doc. 747.

Alexander, Joseph H. *Across the Reef: The Marine Assault on Tarawa.* Marines in World War II Commemorative Series. Washington, DC: U.S. Marine Corps, 1993.

——. *The Final Campaign: Marines in the Victory on Okinawa.* Marines in World War II Commemorative Series. Washington, DC: Marine Corps Historical Center, 1996.

——. "Hellish Prelude at Okinawa." *Naval History Magazine,* April 2005.

——. *Storm Landings: Epic Amphibious Battles in the Central Pacific.* Annapolis, MD: Naval Institute Press, 1997.

——. *Utmost Savagery: The Three Days of Tarawa.* Annapolis, MD: Naval Institute Press, 1995.

Alexander, Joseph H., Don Horan, and Norman Stahl. *A Fellowship of Valor: The Battle History of the United States Marines.* New York: HarperCollins, 1997.

Alinsky, Saul. *John L. Lewis: An Unauthorized Biography.* Papamoa Press, 2017.

Allied Translator and Interpreter Section, South West Pacific Area. *The Exploitation of Japanese Documents.* Allied Translator and Interpreter Section, South West Pacific Area, 1944.

Allis, Frederick S., Jr. *Youth from Every Quarter.* Andover, MA: Phillips Academy, 1979. http://www.pa59ers.com/library/Allis/youth18b.html.

Altman, Lawrence K. *Who Goes First?: The Story of Self-Experimentation in Medicine.* Berkeley: University of California Press, 1998.

Alvarez, Eugene. *Parris Island: Once a Recruit, Always a Marine.* Charleston, SC: History Press, 2007.

Ambrose, Stephen E. *Nothing Like It in the World: The Men Who Built the Transcontinental Railroad, 1863–1869.* New York: Simon & Schuster, 2000.

Anderson, Irvine H., Jr. "The 1941 de Facto Embargo on Oil to Japan: A Bureaucratic Reflex." *Pacific Historical Review* 44, no. 2 (May 1975): 201–31. https://www.jstor.org/stable/3638003.

Angle, Paul M. *Bloody Williamson: A Chapter in American Lawlessness.* Champaign-Urbana: University of Illinois Press, 1992.

Antill, P. "Operation Iceberg: The Assault on Okinawa—the Last Battle of World War II (Part 1) April–June 1945." History of War, 2003. http://www.historyofwar.org/articles/battles_okinawa1.html.

———. "Operation Iceberg: The Assault on Okinawa—the Last Battle of World War II (Part 2) April–June 1945." History of War, 2003. http://www.historyofwar.org/articles/battles_okinawa2.html.

Appleman, Roy Edgar, James M. Burns, Russell A. Gugeler, and John Stevens. *Okinawa: The Last Battle.* Washington, DC: Historical Division, Department of the Army, 1948.

Army Bureau of Current Affairs. *Japs: British Views on Japan During the Second World War.* Northern Ireland: Books Ulster, 2012.

Army Dissemination Division, G-2 Section. *Artillery Bulletin Number 1: U.S. Army Forces in Middle Pacific.* N-11318. Washington, DC: Army Dissemination Division, 1945.

Army War College. *Report on the Okinawa Operation.* N-11293. Washington, DC: Army War College, 1945.

Astor, Gerald. *Operation Iceberg: The Invasion and Conquest of Okinawa in World War II.* New York: D. I. Fine, 1995.

Atu, William T. "Fishing for Drummerfish (Kyphosidae) with Termites and Spider Webs on the Weather Coast of Guadalcanal, Solomon Islands." *SPC Traditional Marine Resource Management and Knowledge Information Bulletin* 18 (2005): 3–8.

Axell, Albert, and Hideaki Kaze. *Kamikaze: Japan's Suicide Gods.* Harlow, UK: Pearson Education, 2002.

Bailey, Gilbert P. *Boot: A Marine in the Making.* Columbia, SC: Bostick & Thornley, 1943.

Barnhart, Michael A. *Japan Prepares for Total War: The Search for Economic Security, 1919–1941.* Cornell Studies in Security Affairs. Ithaca, NY: Cornell University Press, 1987.

Barrows, R. M. *The Kit Book for Soldiers, Sailors and Marines.* Chicago: Consolidated Book Publishers, 1942.

Bartlett, Merrill L. *Assault from the Sea: Essays on the History of Amphibious Warfare.* Annapolis, MD: Naval Institute Press, 1983.

Bate, Roger. "The Rise, Fall, Rise, and Imminent Fall of DDT." *Health Policy Outlook* 14 (November 2007). https://www.aei.org/wp-content/uploads/2011/10/2007110 2_22368HPO14Bate_g.pdf?x91208.

Bayor, Ronald H. *Encountering Ellis Island: How European Immigrants Entered America.* Baltimore: Johns Hopkins University Press, 2014.

Belden, Jack. *Still Time to Die.* New York: Harper & Brothers, 1944.

Benedict, Ruth. *The Chrysanthemum and the Sword: Patterns of Japanese Culture.* Cleveland: Meridian Books, 1967.

Bennett, Judith A. *Natives and Exotics: World War II and Environment in the Southern Pacific.* Honolulu: University of Hawaii Press, 2009.

Benton-Cohen, Katherine. *Inventing the Immigration Problem: The Dillingham Commission and Its Legacy.* Cambridge, MA: Harvard University Press, 2018.

Bérubé, Allan. *Coming Out Under Fire: The History of Gay Men and Women in World War II.* Twentieth anniversary ed. Chapel Hill: University of North Carolina Press, 2010.

The Best from Yank, the Army Weekly. New York: E. P. Dutton, 1945.

Bigger, Margaret G., ed. *World War II—Hometown and Home Front Heroes: Life-Experience Stories from the Carolinas' Piedmont.* Charlotte, NC: A. Borough Books, 2004.

Birn, Anne-Emanuelle. "Six Seconds per Eyelid: The Medical Inspection of Immigrants at Ellis Island, 1892–1914." *Dynamis* 17 (1997): 281–316.

Bix, Herbert P. *Hirohito and the Making of Modern Japan.* New York: Harper Perennial, 2016.

Black, Jeremy. *The Second World War.* Burlington, VT: Ashgate, 2007.

The Black Diamond. Chicago: National Coal Exchange, 1885.

Blackmon, Douglas A. *Slavery by Another Name: The Re-enslavement of Black People in America from the Civil War to World War II.* New York: Doubleday, 2008.

Blantz, Thomas E. *The University of Notre Dame: A History.* Notre Dame, IN: University of Notre Dame Press, 2020.

Blantz, Thomas E., and George N. Shuster. *George N. Shuster: On the Side of Truth.* Notre Dame, IN: University of Notre Dame Press, 1993.

Blum, Albert A. "The Army and Student Deferments During the Second World War." *Journal of Higher Education* 31, no. 1 (January 1960): 41–45.

Blume, Lesley M. M. *Fallout.* New York: Simon & Schuster, 2020.

Bodnar, John E. *The Transplanted: A History of Immigrants in Urban America.* Interdisciplinary Studies in History. Bloomington: Indiana University Press, 1985.

Boister, Neil, and Robert Cryer, eds. *Documents on the Tokyo International Military Tribunal: Charter, Indictment and Judgments.* Oxford, UK: Oxford University Press, 2008.

Boomhower, Ray E. *Dispatches from the Pacific: The World War II Reporting of Robert L. Sherrod.* Bloomington: Indiana University Press, 2017.

Borneman, Walter R. *The Admirals: Nimitz, Halsey, Leahy, and King—the Five-Star Admirals Who Won the War at Sea.* New York: Little, Brown, 2012.

Brackman, Arnold C. *The Other Nuremberg: The Untold Story of the Tokyo War Crimes Trials.* New York: Morrow, 1987.

Bradley, John H., and Jack W. Dice. *The Second World War: Asia and the Pacific.* West Point Military History Series. Garden City Park, NY: Square One Publishers, 2002.

Brandenburg, Broughton. *Imported Americans: The Story of the Experiences of a Disguised American and His Wife Studying the Immigration Question.* New York: Stokes, 1904.

Brands, H. W. *Dreams of El Dorado: A History of the American West.* New York: Basic Books, 2019.

Bresnahan, James C. *Refighting the Pacific War: An Alternative History of World War II.* Annapolis, MD: Naval Institute Press, 2011.

Bridgman, Leonard. *Jane's Fighting Aircraft of World War II.* London: Bracken Books, 1989.

Brinkley, Douglas, and Michael E. Haskew, eds., with the Eisenhower Center for American Studies. *The World War II Desk Reference.* New York: HarperResource, 2004.

Brondfield, Jerry. *Rockne, the Coach, the Man, the Legend.* New York: Random House, 1976.

Brooks, William Allan. *Keep 'Em Laughing, a Fun Manual for Men in the Military Service.* New York: Knickerbocker Publishing Co., 1942.

Brophy, Leo P., Wyndham D. Miles, and Rexmond C. Cochrane. *The Chemical Warfare Service: From Laboratory to Field.* United States Army in World War II: The Technical Services. Washington, DC: Office of the Chief of Military History, Department of the Army, 1959.

Broughton, Philip S. *Prostitution and the War.* New York: Public Affairs Committee, 1943.

Brown, Cecil. *Suez to Singapore.* New York: Random House, 1942.

Brownstone, David M., Irene M. Franck, and Douglass L. Brownstone. *Island of Hope, Island of Tears.* New York: Penguin, 1986.

Brunnbauer, Ulf. *Globalizing Southeastern Europe: Emigrants, America, and the State Since the Late Nineteenth Century.* Lanham, MD: Lexington Books, 2016.

Buckner, Simon Bolivar, Jr. *Tales of the Philippines: In the Early 1900's.* BookBaby, 2019.

Buckner, Simon Bolivar, Jr., and Joseph Warren Stilwell. *Seven Stars: The Okinawa Battle Diaries of Simon Bolivar Buckner, Jr., and Joseph Stilwell,* edited by Nicholas Evan Sarantakes. Texas A&M Military History Series 93. College Station: Texas A&M University Press, 2004.

Buell, Raymond Leslie. "Japanese Immigration." World Peace Foundation Pamphlets, vol. 7, nos. 5–6 (1924): 287–305, 314–18. Boston: World Peace Foundation, 1924. Immigration to the United States, 1789–1930, Harvard Library.

Buell, Thomas B. *The Quiet Warrior: A Biography of Admiral Raymond A. Spruance.* Annapolis, MD: Naval Institute Press, 2009.

Bull, Stephen. *World War II Jungle Warfare Tactics.* Oxford, UK: Osprey Publishing, 2007.

Bureau of Naval Personnel, Department of the Navy. *Booby Traps.* Washington, DC: Bureau of Naval Personnel, 1944.

———. *Bureau of Naval Personnel Information Bulletin* 312 (March 1945). Washington, DC: U.S. Government Printing Office, 1945.

Burns, Bonner F. *Psychology of the Japanese Soldier.* Creative Media Partners, 2015.

Burns, Robert E. *Being Catholic, Being American: The Notre Dame Story 1934–1952.* 2 vols. Mary and Tim Gray Series for the Study of Catholic Higher Education. Notre Dame, IN: University of Notre Dame Press, 2000.

Buruma, Ian. *A Japanese Mirror: Heroes and Villains of Japanese Culture.* London: Atlantic Books, 2015.

———. *A Tokyo Romance: A Memoir.* New York: Penguin Press, 2018.

———. *The Wages of Guilt: Memories of War in Germany and Japan.* New York: New York Review of Books, 2015.

———. *Year Zero: A History of 1945.* New York: Penguin, 2013.

Butler, Smedley D. *War Is a Racket.* New York: Round Table Press, 1935.

Byas, Hugh. *The Japanese Enemy: His Power and His Vulnerability.* London: Hodder & Stoughton, 1942.

Byrd, Gregory Dean. "General Ishii Shiro: His Legacy Is That of Genius and Madman." Master's thesis, East Tennessee State University, 2005.

Byrnes, James F. *All in One Lifetime.* New York: Harper, 1958.

Camp, Richard D. *Battleship Arizona's Marines at War: Making the Ultimate Sacrifice, December 7, 1941*. St. Paul, MN: MBI Publishing, 2006.

Campbell, David. *Russian Soldier Versus Japanese Soldier: Manchuria 1904–05*. Oxford, UK: Osprey Publishing, 2019.

Campbell, Tracy. *The Year of Peril: America in 1942*. New Haven, CT: Yale University Press, 2020.

Canfield, Bruce N. *U.S. Infantry Weapons of World War II*. Improved 3rd ed. Lincoln, RI: Andrew Mowbray Pub., 1998.

Cannato, Vincent J. "Immigration and the Brahmins." *Humanities* 30, no. 3 (May–June 2009): 12–17.

Cardozier, V. R. *Colleges and Universities in World War II*. Westport, CT: Praeger, 1993.

Carleton, Philips D. *The Conquest of Okinawa: An Account of the Sixth Marine Division*. Washington, DC: Marine Corps Historical Division, 1946.

Cass, Bevan G., ed. *History of the Sixth Marine Division*. Washington, DC: Infantry Journal Press, 1948.

Cavanaugh, Jack. *Mr. Inside and Mr. Outside: World War II, Army's Undefeated Teams, and College Football's Greatest Backfield Duo*. Chicago: Triumph Books, 2014.

Center of Military History, United States Army. *Aleutian Islands*. The Campaigns of World War II, no. 72–7. Washington, DC: Center of Military History, 2003.

———. *Guadalcanal*. The Campaigns of World War II, no. 72–8. Washington, DC: U.S. Army Center of Military History, 2003.

———. *Guam: Operations of the 77th Division, 21 July–10 August 1944*. Washington, DC: U.S. Army Center of Military History, 1990.

Central Junior-Senior High School. *Interlude*. South Bend, IN: 1937.

Central Junior-Senior High School. *Interlude*. South Bend, IN: 1939.

"Changes in Bodily Form of Descendants of Immigrants." In US Senate, *Reports of the Immigration Commission*, 61st Cong., 2nd sess., June 8, 1911. Doc. 208.

Chapin, John C. *Breaching the Marianas: The Battle for Saipan*. Marines in World War II Commemorative Series. Washington, DC: History and Museums Division, U.S. Marine Corps, 1994.

Chappell, John D. *Before the Bomb: How America Approached the End of the Pacific War*. Lexington: University Press of Kentucky, 1997.

Charles, Roland W. *Troopships of World War II*. Washington, DC: Army Transportation Association, 1947.

Charles River Editors. *The Aleutian Islands Campaign: The History of Japan's Invasion of Alaska During World War II*. Charles River Editors, 2016.

Chemical Warfare Bulletin 29, no. 2 (April 1943).

Chesneau, Roger, Eugène M. Koleśnik, and N. J. M. Campbell. *Conway's All the World's Fighting Ships, 1860–1905*. London: Conway Maritime Press, 1979.

Childers, Thomas. *Soldier from the War Returning: The Greatest Generation's Troubled Homecoming from World War II*. Boston: Houghton Mifflin Harcourt, 2009.

Christopher, Robert C. *The Japanese Mind*. New York: Ballantine, 1984.

Chun, Clayton K. S. *Japan 1945: From Operation Downfall to Hiroshima and Nagasaki*. Campaign 200. Oxford, UK: Osprey Publishing, 2008.

Clark, George B. *The Six Marine Divisions in the Pacific: Every Campaign of World War II*. Jefferson, NC: McFarland, 2006.

Clark, Helen Hollandsworth, ed. *A History of Fulton County Illinois in Spoon River Country, 1818–1968*. Fulton County, IL: Fulton County Board of Supervisors, 1969.

Clodfelter, Michael. *Warfare and Armed Conflicts: A Statistical Encyclopedia of Casualty and Other Figures, 1492–2015.* 4th ed. Jefferson, NC: McFarland, 2017.

Cloe, John Haile, and National Parks Service. *Attu: The Forgotten Battle.* Washington, DC: Department of the Interior, 2017.

Coan, Peter Morton. *Ellis Island Interviews.* New York: Barnes & Noble Books, 1997.

Coen, Ross Allen. *Fu-go: The Curious History of Japan's Balloon Bomb Attack on America. Studies in War, Society, and the Military.* Lincoln: University of Nebraska Press, 2014.

Cohen, Jerome Bernard. *Japan's Economy in War and Reconstruction.* Minneapolis: University of Minnesota Press, 1949.

Cohen, Robin. *The Cambridge Survey of World Migration.* Cambridge, UK: Cambridge University Press, 1995.

Cohn, Raymond L. "The Transition from Sail to Steam in Immigration to the United States." *The Journal of Economic History* 65, no. 2 (2005): 469–95. http://www.jstor.org/stable/3875069.

Cole, Terrence M. "Jim Crow in Alaska: The Passage of the Alaska Equal Rights Act of 1945." *Western Historical Quarterly* 23, no. 4 (1992): 429–49. https://doi.org/10.2307/970301.

Coleman, Kent Stephen. "Halsey at Leyte Gulf: Command Decision and Disunity of Effort." Master of Military Art and

Science thesis, US Army Command and General Staff College, 2006.

Collingham, E. M. *The Taste of War: World War II and the Battle for Food.* New York: Penguin Press, 2012.

Colwell, Robert N. "Intelligence and the Okinawa Battle." *Naval War College Review* 38, no. 2 (1985): article 9.

Combat Lessons Gained from Overseas Observations. AGF Observers Report (Resume) POA 23 June 45. Fort Leavenworth, KS: Department of the Army, 1945.

Commander, Amphibious Group Four. Report of Participation in the Capture of Okinawa Gunto—Phases I and II, July 20, 1945.

Commander, Fifth Fleet. Action Report, Ryukyus Operation Through 27 May 1945, June 21, 1945.

Commander in Chief, Pacific Fleet. Commander in Chief War Diary for the Month of June 1945, November 21, 1945.

Commission on Wartime Relocation and Internment of Civilians. *Personal Justice Denied: Report of the Commission on Wartime Relocation and Internment of Civilians.* Seattle: University of Washington Press, 2012.

Commons, John R. *Races and Immigrants in America.* New York: Macmillan, 1907.

Conant, Jennet. *Man of the Hour: James B. Conant, Warrior Scientist.* New York: Simon & Schuster, 2017.

Condit, Kenneth W., and Edwin T. Turnbladh, Historical Branch, G-3 Division, Headquarters, U.S. Marine Corps. *Hold High the Torch: A History of the 4th Marines.* Washington, DC: U.S. Government Printing Office, 1960.

Congressional Record. Vol. 91, pt. 12. Appendix. 79th Cong., 1st sess., 1945.

Conis, Elena. "Beyond Silent Spring: An Alternate History of DDT." Science History Institute, February 14, 2017. https://www.sciencehistory.org/distillations/beyond-silent-spring-an-alternate-history-of-ddt.

Connaughton, R. M. *Rising Sun and Tumbling Bear: Russia's War with Japan.* London: Cassell, 2003.

Connor, Jack. *Leahy's Lads: The Story of the Famous Notre Dame Football Teams of the 1940s.* South Bend, IN: Diamond Communications, 1997.

Cook, Haruko Taya, and Theodore Failor Cook. *Japan at War: An Oral History.* New York: New Press, 1992.

Coram, Robert. *Brute: The Life of Victor Krulak, U.S. Marine.* New York: Little, Brown, 2010.

Corbett, G. Vance. "Operation Iceberg: Campaigning in the Ryukyus." Joint Military Operations, Naval War College, 1998.

Costello, John. *The Pacific War.* New York: Quill, 1982.

Couffer, Jack. *Bat Bomb: World War II's Other Secret Weapon.* Austin: University of Texas Press, 1992.

Cowdrey, Albert E. *Fighting for Life: American Military Medicine in World War II.* New York: Free Press, 1994.

Craig, Berry. *Hidden History of Kentucky Soldiers.* Charleston, SC: History Press, 2011.

Craig, William. *The Fall of Japan.* New York: Dial Press, 1967.

Cunningham, Paul E., II. "Command and Control of the U.S. Tenth Army During the Battle of Okinawa." Master of Military Art and Science thesis, Military History, U.S. Army Command and General Staff College, 2009.

———. *Command and Control of the U.S. Tenth Army During the Battle of Okinawa.* Verdun Press, 2014.

Cushing, Emory C. *Unseen Enemies: The Fight to Control Mosquitoes, Lice, Flies and Other Deadly Insects in World War II.* Barajima Books, 2020.

D'Ambrosio, Brian. *Montana and the NFL.* Charleston, SC: History Press, 2017.

Daniels, Roger. *Coming to America: A History of Immigration and Ethnicity in American Life.* 2nd ed. New York: Perennial, 2002.

Danzig, Allison. *The History of American Football: Its Great Teams, Players, and Coaches.* Englewood Cliffs, NJ: Prentice-Hall, 1956.

Daugherty, Leo J. *Fighting Techniques of a Japanese Infantryman, 1941–1945: Training, Techniques and Weapons.* St. Paul, MN: MBI Publishing, 2002.

——. *Pioneers of Amphibious Warfare, 1898–1945: Profiles of Fourteen American Military Strategists.* Jefferson, NC: McFarland, 2009.

Daye, John. *Encyclopedia of Armed Forces Football: The Complete History of the Glory Years.* Haworth, NJ: St. Johann Press, 2014.

Debouzy, Marianne. *In the Shadow of the Statue of Liberty: Immigrants, Workers, and Citizens in the American Republic, 1880–1920.* Urbana: University of Illinois Press, 1992.

Del Valle, Pedro A. *Semper Fidelis: An Autobiography.* Hawthorne, CA: Christian Book Club of America, 1976.

Delsohn, Steve. *Talking Irish: The Oral History of Notre Dame Football.* New York: Avon, 1998.

Diamond, Jon. *The Battle of Okinawa 1945: The Pacific War's Last Invasion.* Images of War. South Yorkshire, UK: Pen & Sword Military, 2019.

Diamond, Leland. *Notes on Jungle Warfare.* Iowa City, IA: Middle Coast Publishing, 2020.

Dillingham, William P., W. Jett Lauck, Alexander E. Cance, and Harry A. Millis. *Immigrants in Industries.* Reports of the Immigration Commission, vols. 6–25. Washington, DC: U.S. Government Printing Office, 1911.

Dissemination Division, G-2 Section, Headquarters Army Ground Forces, Army War College. *Information on Japanese*

Defensive Installations and Tactics. 1569–45. Washington, DC: Army War College, 1945.

Division of Naval Intelligence. *ONI 222-J: The Japanese Navy.* Washington, DC: Office of the Chief of Naval Operations, 1945.

Dixon, Chris. *African Americans and the Pacific War, 1941–1945: Race, Nationality, and the Fight for Freedom.* Cambridge, UK: Cambridge University Press, 2018.

Doody, Scott. *Herrin Massacre.* Morrisville, NC: Lulu Press, 2014.

Dower, John W. *Cultures of War: Pearl Harbor/Hiroshima/9–11/ Iraq.* New York: Norton, 2010.

———. *Embracing Defeat: Japan in the Wake of World War II.* New York: Norton, 1999.

———. *Japan in War and Peace: Selected Essays.* New York: New Press, Norton, 1993.

———. *War Without Mercy: Race and Power in the Pacific War.* New York: Pantheon, 1986.

Drea, Edward J. *In the Service of the Emperor: Essays on the Imperial Japanese Army.* Studies in War, Society, and the Military. Lincoln: University of Nebraska Press, 1998.

———. *Japan's Imperial Army: Its Rise and Fall, 1853–1945.* Modern War Studies. Lawrence: University Press of Kansas, 2009.

Drea, Edward, Greg Bradsher, Robert Hanyok, James Lide, Michael Petersen, and Daqing Yang. *Researching Japanese War Crimes Records: Introductory Essays.* Washington, DC: Nazi War Crimes and Japanese Imperial Government Records Interagency Working Group, 2006.

Driscoll, Joseph. *War Discovers Alaska.* Philadelphia: Lippincott, 1943.

Drury, John. *This Is Fulton County, Illinois.* American Aerial County History Series, no. 2. Chicago: Loree, 1954.

Dupuy, Trevor N. *Dictionary of Military Terms: A Guide to the Language of Warfare and Military Institutions.* 2nd ed. New York: H. W. Wilson, 2003.

Duus, Masayo Umezawa. *The Japanese Conspiracy: The Oahu Sugar Strike of 1920.* Berkeley: University of California Press, 1999.

Dwyer, James F. *Annihilation Beach: A Story About the Horrific Marine Battle for Tarawa, Day One.* North Charleston, SC: CreateSpace Independent Publishing Platform, 2014.

Dyer, George C. *The Amphibians Came to Conquer: The Story of Richmond Kelly Turner.* 2 vols. Verdun Press, 2015.

Echevarria, Antulio J. *Military Strategy: A Very Short Introduction.* Oxford, UK: Oxford University Press, 2017.

Editors of *Yank*, ed. *Yank: The Story of World War II as Written by the Soldiers.* New York: Random House Value Publishing, 1984.

Elias, Robert. *The Empire Strikes Out: How Baseball Sold U.S. Foreign Policy and Promoted the American Way Abroad.* New York: New Press, 2010.

Ellis, Earl H. *21st Century Ellis: Operational Art and Strategic Prophecy for the Modern Era.* Edited by B. A. Friedman. Annapolis, MD: Naval Institute Press, 2015.

Ellis, John. *The Sharp End: The Fighting Man in World War II.* New York: Scribner, 1980.

———. *The World War II Databook: The Essential Facts and Figures for All the Combatants.* London: Aurum Press, 1993.

Eparvier, Jean. *Miracles of Surgery.* Translated by Ann Lindsay. London: Elek Books, 1952.

Erickson, Vernon D. *Genealogical Events from Newspapers for Crawford, Vernon, and Grant Counties, Wisconsin, 1870–1901.* Bowie, MD: Heritage Books, 2001.

Estes, Kenneth W. *US Marine Corps Tank Crewman, 1941–45.* Oxford, UK: Osprey Publishing, 2005.

Eterovich, Francis H., and Christopher Spalatin. *Croatia: Land, People, Culture.* Vol. 2. Toronto: University of Toronto Press, 1970.

Evans, David C., and Mark R. Peattie. *Kaigun: Strategy, Tactics, and Technology in the Imperial Japanese Navy, 1887–1941.* Annapolis, MD: Naval Institute Press, 2012.

Farley, John. "The Aleutian Islands Campaign: An Operational Perspective." Naval War College, Newport, RI, 1997.

Feffer, Mary Gertina. "American Attitude Toward World War II During the Period from September 1939, to December, 1941." Master's thesis, Loyola University Chicago, 1951.

Feifer, George. *The Battle of Okinawa: The Blood and the Bomb.* Guilford, CT: Lyons Press, 2001.

Fellers, Bonner F. *Psychology of the Japanese Soldier*, Part 1. Creative Media Partners, 2015.

Field, Norma. *In the Realm of a Dying Emperor.* New York: Pantheon, 1991.

Fieser, Louis F. *The Scientific Method: A Personal Account of Unusual Projects in War and in Peace.* New York: Reinhold, 1964.

Fieser, Louis F., et al. "Napalm." *Industrial & Engineering Chemistry* 38, no. 8 (1946): 768–73.

Fifth Amphibious Corps, Marine Corps. *Report on Galvanic*, Enclosures A–H: Corps Operation Plan I-43; G-3 Report; G-2 Report; G-4 Report; Special Staff Officers Reports; Special Observers Reports; Corps Reconnaissance Company Report. January 11, 1944.

First Marine Division, Marine Corps. Special Action Report: Nansei-Shoto Operation 1 April–30 June, 1945. July 10, 1945.

First Marine Division Association. *Membership Directory, 2009.* Bloomington, IN: AuthorHouse, 2009.

Fisch, Arnold G., Jr. *Military Government in the Ryukyu Islands 1945–1950.* Washington, DC: U.S. Army Center of Military History, 1988.

——. *Ryukyus.* The U.S. Army Campaigns of World War II. Washington, DC: Center for Military History, 1995.

Flynn, George Q. *The Draft, 1940–1973.* Modern War Studies. Lawrence: University Press of Kansas, 1993.

Foner, Jack D. *Blacks and the Military in American History.* New Perspectives in American History, edited by James P. Shenton. New York: Praeger Publishers, 1974.

Ford, Douglas. "US Assessments of Japanese Ground Warfare Tactics and the Army's Campaigns in the Pacific Theatres, 1943–1945: Lessons Learned and Methods Applied." *War in History* 16, no. 3 (2009): 325–58. https://doi.org/10.1177/0968344509104195.

Francis, Timothy Lang. "'To Dispose of the Prisoners': The Japanese Executions of American Aircrew at Fukuoka, Japan, During 1945." *Pacific Historical Review* 66, no. 4 (1997): 469–501.

Frank, Benis M., and Henry I. Shaw, Jr. *History of the U.S. Marine Corps Operations in World War II: Victory and Occu-*

pation. Vol. 5. Washington, DC: U.S. Marine Corps, Historical Branch, 1968.

Frank, Richard B. *Tower of Skulls: A History of the Asia-Pacific War.* New York: Norton, 2020.

Frei, Terry. *Third Down and a War to Go: The All-American 1942 Wisconsin Badgers.* Madison: Wisconsin Historical Society Press, 2007.

Fuess, Claude M. *In My Time: A Medley of Andover Reminiscences.* Andover, MA: Phillips Academy, 1959.

Fulton County Historical and Genealogical Society. *Fulton County Heritage.* Dallas: Curtis Media Corporation, 1988.

Fussell, Paul. *Wartime: Understanding and Behavior in the Second World War.* Oxford, UK: Oxford University Press, 1989.

Gabriel, Richard A. *Between Flesh and Steel: A History of Military Medicine from the Middle Ages to the War in Afghanistan.* Washington, DC: Potomac Books, an imprint of the University of Nebraska Press, 2016.

Gaddis, John Lewis. *On Grand Strategy.* New York: Penguin, 2018.

Gailey, Harry A. *Bougainville, 1943–1945: The Forgotten Campaign.* Lexington: University Press of Kentucky, 1991.

———. *Howlin' Mad vs. the Army: Conflict in Command, Saipan, 1944.* Novato, CA: Presidio, 1986.

Gallant, Thomas Grady. *On Valor's Side*. Garden City, NY: Doubleday, 1963.

Gallicchio, Marc. *Unconditional: The Japanese Surrender in World War II*. New York: Oxford University Press, 2020.

Garand, George W., and Truman R. Strobridge. *Western Pacific Operations*. Vol. 4, *History of U.S. Marine Corps Operations in World War II*. Washington, DC: U.S. Marine Corps, 1971.

Gard, Rosemary. *Destiny's Design*. St. Petersburg, FL: BookLocker.com, 2016.

Garfield, Brian. *The Thousand-Mile War: World War II in Alaska and the Aleutians*. Fairbanks: University of Alaska Press, 1995.

Garvey, Harold R. *A Replacement on Okinawa: The Last Letters of Private Harold R. Garvey*. Edited by Nicholas Efstathiou. W. K. Hawthorne, 2015.

Gatchel, Theodore L. *At the Water's Edge: Defending Against the Modern Amphibious Assault*. Annapolis, MD: Naval Institute Press, 1996.

Gawne, Jonathan. *Finding Your Father's War: A Practical Guide to Researching and Understanding Service in the World War II U.S. Army*. Philadelphia: Casemate, 2006.

General Headquarters, Far East Command, Military Intelligence Section, Historical Division. *Statements of Japanese Officials on World War II (English Translations)*. Washington, DC: U.S. Government Printing Office, 1950.

Gibney, Frank. *Five Gentlemen of Japan: The Portrait of a Nation's Character.* 4th ed. Norwalk, CT: EastBridge, 2003.

Gibney, Frank, ed. *Sensō: The Japanese Remember the Pacific War.* Expanded ed. Translated by Beth Cary. London: Routledge, 2015.

Gilman, William. *Our Hidden Front.* New York: Reynal & Hitchcock, 1944.

Gilmore, Allison B. *You Can't Fight Tanks with Bayonets: Psychological Warfare Against the Japanese Army in the Southwest Pacific.* Studies in War, Society, and the Military. Lincoln: University of Nebraska Press, 1998.

Ginzberg, Eli, James K. Anderson, Sol W. Ginsburg, and John L. Herma. *The Lost Divisions.* New York: Columbia University Press, 1959.

Goldberg, Harold J. *D-Day in the Pacific: The Battle of Saipan.* Twentieth-Century Battles. Bloomington: Indiana University Press, 2007.

Goodenough, Simon. *War Maps: World War II, from September 1939 to August 1945, Air, Sea, and Land, Battle by Battle.* New York: St. Martin's Press, 1982.

Grandin, Greg. *The End of the Myth: From the Frontier to the Border Wall in the Mind of America.* New York: Metropolitan Books, 2019.

Grant, Madison. *The Passing of the Great Race.* The American Immigration Collection Series II. New York: Arno Press, 1970.

Greene, Victor R. "A Study in Slavs, Strikes, and Unions: The Anthracite Strike of 1897." *Pennsylvania History: A Journal of Mid-Atlantic Studies* 31, no. 2 (1964): 199–215. https://www.jstor.org/stable/27770252.

Grew, Joseph C. *Ten Years in Japan: A Contemporary Record Drawn from the Diaries and Private and Official Papers of Joseph G. Grew, United States Ambassador to Japan, 1932–1942.* New York: Simon & Schuster, 1944.

Griswold, John. *Herrin: The Brief History of an Infamous American City.* Charleston, SC: History Press, 2009.

Groom, Winston. *1942: The Year That Tried Men's Souls.* New York: Atlantic Monthly Press, 2005.

Gross, Jonathan J. *Imperial Japanese Navy Campaign Planning and Design of the Aleutian-Midway Campaign.* Fort Leavenworth, KS: School of Advanced Military Studies, United States Army Command and General Staff College, 2013.

Gruening, Ernest. *Many Battles: The Autobiography of Ernest Gruening.* New York: Liveright, 1973.

Guard, Harold, and John Tring. *The Pacific War Uncensored: A War Correspondent's Unvarnished Account of the Fight Against Japan.* Philadelphia: Casemate, 2011.

Guillain, Robert. *I Saw Tokyo Burning: An Eyewitness Narrative from Pearl Harbor to Hiroshima*. Garden City, NY: Doubleday, 1981.

Guillaume, Marine. "Napalm in US Bombing Doctrine and Practice, 1942–1975." *The Asia-Pacific Journal* 14, no. 23 (2016): article 4983.

Gulick, Sidney Lewis. *The American Japanese Problem: A Study of the Racial Relations of the East and the West*. New York: Charles Scribner's Sons, 1914.

Gunn, John. *The Old Core: Parris Island, San Diego, the All-Marines, the Great Goettge, President's Cup Series, Mare Island, the Rose Bowl Games, Swede Larson, John Beckett, and More*. Costa Mesa, CA: J&J Publishing, 1992.

———. *(Quite) A Few Good Men*. Costa Mesa, CA: J&J Publishing, 1992.

Guppy, H. B. *The Solomon Islands and Their Natives*. London: S. Sonnenschein, Lowrey & Co., 1887.

Guzda, Henry P. "Keeper of the Gate: Ellis Island a Welcome Site? Only After Years of Reform." *Monthly Labor Review* 109, no. 7 (1986): 30–36. http://www.jstor.org/stable/41842797.

Hadlow, Martin. "The Mosquito Network: American Military Broadcasting in the South West Pacific During World War Two." *Journal of Radio Studies* 11, no. 4 (2004): 73–86.

Hall, John Whitney. *The Cambridge History of Japan*. Reprint ed. 6 vols. Cambridge, UK: Cambridge University Press, 1989.

Hallas, James H. *The Devil's Anvil: The Assault on Peleliu*. Westport, CT: Praeger, 1994.

———. *Killing Ground on Okinawa: The Battle for Sugar Loaf Hill*. Annapolis, MD: Naval Institute Press, 2007.

———. *Saipan: The Battle That Doomed Japan in World War II*. Guilford, CT: Stackpole Books, 2019.

Hallwas, John E., ed. *The Legacy of the Mines: Memoirs of Coal Mining in Fulton County, Illinois*. Canton, IL: Spoon River College, 1993.

Halsey, William Frederick. *Admiral Halsey's Story*. New York: McGraw-Hill, 1947.

Halstead, James A. "Gastrointestinal Disorders of Psychogenic Origin: Management in Forward Areas." *Bulletin of the U.S. Army Medical Department* 9, suppl. (1949): 163–80.

Hamilton, Nigel. *The Mantle of Command: FDR at War, 1941–1942*. Boston: Houghton Mifflin Harcourt, 2014.

Hammel, Eric. *Marines at War: 20 True Heroic Tales of Marines in Combat, 1942–1983*. Pacifica, CA: Pacifica Military History, 2008.

Handlin, Oscar. *The Uprooted: The Epic Story of the Great Migrations That Made the American People*. Boston: Little, Brown, 1951.

Hanson, Frederick R., ed. *Combat Psychiatry: Experiences in the North African and Mediterranean Theaters of Operation, American Ground Forces, World War II*. Washington, DC: U.S. Government Printing Office, 1949. https://achh.army.mil/history/book-wwii-combatphsych-default.

———. "The Factor of Fatigue in the Neuroses of Combat." *Bulletin of the U.S. Army Medical Department* 9, suppl. (1949): 147–50.

Hanson, Victor Davis. *Ripples of Battle: How Wars of the Past Still Determine How We Fight, How We Live, and How We Think*. New York: Doubleday, 2003.

———. *The Second World Wars: How the First Global Conflict Was Fought and Won*. New York: Basic Books, 2017.

Hara, Tameichi. *Japanese Destroyer Captain*. New York: Ballantine, 1961.

Harada, Tasuku, ed. *The Japanese Problem in California: Answers (by Representative Americans) to Questionnaire*. San Francisco: Printed for private circulation, 1922.

Hargrove, Marion. *See Here, Private Hargrove*. New York: H. Holt and Company, 1942.

Harmsen, Peter. *Storm Clouds Over the Pacific, 1931–1941*. War in the Far East. Philadelphia: Casemate, 2018.

Harries, Meirion, and Susie Harries. *Soldiers of the Sun: The*

Rise and Fall of the Imperial Japanese Army, 1868–1945. London: Heinemann, 1991.

Harris, Sheldon H. "Japanese Biomedical Experimentation During the World-War-II Era." In *Military Medical Ethics*, vol. 2, edited by Dave E. Lounsbury, 463–506. Washington, DC: Department of the Army, 2003.

Harrison, Richard Edes. *A War Atlas for Americans*. New York: Simon and Schuster, 1944.

Hart, Peter. *Gallipoli*. New York: Oxford University Press, 2011.

Hastings, Max. *Inferno: The World at War, 1939–1945*. New York: Vintage, 2012.

Hayashi, Saburō, and Alvin D. Cook. *KōGun: The Japanese Army in the Pacific War*. Westport, CT: Greenwood Press, 1978.

Headquarters, United States Army Japan, Assistant Chief of Staff, G3, Foreign Histories Division. *History of Imperial General Headquarters, Army Section (Revised Edition)*. Japanese Monograph No. 45. Washington, DC: War Department, 1946.

Headquarters ISCOM Okinawa. Joint Communications Activities. *Action Report: Phase I Nansei Shoto, Report of Operations Against Okinawa Gunto 28 January to 30 June 1945*.

Headquarters Tenth Army, Office of the Commanding General. *Tentative Operations Plan I-45, Iceberg*. N-8633. 1945.

Hearings Before the Committee on Immigration on S. 2576, a Bill to Limit the Immigration of Aliens into the United States, and for Other Purposes, March 11, 12, 13, and 15, 1924. 68th Cong., 1st sess., 1924.

Hearn, Lafcadio. *Japan: An Attempt at Interpretation.* New York: Macmillan, 1905.

Heinrichs, Waldo H., and Marc Gallicchio. *Implacable Foes: War in the Pacific, 1944–1945.* New York: Oxford University Press, 2017.

Helling, Thomas. *Desperate Surgery in the Pacific War: Doctors and Damage Control for American Wounded, 1941–1945.* Jefferson, NC: McFarland, 2017.

Helms, Doan, Jr. *Bougainville: A Marine's Story.* Bloomington, IN: AuthorHouse, 2011.

Herge, Henry C. *Navy V-12.* Paducah, KY: Turner Publishing, 1996.

Herman, Arthur. *Freedom's Forge: How American Business Produced Victory in World War II.* New York: Random House, 2012.

Hersey, Harold Brainerd. *More G.I. Laughs, Real Army Humor.* New York: Sheridan House, 1944.

Hersey, John. *Into the Valley: A Skirmish of the Marines.* New York: Knopf, 1943.

Hershberg, James G. *James B. Conant: Harvard to Hiroshima and the Making of the Nuclear Age.* Stanford Nuclear Age Series. Stanford, CA: Stanford University Press, 1995.

Hervieux, Linda. *Forgotten: The Untold Story of D-Day's Black Heroes, at Home and at War.* New York: Harper, 2015.

Hicken, Victor. "The Virden and Pana Mine Wars of 1898." *Journal of the Illinois State Historical Society* 52, no. 2 (1959): 263–78.

Higham, John. *Strangers in the Land: Patterns of American Nativism, 1860–1925.* New Brunswick, NJ: Rutgers University Press, 2002.

Hillenbrand, Laura. *Unbroken: A World War II Story of Survival, Resilience, and Redemption.* New York: Random House, 2010.

Hirobe, Izumi. "American Attitudes Toward the Japanese Immigration Question, 1924–1931." *The Journal of American–East Asian Relations* 2, no. 3 (1993): 275–301.

———. *Japanese Pride, American Prejudice: Modifying the Exclusion Clause of the 1924 Immigration Act.* Stanford, CA: Stanford University Press, 2001.

Historical Branch, G-3 Division, Headquarters, U.S. Marine Corps. *History of U.S. Marine Corps Operations in World*

War II. 5 vols. Washington, DC: U.S. Government Printing Office, 1958.

History of Fulton County. Peoria, IL: Chapman, 1879.

History of McHenry County, Illinois. Vol. 2. Chicago: Munsell, 1922.

Hoffman, Jon T. *Chesty: The Story of Lieutenant General Lewis B. Puller, USMC.* New York: Random House, 2001.

Holmes, Richard, Hew Strachan, Chris Bellamy, and Hugh Bicheno. *The Oxford Companion to Military History.* Oxford, UK: Oxford University Press, 2001.

Horan, James David, and Gerold Frank. *Out in the Boondocks: Marines in Action in the Pacific: 21 U. S. Marines Tell Their Stories.* New York: G. P. Putnam, 1943.

Horne, Gerald. *Facing the Rising Sun: African Americans, Japan, and the Rise of Afro-Asian Solidarity.* New York: New York University Press, 2018.

Hornfischer, James D. *The Fleet at Flood Tide: America at Total War in the Pacific, 1944–1945.* New York: Bantam, 2016.

Hotta, Eri. *Japan 1941: Countdown to Infamy.* New York: Knopf, 2013.

Hough, Frank O. *The Island War: The United States Marine Corps in the Pacific.* Philadelphia: Lippincott, 1947.

Huber, Thomas M. *Japan's Battle of Okinawa, April–June 1945.* Leavenworth Papers, vol. 18. Washington, DC: U.S. Government Printing Office, 1990.

Hudak, Josh. "Through Crimson Tides: Tarawa's Effect on Military Tactics and Public Perception of War." Master's thesis, Clemson University, 2014.

Huggins, Ken, and Lori McLouth. *The Illustrated Book of Fulton County Illinois.* Canton: West Central Publications of Illinois, 2014.

Huie, William Bradford. *Can Do! The Story of the Seabees.* New York: E. P. Dutton, 1944.

———. *From Omaha to Okinawa.* New York: Dutton, 1945.

Hunt, George Pinney. *Coral Comes High.* New York: Harper & Brothers, 1946.

Ienaga, Saburō. *The Pacific War: World War II and the Japanese, 1931–1945.* The Pantheon Asia Library. New York: Pantheon Books, 1978.

"Immigrants in Industries. Part 1: Bituminous Coal Mining, vol. 1." In US Senate, *Reports of the Immigration Commission,* 61st Cong., 2nd sess., June 15, 1911.

Inoguchi, Rikihei, Tadashi Nakajima, and Roger Pineau. *The Divine Wind: Japan's Kamikaze Force in World War II.* Westport, CT: Greenwood Press, 1978.

Intelligence and Leaflet Unit, Area III, Office of War Information. *Leaflet Newsletter* 1, no. 9. Washington, DC: Intelligence and Leaflet Unit, 1945.

———. *Leaflet Newsletter* 1, no. 10. Washington, DC: Intelligence and Leaflet Unit, 1945.

International Military Tribunal for the Far East. *Judgment of the International Military Tribunal for the Far East.* 4 vols. 1948. https://www.loc.gov/rr/frd/Military_Law/pdf/Judgment-IMTFE-Vol-I-PartA.pdf.

Ireland, Bernard. *The World Encyclopedia of Amphibious Warfare Vessels: An Illustrated History of Modern Amphibious Warfare.* London: Lorenz Books, 2011.

Isely, Jeter Allen, and Philip A. Crowl. *The U.S. Marines and Amphibious War: Its Theory, and Its Practice in the Pacific.* Princeton, NJ: Princeton University Press, 1951.

Ishida, Jintarō. *The Remains of War: Apology and Forgiveness.* Quezon City, Philippines: Megabooks, 2001.

Janken, Kenneth Robert. *White: The Biography of Walter White, Mr. NAACP.* New York: New Press, 2003.

Jansen, Marius B. *The Making of Modern Japan.* Cambridge, MA: Belknap Press of Harvard University Press, 2000.

Japanese Antitank Warfare: "Know Your Enemy!" CinCPac-CinCPOA Bulletin 144–45. N-9846. Washington, DC: CinCPac-CinCPOA, 1945.

Jefferis, B. G., and J. L. Nichols. "The Science of Eugenics." In *Safe Counsel or Practical Eugenics, to Which Has Been Added: The Story of Life.* 40th ed., 9–35. Chicago: Franklin Publishing Company, 1930.

Jenkins, A. P., ed. "Lt. Gen. Simon Bolivar Buckner: Private Letters Relating to the Battle of Okinawa." *Ryudai Review of Euro-American Studies* 42 (1997): 63–113. https://core.ac.uk/download/pdf/59154188.pdf.

Jenks, Jeremiah W., and W. Jett Lauck. *The Immigration Problem: A Study of American Immigration Conditions and Needs.* New York: Funk & Wagnalls Company, 1922.

Johnson, Osa. *Bride in the Solomons.* Boston: Houghton Mifflin, 1944.

Johnson, Robert David. *Ernest Gruening and the American Dissenting Tradition.* Harvard Historical Studies 132. Cambridge, MA: Harvard University Press, 1998.

Johnson, William Bruce. *The Pacific Campaign in World War II: From Pearl Harbor to Guadalcanal.* Cass Series—Naval Policy and History 35. London: Routledge/Taylor & Francis Group, 2006.

Johnston, George Henry. *The Toughest Fighting in the World.* New York: Duell, 1943.

Joint Army-Navy Assessment Committee. *Japanese Naval and Merchant Shipping Losses During World War II by All*

Causes. Washington, DC: U.S. Government Printing Office, 1947.

Joint History Office. *World War II Inter-Allied Conferences.* Washington, DC: Joint Chiefs of Staff, 2003.

Jones, Charles. *War Shots: Norm Hatch and the U.S. Marine Corps Combat Cameramen of World War II.* Mechanicsburg, PA: Stackpole Books, 2011.

Jones, James. *From Here to Eternity: A Novel.* Complete uncensored edition. New York: Dial Press Trade Paperbacks, 2012.

Jones, Wilbur D. *"Football! Navy! War!": How Military "Lend-Lease" Players Saved the College Game and Helped Win World War II.* Jefferson, NC: McFarland, 2009.

———. *Gyrene: The World War II United States Marine.* Shippensburg, PA: White Mane Books, 1998.

Jukes, Geoffrey. *The Russo-Japanese War, 1904–1905.* Essential Histories, vol. 31. Oxford, UK: Osprey Publishing, 2002.

Kaplan, Alice Yaeger. *The Interpreter.* New York: Free Press, 2005.

Kapphahn, Catherine. *Immigrant Daughter: Stories You Never Told Me.* Catherine Kapphahn, 2019.

Kato, Masuo. *The Lost War: A Japanese Reporter's Inside Story.* New York: Knopf, 1946.

Kaune, Charles S. "The National Guard in War: An Historical

Analysis of the 27th Infantry Division (New York National Guard) in World War II." Master's thesis, U.S. Army Command and General Staff College, 1990.

Keefer, Louis E. "Birth and Death of the Army Specialized Training Program." *Army History*, no. 33 (Winter 1995): 1–7. http://jstor.com/stable/26304217.

Keegan, John. *The Face of Battle: A Study of Agincourt, Waterloo, and the Somme.* London: Barrie & Jenkins, 1988.

Keeling, Drew. *The Business of Transatlantic Migration Between Europe and the United States, 1900–1914.* Zurich: Chronos, 2012.

Kelly, Brian W. *Great Moments in Army Football: From the Beginning of Football All the Way to Army's Great 2017 Team.* Let's Go Publish!, 2017.

Kemper, Kurt Edward. *College Football and American Culture in the Cold War Era.* Sport and Society. Champaign-Urbana: University of Illinois Press, 2009.

Kendall, Park. *Dictionary of Service Slang.* New York: Mill, 1944.

Kennard, Richard. *Combat Letters Home.* Pittsburgh: Dorrance, 1985.

Kennedy, David M. *Freedom from Fear: The American People in Depression and War, 1929–1945.* Oxford History of the United States 9. Oxford, UK: Oxford University Press, 2004.

Kennedy, Malcolm Duncan. *Some Aspects of Japan and Her Defence Forces.* London: K. Paul, Trench, Trubner & Co., 1928.

Kennedy, Maxwell Taylor. *Danger's Hour: The Story of the USS Bunker Hill and the Kamikaze Pilot Who Crippled Her.* New York: Simon & Schuster, 2008.

Kerr, Alex. *Lost Japan.* Oakland, CA: Lonely Planet Publications, 2009.

King, Dan. *A Tomb Called Iwo Jima, Firsthand Accounts of Japanese Survivors.* Nampa, ID: Pacific Press, 2014.

King, Ernest J. *Our Navy at War, a Report to the Secretary of the Navy, Covering Our Peacetime Navy and Our Wartime Navy and Including Combat Operations up to March 1, 1944.* Washington, DC: U.S. Government Printing Office, 1944.

Kingseed, Cole C. *Old Glory Stories: American Combat Leadership in World War II.* Annapolis, MD: Naval Institute Press, 2006.

Kleber, Brooks E., and Dale Birdsell. *The Chemical Warfare Service: Chemicals in Combat.* United States Army in World War II: The Technical Services. Washington, DC: Office of the Chief of Military History, United States Army, 1966.

Krohe, James. *Corn Kings and One-Horse Thieves: A Plain-Spoken History of Mid-Illinois.* Carbondale: Southern Illinois University Press, 2017.

Krulak, Victor H. *First to Fight: An Inside View of the U.S. Marine Corps.* Annapolis, MD: Naval Institute Press, 1999.

Kühl, Stefan. *The Nazi Connection: Eugenics, American Racism, and German National Socialism.* New York: Oxford University Press, 1994.

Kume, Kunitake. *Japan Rising: The Iwakura Embassy to the USA and Europe, 1871–1873.* Edited by Chushichi Tsuzuki and R. Jules Young. Cambridge, UK: Cambridge University Press, 2009.

Kuramoto, Kazuko. *Manchurian Legacy: Memoirs of a Japanese Colonist.* East Lansing: Michigan State University Press, 1999.

Kushner, Barak. *The Thought War: Japanese Imperial Propaganda.* Honolulu: University of Hawaii Press, 2006.

Kuwahara, Yasuo, and Gordon T. Allred. *Kamikaze.* New York: Ballantine, 1957.

La Bree, Clifton. *The Gentle Warrior: General Oliver Prince Smith, USMC.* Kent, OH: Kent State University Press, 2001.

Lacey, Laura Homan. *Stay Off the Skyline: The Sixth Marine Division on Okinawa: An Oral History.* Washington, DC: Potomac Books, 2005.

Lacey, Sharon Tosi. *Pacific Blitzkrieg: World War II in the Central Pacific.* Denton: University of North Texas Press, 2013.

———. "The Peacemaker." *World War II* (August 2013): 40–47.

Ladd, James D. *Assault from the Sea, 1939–45: The Craft, the Landings, the Men.* Newton Abbot, UK: David & Charles, 1976.

Lai, Benjamin. *Chinese Soldier vs Japanese Soldier: China 1937–38.* Combat. Oxford, UK: Osprey Publishing, 2018.

Landing Craft School, Amphibious Training Base, Coronado, California. *Skill in the Surf: A Landing Boat Manual.* Coronado, CA: Bureau of Naval Personnel, 1945.

Lauck, W. Jett, and Edgar Sydenstricker. *Conditions of Labor in American Industries: A Summarization of the Results of Recent Investigations.* New York: Funk & Wagnalls, 1917. http://nrs.harvard.edu/urn-3:FHCL:446772.

Leavitt, Howard J. *Semper—Chai!: Marines of Blue and White (and Red).* Philadelphia: Xlibris, 2002.

Leckie, Robert. *Helmet for My Pillow: From Parris Island to the Pacific.* New York: Random House, 1957.

———. *Okinawa: The Last Battle of World War II.* New York: Viking, 1995.

———. *Strong Men Armed: The United States Marines Against Japan.* New York: Random House, 1962.

Lee, Erika. *America for Americans: A History of Xenophobia in the United States.* New York: Basic Books, 2019.

Leonard, Thomas C. "Retrospectives: Eugenics and Economics in the Progressive Era." *Journal of Economic Perspectives* 19, no. 4 (2005): 207–24.

Lewis, Adrian R. *Omaha Beach: A Flawed Victory*. Chapel Hill: University of North Carolina Press, 2001.

Lilly, J. Robert. "Death Penalty Cases in WWII Military Courts: Lessons Learned from North Africa and Italy." Paper presented at the 41st Annual Meeting of the Academy of Criminal Justice Sciences, Las Vegas, NV, March 10–13, 2004.

Linderman, Gerald F. *The World Within War: America's Combat Experience in World War II*. New York: Free Press, 1997.

Lodge, O. R. *The Recapture of Guam*. Washington, DC: Historical Branch, G-3 Division, Headquarters, U.S. Marine Corps, 1954.

Long, Kenneth J., ed. *Okinawa 1945: Personal Recollections of the Battle of Okinawa by Marines of the Sixth Marine Division*. 4 vols. Sixth Marine Division Association.

Lord, Walter. *Incredible Victory*. New York: Harper & Row, 1967.

Lory, Hillis. *Japan's Military Masters: The Army in Japanese Life*. New York: Viking Press, 1943.

Love, Edmund. *The 27th Infantry Division in World War II*. Washington, DC: Infantry Journal Press, 1949.

Lovelace, Alexander G. "'Slap Heard Around the World': George Patton and Shell Shock." *Parameters* 49, no. 3 (2019): 79–91. https://press.armywarcollege.edu/parameters/vol49/iss3/9.

Ludwig, Alfred O. "Malingering in Combat Soldiers." *Bulletin of the U.S. Army Medical Department* 9, suppl. (1949): 26–32.

Lukens, Patrick D. "Nativists and Immigration Law to 1924." In *A Quiet Victory for Latino Rights: FDR and the Controversy over "Whiteness,"* 18–32. Tucson: University of Arizona Press, 2012. http://www.jstor.org/stable/j.ctt1814jgg.7.

Lundstrom, John B. *Black Shoe Carrier Admiral: Frank Jack Fletcher at Coral Sea, Midway, and Guadalcanal.* Annapolis, MD: Naval Institute Press, 2006.

Lynd, Staughton. *"We Are All Leaders": The Alternative Unionism of the Early 1930s.* The Working Class in American History. Champaign-Urbana: University of Illinois Press, 1996.

MacCambridge, Michael. *America's Game: The Epic Story of How Pro Football Captured a Nation.* New York: Random House, 2004.

MacDonald, Charles B. *United States Army in World War II: The European Theater of Operations, The Last Offensive.* Washington, DC: Center of Military History, 1993.

Mackenzie, De Witt, Clarence Worden, and Abbott Laboratories. *Men Without Guns.* Philadelphia: Blakiston, 1945.

MacMillan, Margaret. *War: How Conflict Shaped Us.* New York: Random House, 2020.

Manchester, William. *American Caesar: Douglas MacArthur, 1880–1964.* New York: Back Bay Books, 2008.

Manning, Molly Guptill. *When Books Went to War: The Stories*

That Helped Us Win World War II. Boston: Houghton Mifflin Harcourt, 2014.

Mansberger, Floyd, and Christopher Stratton. *"Pick, Shovel, Wedge, and Sledge": A Historical Context for Evaluating Coal Mining Resources in Illinois.* Springfield, IL: Fever River Research, 2005.

Margaritis, Peter. *Landing in Hell: The Pyrrhic Victory of the First Marine Division on Peleliu, 1944.* Philadelphia: Casemate, 2018.

Margolin, Leo J. *Paper Bullets, A Brief Story of Psychological Warfare in World War II.* New York: Froben Press, 1946.

Marine Corps Schools. *The Marine Rifle Squad in Combat.* Quantico, VA: Marine Corps Schools, 1945.

Marion Cross School Sixth Graders and Marguerite J. Ames. *World War II Memories from Home and Abroad.* Edited by Marguerite J. Ames. 2006.

Marshall, George C. *Biennial Report of the Chief of Staff of the United States Army, July 1, 1941, to June 30, 1943, to the Secretary of War.* Washington, DC: U.S. Government Printing Office, 1943.

———. *The Papers of George Catlett Marshall.* Edited by Larry I. Bland and Sharon Ritenour Stevens. Lexington, VA: George C. Marshall Foundation, 1981.

Marshall, S. L. A. *Men Against Fire: The Problem of Battle Command.* Norman: University of Oklahoma Press, 2000.

Marston, Muktuk. *Men of the Tundra: Alaska Eskimos at War.* New York: October House, 1969.

Martin, Robert Akers. *Remembering Okinawa.* Morrisville, NC: Lulu Press, 2014.

Marx de Salcedo, Anastacia. *Combat-Ready Kitchen: How the U.S. Military Shapes the Way You Eat.* New York: Current, 2015.

Masterson, Karen. *The Malaria Project: The U.S. Government's Secret Mission to Find a Miracle Cure.* New York: New American Library, 2014.

Matsuo, Kinoaki. *How Japan Plans to Win.* Translated by Kilsoo K. Haan. London: Harrap, 1942.

Mauldin, Bill. *Up Front.* New York: Holt, 1945.

Mauldin, Bill, and Todd DePastino. *Willie & Joe: Back Home.* Seattle, WA: Fantagraphics Books, 2011.

Maurer, John H., and Christopher M. Bell. *At the Crossroads Between Peace and War: The London Naval Conference of 1930.* Annapolis, MD: Naval Institute Press, 2013.

McGuire, Phillip. "Desegregation of the Armed Forces: Black Leadership, Protest and World War II." *Journal of Negro History* 68, no. 2 (Spring 1983): 147–58.

———, ed. *Taps for a Jim Crow Army: Letters from Black Soldiers in World War II*. Lexington: University Press of Kentucky, 1993.

McGurn, Barrett. *Yank, the Army Weekly: Reporting the Greatest Generation*. Golden, CO: Fulcrum, 2004.

McHenry County. *Biographical Directory of the Tax-payers and Voters of McHenry County: Containing Also a Condensed History of Illinois, Sketch of the County, Etc.* Chicago: Walker, 1876.

McKinney, Leonard L., and Chemical Corps Historical Studies. *Portable Flame Thrower Operations in World War II*. Washington, DC: Department of the Army, 1949.

McLaurin, Melton A. *The Marines of Montford Point: America's First Black Marines*. Chapel Hill: University of North Carolina Press, 2007.

McManus, John C. *The Deadly Brotherhood: The American Combat Soldier in World War II*. Novato, CA: Presidio, 1998.

———. *Grunts: Inside the American Infantry Combat Experience: World War II Through Iraq*. New York: NAL Caliber, 2010.

McNab, Chris. *The Flamethrower*. Oxford, UK: Osprey Publishing, 2015.

Mears, Helen. *Mirror for Americans, Japan*. Boston: Houghton, Mifflin, 1948.

Merritt, Ed, et al. *World War II: Map by Map*. New York: DK Publishing, 2019.

Metcalf, Clyde Hill. *The Marine Corps Reader.* New York: G. P. Putnam's Sons, 1944.

Michno, Gregory. *Death on the Hellships: Prisoners at Sea in the Pacific War.* Annapolis, MD: Naval Institute Press, 2001.

Mikesh, Robert C. *Japan's World War II Balloon Bomb Attacks on North America.* Smithsonian Annals of Flight. Washington, DC: Smithsonian Institution Press, 1973.

Military Intelligence Service, War Department. *Morale-Building Activities in Foreign Armies.* Washington, DC: Military Intelligence Service, 1943.

Military Review 25, no. 7 (October 1945). Fort Leavenworth, KS: Command and General Staff School, 1945.

Miller, Donald L. *D-Days in the Pacific.* New York: Simon & Schuster, 2005.

Miller, Edward S. *War Plan Orange: The U.S. Strategy to Defeat Japan, 1897–1945.* Annapolis, MD: Naval Institute Press, 1991.

Miller, John, Jr. *Guadalcanal: The First Offensive.* United States Army in World War II: The War in the Pacific. Edited by Kent Roberts Greenfield. Washington, DC: Center of Military History, 1995.

Millett, Allan Reed. *Semper Fidelis: The History of the United States Marine Corps.* Macmillan Wars of the United States. Toronto: Free Press, 1991.

Millett, Allan Reed, and Williamson Murray. *Military Effectiveness*. New ed. 3 vols. Cambridge, UK: Cambridge University Press, 2010.

Miner's Magazine. Western Federation of Miners, 1903.

Mitchell, Robert J., Sewell T. Tyng, and Nelson L. Drummond. *The Capture of Attu: A World War II Battle as Told by the Men Who Fought There*. Lincoln: University of Nebraska Press, 2000.

Mitter, Rana. *Forgotten Ally: China's World War II, 1937–1945*. Boston: Houghton Mifflin Harcourt, 2013.

Mizuki, Shigeru. *Onward Towards Our Noble Deaths*. Translated by Jocelyne Allen. Montreal: Drawn & Quarterly, 2011.

———. *Showa 1939–1944: A History of Japan*. Translated by Zack Davisson. Montreal: Drawn & Quarterly, 2014.

Molek, Ivan. *Slovene Immigrant History, 1900–1950: Autobiographical Sketches*. Dover, DE: Molek, 1979.

Moore, Christopher Paul. *Fighting for America: Black Soldiers, The Unsung Heroes of World War II*. New York: One World, 2005.

Moorehead, Alan. *Gallipoli*. New ed. London: H. Hamilton, 1967.

Moran, Baron, and Charles McMoran Wilson. *The Anatomy of Courage*. London: Constable, 1945.

Moran, Jim, and Gordon L. Rottman. *Peleliu 1944: The Forgotten Corner of Hell.* Praeger Illustrated Military History Series. Westport, CT: Praeger, 2004.

Morehouse, Maggi M. *Fighting in the Jim Crow Army: Black Men and Women Remember World War II.* Lanham, MD: Rowman & Littlefield, 2000.

Moreland, Wallace Sheldon. *A Practical Guide to Successful Farming.* Garden City, NY: Halcyon House, 1943.

Mori, Jūzō. *The Miraculous Torpedo Squadron.* Translated by Nicholas Voge. Kindle edition, 2015.

Morison, Samuel Eliot. *The Struggle for Guadalcanal, August 1942–February 1943.* History of United States Naval Operations in World War II, vol. 5. Boston: Little, Brown, 1960.

———. *Victory in the Pacific, 1945.* History of United States Naval Operations in World War II, vol. 14. Boston: Little, Brown, 1960.

Morton, G. M. *Brown University Athletics: From the Bruins to the Bears.* Images of Sports. Mount Pleasant, SC: Arcadia Publishing, 2003.

Motomura, Hiroshi. *Americans in Waiting: The Lost Story of Immigration and Citizenship in the United States.* Oxford, UK: Oxford University Press, 2006.

Mountcastle, John Wyndham. *Flame On: U.S. Incendiary Weapons, 1918–1945.* Stackpole Military History Series. Mechanicsburg, PA: Stackpole Books, 2016.

Mullener, Elizabeth. *War Stories: Remembering World War II.* Baton Rouge: Louisiana State University Press, 2002.

Murphy, R. Taggart. *Japan and the Shackles of the Past.* Oxford, UK: Oxford University Press, 2014.

Murray, Williamson, and Allan Reed Millett. *Military Innovation in the Interwar Period.* Cambridge, UK: Cambridge University Press, 1996.

Nagatsuka, Ryūji. *I Was a Kamikaze.* Eyewitness Accounts. Stroud, Gloucestershire, UK: Amberley, 2014.

Nalty, Bernard C. *The Right to Fight: African-American Marines in World War II.* Marines in World War II Commemorative Series. Washington, DC: U.S. Marine Corps, History and Museums Division, U.S. Government Printing Office, distributor, 1995.

Naske, Claus-M. "The Battle of Alaska Has Ended and . . . the Japs Won It." *Military Affairs* 49, no. 3 (1985): 144–51.

Ness, Leland S. *Rikugun: Guide to Japanese Ground Forces, 1937–1945: Tactical Organization of Imperial Japanese Army and Navy Ground Forces.* Solihull, UK: Helion, 2014.

Neushul, Peter. "Andrew Jackson Higgins and the Mass Production of World War II Landing Craft." *Louisiana History: The Journal of the Louisiana Historical Association* 39, no. 2 (1998): 133–66. http://www.jstor.org/stable/4233491.

Nichols, Charles S., Jr., and Henry I. Shaw, Jr., Historical Branch, G-3 Division, Headquarters, U.S. Marine Corps. *Okinawa: Victory in the Pacific.* Washington, DC: U.S. Government Printing Office, 1955.

Nolan, Cathal J. *The Allure of Battle: A History of How Wars Have Been Won and Lost.* Oxford, UK: Oxford University Press, 2017.

Nolan, Tom. *Three Chords for Beauty's Sake: The Life of Artie Shaw.* New York: Norton, 2010.

Northern Illinois State Teachers College. *The Norther.* DeKalb, IL: 1942.

Northern Illinois State Teachers College. *The Norther.* DeKalb, IL: 1951.

Notes on Jungle Warfare from the U. S. Marines and U. S. Infantry on Guadalcanal Island. R-14296. Washington, DC: United States Marines, 1942.

Oblinger, Carl D. *Divided Kingdom: Work, Community, and the Mining Wars in the Central Illinois Coal Fields During the Great Depression.* Springfield: Illinois State Historical Society, 1991.

"Occupational Deferments." *Indiana Law Journal* 17, no. 4 (April 1942): 316.

O'Donnell, Patrick K. *Into the Rising Sun: In Their Own Words,*

World War II's Pacific Veterans Reveal the Heart of Combat. New York: Free Press, 2002.

Office of Armed Forces Information and Education, United States Department of Defense. *A Pocket Guide to Japan.* Washington, DC: U.S. Government Printing Office, 1961.

Office, Director of Intelligence, Army Service Forces. *Cave War.* Washington, DC: Office, Director of Intelligence, 1945.

———. *Flame!* Special Technical Intelligence Bulletin no. 9. Washington, DC: Office, Director of Intelligence, 1945.

Office of Scientific Research and Development, National Defense Research Committee, and Division 11. *Fire Warfare: Incendiaries and Flame Throwers.* Vol. 3, *Summary Technical Report of Division 11, NDRC.* Washington, DC: Joint Research and Development Board, 1946.

Office of the Chief of Naval Operations. *Distribution of CinCPOA Serial 0005748 of 15 July 1945. (Subject: CinCPac War Diary for JUNE 1945.)* March 4, 1946.

Office of the Chief of Naval Operations, Division of Fleet Training. *Landing Operations Doctrine.* F.T.P. 167. Washington, DC: U.S. Government Printing Office, 1938.

Office of the Surgeon General. *Annual Report of the Surgeon General of the Army for the Commanding General, Army Service Forces.* Washington, DC: U.S. Government Printing Office, 1944.

Official Register of the Officers and Cadets of the U.S. Military Academy, June 1908. West Point, NY: U.S.M.A. Press and Bindery, 1908.

Official Register of the Officers and Cadets of the U.S. Military Academy for the Academic Year Ending June 30, 1942. West Point, NY: United States Military Academy Printing Office, 1942.

Official Register of the Officers and Cadets of the U.S. Military Academy for the Academic Year Ending June 30, 1946. West Point, NY: United States Military Academy Printing Office, 1946.

Ohkubo, Kristine. *The Sun Will Rise Again.* Kristine Ohkubo, 2016.

Ohnuki-Tierney, Emiko. *Kamikaze Diaries: Reflections of Japanese Student Soldiers.* Chicago: University of Chicago Press, 2006.

———. *Kamikaze, Cherry Blossoms, and Nationalisms: The Militarization of Aesthetics in Japanese History.* Chicago: University of Chicago Press, 2002.

Okrent, Daniel. *The Guarded Gate: Bigotry, Eugenics, and the Law That Kept Two Generations of Jews, Italians, and Other European Immigrants Out of America.* New York: Scribner, 2019.

Okumiya, Masatake, and Jirō Horikoshi. *Zero!* New York: Dutton, 1956.

Olson, Lynne. *Those Angry Days: Roosevelt, Lindbergh, and America's Fight over World War II, 1939–1941*. New York: Random House, 2013.

Onoda, Hiroo. *No Surrender: My Thirty-Year War*. London: Deutsch, 1975.

Orr, James J. *The Victim as Hero: Ideologies of Peace and National Identity in Postwar Japan*. Honolulu: University of Hawaii Press, 2001.

Ōta, Masahide. *This Was the Battle of Okinawa*. Naha, Japan: Naha Publishing Company, 1981.

Over, Richard, ed. *New York Times Complete World War II: The Coverage of the Entire Conflict*. Philadelphia: Running Press, 2016.

Owens, Ben H. "Marine Public Affairs and the Battle of Iwo Jima." Master of Military Studies thesis, Marine Corps University, 2001.

Packard, Randall M. *The Making of a Tropical Disease: A Short History of Malaria*. 2nd ed. Johns Hopkins Biographies of Disease. Baltimore: Johns Hopkins University Press, 2021.

Paine, S. C. M. *The Wars for Asia, 1911–1949*. New York: Cambridge University Press, 2012.

Parrish, Thomas, and S. L. A. Marshall. *The Simon and Schuster Encyclopedia of World War II*. New York: Simon and Schuster, 1978.

Parshall, Jonathan B., and Anthony P. Tully. *Shattered Sword: The Untold Story of the Battle of Midway.* Washington, DC: Potomac Books, 2005.

Persico, Joseph E. *Roosevelt's Centurions: FDR and the Commanders He Led to Victory in World War II.* New York: Random House, 2014.

Petty, Bruce M. *At War in the Pacific: Personal Accounts of World War II Navy and Marine Corps Officers.* Jefferson, NC: McFarland, 2006.

Phillips, Sid. *You'll Be Sor-Ree: A Guadalcanal Marine Remembers the Pacific War.* New York: Dutton Caliber, 2010.

Pike, Francis. "The Development of a Death Cult in 1930s Japan and the Decision to Drop the Atom Bomb." *Asian Affairs* 47, no. 1 (2016): 1–31. https://doi.org/10.1080/03068374.2015.112 8682.

Pogue, Forrest C. *George C. Marshall: Organizer of Victory, 1943–1945.* Vol. 3. New York: Viking, 1963.

Pols, Hans, and Stephanie Oak. "War & Military Mental Health: The US Psychiatric Response in the 20th Century." *American Journal of Public Health* 97, no. 12 (2007): 2132–42.

Porch, Douglas. "'No Bad Stories': The American Media-Military Relationship." *Naval War College Review* 55, no. 1 (2002).

Potter, E. B. *Nimitz.* Annapolis, MD: Naval Institute Press, 2008.

Prange, Gordon W., Donald M. Goldstein, and Katherine V. Dillon. *Miracle at Midway*. New York: McGraw-Hill, 1982.

Pratt, Fletcher. *The Marines' War: An Account of the Struggle for the Pacific from Both American and Japanese Sources*. New York: Sloane, 1948.

Preventive Medicine in World War II. Washington, DC: U.S. Government Printing Office, 1955.

Prpic, George J. *The Croatian Immigrants in America*. New York: Philosophical Library, 1971.

Purdue University. *Debris*. West Lafayette, IN: 1943.

Purdue University. *Debris*. West Lafayette, IN: 1944.

Reece, Chester Abraham. *Things Remembered*. Morrisville, NC: Lulu Press, 2008.

Rees, Laurence. *Horror in the East: Japan and the Atrocities of World War 2*. London: BBC Books, 2001.

Reischauer, Edwin O., and Ichirō Katō. *Japan: An Illustrated Encyclopedia*. 2 vols. Tokyo: Kodansha, 1993.

Reporting World War II. Part I: American Journalism, 1938–1944. New York: Library of America, 1995.

Reporting World War II. Part 2: American Journalism, 1944–1946. New York: Library of America, 1995.

Restriction of Immigration: Hearings Before the Committee on Immigration and Naturalization, House of Representatives,

Sixty-eighth Congress, First Session, on H.R.5, H.R.101, H.R.561 [H.R.6540], 68th Cong., 1st sess., 1924.

Richie, Donald. *The Inland Sea.* Berkeley, CA: Stone Bridge Press, 2002.

Ricks, Thomas E. *The Generals: American Military Command from World War II to Today.* New York: Penguin, 2012.

Rider, Dwight R. *Japan's Biological and Chemical Weapons Programs: War Crimes and Atrocities—Who's Who, What's What, Where's Where. 1928–1945.* Los Altos, CA: Center for Research: Allied POWs Under the Japanese, 2015.

Rielly, Robin L. *Kamikaze Attacks of World War II: A Complete History of Japanese Suicide Strikes on American Ships, by Aircraft and Other Means.* Jefferson, NC: McFarland, 2010.

Riess, Steven A. *Sport in Industrial America, 1850–1920.* 2nd ed. Chichester, West Sussex, UK: Wiley-Blackwell, 2013.

Rigg, Bryan Mark. *Flamethrower: Iwo Jima Medal of Honor Recipient and U.S. Marine Woody Williams and His Controversial Award, Japan's Holocaust and the Pacific War.* Addison, TX: Fidelis, 2020.

Riis, Jacob A., and Hasia R. Diner. *How the Other Half Lives: Authoritative Text, Contexts, Criticism.* New York: Norton, 2010.

Roan, Richard W. *Roebling's Amphibian: The Origin of the Assault Amphibian.* Quantico, VA: Marine Corps Development and Education Command, 1987.

Roberts, Howard. *The Big Nine: The Story of Football in the Western Conference.* New York: G. P. Putnam's Sons, 1948.

Roberts, Mary Louise. *What Soldiers Do: Sex and the American GI in World War II France.* Chicago: University of Chicago Press, 2013.

Roberts, Randy. *A Team for America: The Army-Navy Game That Rallied a Nation at War.* Boston: Mariner Books, 2012.

Robinson, Ray. *Rockne of Notre Dame: The Making of a Football Legend.* New York: Oxford University Press, 1999.

Robson, Robert William. *The Pacific Islands Handbook.* New York: Macmillan, 1944.

Rocco, Fiammetta. *The Miraculous Fever Tree: Malaria and the Quest for a Cure That Changed the World.* New York: HarperCollins, 2003.

Roebling, Washington Augustus, and Donald Sayenga. *Washington Roebling's Father: A Memoir of John A. Roebling.* Reston, VA: ASCE Press, 2009.

Roediger, David R. *Working Toward Whiteness: How America's Immigrants Became White—The Strange Journey from Ellis Island to the Suburbs.* 2nd ed. New York: Basic Books, 2018.

Rogers, J. David. "Donald Roebling and the Origins of the Amphibious Tractor." Paper given at American Society of Civil Engineers, World Environmental and Water Resources Congress, 2016.

Rominger, Donald W., Jr., "From Playing Field to Battleground: The United States Navy V-5 Preflight Program in World War II." *Journal of Sport History* 12, no. 3 (1985): 252–64.

Rose, Kenneth D. *Myth and the Greatest Generation: A Social History of Americans in World War II.* New York: Routledge, 2008.

Rottman, Gordon L. *The Hand Grenade.* Oxford, UK: Osprey Publishing, 2015.

———. *Landing Ship, Tank (LST), 1942–2002.* Oxford, UK: Osprey Publishing, 2012.

———. *Okinawa, 1945: The Last Battle.* Edited by Lee Johnson. Oxford, UK: Osprey Publishing, 2002.

———. *U.S. Marine Corps World War II Order of Battle: Ground and Air Units in the Pacific War, 1939–1945.* Westport, CT: Greenwood Press, 2001.

———. *US Marine Rifleman, 1939–45: Pacific Theater.* Oxford, UK: Osprey Publishing, 2006.

———. *US Marine versus Japanese Infantryman: Guadalcanal 1942–43.* Oxford, UK: Osprey Publishing, 2014.

———. *US World War II Amphibious Tactics, Army and Marine Corps: Pacific Theater.* Oxford, UK: Osprey Publishing, 2012.

———. *US World War II Amphibious Tactics: Mediterranean &*

European Theaters. New York: Osprey Publishing, 2006.

———. *World War II Pacific Island Guide: A Geo-Military Study.* Westport, CT: Greenwood Press, 2002.

———. *World War II US Marine Infantry Regiments*. Oxford, UK: Osprey Publishing, 2018.

Rottman, Gordon L., and Peter Dennis. *World War II Allied Sabotage Devices and Booby Traps*. Oxford, UK: Osprey Publishing, 2010.

Rowell, Chester H. "Chinese and Japanese Immigrants—A Comparison." *Annals of the American Academy of Political and Social Science* 34, no. 2 (September 1909): 223.

Rozell, Matthew Anthony. *The Things Our Fathers Saw: The Untold Stories of the World War II Generation*. Vol. 1, *Voices of the Pacific Theater*. Hartford, NY: Woodchuck Hollow Press, 2015.

———. *The Things Our Fathers Saw: The Untold Stories of the World War II Generation*. Vol. 2, *War in the Air*. Hartford, NY: Woodchuck Hollow Press, 2017.

Rubin, Jay, ed. *The Penguin Book of Japanese Short Stories*. London: Penguin, 2018.

Ruffner, Frederick G., and Robert C. Thomas. *Code Names Dictionary: A Guide to Code Names, Slang, Nicknames, Journalese, and Similar Terms*. Detroit: Gale Research, 1963.

Rutenberg, Amy J. *Rough Draft: Cold War Military Manpower*

Policy and the Origins of Vietnam-Era Draft Resistance. Ithaca, NY: Cornell University Press, 2019.

Ryan, Joseph W., and Samuel A. Stouffer. *Samuel Stouffer and the GI Survey: Sociologists and Soldiers During the Second World War.* Legacies of War Series. Knoxville: University of Tennessee Press, 2013.

Ryukyu Shimpo. Descent into Hell: Civilian Memories of the Battle of Okinawa. Translated by Mark Ealey and Alastair McLauchlan. Portland, ME: MerwinAsia, 2014.

Said, Edward W. *Orientalism.* New York: Vintage Books, 1979.

Salter, James. *Burning the Days: Recollection.* New York: Random House, 1997.

Sarantakes, Nicholas Evan. "Keystone: The American Occupation of Okinawa, and U.S.-Japanese Relations, 1945–1972." Doctor of Philosophy diss., University of Southern California, 1996.

———. "Warriors of Word and Sword: The Battle of Okinawa, Media Coverage, and Truman's Reevaluation of Strategy in the Pacific." *Journal of American–East Asian Relations* 23, no. 4 (2016): 334–67.

Satterfield, John R. *Saving Big Ben: The USS Franklin and Father Joseph T. O'Callahan.* Annapolis, MD: Naval Institute Press, 2011.

Schindler, David, and Mark Westcott. "Shocking Racial Attitudes: Black G.I.s in Europe." *Review of Economic Studies* 88, no. 1 (January 2021): 489–520.

Schmahl, Helmut. "Transplanted but Not Uprooted: 19th-Century Immigrants from Hessen-Darmstadt in Wisconsin." Paper presented at Defining Tensions: A Fresh Look at Germans in Wisconsin, Max Kade Institute for German-American Studies, University of Wisconsin–Madison, October 15–17, 1998.

Schmidt, David A. *Ianfu, The Comfort Women of the Japanese Imperial Army of the Pacific War: Broken Silence.* Japanese Studies, vol. 10. Lewiston, NY: Edwin Mellen Press, 2000.

Schmidt, Raymond. *Football's Stars of Summer: A History of the College All-Star Football Game Series of 1934–1976.* American Sports History Series, vol. 21. Lanham, MD: Scarecrow Press, 2001.

Schneider, James G. *The Navy V-12 Program: Leadership for a Lifetime.* Champaign, IL: Marlow Books, 1987.

Scott, Benjamin S. *Operational Art and Sustainment of US Campaigns to Seize the Philippines and Okinawa in 1944–1945.* Fort Leavenworth, KS: Command and General Staff College, 2018.

Scott, James. *Rampage: MacArthur, Yamashita, and the Battle of Manila.* New York: Norton, 2018.

Scott, Robert J., and Myles A. Pocta. *Honor on the Line: The*

Fifth Down and the Spectacular 1940 College Football Season. iUniverse, 2012.

Shapiro, Miles. *Charles Drew: Life-Saving Scientist.* Innovative Minds. Austin, TX: Raintree Steck-Vaughn, 1997.

Shaw, Henry L., Jr., Bernard C. Nalty, and Edwin T. Turnbladh. *Central Pacific Drive: History of U.S. Marine Corps Operations in World War II.* Washington, DC: Historical Branch, G-3 Division, Headquarters, U.S. Marine Corps, 1966.

Sheftall, Mordecai G. *Blossoms in the Wind: The Human Legacy of the Kamikaze.* New York: NAL Caliber, 2005.

Sheidlower, Jesse. *The F-Word.* 3rd ed. Oxford, UK: Oxford University Press, 2009.

Sherrod, Robert. *Tarawa: The Incredible Story of One of World War II's Bloodiest Battles.* New York: Skyhorse, 2013 (originally published 1944).

Shigeru, Mizuki. *Showa 1926–1939: A History of Japan.* Translated by Zack Davisson. Montreal: Drawn & Quarterly, 2013.

Shillony, Ben-Ami. *Revolt in Japan: The Young Officers and the February 26, 1936 Incident.* Princeton, NJ: Princeton University Press, 1973.

Shisler, Gail B. *For Country and Corps: The Life of General Oliver P. Smith.* Annapolis, MD: Naval Institute Press, 2009.

Shively, Donald H., and Carmen Blacker. *Tradition and Modern-*

ization in Japanese Culture. Studies in the Modernization of Japan. Vol. 5. Princeton, NJ: Princeton University Press, 1971.

Shribman, David M., and Jack DeGange. *Dartmouth College Football: Green Fields of Autumn.* Images of Sports. Charleston, SC: Arcadia Publishing, 2004.

Simmons, Edwin H. *The United States Marines: The First 200 Years, 1775–1975.* New York: Viking Adult, 1976.

Sixth Marine Division, Marine Corps. Regimental Weapons Company, Fourth Marines. Special Action Report. June 27, 1945.

——. Special Action Report, Phase III: Okinawa Operation. June 30, 1945.

——. Special Action Report, Phase III: Okinawa Operation; Annexes A-K (4th Marines; 22nd Marines; 29th Marines; 15th Marines; 6th Tank Battalion; 6th Engineer Battalion; 6th Pioneer Battalion; 1st Armored Amphibian Battalion; 4th Amphibian Tractor Battalion; 9th Amphibian Tractor Battalion; 6th Medical Battalion). June 30, 1945.

——. Special Action Report, Phases I and II, Okinawa Operation. April 30, 1945.

——. Special Action Report, Phases I and II, Okinawa Operation; Annexes A-K (4th Marines; 22nd Marines, 29th Marines; Division Artillery Report; 6th Tank Battalion; 6th Engineer Battalion; Division Shore Party Report; 6th Medical

Battalion Report; 1st Armored Amphibian Battalion; 4th Amphibian Tractor Battalion; 9th Amphibian Tractor Battalion). April 30, 1945.

———, Third Battalion, Fourth Regiment. Special Action Report, Phase III: Okinawa Operation. June 29, 1945.

Sixth Marine Division Association. *Sixth Marine Division: The Striking Sixth.* Paducah, KY: Turner Publishing, 1987.

Sledge, E. B. *With the Old Breed at Peleliu and Okinawa.* New York: Presidio, 2010.

Sloan, Bill. *Brotherhood of Heroes: The Marines at Peleliu, 1944—The Bloodiest Battle of the Pacific War.* New York: Simon & Schuster, 2005.

———. *The Ultimate Battle: Okinawa 1945—The Last Epic Struggle of World War II.* New York: Simon & Schuster, 2008.

Smith, Holland M., and Percy Finch. *Coral and Brass.* New York: Charles Scribner's Sons, 1949.

Smith, Perry. *Courage, Compassion, Marine: The Unique Story of Jimmie Dyess.* iUniverse, 2015.

Smith, Peter C. *Kamikaze: To Die for the Emperor.* Barnsley, South Yorkshire, UK: Pen & Sword Aviation, 2014.

Smith, S. E. *The United States Marine Corps in World War II: The One-Volume History, from Wake to Tsingtao, by the Men Who Fought in the Pacific and by Distinguished Marine Experts, Authors, and Newspapermen.* New York: Random

House, 1969.

Sobel, Raymond. "Anxiety-Depressive Reactions After Prolonged Combat Experience—the 'Old Sergeant Syndrome.'" *Bulletin of the U.S. Army Medical Department* (1949): 137–46.

Solberg, Winton U. *Creating the Big Ten: Courage, Corruption, and Commercialization.* Urbana: University of Illinois Press, 2018.

Spector, Ronald H. *Eagle Against the Sun: The American War with Japan.* Norwalk, CT: Easton Press, 1989.

Speller, Ian, and Christopher Tuck. *Amphibious Warfare: Strategy and Tactics.* Staplehurst, Kent, UK: Spellmount, 2001.

Sperber, Murray A. *Onward to Victory: The Crises That Shaped College Sports.* New York: Holt, 1998.

———. *Shake Down the Thunder: The Creation of Notre Dame Football.* Bloomington: Indiana University Press, 2002 (originally published 1993).

Spiegel, Hart H. Unpublished memoir. San Francisco, CA, 1943.

Spielman, A., and Michael D'Antonio. *Mosquito: A Natural History of Our Most Persistent and Deadly Foe.* New York: Hyperion, 2001.

Spiller, Harry. *Sheriff: A Memoir of a Lawman from Bloody Williamson County, Illinois.* Paducah, KY: Turner Publishing Company, 1999.

Springer, Joseph A. *Inferno: The Epic Life and Death Struggle of the USS* Franklin *in World War II.* St. Paul, MN: Zenith Press, 2007.

Stalker, Nancy. "Suicide, Boycotts and Embracing Tagore: The Japanese Popular Response to the 1924 US Immigration Exclusion Act." *Japanese Studies* 26, no. 2 (2007): 153–70.

"Steerage Conditions, Importation and Harboring of Women for Immoral Purposes, Immigrant Homes and Aid Societies, Immigrant Banks." In US Senate, *Reports of the Immigration Commission,* 61st Cong., 3rd sess., December 5, 1910. Doc. 753.

Stephenson, Michael. *The Last Full Measure: How Soldiers Die in Battle.* New York: Crown, 2012.

Stickles, Arndt Mathis. *Simon Bolivar Buckner: Borderland Knight.* Chapel Hill: University of North Carolina Press, 1940.

Stille, Mark. *US Navy Ships vs Japanese Attack Aircraft: 1941–42.* Oxford, UK: Osprey Publishing, 2020.

Stimson, Henry L., and McGeorge Bundy. *On Active Service in Peace and War.* New York: Harper, 1948.

Stockman, James R. *The Battle for Tarawa.* Washington, DC: Historical Section, Division of Public Information, U.S. Marine Corps, 1947.

Stoddard, Lothrop. *The Revolt Against Civilization: The Menace of the Under Man.* New York: Charles Scribner's Sons, 1922.

———. *The Rising Tide of Color: Against White World-*

Supremacy. New York: Charles Scribner's Sons, 1922.

Stouffer, Samuel A. *The American Soldier: Combat and Its Aftermath.* 2 vols. Studies in Social Psychology in World War II. Princeton, NJ: Princeton University Press, 1949.

Strahan, Jerry E. *Andrew Jackson Higgins and the Boats That Won World War II.* Baton Rouge: Louisiana State University Press, 1994.

Stratton, Donald, and Ken Gire. *All the Gallant Men: An American Sailor's Firsthand Account of Pearl Harbor.* New York: William Morrow, 2017.

Straus, Ulrich. *The Anguish of Surrender: Japanese POWs of World War II.* Seattle: University of Washington Press, 2003.

Styron, William. *A Tidewater Morning: Three Tales from Youth.* New York: Random House, 1993.

Styron, William, and James L. W. West. *The Suicide Run: Five Tales of the Marine Corps.* New York: Random House, 2009.

Sullivan, John M., Jr. "Why Gallipoli Matters: Interpreting Different Lessons." Newport, RI: Naval War College, 2003.

Sweetman, Jack. *Great American Naval Battles.* Annapolis, MD: Naval Institute Press, 1998.

Symonds, Craig L. *World War II at Sea: A Global History.* Oxford, UK: Oxford University Press, 2018.

Taglianetti, Rob. "'Denig's Demons': Marine News Reporters, Artists, Radio Personalities and Photographers in World War II." *Leatherneck* 52 (September 2007).

Tamayama, Kazuo, and John Nunneley. *Tales by Japanese Soldiers of the Burma Campaign, 1942–1945.* London: Cassell, 2001.

Tanaka, Toshiyuki. *Hidden Horrors: Japanese War Crimes in World War II.* Boulder, CO: Westview, 1996.

Taylor, Alan. "World War II: The Pacific Islands." *The Atlantic*, September 25, 2011. https://www.theatlantic.com/photo/2011/09/world-war-ii-the-pacific-islands/100155/.

Taylor, Anna Marjorie. *The Language of World War II: Abbreviations, Captions, Quotations, Slogans, Titles and Other Terms and Phrases.* Revised and enlarged ed. New York: Wilson, 1948.

Taylor, Pat, Dave Bishop, Brooks Carver, and Sue Rusch, eds. *Spoon River Country: The Immigrant Story.* Canton, IL: Prairie Sky Press.

Technical Staff, Dugway Proving Ground. *Attack Against Cave-Type Fortifications.* Tooele, UT: Chemical Warfare Service, 1945.

Terkel, Studs. *The Good War: An Oral History of World War Two.* New York: New Press, 1997.

Terry, Howard. *Terrible Terry: Just a Marine.* Bloomington, IN: Xlibris, 2009.

Third Amphibious Corps, Marine Corps. Action Report: Ryukyus Operation, Appendices, Corps Operation Orders and G-3 Periodic Reports. July 1, 1945.

——. Action Report: Ryukyus Operation, Phases I & II (Okinawa). July 1, 1945.

Thobaben, Robert G. *For Comrade and Country: Oral Histories of World War II Veterans.* Jefferson, NC: MacFarland, 2003.

Thomason, John W. *. . . and a Few Marines.* New York: Charles Scribner's Sons, 1943.

Thompson, George. *82 Days of Hell and Glory: The Okinawa Campaign with the Sixth Marine Division.* Washington, DC: War Department, 1945.

Toland, John. *The Rising Sun: The Decline and Fall of the Japanese Empire, 1936–1945.* New York: Random House, 1970.

Toll, Ian W. *The Conquering Tide: War in the Pacific Islands, 1942–1944.* New York: Norton, 2015.

Travers, Timothy. *The Killing Ground: The British Army, The Western Front, and the Emergence of Modern Warfare, 1900–1918.* Barnsley, South Yorkshire, UK: Pen & Sword Military, 2009.

Tregaskis, Richard. *Guadalcanal Diary.* Redhill, Surrey, UK: Wells, Darton & Co., 1943.

Tunney, Christopher. *A Biographical Dictionary of World War II.* London: Dent, 1972.

Ugaki, Matome, Donald M. Goldstein, and Katherine V. Dillon. *Fading Victory: The Diary of Admiral Matome Ugaki, 1941–1945.* Annapolis, MD: Naval Institute Press, 2008.

United States Army. *Intelligence Bulletin* 1, no. 3, November 1942.

——. *Intelligence Bulletin* 2, no. 3, November 1943.

——. *Intelligence Bulletin* 2, no. 5, January 1944.

——. *Intelligence Bulletin* 2, no. 7, March 1944.

——. *Intelligence Bulletin* 3, no. 3, November 1944.

——. *Intelligence Bulletin* 3, no. 4, December 1944.

——. *Intelligence Bulletin* 3, no. 5, January 1945.

——. *Intelligence Bulletin* 3, no. 6, February 1945.

——. *Intelligence Bulletin* 3, no. 8, April 1945.

——. *Intelligence Bulletin* 3, no. 9, May 1945.

——. *Intelligence Bulletin* 3, no. 10, June 1945.

——. *Intelligence Bulletin* 3, no. 12, August 1945.

United States Army, 27th Infantry Division. *Report of Intelligence Activities 27th Infantry Division, Saipan Operation.* April 1–August 6, 1944.

United States Army, 77th Infantry Division. *G-2 Periodic Report,* nos. 1–6, March 1945.

——. *G-2 Periodic Report,* nos. 7–36, April 1945.

——. *G-2 Periodic Report,* nos. 37–68, May 1945.

——. *G-2 Periodic Report*, nos. 69–91, June 1945.

United States Army, 96th Infantry Division. Action Report, Ryukyu Campaign, Headquarters US Army XXIV Corps. TFGOG 314.7, July 28, 1945.

United States Army, 713th Tank Battalion. After Action Report: 713th Tank Battalion, Armored Flame Thrower Provisional. November 10, 1944–June 30, 1945.

United States Army Forces, Pacific Ocean Areas. *G-2 Periodic Report*, no. 54 for the Period 30 Dec. 1944 to 6 Jan. 1945.

——. *G-2 Periodic Report*, no. 78. N-7660, June 12, 1945.

——. *Intelligence Bulletin*, no. 7, January 1, 1945.

——. *Intelligence Bulletin*, no. 10, February 19, 1945.

——. *Intelligence Bulletin*, no. 14, April 20, 1945.

——. *Intelligence Bulletin*, no. 15, May 4, 1945.

——. *Intelligence Bulletin*, no. 16, May 18, 1945.

——. *Intelligence Bulletin*, May 1946.

United States Army Medical Department. *Report of 61st Medical Battalion, Annual Report for 1944 Medical Department Activities in Pacific Ocean Areas.* Washington, DC: United States Army Medical Department, 1944.

United States Army Service Forces. *Civil Affairs Handbook: Japan.* M 354–1. Washington, DC: United States Army Service Forces, 1944.

United States Army Service Forces, Office of the Surgeon General. *Care of the Wounded in Theaters of Operation.* Washington, DC: Office of the Surgeon General, 1943.

United States Bureau of the Census. *Thirteenth Census of the United States Taken in the Year 1910.* Prepared under the supervision of Edward Dana Durand, William J. Harris, William C. Hunt, John Lee Coulter, Le Grand Powers, R. P. Teele, William M. Steuart, and Isaac A. Hourwich. 11 vols. Washington, DC: U.S. Government Printing Office, 1912.

United States Bureau of Medicine and Surgery. *The History of the Medical Department of the United States Navy in World War II.* 3 vols. Washington, DC: U.S. Government Printing Office, 1953.

United States Department of Defense. *The Dictionary of Military Terms.* New York: Skyhorse, 2009.

United States Fleet, Headquarters of the Commander in Chief. Antiaircraft Action Summary: Suicide Attacks. N-4731 (APR45). April 1945.

United States Military Academy. *The Howitzer.* West Point, NY: 1908.

United States Office of the Chief of Naval Operations. *Amphibious Operations: Capture of Okinawa (Ryukyus Operation), 27 March to 21 June 1945.* January 22, 1946.

United States Pacific Fleet and Pacific Ocean Areas. *Okinawa Gunto Second Supplement: CINCPAC-CINCPOA Bulletin No. 53–45.* N-12283. February 28, 1945.

United States Strategic Bombing Survey, Over-all Economic Effects Division. *The Effects of Strategic Bombing on Japan's War Economy.* Washington, DC: U.S. Government Printing Office, 1946.

United States War Department. *Army Battle Casualties and Nonbattle Deaths in World War II: Final Report, 7 December 1941–31 December 1945.* N-5851–2. December 31, 1946.

United States War Department. *Artillery Ammunition.* War Department Technical Manual TM9–1901. Washington, DC: War Department, 1944.

United States War Department. *Battle Experiences Against the Japanese.* N-10228. Washington, DC: War Department, 1945.

United States War Department. *Combat Lessons,* no. 2. N-14362.1. Washington, DC: War Department, 1944.

United States War Department. *Combat Lessons,* no. 8. N-14362.7. Washington, DC: War Department, 1944.

United States War Department. *Combat Lessons,* no. 9. N-14362.8. Washington, DC: War Department, 1944.

United States War Department. *Japanese Phrase Book.* Washington, DC: War Department, 1943.

United States War Department. *Jungle Warfare: War Department*

Field Manual. Washington, DC: U.S. Government Printing Office, 1944.

United States War Department. *Notes on Care of Battle Casualties.* Washington, DC: War Department, 1943.

United States War Department. *Technical Manual: Handbook on Japanese Military Forces.* TM-E 30–480. Washington, DC: War Department, 1944.

United States War Department, Military Intelligence Division. *Japanese Ground Forces Order of Battle Bulletins (7 April–2 June 1945).* SRH-195 (Part I). Washington, DC: War Department, 1945.

United States War Department and British War Office. *The Jungle Survival Manual, 1939–1945: Instructions on Warfare, Terrain, Endurance, and the Dangers of the Tropics.* Edited by Alan Jeffreys. Washington, DC: War Department, 1945.

University of Wisconsin. *The Badger.* Madison, WI: 1943.

US Joint Chiefs of Staff. *Joint War Plans Committee (J.W.P.C) 116/14 Plan for Seizure of the Ryukyus 116/4.* N-R13673R.

USS *Bush* Action Report—Okinawa Operation, March 15 to April 6, 1945.

USS *Harry Lee* Report of Operations at Tarawa (GALVANIC), January 9, 1944.

Vandegrift, A. A., and Robert B. Asprey. *Once a Marine: The*

Memoirs of General A. A. Vandegrift, United States Marine Corps. New York: Norton, 1964.

Van Wyck, David W. "Beyond the Burn: Studies on the Physiological Effects of Flamethrowers During World War II." *Military Medical Research* 7, no. 8 (2020). https://doi.org/10.1186/s40779-020-00237-9.

Vasquez, Joseph Paul, III. "America and the Garrison Stadium: How the US Armed Forces Shaped College Football." *Armed Forces & Society* 38, no. 3 (July 2012): 353–72.

Venable, Heather P. *How the Few Became the Proud: Crafting the Marine Corps Mystique, 1874–1918.* Transforming War. Annapolis, MD: Naval Institute Press, 2019.

Venzon, Anne Cipriano. *From Whaleboats to Amphibious Warfare: Lt. Gen. "Howling Mad" Smith and the U.S. Marine Corps.* Westport, CT: Praeger, 2003.

Virtue, John. *The Black Soldiers Who Built the Alaska Highway: A History of Four Army Regiments in the North, 1942–1943.* Jefferson, NC: McFarland, 2013.

Wakabayashi, Bob Tadashi. "The Nanking 100-Man Killing Contest Debate: War Guilt amid Fabricated Illusions, 1971–75." *Journal of Japanese Studies* 26, no. 2 (2000): 307–40.

Ward, Arch. *Frank Leahy and the Fighting Irish: The Story of Notre Dame Football.* New York: G. P. Putnam's Sons, 1944.

Warne, Frank Julian. *The Immigrant Invasion*. New York: Dodd, Mead, 1913.

———. *The Slav Invasion and the Mine Workers: A Study in Immigration*. Philadelphia: Lippincott, 1904. http://hdl.loc.gov/loc.gdc/scd0001.00158703658.

Warren, Paul. *Adventurer Floyd Gibbons: Eye Street's Eyewitness to History*. CreateSpace Independent Publishing Platform, 2016.

Watterson, John Sayle. *College Football: History, Spectacle, Controversy*. Baltimore: Johns Hopkins University Press, 2000.

Waugh, Isami Arifuku, Alex Yamato, and Raymond Y. Okamura. "A History of Japanese Americans in California: Immigration." *Five Views: An Ethnic Historic Site Survey for California*. National Park Service, 2004. http://nps.gov/parkhistory/online_books/5views/5views4a.htm.

Wawro, Geoffrey. *A Mad Catastrophe: The Outbreak of World War I and the Collapse of the Habsburg Empire*. New York: Basic Books, 2014.

Weinberg, Gerhard L. *A World at Arms: A Global History of World War II*. 2nd ed. Cambridge, UK: Cambridge University Press, 2005.

Weller, George. *Cruise of Death: 49 Days of Death and Madness Aboard Japanese Hell Ships*. Lexington, KY: Uncommon Valor Press, 2015.

Wells, Ed. *Hey Doc!: The Battle of Okinawa as Remembered by a Marine Corpsman.* Edited by Shannon D. Wells. Pearl Handle Press, 2017.

Wertz, Jay. *The Pacific: Pearl Harbor to Guadalcanal.* Vol. 1, *War Stories: World War II Firsthand.* Leesburg, VA: Weider History Publications, 2010.

Wheelan, Joseph. *Bloody Okinawa: The Last Great Battle of World War II.* New York: Hachette, 2020.

Wheeler, Richard. *A Special Valor: The U.S. Marines and the Pacific War.* Annapolis, MD: Naval Institute Press, 2006.

White, Matthew. *The Great Big Book of Horrible Things: The Definitive Chronicle of History's 100 Worst Atrocities.* New York: Norton, 2012.

White, Walter. *A Man Called White: The Autobiography of Walter White.* New York: Viking Press, 1948.

Whitman, James Q. *Hitler's American Model: The United States and the Making of Nazi Race Law.* Princeton, NJ: Princeton University Press, 2018.

Willard, Warren Wyeth. *The Leathernecks Come Through.* New York: Revell, 1944.

Williams, B. J., and Leslie O. Read. *Iron Desire: The Legacy of Notre Dame Football Coach Frank Leahy.* Edited by K. Raven Rozier. Morrisville, NC: Lulu Press, 2009.

Wilson, Jennifer. *Running Away to Home: Our Family's Journey* to Croatia in Search of Who We Are, Where We Came From, and What Really Matters. New York: St. Martin's Press, 2011.

Winegard, Timothy C. The Mosquito: A Human History of Our Deadliest Predator. New York: Dutton, 2019.

Wolmar, Christian. The Great Railroad Revolution: The History of Trains in America. New York: PublicAffairs, 2012.

Wood, Karen Marie. "Gridiron Courage: The Navy, Purdue, and World War II." Master's thesis, Indiana University, 2011.

Wukovits, John F. One Square Mile of Hell: The Battle for Tarawa. New York: NAL Caliber, 2006.

Yahara, Hiromichi. The Battle for Okinawa: A Japanese Officer's Eyewitness Account of the Last Great Campaign of World War II. New York: John Wiley & Sons, 1995.

Yamada, Otozō. Materials on the Trial of Former Servicemen of the Japanese Army Charged with Manufacturing and Employing Bacteriological Weapons. Moscow: Foreign Languages Publishing House, 1950.

Yang, Jia Lynn. One Mighty and Irresistible Tide: The Epic Struggle over American Immigration, 1924–1965. New York: Norton, 2020.

Yeide, Harry. The Tank Killers: A History of America's World War II Tank Destroyer Force. Havertown, PA: Casemate, 2004.

Yellen, Jeremy A. The Greater East Asia Co-Prosperity Sphere:

When Total Empire Met Total War. Studies of the Weatherhead East Asian Institute, Columbia University. Ithaca, NY: Cornell University Press, 2019.

Yellin, Emily. *Our Mothers' War: American Women at Home and at the Front During World War II.* New York: Free Press, 2004.

Yoshida, Mitsuru, and Richard H. Minear. *Requiem for Battleship Yamato.* Seattle: University of Washington Press, 1985.

Yoshida, Shigeru. *The Yoshida Memoirs: the Story of Japan in Crisis.* Translated by Kenichi Yoshida. Boston: Houghton Mifflin, 1962.

Young, Dallas M. "Origin of the Progressive Mine Workers of America." *Journal of the Illinois State Historical Society* 40, no. 3 (September 1947): 313–30.

Zaloga, Steven J. *US Flamethrower Tanks of World War II.* Oxford, UK: Osprey Publishing, 2013.

NEWSPAPERS AND PERIODICALS

Akron Beacon Journal

Altoona Tribune

American Heritage

Argus-Leader (Sioux Falls, SD)

Arizona Republic

Austin American

Baltimore Sun

Beckley Post-Herald (Beckley, WV)

Biloxi Daily Herald (Biloxi, MS)

Bismarck Tribune

Boston Globe

Brown Daily Herald

Canton Daily Ledger (Canton, IL)

Capital Journal (Salem, OR)

Capital Times (Madison, WI)

Chicago Daily Tribune

Chillicothe Gazette (OH)

Christian Science Monitor

Columbia Spectator

Cornell Alumni News

Cornell Daily Sun

Courier-Journal (Louisville, KY)

Daily Cardinal (Madison, WI)

Daily Illini (Urbana-Champaign, IL)

Daily News (New York)

Daily Sentinel (Woodstock, IL)

Daily Times (New Philadelphia, OH)

Dartmouth (Dartmouth College, Hanover, NH)

Decatur Daily Review (Decatur, IL)

Decatur Herald (Decatur, IL)

Des Moines Register

Detroit Free Press

Dispatch (Moline, IA)

Duquesne Duke (Duquesne University, Pittsburgh, PA)

Eagle (Bryan, TX)

Fort Worth Star-Telegram

Freeport Journal-Standard (Freeport, IL)

Fulton Democrat (Lewistown, IL)

Galesburg Register-Mail (Galesburg, IL)

Globe-Gazette (Mason City, Iowa)

Golden Football Magazine

Grant County Herald (Lancaster, WI)

Green Bay Press-Gazette

Harvard Crimson

Harvey Tribune (Harvey, IL)

Idaho Statesman

Indianapolis Star

Intelligencer Record (Doylestown, PA)

Ironwood Daily Globe (Ironwood, MI)

Journal and Courier (Lafayette, LA)

Lansing State Journal

Leatherneck

Los Angeles Times

Lubbock Morning Avalanche

Marine Chevron

Marine Corps Gazette

Michigan Daily

Milwaukee Journal

Milwaukee Sentinel

Mississippi Press

Missoulian

Naval History Magazine

New York Herald-Tribune

New York Times

Notre Dame Scholastic

Oakland Tribune

Oklahoman

Pantagraph (Bloomington, IL)

Philadelphia Inquirer

Phillipian (Phillips Academy, Andover, MA)

Pittsburgh Courier

Pittsburgh Post-Gazette

Pittsburgh Press

Pittsburgh Sun-Telegraph

Plain Speaker (Hazleton, PA)

Post-Standard (Syracuse, NY)

Purdue Exponent (Purdue University, West Lafayette, IN)

Racine Journal (Racine, WI)

Register-Republic (Rockford, IL)

Sacramento Bee

Salt Lake Tribune

San Francisco Examiner

Santa Barbara College El Gaucho

Sioux City Journal

South Bend Tribune

Star Press (Muncie, IN)

Statesman Journal (Salem, OR)

Times (Shreveport, LA)

Times (Streator, IL)

Times Herald (Port Huron, MI)

Tulsa World

Tyler Morning Telegraph (Tyler, TX)

Valley News Dispatch

Washington C.H. Record Herald (Washington Court House, OH)

Washington Post

Wilkes-Barre Times Leader

Wisconsin State Journal (Madison, WI)

Yale Daily News

Yank

FOOTBALL PROGRAMS AND YEARBOOKS

Army v. Duke game program, October 27, 1945.

Army v. Notre Dame game program, November 7, 1942.

Army v. Notre Dame game program, November 11, 1944.

Army v. University of Pennsylvania game program, October 30, 1943.

Army v. University of Pennsylvania game program, November 17, 1945.

Brown v. Harvard game program, October 1, 1938.

East-West Annual All-Star Football Game game program, January 1, 1943.

Eastern College All-Stars v. New York Giants game program, September 4, 1940.

Illinois v. Minnesota game program, October 10, 1942.

Navy v. Notre Dame game program, October 31, 1942.

Notre Dame v. Illinois game program, October 24, 1942.

Purdue v. Illinois game program, October 2, 1943.

Stanford v. Notre Dame game program, October 10, 1942.

Street & Smith's Football Year Book, 1941.

Street & Smith's Football Year Book, 1942.

Street & Smith's Football Year Book, 1943.

Wisconsin v. Iowa game program, November 7, 1942.

Wisconsin v. Minnesota game program, November 21, 1942.

Wisconsin v. Notre Dame game program, September 26, 1942.

Acknowledgments

The Mosquito Bowl never would have hatched without the support of the Sixth Marine Division Association and its board of directors: Connie Houseweart, Lisa Benedetti, Sharon Woodhouse, Carroll McGowan, Bob McGowan, Jim Monbeck, Patty Payne, Harry McKnight, and Watson Crumbie. They supplied names and emails of veterans of the 6th Division to interview, gave me a superb multiple-volume set of oral interviews, shared with me their own stories, answered all my questions sublime and ridiculous, and have become dear friends for life. Other members of the association I would like to thank include Anita and Melinda Benedetti (the other two-thirds of the famous Benedetti sisters), Dolores Bertram, Mary Brauer, Dave Hilner, Joe Kite, Louise Lutts, Frank and Christine McBride, Bob and Jane McCalmont, Kay Newill, D. C. Rigby and son Jim Rigby, Bill and Jean Steed, Mary Beth Tierney, and Leonard Turner and daughter, Karen Turner. I also want to acknowledge Gregg Woodhouse, who so sadly is no longer with us.

I cannot say enough about the contribution of 6th Division and Okinawa veteran Neal McCallum. He is one of the smartest men I have ever met and has an encyclopedic knowledge of Okinawa. He was instrumental in helping me separate the wheat (what really happened) from the chaff (what has been embellished over time). Whether in person or by email or text, I spoke with Neal close to fifty times. He is ninety-five years young, in large part because of his wonderful mate, Pfuong Riles.

Other veterans of Okinawa and their families who were so gracious with their time, in some cases supplying me with personal letters of their war experiences and other artifacts, include John Baird, Harry Grover, Melvin Heckt, Melvin Kabik, Ed Marsalek, Dave Mears, John McCulloch, Les Penny, the family of Warren Rudkin, Oscar Soifer, Maurice Vail, Ken and Natalie Wells, Ed Whitten, Dick Whitaker, and Jim White. Helen Simmons allowed me full access to the letters of her father, Fred Abbott. Gloria Taylor did the same with the letters of her father, Gerald Strohacker.

So did marvelous Mary Walker with letters and other material from her husband, Jack Walker. Not to mention the North Carolina hospitality of both Mary and her daughter, Lynne Warren, when I visited. Laura Lacey, the historian for the Sixth Marine Division Association and author of a hair-raising book about Okinawa called *Stay off the Skyline*, could not have been more giving. Bill Beigel made the process of obtaining military records about ten times easier than I expected. Penny Stark knows exactly why she is here.

Richard McLaughry and Marguerite Ames allowed access to a treasure trove of material on their father, John, dating back to his childhood: to simply acknowledge and offer thanks in no way conveys my debt to them. Patti and Brett Margaron shared hundreds of letters and documents in helping me to draw a portrait of Bob and Frank Bauman (Patti's father). Their sons, Matt and Frank, offered observations on the impact of Bob's life on their grandfather. Their daughter, Hana, and her husband, Dan, are just really cool.

Judy Corfield gave me a box filled to the brim with letters from her uncle, Dave Schreiner. Ann Norman so willingly shared letters and other material relating to the engagement between her mother, Odette, and Schreiner during the war. Terry Frei's book, *Third Down and a War to Go*, about the Wisconsin football team of 1942, was enormously helpful in depicting Schreiner and Bauman and is also a great read that I highly recommend. Terry gave me access to his notes and went above and beyond the call of duty in supplying names and emails of people to interview. Larry Krulac, Jim Starcevic, and Roger Parmenter greatly helped in learning about Tony Butkovich and his family. Local historian Bruce Weirauch was indispensable in helping to depict the coal era of Fulton County. In writing about George Murphy, a big thank-you to the Steele family, including John, Brian, Emily, Theresa Steele Butts, and Tim Butts.

In fact-checking the book, I could not have done better than David Georgi. A former colleague from *Vanity Fair*, he is a heat-seeking missile when it comes to finding mistakes. He is beyond thorough, to put it mildly. Because of the amount of material within the book, Ben Kalin, another former *Vanity Fair* colleague, came in at the end to assist and was superb. Anne Metcalf was not only a genius in compiling the notes on sources and bibliography within a limited time frame but one of the nicest people I have ever met. Researchers Maria Spano, Julia Bell, and Colin Lodewick were meticulous in their work, and I was lucky to have them.

HarperCollins showed total faith from beginning to end, not flinching for a second when I asked for several deadline extensions, and then doing everything possible to make the book as good as possible. Thanks to the following: president and publisher Jonathan Burnham; deputy publisher Doug Jones; Elina Cohen, who did the interior design; Robin Bilardello, who did the cover; Tina Andreadis and Kate D'Esmond in publicity; Leah Waslielewski and Katie O'Callaghan in marketing.

Which brings me to my editor at HarperCollins, Noah Eaker. What can I say? Bright, hardworking, a deft editing touch, fun, patiently putting up with panicked and prickly emails born of insecurity and five years of tackling the beast in isolation. He has many great years ahead as an editor and could definitely work up a side practice in psychiatry. His assistant, Mary Gaule, and her replacement, Edie Astley, were great.

My agent at WME, Eric Simonoff, was an excited supporter of the project when it was nothing more than a few at-random thoughts. He is straight to the point, no-nonsense, smart as hell, and also graced with a superb sense of humor (he laughed at my quips). Eric's former assistant, Jessica Spitz, and current one, Criss Moon, were both terrific to work with. Sylvie Rabineau and Elizabeth Wachtel, who specialize in literary packaging for WME, were inexhaustible champions of the book.

For the first time ever in my career, I put my over-sensitivity aside and had several people read the first draft of the manuscript. Two of them were colleagues from my former days at the *Philadelphia Inquirer*, Vernon Loeb and Fen Montaigne. They pushed me to revisit the manuscript and do some major surgery that ultimately meant tearing out months and months of research. My son Caleb read the manuscript and, armed with an intuitive touch on how to shape narrative, had many terrific suggestions and insights. To tell the truth, I was a little bit in awe, that moment in life when what you suspected is now officially true: your son is smarter than you. My other sons, twins Gerry and Zach, are old hands at dealing with Dad when he is writing a book and not taking it personally when he gets that look on his face as if he is smelling something rotten.

My wife, Lisa, is warm, funny, beautiful, supportive, patient, smart as hell, and everything else. She, too, is a gifted editor and in a very early iteration suggested a structural change that helped the book to coalesce. I tend to bad-mouth my work, and since it was the pandemic with nowhere to go and no one else around, she bore the brunt of my foaming until she told me to stop feeling sorry for myself and get to work, and when I really drove her nuts, to "shut the fuck up." Which worked quite effectively.

I would like to close by thanking Pippin. He came into our lives as an older rescue at the age of fourteen. He weighed all of five pounds with a coat of mottled gray and ears shooting up like the pyramids. Although like most small dogs he fancied himself ten times bigger than he was, his nature was gentle, affectionate, and vulnerable. He was beautiful because he wasn't classically beautiful at all and at times beautifully silly.

Your mind plays terrible tricks when you write a book: What seemed so good on the first read turns to shit on the second. Every afternoon, as the writing spigot went dry and fear set in, I escaped to my favorite chair. Pip would climb into my lap, take what seemed like two hours to find the perfect angle of repose, and together we would both fall asleep. He gave me the love and warmth and reassurance needed to go back at it the following morning. It went on like this for nearly two years until the writing was completed.

Lisa and I knew the end was coming after he was diagnosed with cancer. We hoped for miracles when there weren't any. We tried to prepare ourselves when we could not. Our hearts will eventually heal but they will never fully mend. And so we wait, until our own time comes to cross the Rainbow Bridge.

About the Author

BUZZ BISSINGER was born in New York City in 1954. He is a graduate of Phillips Academy in Andover and the University of Pennsylvania. He won a Pulitzer Prize for investigative reporting along with two other reporters at the *Philadelphia Inquirer* and was a Nieman Fellow at Harvard University. He is the author of six books, including *Friday Night Lights*, which has sold close to two million copies and spawned a film and television show of the same name. He has been a contributing editor at *Vanity Fair* for more than two decades and teaches a seminar in advanced narrative nonfiction at the University of Pennsylvania.

He and his wife, Lisa, split their time between the Long Beach Peninsula in Washington State and Philadelphia.